DEMOCRATIZATIONS

DEMOCRATIZATIONS:
Comparisons, Confrontations, and Contrasts

Jose V. Ciprut, Editor

The MIT Press
Cambridge, Massachusetts
London, England

Egg in one hand: Akan (Ghana and Côte d'Ivoire) people's symbol for insinu-
ating that "Power is fragile. Like an egg. Hold it too tightly, and it might break
and spill all over the hand. Yet hold it too loosely, and it might fall, break, and
splatter all over the floor."—*Ed.*

Graphic: *Akan Cultural Symbols Project*, G. F. Kojo Arthur
and Robert Rowe. © 1998–2001 (Courtesy Jose V. Ciprut)

Cover Concept and Design: Jose V. Ciprut

MIT Press books may be purchased at special quantity discounts for business or sales
promotional use. For information, please e-mail special_sales@mitpress.mit.edu or
write to Special Sales Department, The MIT Press, 55 Hayward Street, Cambridge,
MA 02142.

This book was set in Palatino by SNP Best-set Typesetter Ltd., Hong Kong, and was
printed and bound in the United States of America.

Library of Congress Cataloging-in-Publication Data

Democratizations : comparisons, confrontations, and contrasts / edited by Jose V. Ciprut
    p.   cm.
Includes bibliographical references and index.
ISBN 978-0-262-03385-5 (hardcover : alk. paper)—ISBN 978-0-262-53308-9 (pbk. : alk.
paper)
1. Democracy—Case studies. 2. Democratization—Case studies. 3. Comparative
government. I. Ciprut, Jose V.
JC423.D47818   2009
320.9—dc22
                                                                      2008014046

10 9 8 7 6 5 4 3 2 1

*For Raymond, Félicie-Yvonne, and their much-loved
daughter Marie-José (Josie) Norrenberg*

**Courageous Members of the Belgian Civilian
Resistance, Fighters for Democracy in WWII**

DER SPIEGEL 32/2005–August 8, 2005

Excerpt from: SPIEGEL Interview with Singapore's Lee Kuan Yew
[URL: http://www.spiegel.de/international/spiegel/0,1518,369128,00.html]

SPIEGEL: During your career, you have kept your distance from Western style democracy. Are you still convinced that an authoritarian system is the future for Asia?

Mr. Lee: Why should I be against democracy? The British came here, never gave me democracy, except when they were about to leave. But I cannot run my system based on their rules. I have to amend it to fit my people's position. In multiracial societies, you don't vote in accordance with your economic interests and social interests, you vote in accordance with race and religion. Supposing I'd run their system here, Malays would vote for Muslims, Indians would vote for Indians, Chinese would vote for Chinese. I would have a constant clash in my Parliament which cannot be resolved because the Chinese majority would always overrule them. So I found a formula that changes that . . .

SPIEGEL: . . . and that turned Singapore de facto into a one-party state. Critics say that Singapore resembles a Lee Family Enterprise. Your son is the Prime Minister, your daughter-in-law heads the powerful Development Agency . . .

Mr. Lee: . . . and my other son is CEO of Singapore Telecoms, my daughter is head of the National Institute for Neurology. This is a very small community of 4 million people. We run a meritocracy. If the Lee Family set an example of nepotism, that system would collapse. If I were not the prime minister, my son could have become Prime Minister several years earlier. It is against my interest to allow any family member who's incompetent to hold an important job because that would be a disaster for Singapore and my legacy. That cannot be allowed.

The interview was conducted by editors Hans Hoyng and Andreas Lorenz. *Translated from the German by Christoper Sultan.*

Bolívar died aged 47, disillusioned at his failure to form a unified Latin American republic, but today "El Libertador" is revered as a saint. Passing his statue, I cross the street to a small café where, over a delicious guava milkshake, I ponder our own lack of equivalent heroes. Britons have nobody like Bolívar to look up to. Cubans are lucky, with several giants to worship—not lightweight media celebrities, but principled, visionary reformers. Like him or loathe him, Fidel Castro is one of them. There are few photographs of him, and no statues, but for most Cubans, Castro is a living legend who has maintained his communist ideals despite the collapse of communism elsewhere, and despite sanctions and embargoes from the 'Enemy' to the north. The Cubans I speak to all share Castro's patriotism and his distrust of democracy, and are intensely proud of Cuba's egalitarianism, education, health care and sporting achievements. None of them mention human rights or freedom of expression. [They] hope that tourism and foreign investment will help to alleviate poverty, but admit that the tourist peso, worth 20 times the local peso, is itself creating class divisions between those with access to it and those without. But despite this, Cubans remain cheerfully egalitarian, and as enthralled as ever by their most famous hero. I remember my own Che Guevara poster, pinned to my bedroom wall 35 years ago. Sixth-form pupils at the school where I teach have an identical poster in their common-room today—but nothing prepares me for his iconic importance in Cuba.

Sarah Shuckburg, "A Little Local Colour,"
Telegraph (UK), Travel, March 5, 2006

Contents

Preface and Acknowledgments   xi

1. **Democratizations: Perspectives and Contexts**   1
   Jose V. Ciprut

2. **From Rule of Law to Freedoms to Enlightened Self-Government: Emplacement of Value in Democratization**   31
   Charles F. Doran

3. **Liberal Democracy: Interrogating the Premises and Inferences**   53
   Aryeh Botwinick

4. **Globalizations and Democratizations: Forces, Counterforces**   73
   Henry Teune

5. **Federalism: The Highest Stage of Democracy?**   93
   John Kincaid

6. **Democratizing the European Union: With or without Popular Sovereignty?**   119
   Andreas Heinemann-Grüder

7. **Democratizations in Central Europe: Comparative Perspectives**   145
   Jerzy J. Wiatr

8. **Russian Civil Society: Elite Versus Mass Attitudes
    to the Democratization of Russia**   165
    Vladimir Shlapentokh

9. **Development without Democratization? China, Law,
    and the East Asian Model**   197
    Jacques deLisle

10. **Democratizations in Africa: Attempts, Hindrances, and
    Prospects**   233
    Stephen Brown and Paul Kaiser

11. **Immigration from and Democratizations in Latin America:
    Crossing the Mexico-U.S. Border**   259
    Douglas S. Massey and S. Mara Pérez

12. **Voice, Participation, and the Globalization of
    Communication Systems**   281
    James Patrick McDaniel, Timothy Kuhn, and Stanley Deetz

13. **Democratic Prospects in Undemocratic Times**   301
    Patrick J. Deneen

14. **Pictures at an Exhibition in the Guise of an Epilogue**   321
    Jose V. Ciprut

    About the Authors   339
    Name Index   343
    Subject Index   353

Preface and
Acknowledgments

This book offers intrasystemic reassessments of democratized and democratizing civic cultures that have evolved and are continuing to proliferate around the globe. Not all of the countries scrutinized assure the emancipation of their citizens. Nor, indeed, do all of the citizenries examined show an innate capacity for self-transformation via self-characterizing means to self-actualizing ends by initiatives that they truthfully can boast to be their very own. As is typical of nonlinear processes, initial conditions seem to matter significantly, as do also the situational contexts and the propelling values, which, as they evolve, individualize trajectories, characterize directional pursuits, and have an impact on basic approaches, thereby imparting idiosyncratic destiny to predetermined destination and particularity to generality.

Our initiative finds its inspiration and drive in our perception that civic awareness fosters self-emancipation and in our observation that active civic participation generates a more palpably practical sense of belonging, crucial for equality and justice on the level of the citizen and vital to legitimacy of sovereignty on the level of the citizenry's government.

In that sense, this book constitutes a serendipitous tribute to Thomas Jefferson, who knew of "no safe depository of the ultimate powers of society but the people themselves" and who suggested that even when one should judge the plebe to be "not enlightened enough" to exercise the control of the powers vested in it with "wholesome discretion," the proper action ought not to involve acts that deprive the populace of its powers, but rather, initiatives tailored to edify a people-in-becoming or a citizenry-in-the-making, of its discretion. Thus more specifically, this book seeks to inform semicitizens and subjects around the globe and possibly to assist them in reorienting their pursuits, in disincentivizing their deferrals, in dissipating their dormancies, and in daring themselves to take charge of their human condition. Would that the pages ahead offer choice of direction and force of will, but above all courage of action to the many around the world still too resignedly awaiting to be made into whom they can be or too perplexed to figure out where and how to start the journey into what they would elect to become once they realize whom they are not.

To that end, we bring together seasoned practitioners and senior scholars from a variety of pertinent disciplines. We interconnect our perspectives, to enable ourselves synergetically to scrutinize the makings and failings of institutions, constitutions, and practices in the domains of that elusive idea commonly referred to as *democracy*. We weigh the relative merits of some select methods of and approaches to democratizations, taking extreme care not to lump these under one and the same rationale. We braid our analytic strands in ways that should allow the reader to draw from our comparative syntheses cogent contextualized perspectives at each of three levels of overview: the theoretical-conceptual; the geopolitical/macrospatial; and the micro-issue/macro-policy-specific epiphenomenal. This we do by striking a balance between several chapters under each dimension. Ideas, forms, pursuits, practices, and problems come alive as we circumnavigate the globe hand in hand with our readers. In virtue of its ambitious reach and its enveloping embrace, our book seeks to inform the novice and to alert the expert via clarity of thought and limpidity of language. It hence is written to serve a broad range of readership—students, researchers, practitioners, teachers, analysts, policy makers, and not least, the ubiquitous, intelligent, well-read eclectic individual with an inquisitive spirit and an inquiring mind.

I wish herewith to express my sincere appreciation and thanks to Dr. Brian Spooner—Professor of Anthropology and then-Acting Director of the Middle East Center at Penn—who appointed me Research Fellow at the Center, in order to protect our transdisciplinary series of inter-faculty seminars titled *Cross-Campus Conversations at Penn* and to facilitate the materialization of this book project. I thank also Dr. Jay C. Treat, Director of Instructional Computing at Penn's School of Arts and Sciences, for his gracious facilitation of our internal communication and electronic-blackboard postings in time-efficient and cost-effective ways. To Ms. Adela Smith, Executive Assistant to the Vice Provost and Director of Libraries at Penn, who always helped me secure the most appropriate seminar spaces I could reconnoiter and request in advance, I convey my appreciation and amity. I reserve my highest admiration and especial thanks for my fellow travelers who endowed this project with superb intellectual qualities. To my loved ones, deservedly, I offer my deepest gratitude for their sustained share of the selfless sacrifice.

This project completes the work of the third academic cycle in the series of cross-disciplinary interfaculty exchanges founded by the Editor on the Campus of the University of Pennsylvania under the title *Cross-Campus Conversations at Penn*—an initiative that has been able meanwhile to transgress the boundaries of a single campus, the borders of a single country, and yes, also the disciplinary confines of single-minded inquiries into subject matters of compound complexity.

Jose V. Ciprut

1 Democratizations: Perspectives and Contexts

Jose V. Ciprut

Democracy is not in steady state, and democratizations are open-ended processes; they depend on structures and functions in systemic contexts that idiosyncratically evolve in tone, tenor, direction, and pace over time. They also affect and are in turn affected by scores of determinants—both perceived and hypothetical—presumed to inform outcomes. These factors include distinct socioeconomic or cultural/normative prerequisites, historical "path dependency" arguments, homogeneity versus heterogeneity considerations, and, not least, actors' choices. All of these relate to external and internal environments that, deliberately or not, shape the evolution of human development and have an impact on personal and societal emancipation in idiosyncratic ways.

Power-analytical understandings of idealistic explanations and hybrid formulations for democratizations abound. As is evident from its title, the premise of this book is that, although certain basic traits tend to characterize democracy[1] as "ideology,"[2] not all of the practicable paths to it offer the same vistas and vicissitudes, and not all roads lead to the same putative terminus, smack at the center of a movable end station. In fact, precipitous starts, unpreventable breakdowns, contingent digressions, parallel pursuits, and fundamental changes in circumstances—whether by redirecting journeys or renaming destinations—can transform democratizations, in theory and practice. Among factors that complicate facile explanations are the perceived

---

1. "Be nice to America," reads teasingly a red, white, and blue bumper sticker placed on the tail end of a 1966 Imperial Crown convertible proudly kept alive in an oil-poor country known for its populist slogans, "or we'll bring democracy to your country."
2. On the linguistic merits of the context-specific use and avoidance of this multifaceted term, please see Ciprut, "Citizenship: Mere Contract, or Construct for Conduct?" and Schiffman, "Language, Language Policy, and Citizenship: Three Views Compared," both in Ciprut (2008).

correlative relationship between democracy and diversity/asymmetry on the one hand and democracy and equality versus uniformity on the other.

In a few interlinked chapters, this book reexamines the basic traits, the comparable outcomes, and the self-defining dynamics of some of the more widely attempted versions of democracy across the world. It discusses several of the more pressing if less understood controversies that can speed up or retard democratizations, depending on the systemic structures, functions, processes, and contexts at play inside, outside, and across political boundaries. And it concludes with an eye to 'the future'. Of particular focus are the comparable merits of democracy's long-alleged pursuits and destinations, their distinct implications and consequences for a mode of citizenship exercisable in a viable ethic of freedom, and the role of settings in many of which masses of human beings still today somehow find themselves struggling under less than adequate conditions of liberty.

If, as purported, democratizations truly are about dissipating asymmetries, decreasing top-down dominations, encouraging and even speeding up asymptotic approaches to ideals of self-liberty pregnant with collective progress, without danger of internal contradictions on questions of egalitarianism and "social leveling," might it not be useful to revisit the thoughts and the practices that have, and still very much do, foster such emancipation? Hence the cross-disciplinary investigation in this book, the innate logic of which—reflected via the sequence of its chapters—pursues the questions of how democratizations might have an impact on the future of citizenship and in which ways, under what proper circumstances, they might even lead to a political ethic of freedom.

From Rule of Law to Freedoms to Enlightened Self-Government

In his chapter, International Relations specialist Charles Doran holds that democratic pluralism in contemporary democratic polities will become even more crucial as immigration and especially differential birth rates make those societies more diverse. Tolerance enhances the capacity of democratic pluralism to create within the global polity of the twenty-first century what its members will identify as the 'just society'. How so, one may ask. Doran provides a plausibly clear and detailed argument: 'Democratization' is the process of becoming democratic, whereas 'law' within democracy is institutionalized democratization. Democratization is thus the foremost political process in the twenty-first century. But among countries (because many are still undemocratic) as well as within any single country (because the process is still unperfected), processes of democratization are far from complete, although admittedly unending. Three primary values underlie democratization: equality before the law, freedom, and tolerance.[3] In historical time, the achievement of individual freedom and the freedom of the nation state (autonomy) for the most part precedes the achievement of equality before the law, not only inside the state but also outside of it—within the international system. But tolerance is the laggard political value, an "unfulfilled idea" in many modern polities and one not forthrightly attempted in many illiberal states.

Democratic pluralism, which encourages political tolerance among individuals and communities, is therefore central to greater levels of democratization today. Focus on democratic pluralism will become more important as the great democratic polities become more culturally and ethnically diverse via the impact of immigration and as a consequence of differential birth rates among communal groups. But reforms of democratic institutions of democracy cannot yield greater benefit until and unless democratic pluralism enhances political tolerance and in turn can be enhanced by newfound tolerance inside the modern democratic polity. Critiques on issues of tolerance aside, might the time not have come for a critical reassessment of the forms of liberal democracy, in its various theoretical and practical modes?

Liberal Democracy: Interrogating the Premises and the Inferences

Political philosopher and theorist Aryeh Botwinick's chapter examines the theoretical considerations of democratizations under the processes of representative versus participatory democracy. Liberal democracy— the present form of government of, by, and for the citizens of the United States, for instance—represents the institutionalization of a delicate balance of tensions. 'Democracy' connotes popular rule, a mode of direct input by citizens in the formation of their country's government. 'Liberal', by contrast, conjures up a multitude of ways in which democracy is deflected, channeled, and even blocked, the better to protect

---

3. Tolerance may be mistaken for a high-handed mannerism of condescendence, which it is not, when "toleration" is mutual and practiced in reciprocation. An in-depth overview of its dilemmas is offered in Heyd (1996).

minority rights. As Madison classically argued in *Federalist No. 10*, representation itself is a key device for frustrating popular rule because it places political decision making in the hands of a cadre of professional politicians who are already removed from the scene of popular agitation and whose routine professional ethos consists of reaching compromises with other similarly situated individuals. Political theorist Sheldon Wolin has been an eloquent critic of liberal democracy, at least partially because of the ways it plays into the hands of corporate elites bent on thwarting majority rule for the sake of enhancing their economic interests.[4] Robert Dahl, in the later stages of his career, has argued in favor of a natural extension of the logic of democracy, from the exclusions sanctioned by 'liberal' democracy to the greater inclusiveness promoted and nurtured by 'participatory' democracy. He went so far as to suggest that the next area for the application of participatory democracy ought to be none other than the workplace. Because so much of that space had already become public, he reasoned, did it not make sense to go the distance (of politicization) and enforce democratic norms throughout the vast interior of that expanse.

Peter Bachrach and Aryeh Botwinick, too, have argued that, as concerns democracy, the workplace needs to be theorized and designed as a locus for raising the consciousness of ordinary citizens about justifications for greater equality in decision-making procedures and for greater equality in the distribution of the wealth of the society across its life space, in the belief that ultimately this development should likely generate rippling restructuring effects on political governance as a whole. Dahl, Bachrach, and Botwinick have been deeply concerned with sustaining the liberal guarantees of minority rights even as they went on encouraging exertions of majority rule to become more efficacious and also more egalitarian. By contrast, Wolin has become more apocalyptic in his willingness to dispense with these liberal protections.[5]

In chapter 3, Botwinick considers the question of the metaphysical backdrop to liberal democracy: Does it grow out of certainty or skepti-

---

4. Cf. Shlapentokh, chapter 8 in this book, on elites' roles in, and popular appetites for, democracy within state-led pursuits of democratization across Russia today.

5. As a participant in our cross-disciplinary seminar, Dr. Andreas Heinemann-Grüder, deemed it useful to remind us, focus on the liberal defense of minority rights may not be seen inadvertently to conflate two very distinct notions: that (1) liberalism is more about individual rights and the right to be different and (2) the concept of minority rights is practically always exclusively on group rights. Need one here overemphasize that liberalism usually prefers individual rights over group rights?

cism? What varieties of certainty and which types of skepticism? Might reorienting one's concerns over the theoretical bearings of liberal democracy help in achieving greater clarity with regard to questions of institutional design and efficacy? In an era of rampant globalization, which often serves as a veiled reference to the speed and efficacy with which 'Western' (read 'American') political and economic models penetrate the far corners of the world, this chapter provides a theoretical exploration of what in essence the political project of postmodern and postindustrial society might be about in an epoch of broader democratization and faster globalization.

Globalizations and Democratizations: Forces, Counterforces

The dynamics of social development by which systems increase their scale (i.e., the level of their integrated diversity) are the forces that also underlie both globalization and democratization. The globalization experienced in our epoch began in the mid-1970s and was 'pushed' initially by market integration; it subsequently began to fuse gradually with processes of democratization. Globalization and democratization remain two important parts of human society's developmental processes worldwide. So argues, in chapter 4, political scientist Henry Teune, who has studied these forces for a long time.

Teune uses three theoretical approaches to explain globalization at different levels of generality. First, he argues that social systems have a developmental logic of generating variety, by dispersing the resultant diversity, then integrating it, and as a result increasing their own scale. This increased scale becomes an environment that speeds up the creation of variety, the spread of diversity, and the integration of that diversity. Second, individuals, groups, and organizations seek in the long run to maximize their contacts with other such entities, through the fewest nodes possible. And over time, this process, which is one of rational learning, evolves into a structure of highly integrated components on a worldwide basis. Third, both globalization and democratization have come about through confluences of historical events, and this state of affairs has led to more political systems seeking to open themselves to the benefits of 'the rest of the world' and, of necessity, basing their legitimacy on democratic processes that receive approval from other political systems.

Teune's chapter discusses myriad resistances to the forces of globalization in terms of general dialectics and specific conflicts. The two main dialectical dynamics that carry potential to destabilize processes of globalization and democratization are argued to be (1) between levels of development [here, diversity spreads among levels within the system (and world)], which have the greatest extant diversity but also to levels with little or no diversity; the first kind of flow is faster than the second and hence accelerates inequalities; and (2) between the rates of diversification and those of integration [note that here, because it occurs much quicker than its integration, diversity pulls a system (and world) apart in the process of accommodating what is novel].

These dialectics lead to conflicts among economic and social strata, regions, and the old and new developmental elites. Teune sees the forces of globalization winning in the long run, despite battles that may take place between pushes of the global and pulls of the local threatened by it, in new modes of wars of resistance worldwide. Might a more accommodating category of inclusive governance provide a long-term resolution of the shorter-term and medium-term difficulties prognosticated by this chapter, in preemptive ways? Might not, say, federalism, in its growing array of forms, provide a timely answer?

Federalism: The Highest Stage of Democracy?

For veteran of the subject and seasoned political scientist John Kincaid, federalism is arguably the highest stage of democracy because it makes democracy possible on a large scale and in a wide variety of ways that combine the advantages of large and small republics. The world's twenty-five federal countries already encompass 39 percent of the world's population. The average land area and population of federal countries are much larger than those of other nations, and federal countries are also the most culturally heterogeneous. On indicators of democracy, freedom, rights, economic development, and quality of life, federal countries seem to perform better than unitary countries and as well as or better than decentralized unitary countries. Through dispersed power and multiple arenas of government—national, regional, and local—federalism seems to enhance opportunities for citizen participation, to offer multiple forums for citizen voice, to protect the liberties of both persons and cultural communities, to accommodate cultural heterogeneity through regional and local self-government without insisting on uniformity, and to provide means to hold public officials accountable to the people, while also promoting justice by better matching public benefits to public burdens and by allowing some diversity of ideas of justice where universal agreement is not possible. Although federalism by itself is neither a panacea nor a guarantor of democracy, argues Kincaid, for some countries, it is the only viable form of democracy, whereas in others it enhances democracy. And he deploys comparative figures to buttress his considered contention.

But, then, how do the theoretical considerations covered so far manifest themselves around the world and with what typical concerns and consequences?

Democratizing the European Union: With or without a Sovereign Demos?

There still is no model for democracy on the supranational level in the European Union.[6] Yet, the debate about the Union's so-called 'democratic deficit' is coming of age. Democracy is commonly assumed to be

---

6. The European Union (EU) was formed by the Treaty of Maastricht in 1993 as a political-economic union across a geocultural space that constitutes almost all of Greater Christian Europe. It holds a population of almost 500 million, over a space of 4.3 million km^2; spanning 27 member states (Austria, Belgium, Bulgaria, Cyprus, the Czech Republic, Denmark, Estonia, Finland, France, Germany, Greece, Hungary, Ireland, Italy, Latvia, Lithuania, Luxemburg, Malta, the Netherlands, Poland, Portugal, Romania, Slovakia, Slovenia, Spain, Sweden, and the United Kingdom). It generates approximately 30 percent of the world's nominal gross domestic product. On a waiting list are three *official candidate* countries (Croatia, the former-Yugoslav Republic of Macedonia, and a secular Muslim democracy—the Republic of Turkey). Officially recognized *potential candidate* countries are Albania, Bosnia and Herzegovina, Montenegro, Serbia, and now Kosovo as well. The EU rises on the foundations of the pre-existing European Economic Community (EEC), itself created by the Treaty of Paris on July 23, 1952, among France, West Germany, the Netherlands, Belgium, Luxemburg, and Italy—dubbed the 'inner six', for being the founding members also of the Union's de facto predecessor, the European Coal and Steel Community (ECSC), established in 1951, and for having ratified the Treaties of Rome on March 25, 1957. Of the 'outer seven' (UK, Denmark, Sweden, Norway, Portugal, Austria, and Switzerland), who, on January 4, 1960, had signed the European Free Trade Association (EFTA) Convention in Stockholm (taking effect on May 3, 1960) and later admitted Finland as a full member, the UK (with it, the British Overseas Territory of Gibraltar) and Denmark joined *The Community* in 1973, the year Ireland adhered. After gaining home rule from Denmark and conducting a referendum, Greenland left the community in 1985, remaining an overseas territory. If Greece joined in 1981, Portugal did so only in 1986, the year Spain became a member; and Austria, Sweden, and Finland became members in 1995, but Norway had to withdraw its (accepted) application for membership when its people voted against joining. Following 'the fall of the Berlin Wall', the Czech Republic, Estonia, Hungary, Latvia, Lithuania, Poland, Slovakia, and Slovenia, on one hand, and, on the other hand, the island countries of Malta and Cyprus, joined at the same time, on May 1, 2004. Bulgaria and Romania would follow suit in January

based on certain prerequisites still regarded to be missing in the EU: statehood, well-defined territorial boundaries, a supreme decision-making authority, a clearly delineated citizenry as the subject of law, and a preexisting politicocultural identity of sorts, among them. The failure of member states to adopt a binding constitution for the European Union in 2005, and the Irish reticence in 2008 to ratify the Lisbon Treaty[7] of December, 12, 2007, warrant political scientist and historian Andreas Heinemann-Grüder's critical comparison of the merits of the dominant modes of dealing with the 'democratic deficit' of the European Union. Many rivalries seem at play:

Adherents of a collectivist or communitarian conception of the demos conventionally assume that, in order to occur and survive, a democracy requires not only a good measure of cultural and social homogeneity but a vibrant civilian society as well. As long as these prerequisites are

---

2007. The European Economic Area (EEA), created by the EC and EFTA on January 1, 1994, and extending to all of the EU members since, now allows residual EFTA countries (Iceland, Liechtenstein, Norway, and Switzerland), bound among themselves by the Vaduz Convention, which has long replaced the Stockholm Convention, to participate also in the *European Single Market* without joining the EU. Switzerland enjoys bilateral treaties. And a very effective cooperation including privileged use of the Euro extends to Europe's micro-city-states (Andorra, Monaco, San Marino, and Vatican City), as well. Although the marathon negotiations brokered as a last hurrah by the outgoing EU President, German Chancellor Angela Merkel, in Brussels, at dawn, on Saturday, June 23, 2007, had somehow succeeded in transmuting longstanding reservations into last-minute concessions toward producing a draft Reform Treaty—hard-nosed pursuits of self-interest by the UK, the Netherlands, and Poland, notwithstanding—the way things have developed since provides a good example of the great many difficulties intrinsic to the political process of translating ideas to intents, intents to will, will to attitude, to signatures, and to action capable of transforming an aggregate into a functioning system.

7. The Lisbon treaty was conceived as 'Plan B', following the French and Dutch "non"/ "nee" to a European Constitution. It was drawn with the intent of streamlining decision-making across an enlarged EU. On June 13, 2008, it was rejected (by a vote of 53.4 percent) by the Irish. As this volume goes to press, only 21 of the 27 EU members have ratified it. It remains dependent on parliamentary approval in the Czech Republic, Italy, Spain, and Sweden, and still awaits formal presidential signature in Germany and Poland. This development promises to provide another significant test for the ends and means of European-wide democratization. On July 16, 2008, rumors were that under the newly inaugurated French Presidency, there might exist "a plan to stage a rerun of the vote backed by guarantees that Ireland will keep its EU commissioner as well as its military neutrality, its veto over tax policy and its right to set its abortion laws." More on this is available at http://www.timesonline.co.uk/tol/news/world/europe/article4340086.ece. A visit to Ireland by the newly elected EU President, Mr. Sarkozy, could not afford to be seen as anything other than a courtesy visit. And not much more than that it certainly ended up being. The transformation of an aggregate into a system will likely require a broader sense of citizenship by a few inclined to cater to their narrow national interests first.

missing on the European level, they tend to argue, national statehood at the member state level should remain by far the more appropriate institutional framework for democracy. From a liberalist point of view, it has been argued moreover that further supranational state building in the European Union would undermine accountability, participatory rights, and, above all, freedom, were it for creating a Leviathan ever more detached from its populaces. According to this 'Euroskeptical-liberalist' point of view, the EU should embody and further 'broaden' the space governed by liberal rights while refraining from 'deepening' further. 'Intergovernmentalists' in principle deny democracy any possibility for legitimizing inputs, concentrating instead on output legitimization. In sum, as long as the EU's policy output does not fundamentally dissatisfy the electorates, they deem that the EU can be regarded as legitimate, whether democratic or not.

In contrast, the Euro-optimists claim to see a solution to the democratic deficit: in institution building or in the strengthening of existing institutions. At the core of this institutional approach is the call for parliamentarizing the EU, for instance by holding the EU executive accountable, by broadening the law-making capacities of the European Parliament, by strengthening the decision-making capacities in the Council, and by emboldening the citizenries through arrangements easing a pan-European mode of direct democracy (via referenda, plebiscites, consultations of all sorts at all levels, for example).

Still others do not even care about the democratic credentials of the EU and argue in favor of 'a European empire' as an alternative to U.S. hegemony, something able to copy while capably checking and balancing 'It'. There exists also a loose camp, one imbued with republican views for democratizing the EU, pursuing by and large the considerations originally laid out by German philosopher and sociologist Jürgen Habermas. This camp starts with the sweeping observation that the traditional premises of national homogeneity erode the coherence of traditional group interests, the overlap of social milieus, political parties, and hence of national identities. Multilevel governance, 'deliberative politics', pan-European media, transnational networks, transnational public discourses, surely also transnational grass-root movements, and party systems, they argue, would constitute a new form of communitarization 'beyond the nation-state'. Somehow, it seems assumed, expected, or hoped that the prerequisites of democracy are already in place, in a state of infancy but progressively evolving. The failure of the referenda on the EU Constitution in France and in the Netherlands brought the mainly elite-guided and "ideology"-driven pattern of legitimizing the EU to a sudden halt. For the time being—that is, for the next five to ten years—it seems that there will not be any further widening or deepening of the EU but rather a protracted lapse permitting 'digestion', the better to cope with the EU's (hasty?) expansion into Eastern Europe and into a few more Southern European countries too. True, some unpredictable external factors may intervene: shared manifest challenges or common threat perceptions may 'deepen' the purview of joint decision making, but opposite views among the member states with regard to external threats might prove disruptive for the EU as well. This is my take on Heinemann-Grüder's thoughts on what is a complex matter laden with compounding, interlacing, and overlapping considerations.

It is only following the ongoing period of slow digestion that yet another attempt to 'constitutionalize' the EU might well be undertaken.[8] In the meantime, however, the Europeanization of lawmaking and justice will proceed—at creeping pace. And although the prospects that extra rounds of enlargement—after the Balkans, next to the Ukraine, Belarus, and (why not![9]) Turkey, or the Caucasus—may beget

8. The agreements reached in Brussels on June 23, 2007, over a Reform Treaty had come up with something to satisfy everyone: for instance, the UK (adamant on maintaining national control over foreign policy, justice, and home affairs) *because* it made it "absolutely clear that the charter on fundamental rights [was] not going to be justiciable in British courts or alter British law," as publicly stated by the outgoing British Prime Minister Tony Blair; they pleased also the Netherlands, *because* the role of national parliaments in Europe would be thereby strengthened and *because* the criteria for new members eager to join the EU were explicitly included in the treaty. Yet one still was not quite certain that these quasi-accords at long last did suit *all* members. Why? *Because* the new system labeled 'double majority', and earmarked for phase-in as of 2014 for full implementation in 2017, requires that fully a 55 percent majority of EU member states and at least 65 percent of the EU population approve a change by their vote; and *because* it also vies to include most of the central points of the aborted Constitution, such as fewer national veto powers, more and greater powers for the European Parliament, a slimmer European Commission, and a singular role and budget for a Foreign Affairs Chief, as also a longer-term/full-time President of the European Council (the venue where the presidents and prime ministers of the twenty-seven member states consult regularly). In addition, the time span allowed until full implementation (ten very long years, until 2017) should offer inordinate space and latitude for spoilers to renegotiate the Brussels agreement—let alone that the debate over a Constitution is far from over, appearances to the contrary (catchy leitmotiv "that book is forever closed"), quite aside.
9. "Why not? Well, because this great nation is in Asia Minor, not in Europe," retorted candidate to the French Presidency Nicolas Sarkozy in a televised debate, on May 2, 2007, to his competitor Ségolène Royal, who somehow failed to ask him why then, Cyprus—an island situated in the south of Turkey, but unlike Turkey, with no national territory on European soil—was allowed into the EU. (Readers may recall that it was Greece's

liberalizing-democratizing impacts and outcomes in each of these countries situated on Europe's anecdotal fringes, a too convenient way of stemming the periphery-to-center flow of economic migrants into the Metropole will remain a priority to address in defensive postures for the foreseeable future. The political activities of some of the naturalized EU citizens who were not so long ago subjects of the countries they emigrated from would seem to indicate that some of these good folk tend to become more and more like who they once were as they come to acquaint themselves with greater freedoms. And as to the EU, it is our view that it is unlikely to overcome soon or in any substantial manner its still weak 'input legitimacy', its flawed checks and balances, and—disconcerting in its own right—its conspicuous lack of intermediary organizations so essential for articulating manifest forms of sovereign democratic governance. It is, however, one's thoughtful wishing that ultimately the truth—and nothing but the ever-evolving truths in and around it—shall set the EU free . . . of itself.[10]

Democratizations in Central Europe: Comparative Aspects

Central Europe has merited and received much attention in reference to its experiments with democracy and democratization, even well before the definitive dismemberment of the Soviet Empire. Among the questions examined, issues of transitions from dictatorship (McFaul 2005), of noncooperative or 'compromise' switch overs (McFaul 2002), of preemptive stances (Silitski 2005), of the innate dynamics (Way 2006), of international linkages (Levitsky and Way 2005), and of the factor of youth and societal mobilization (Kuzio 2006) have generated interest, as have debates toward explaining successes and failures (D'Anieri 2006), fathoming 'international diffusion' (Bunce and Wolchik 2006),

---

attempts to encourage Cyprus' annexation to itself that had in last recourse compelled Turkey to create a Turkish entity in the north of Cyprus. Instead, Greek Cyprus was annexed to the EU.)

10. Further expansion—be it to the East or to the South, even after the recommended period of "digestive integration"—seems to fuel, still today, especially among the pursuers of a "political Europe," preemptive fears of "dilution and death" of that very ideal, itself an elite-entertained aspiration of what for these minds is but Europe's eternal and unalienable reason to be. In that view, an at long last thoroughly democratically integrated political EU should gain even greater security if democratizations occurred at its fringes through special partnerships across a *nova mare nostrum*, textured by accords throughout the Mediterranean Basin and, with time, maybe even beyond—for as long as little if any reason is left or allowed for immigration.

remembering 'the origins of the Ukraine's democratic breakthrough' (Aslund and McFaul 2006), and understanding the challenges of 'reclaiming democracy' in Central and Eastern Europe (Forbrig and Demeš 2007).

For Polish military sociologist Jerzy Wiatr, the states still referred to as 'post-communist', in East and Central Europe, comprise a great variety of cases, which differ from each other on account of factors including: (1) the nature of the old regime (say, from rigid totalitarian to benign authoritarian), (2) the type of economy (from the fully nationalized 'command' types to manifold forms of 'mixed' practice), (3) the degree of 'latitude' for autonomy (from independent national communist regimes, to communist regimes dependent on Moscow, to the former Republics of the USSR), and (4) the ethnic makeup or general composition (from multiethnic state, to national entity with strong ethnic minorities, to homogeneous national state), although these countries differ also in (5) the way they have swerved from communism (whether through negotiated transition, by a top-down abortive coup, via the collapse of the regime or the disintegration of the multiethnic state), and, not least, (6) the set of policies pursued by the post-communist elites, distinctively during the early years of the transition specific to a particular country.

In the nineteen years since 1989, the democratizations experienced in 'Eastern Europe' have come to offer a range of outcomes, from the more triumphant (exemplified by the core countries of Central Europe, and the Baltics) to the less fortunate results (typified by the Balkans). Perhaps not surprisingly, in the more successful states, the political results of transformation have earned better grades than the socioeconomic consequences. To date, democratic consolidation has taken place practically in all of the states of Central Europe; a few of these states have become members of NATO and the EU, and several more are in the process of consolidating their adsorption into the EU. Economically, however, even the most successful post-communist states (with the probable exception of Slovenia, which has meanwhile even managed to hold the presidency of the EU Council) have faced serious problems resulting from their transition from a relatively egalitarian raw communist welfare state to an even cruder capitalist economy that markedly categorized and separated the 'winners' from the 'losers' in the harsh processes of self-transformation. This has generated considerable skepticism, and even pessimism, in the hearts and minds of populations for which the balance sheet of these transformations was in moral deficit. Politically, public moods and mindsets of the sort can make it more difficult to exercise stable governance, even to sustain enduring majorities, in ways to avoid the disruption of the democratic processes. Understandably, in the least successful states, prospects have been even darker. Among the several still incapable of resolving their most urgent (economic, ethnic, and other) problems, some governments may yet— in last recourse—try to resort to undemocratic means, unless they fall into the stern hands of a legitimately elected authoritarian leadership that can preempt retroversion. And if the pressures being exercised by the EU on Bulgaria in an endeavor to elicit much needed and still pending ethical reforms at the highest echelons of state are any indication, the road to creating a system out of an aggregate in matters pan-European may be long.

In his chapter, Jerzy Wiatr argues that much will depend on the quality of the new elites.[11] Comparative research has shown that Central European leaders are more likely to adapt to the values and modes of behavior that characterize stable democracies than the new leaders in the former Soviet states. Much will depend also on the way in which Western democracies will respond to the needs of the new democracies in the 'post-communist' states. A far more (pro-)active approach, even if it means accepting some sacrifices and costs, would appear to be in the best interests of the democratic world. But how, if at all, does a born-again Russia, in one way or another, compare with its former Communist-Socialist satellites in East and Central Europe?

The Democratization of Russian Civilian Society: Myth and Reality

"Twenty years ago, few would have predicted that Russia would soon experience an economic boom. [Its] economy had been shackled for decades by Soviet rule. It managed to produce oil, nuclear warheads, Kalashnikov rifles, and very little else of interest to the market economies in the West. Then . . . the reforms of former Soviet President Mikhail Gorbachev, perestroika, the revolution of former President Boris Yeltsin, free markets, and billion-dollar fortunes for at least a few. But how are average Russians faring under these changes, and what challenges [lay] ahead in areas like health care, education and

---

11. Cf. Shlapentokh's take on Russia and deLisle's views on China, in this book, as to elite perceptions of threats versus opportunities in the institutional desirability of "rule by law," for divergent pragmatic reasons but to convergent nondemocratic ends in these two countries, the motivating conveniences of which differ at this time.

employment?" queried only last year *Knowledge@Wharton*, that school's newsletter.[12]

Titled "Russia under Putin: Toward Democracy or Dictatorship?" Stephen Kotkin's talk at the Foreign Policy Research Institute (FPRI) in Philadelphia on February 15, 2007, put it succinctly for the audience: "Russia is not a democracy, and it is not a dictatorship. Russia, like most countries of the world, has a ramshackle authoritarian system with some democratic trappings (some of which are meaningful). Russia is not in transition to or from anything. Russia is what it is." Reminding us that, after the United States, Russia comes second "in the number of immigrants it receives each year" ("from former Soviet republics . . . Ukraine, Armenia . . . Tajikistan, though some also come from North Korea and China," "with more than 500,000 and perhaps up to 1 million Muslims" living in Moscow, while "more than a quarter million Russians live in London"), Kotkin stated three major dimensions for understanding Russia's mode of existence and tilt to socio-economic-political inward/outward transformations.[13]

1. "The phenomenon of so-called Kremlin Inc., the now-fashionable notion that the Putin regime is like a big, single-state corporation." Although "to outsiders, the strategy looks like centralization of all power in a disciplined pyramid . . . on the inside, the strategy looks like making sure that the ruling 'team', far from being united, is at each other's throats . . . Kremlin Inc. is a political system of surface stability but turmoil underneath." [Kremlin Inc.'s] "members compete incessantly, and in Russian politics, offense is the best defense, so they proactively go after each other's property and people (in a so-called *naezd*) before waiting for rivals to go after them."

2. "The uncannily stable nature of today's Russian society, something we hear far less about." Despite "an overall decline in [territorial] population at all ages . . . down to 142 million and still shrinking, despite the immigration, [Russia] has a dynamic stable society [that] owns property": "ownership without rule of law" but nonetheless quite "widespread ownership of property," "a stable, dynamic, growing state and corporate middle class that has a tremendous stake in stability." Why? Well . . . "The Russian middle class is smart, and it knows that if it gets political, it could lose its property and status." And "for the most part,

---

12. *Special Report*, April 24, 2007.
13. Professor Kotkin's talk was cosponsored by the Foreign Policy Research Institute and the Mid-Atlantic Russia Business Council. See FPRI's e-note of March 6, 2007.

Russia's middle class is not ready to sacrifice its position to push for the rule of law and democracy; rather, it is interested in preserving its wealth in privileged access for its children to educational institutions and to career paths. So there is no push in Russia for democracy either from the top or the middle, even though much of the middle identifies strongly with European values and institutions."[14] Kotkin argued that "even though there is a strong current in Russian society appreciative of order, few people mistake order for dictatorship. In fact, in conversations, there is quite a lot of criticism in Russia of Putin and of the country's direction, especially from people who comprise the Russian state." In the meantime, "with its hard work, entrepreneurialism, consumption patterns and tastes, demand for education, foreign travel, and networking both domestically and globally," Russian society continues to transform the country's socioeconomic landscape: "Russia's social transformation is a big story, hiding, once again, in plain view."

3. Russia's new-gained "assertiveness, which has taken many people by surprise and which is sometimes perceived as a new threat" [but is not]. "This revived, assertive, resentful Russia is nothing to fear. Russia has state interests that are different from U.S. interests (or Japanese interests or Chinese interests). Russians are more assertive in pressing their perceived state interests, but are they effective in doing so? Have they persuaded Europe that they're a partner in energy security by cutting off the gas to the Ukraine, or are they using their energy muscle in a way that could be compared to stepping on a rake? When you step on a rake, you smack yourself in the forehead. That's Russian foreign policy—smacking oneself in the forehead. Energy supply looks like a point of tremendous leverage for Russia, except energy is a market, which entails a kind of codependency relationship." Kotin went on to remind us that "the old joke about the State Planning Commission, the so-called Gosplan, was that if you put them in charge of the Sahara, there would be a shortage of sand. Well, Gazprom, the gas monopoly, is in charge of the gas in a country that has around 33 percent of world gas reserves, and Russia may be running out of gas. The problem with a market economy is that you actually have to run a company as a business, and if you do not, you will pay the price."

As Kotkin saw it, "the overall picture in Russia, therefore, is, first, a false stability in the regime but actual instability there. The 2008 problem

---

14. Cf. Jacques deLisle, chapter 9, on democratization in China, in this book.

(presidential elections) is one in which everyone sees Putin as a solution but he himself may actually upend their expectations. Second, Russia has a dynamic middle-class society that is stable and mostly apolitical. The middle class in Russia understands that for now, being apolitical is a winning strategy, and so it is deeply apolitical, to the disappointment of human rights and democracy activists. Third, the world will have to get used to the newly assertive Russia. Russia is not what it was in the 1990s, when it was free-falling, in an ongoing post-Soviet collapse, but rather it is a strategic power in a very important location, with its own state interests, interests that are going to conflict with others' interests sometimes. Still, there is no need to be alarmed. The problem with viewing Russia as a major threat is that the threat is mostly to itself, not to the outside world." In addition, remarked Kotkin: "The popular idea of a KGB takeover of the Russian political system makes a certain amount of sense. The Soviet KGB was a huge institution with massive personnel, and so, inevitably, a lot of today's movers and shakers used to work there. But if Putin had worked in the defense ministry, the defense ministry would be "taking over" Russia. If he had worked in the gas industry, those who have made their careers in gas would be "taking over" Russia. It's wrong to assume that because Putin comes from the KGB, and because that's where his loyalists come from, the whole system is moving in the direction of a security regime by design. There is an element of that. Many of Putin's colleagues sometimes do share a certain mentality—distrust of the West—but even more significantly, they belong to competing factions . . . And that's the key point. Whereas "Kremlin Inc." implies a team, united in a collective enterprise, most high Russian officials despise each other. They're rivals, in charge of competing fiefdoms with overlapping jurisdictions, and they're trying to destroy each other. . . . Sometimes, the ruler will impose a temporary truce. Often, though, the ruler will instigate still more conflict, pitting already antagonistic interests against each other, so that they'll run to him for protection and become dependent on him." Keep in mind that "the Russian political system lacks functioning political parties or other institutionalized mechanisms of elite recruitment" and, "instead, it has an extremely personalistic system." Leaders in Russia "appoint to positions of authority those people they went to school with, those from their hometown, those from the places where they used to work. Vladimir Putin came from St. Petersburg. Moreover, he was at the top levels in Moscow for only a short period before he became president. To assert operative control over central state institutions and state-owned corporations, he seeks to appoint people who are loyal to him (sometimes [he's] lucky and gets both competence and loyalty, but often, it's just loyalty). Such people naturally will come from his hometown and former places of work"—they happened to be the Leningrad KGB and the St. Petersburg city government.[15] Well, a year or so later, it turns out that the current Russian President Dmitry Anatolyevich Medvedev did grow up in a suburb of St. Petersburg; did, indeed, serve as now-Prime Minister Vladimir Putin's chief of staff; and did assume the chairmanship of Gazprom's Board of Directors—twice. One may remember the scandals at Gazprom before then-President Putin took matters in hand and restored order. Today, Gazprom is the largest extractor of natural gas in the world, and its Gazprom Media owns Russia's only nationwide state-independent television station, NTV, as well as Russia's influential newspaper Izvestia, both of which have had to traverse major changes in their editorial policies upon being taken over.

As Russian-American sociologist Vladimir Shlapentokh saw things after the collapse of the Soviet Union, the greatest obstacle to the formation of liberal capitalism in Russia was the continuing lack of law and order in that society. In the aftermath of the anti-Communist revolution in 1991, a common illusion emerged in Russia—and also in the West—that the destruction once and for all of the totalitarian state would spontaneously forge a new, truly civil, society, complete with democratic institutions and Western-style economic formations. In reality, during the 1990s, a peculiar pseudofeudal "new" Russian society emerged, which came to comprise a specific mix of three quite strong sectors: the bureaucratic, the oligarchic, and the criminal sectors, and only one, if very weak, 'liberal' sector. The post-Yeltsin regime proclaimed President Vladimir Putin's policy of restoring order to be his main mission, an objective that would seemingly readily sacrifice democratic institutions if need be. What the data suggested, however, is that without recourse to the time-honored instruments of the old Communist state, President Putin might have faced hardships in trying

15. Which is why, suggested the article—perhaps not all that surprisingly—"there are two main public contenders to succeed Putin as president in 2008. Sergei Ivanov, [who] comes from the Leningrad KGB . . . [and] . . . Dimitrii Medvedev, [who] comes from the St. Petersburg city government. Most insiders suspect there will be a last-minute stealth candidate, in keeping with how Putin himself emerged and how he operates; others suspect that any Putin step-aside in 2008 will be more apparent than real. Only one person knows—if he in fact knows—whom he will be put forward as his successor." Today, we all know what ensued, and how of course.

to reach that goal; that he might have had to continue to perpetuate the social and political circumstances that emerged in the mid-1990s.

In chapter 8, Vladimir Shlapentokh updates those early perceptions, focusing instead on more crucial aspects of the current status and longer-term prospects for democratization in Russia along dimensions hinted by elite attitudes in present context. He observes that, by 2007, Russia had lost its early claim to "being"—or being on the way to becoming—a democratic society.

Various theories for explaining the failure of democracy have been advanced since 2000–2002. In the 1990s, when the fate of Russian democracy was not yet clear for many people, the dominant view in Russia and abroad hinged on a belief in the universalism of democracy and on the secondary importance of innate cultural traditions. In the early years of the twenty-first century, the failure of democracy in Russia became so evident that a new concept took over, suggesting that it was in reality Russia's mass-cultural traditions that ultimately gave shape and content to the political order sweeping the country today.

Shlapentokh finds reason to attribute the major role in this backsliding of democracy in Russia to the political elites. For him, it was the elites who chose the avenue to an authoritarian society, not because of mass political culture, but because of their own selfish appetites and ultimately because of the illegitimacy of their ever-cumulating sizeable fortunes, acquired literally overnight.

The illegal and often crude criminal origins of their fortunes caused these spontaneous elites to worry about what law enforcement agencies in the West and inside Russia might do. They have been even more worried about the imaginable reactions of the Russian population, the majority of which remains cynical as to the legality of the property held by big corporations. The nightmare of an "orange revolution" in the making, however unfounded, hounded private elites incessantly. But because of their illicitly acquired property, even the public elites in charge of wholly official positions could not wish upon themselves an independent parliament, let alone a life in an autonomous judicial system. Irrevocably and indubitably brought to light, the insatiable greed of the new elites, private and public, and their comparably conspicuous addictions to demonstrative consumption would rebuff any allegations as to the critical role that Russian cultural traditions might have played in such malign developments. As all too amply illustrated throughout Russian classical literature, Russian masses always were, and—argues Shlapentokh—remain, deeply hostile toward big wealth and social polarization.

Disdainful of many of the values in the Russian tradition, the ruling elites were able to foment certain elements in Russian culture in ways that best suited their own selfish interests and pursuits at any given moment. The dissemination of "authoritarian ideology" among the people is hence a direct result of a Kremlin-orchestrated public propaganda that continues to seek to awaken nostalgia for a long-gone Soviet empire, to foment jungle patriotism, to fuel xenophobia, and to exploit the disenchantment of the Russian masses against the very first cohort of elites—that of post-1991 vintage. It seems unlikely that mere continuity in change may engender a democratic rule of law for as long as the spontaneously overfattened Russian elites remain wary of some "rule of law" catching up to them from above or from the flanks, or worse—a possible if more and more improbable Colored Revolution pulling the carpet out from under their feet.

How has China fared, and can China's democratization in the (much) longer run prove comparable to what purportedly has been already partly attained in Russia under the guise of liberalization?

China: Development without Democratization?

In a talk some time ago at the FPRI in Philadelphia , Victor Mair (2007) reminded the audience that as "one of the most diverse nations on earth," China "linguistically, ethnically, religiously—on virtually any basis . . . has always had an enormous range of populations and cultural phenomena. It is precisely because of this great social and cultural variety that it has been hard to keep the country together. To maintain political unity has invariably necessitated the exercise of heavy-handed government from the center.[16] China's history for the last 3,500 years documents this lesson very clearly. Whenever the central government is weak or relaxes control, the nation rapidly dissolves into a mass of warring regional and ideological factions. The current government in Beijing is no doubt keenly aware of this history and is consequently fiercely determined not to share power with any group or constituency, be it Falun Gong practitioners, Cantonese merchants and

---

16. On the comparative merits of heavy-handed government from the center regarding political foundations of economic development (precisely in a territorially vast span such as China), see Holt and Turner (1966) for a complementary perspective.

manufacturers, or Manchurian labor leaders and industrialists."
Whereas among the ancient Chinese works, Sun Zi's *Art of War* (*Sun
Zi bingfa*) dwells on military and business applications, the *Dao De Jing*,
like nearly all early works of Chinese thought, was intended primarily
as a guidebook for rulers.

"... [It] advised that the most effective way to govern was through
wuwei   (inaction ... 'nonaction' ... 'disinterested   action' ... 'action
without attachment'). It is similar to the principles advocated in the
ancient Indian classic *Bhagavad Gita*." The perspective that Mair contextualizes here is that whereas "virtually all early schools of Chinese
thought accepted *dao* and *de* as basic components of their reasoning ... their interpretations of the terms differed greatly." And while
"for some, *dao* (literally, 'the Way') was a universal, cosmic principle,
like Brahman in the Indian tradition ... for others, *dao* was more like a
method or technique, rather mundane in comparison with the former
approach. The differences in understanding *de* were equally great. For
those like the Taoists, who looked upon *dao* as universal, cosmic principle, *de* was its manifestation in the individual (*'power'* is one popular
translation; I might prefer *'charisma'*), whereas for the Confucians, *de*
was an ethical concept very close to English *virtue*. Unfortunately,
people have a tendency to translate *de* as *virtue* in all cases, and sometimes it is wholly inappropriate, as when we talk of inferior *de* or evil
de. The source of our word *virtue*, Latin *virtus*, would do as a general
translation for *de*, as it means manliness, inner strength of character,
and that is very close to what the old Chinese word *de* meant." Why,
one might ask, this preamble here? Because it will impart cultural
context when interpreting the insights offered in deLisle's chapter 9,
which examines a resilient puzzle (development without democratization?) in China:

"The Confucians and the Taoists were at odds on almost every issue
about how human beings should relate to each other in society. The
Confucians stressed *li* (civility, etiquette, ritual), *ren* (humaneness,
benevolence), and *yi* (justice, righteousness), among other related,
ethical concepts. The Taoists, in contrast, believed either that these
concepts were ineffectual or that they actually jinxed human relationships. They would permit people to behave more naturally, freed of
artificial norms and constraints. But the Taoist and Confucian outlooks
were by no means the only two positions on the spectrum of early
Chinese thought. Among numerous other schools were the Mohists
(followers of Mo Zi [Master Mo]), who displayed great affinity with

Christianity in emphasizing the need for universal love; the egoists (epicureans/hedonists) who advocated self-interest and personal enjoyment above all; the technicians, who believed that skillful methods were all that was necessary to run a smoothly functioning government, and perforce, society; and the Legalists, who insisted that the only way to ensure a peaceful, orderly society was through the rigorous, inflexible application of law. In the end, the Legalists won out, as might well be expected, considering the chaotic situation that had to be overcome. It was the short-lived (221 to 206 B.C.E.), legalistic Qin Dynasty that established the fundamental bureaucratic institutions by means of which China was governed for the next 2,200 years—when it was governed at all, that is, as there was a succession of many dynasties and almost constant contestation for power, often erupting into rebellions, revolutions, and full-scale war," Mair reminds us in his FPRI article. But, one may ask, after so many revolutions and counter-revolutions and the extensive periods of illiteracy that have accompanied each of these shocks and countershocks, how many Chinese have read or still remember their imperial history, their ancient philosophers and ancestral traditions, let alone heed 'old lessons' in a 'new era'? After long decades of Communist rule, was it not surprising how quickly and intensely both the Russian masses and the Russian elites seem to have taken to the elaborate practice of Orthodox rites, and with what joy and pride they seem to have welcomed anew the majestic pageantry that so regally accentuates those private practices in full public view? It remains nevertheless true that China's philosophical ways and Russia's religious fervor cannot be expected to have an impact on their respective societies in identical ways to comparable extents.

Reflecting on the decades traversed by China since Mao to date, Melanie Manion (2007) suggests that if "the phrase that best characterizes the Maoist era is 'never forget class struggle' . . ." by contrast, the mantra (harmonious society) that the Communist Party has endorsed most recently "is distinctly un-Maoist, even somewhat Confucian," for "it is a long way from class struggle to harmonious society." Manion argues that "Mao was able to invoke his cult of personality, control of the army, and historically 'best guesses' to outmaneuver his colleagues, often with end-runs around formal organizations and procedures. This was evident in the rapid pace of agricultural collectivization after 1955, the radicalization of the Great Leap Forward after the Lushan Plenum in 1959, and [in the] destruction of the CCP in the Cultural Revolution." In contrast, today, "there is a tremendous

concentration of decision-making power at the top of the Chinese political system, in fewer than a dozen leaders on the Politburo Standing
Committee. The Party is organized hierarchically and dominates
governance in organizations and localities from top to bottom. . . . And
this concentration of power produces a lack of open debate on policies
and a smaller pool of ideas."

Hence, deems Manion, "today, power is no longer as concentrated as in the Maoist era or even under Deng Xiaoping in the
post-Mao era. Economic power has been significantly decentralized.
Politically, the cult of personality has been officially repudiated and
collective leadership promoted." Indeed, "neither Hu Jintao nor
Wen Jiabao [has] the stature of a Mao or a Deng. In policymaking,
central agencies rely on their own think tanks as well as research
institutes outside the Party and government. Businesses, including
foreign businesses, regularly lobby government departments about
laws and regulations that affect their bottom line. There is greater
transparency in policymaking. Of course, mass media openness has
been severely curtailed in recent years." One might agree with Manion
that this situation is unlikely to improve at a fast pace—it was not
emphatically better after the 17th Party Congress in fall 2007 and problems with Internet access lingered on the late eve of the Olympics in
August 2008. Still, the media is not the slavish Party instrument of the
Maoist era, suggests Manion, and one has to agree.

In chapter 9, jurist and China-specialist Jacques deLisle is unambigu-
ous about China's position in reference to democratization: for more
than a quarter century, the People's Republic of China (PRC) has been
pursuing a distinctive strategy toward achieving economic development while avoiding political democratization. And it has been doing
so in part by relying on law to support development and forestall pressures for democracy. This 'implicit' PRC model poses the greatest of all
contemporary challenges to the post–Cold War conventional wisdom
(which echoes an earlier postwar conventional wisdom) that markets,
democracy, and the rule of law go together.

In many respects, the PRC's approach to pursuing development
without democracy (or a strong rule of law) resembles the East Asian
model that emerged from the industrialization experiences of the four
"tiger" economies (South Korea, Taiwan, Hong Kong, and Singapore)
and, before them, Japan. But there indeed are also significant diver-
gences between the East Asian model (itself, intramurally diverse) and
reform-era China's distinct pursuit of increasingly market-oriented,

internationally open, economic development: its very own version of authoritarian politics and the roles it has expected law to perform.

The implicit Chinese model has been particularly distinctive with respect to the roles of law (this is a point on which the other exemplars of the East Asian model differ greatly): in China, law is to help build frameworks for markets that will foster development and thereby also provide the people with rising wealth—an effect that putatively will 'buy off' pressures for democratization. Law is to substitute for democracy in providing development-sustaining mechanisms (those of monitoring and controlling economically harmful Party-state behavior) and law is to forestall demand for some of democracy's more political functions by providing insulation from (noneconomic) official misbehavior, few and very limited means for accountability of officials, and just as low and limited a popular input into the governance of that people's own country.

The difficulty the East Asian model has encountered in recent years (long after its exemplar states had industrialized) has limited implications for reform-era China's pursuit of development without democracy. Attempts to draw lessons from such developments, and thus to vindicate the post–Cold War conventional wisdom, are made even more problematic by China's lower level of development and belated international integration, its sheer inability to use some classic East Asian model methods, its significantly different modes of pursuing development, its avoidance of democracy, its use of law to just that effect, and other differences in circumstance as well.

But this implicit Chinese model faces growing difficulties in sustaining the pace of development, in avoiding or quelling pressures for democratization, and in building a legal order sufficient for law to fulfill its expected roles. Nonetheless, and even if the post–Cold War conventional wisdom is right, the reform-era Chinese approach, which has survived and adapted for more than two decades now, may yet provide a successful transition or even evolve into a viable long-term solution.

This constructive and positively hopeful perspective by deLisle is not shared by those who see darker connections between a state's pragmatic pursuit of undemocratic governance, a nation's complicit accommodation, and its citizenry's opportunistic indifference to the lack of an ethic of freedom and to the long-term implications of such a void, however. Edward Friedman (2007), for one, deems that "what is growing in China is an authoritarian, patriotic, racially defined,

Confucian Chinese project, which is going to be a formidable challenge not just to the United States but . . . to democracy, freedom, and
human rights all around the world"; that "China's rise means that
freedom is in trouble"; that "the era we're in is very much like the
era after WWI. Authoritarian models are rising and are becoming
more attractive"; that hence, naturally one "can imagine a future
in which unregulated hedge funds lead to an international financial
crisis [which is] seen as coming out of the Anglo-American countries,
London. and New York being the two centers of these monies" ["China
regulates capital, so these things are not allowed in"] and that therefore "the Chinese model may yet look even more attractive than it
does now." Indeed, argues Friedman, "China is going to seem quite
attractive to many people," because "the Chinese regime has fostered
a nationalism to trump democracy. People are taught that they are
threatened by democracy, that democracy would make people weak.
[As Chinese] Party propaganda [phrases] it, 'How did Rwanda
occur? Because they tried to build a democracy. If the Hutus had
simply imposed their will, they never would have had that problem.
[Thus] if it moves in a democratic direction, China is going to fall
apart; [things] will be like what happened to Russia, to Yugoslavia.
Do you [Chinese] want to end up like Chechnya and Bosnia? That's
what the Americans really want. You are fortunate to be Chinese
living in an ethical, authoritarian system.' The TV will show pictures
of say the Los Angeles riots, the Sudan, and people are made fright-
ened and confused. They're proud to be Chinese and want to raise
ethical kids. They want a country they can be proud of, certainly not
like American kids. The Chinese are taught that American youth are
smoking at an early age, use pot, have babies in their teens, watch
pornography on TV, spread AIDS, get divorced, and don't care what
happens to their elderly parents. Why would you want to live in such
an immoral way? This propaganda seems to work with many Chinese"
(Friedman 2007). Whichever the truer, or the more perspicacious,
among these extant perspectives, it likely will take quite some time
for democracy to blossom inside China and for democratization to be
pursued—whether with a bottom-up and/or top-down approach.
While the expectation that China's experience of an instant multifaceted all-encompassing interface of global import on its own home
territory, on the occasion of the 2008 Olympics, might unleash in
it a sudden urge to transform itself into an open society would be
slightly overoptimistic, the very opportunity ought to be seen as

nevertheless enabling yet another small step to be taken in a long march to far happier tomorrows.

Democratizations in Africa: Attempts, Hindrances, and Prospects

Stephen Brown and Paul Kaiser, the authors of chapter 10, are political scientists with an expertise and corresponding field experience in Africa. Their chapter suggests that experiences differ so widely in Africa that one can only speak of democratization in the plural. Although most countries were granted independence under a multi-party system, military rule and one-party states began to typify African regimes all too soon. Some underwent crippling civil wars, from which a few are only beginning to emerge, and some even experienced 'state collapse'. After 1989, however, Africa witnessed a sudden resurgence of democracy. The vast majority of countries in Africa held multiparty elections, albeit of widely divergent quality. In some places, dictators peacefully ceded power to elected opposition leaders. In others, the ruling party controlled the process to ensure it would not lose power. And in a few cases, military coups reversed previous gains. Even if the results were often disappointing or short lived, the continent of Africa during the 1990s was swept by a wave of democratization unseen for a generation. And this phenomenon warrants much closer study in the framework of our worldwide scrutiny here.

In their chapter on this puzzling topic, Brown and Kaiser survey a representative array of African democratizations. They use as categorical examples four sub-Saharan countries, each of which offers different insights into postcolonial democratic experiences on the African continent: Botswana has enjoyed decades of uninterrupted multiparty politics (but single-party rule) under a political system that mixes Western-style liberal democracy with traditional top-down structures. Benin has democratized rapidly, in relatively successful fashion since 1989, after a long period of dictatorial rule, hence providing a 'transition model' for several other African countries. Kenya's former ruling party reluctantly permitted a multiparty system in 1991 but resisted all further democratization, and thus remained in power for another decade, by manipulating (at times violently) the transition process. In Burundi, on the other hand, democracy was severely undermined in 1993, when army extremists assassinated the new president—(the first one to be freely elected) and raised waves of retributive 'ethnic' violence that have recently subsided but not yet ended. These four cases are drawn from each of the four regions of sub-Saharan Africa (West, East, Central, and Southern), thus also reflecting the main colonial legacies (two former British colonies, one French, and one Belgian) that have marked Africa. Are there any generalizable insights, any "lessons," to harvest here?

After presenting each case, the authors proceed to explore competing explanations for success and failure in democratic pursuits, transitions, and survival, by focusing on voluntaristic and structural factors particularly relevant to the continent. They use a comparative case study approach, supplemented by comparative thematic investigations, and this provides the authors with the opportunity to consider the continent's grave impediments to democratization and to ponder how those might be overcome while also critically evaluating any suitable alternatives to the dominant Western model of liberal democracy, such as those explored by some of the other chapters of this book in other parts of the world, where displacements enter the equation.

Immigration and Democratization: Crossing the Mexico-U.S. Border

Precisely because international migration involves the crossing of borders, it also holds very significant potential for challenging authoritarian rule in migrant-sending countries. It does so—argue demographer-sociologist Douglas Massey and his co-author Mara Pérez, who is also a sociologist with broad expertise on Latin America— by removing large numbers of people from repressive co-optive controls imposed by authoritarian regimes to maintain power. Drawing on many examples from Latin America, Massey and Pérez demonstrate how international migration can produce conditions favorable to political mobilization against repressive regimes. They enumerate the specific characteristics likely to promote a movement for democratization among the members of a diaspora: large numbers, high circularity, a politically open host society, geographic concentration, unmistakable accumulation of resources, and free markets in the country of origin.

Their chapter illustrates all these characteristics with many examples from Cuba, the Dominican Republic, El Salvador, Guatemala, and Colombia. The role played by international migrants in the pro-democracy movement is described in detail for Mexico, a country whose diaspora has been the largest. Mexico's long history of migration and of settlement 'north of the border' created conditions particularly favorable to democratic mobilization.

In the mid-1980s, Mexican migrants in the United States became increasingly active as participants in the struggle for democracy within Mexico. Mexicans living north of the border thus mobilized to support opposition parties of both the left and the right during the 1988, 1994, and 2000 presidential elections, raising money, holding rallies, lobbying U.S. authorities, and establishing nongovernmental organizations to monitor Mexican politics. The diaspora demanded and received recognition of dual nationality, and expatriates were granted the right to vote in national elections, at least in principle, if not yet in practice. Migrants were one of the key constituents pushing for the creation of an electoral institute to manage and supervise elections independently. Such was the influence of the diaspora by the end of the twentieth century that visits on the part of rather important Mexican politicians to large expatriate communities in Los Angeles, Chicago, Houston, and other locations north of the border had become routine.

The movement toward democratization crested in 2000, with the first free election of a Mexican president in decades and the ouster of the political party that had monopolized power for some 70 years. Mexican democracy is now more open than it ever has been, and, in a very real way, Mexican migrants have served as the catalyst for this felicitous transformation. The tangible contribution of international migration to democratization is not limited to Latin America, of course, and the potential for immigrants' diasporas to contribute to democratic transitions elsewhere in the world is very real. *Real* also is the struggle for some categories of peoples in such diasporas to find their niches in their newfound environments[17]: the processes of democratization seem to gain in complexity in sending and receiving countries via the novel conditions created by noncitizen diasporas. And in contexts of compounding heterogeneity, communication becomes a crucial prerequisite in the complex pursuit of democratization.

Voice, Participation, and the Globalization of Communication Systems

Hopes for democratization, both in its small- and large-scale manifestations, hinge fundamentally on communication among citizens. As new communication technologies (NCTs) increasingly procreate and consolidate the globalization of these flows of communication, a

---

17. See Gutiérrez (2008) for an argumentation that provides a complementary perspective by examining diasporaic impact on the receiving country's democratization and on the civic ethic of its home-grown citizenry.

systematic interrogation of the implications for, and the impact on, democracy is required. In chapter 12, the late James P. McDaniel and his colleagues Timothy Kuhn and Stanley Deetz, from the Department of Communication at the University of Colorado-Boulder, examine the development of, and the discourse over, NCTs from a strong theory of communication. The trio draws a useful distinction between concepts of communication as transmission and visions of communication as dialogue, by suggesting that although the former conceptualization is a more prevalent mode of understanding human interaction, the latter offers greater conceptual purchase on the technological shaping of human subjectivities and open communities. From the issues raised by the communication-as-dialogue perspective,[18] they elicit three themes in NCT development discourse with clear implications for democratic participation; with these now in hand, they draw on the pertinent work of Jürgen Habermas to develop a normative foundation for communication technology policy that can contribute to much stronger and future-friendlier versions of democracy.

Democratic Prospects in Undemocratic Times

As the concluding chapter by political theorist Patrick Deneen reminds us, however, the richness of the book's contributions ought not to help buffer the fact that, as processes, democratizations are less plural than may appear at first blush. Beneath the unmistakable diversity of purposeful pursuits of "democratization," there still is nevertheless a clear singular conception of "democracy" that reflects the reigning philosophy of modern liberalism. Resting on the basis of consent (and hence on the view that politics is conventional and that humans are to be conceived as naturally individualistic) and situating as its central goals human autonomy, economic growth, efficiency, and the professionalization of politics, 'modern' forms of democracy might be judged insufficiently democratic when compared and confronted with competing conceptions of democracy. By contrast, ancient political theory used to hold that democracy rested on equal political rule—not merely through periodic elections, but via active participation in self-governance—while at the same time emphasizing the development of a certain 'democratic character' apt to encourage self-governance and mutual concern in the civic sphere.

---

18. Cf. Cooper and Christians (2008).

In light of this comparison, "democratizations" may appear less plausible than is suggested, even though some evidence of this more ancient sense of civic democracy may have been temporarily visible in the aftermath of the tragedy of September 11, 2001—the day the two World Trade Center Towers in New York were destroyed and the Pentagon in Washington, D.C., was attacked by those few for whom the tallest monetary and strongest military symbols of advanced capitalism and the deepest foundations of advanced democracy are but one and the same.

References

Aslund, Anders, and Michael McFaul, Editors (2006) *Revolution in Orange: The Origins of Ukraine's Democratic Breakthrough*, Washington, DC: Carnegie Endowment for International Peace.

Bunce, Valerie J., and Sharon L. Wolchik (2006) "International Diffusion and Post-Communist Electoral Revolutions," *Communist and Post-Communist Studies*, 39(3) (September):283–304.

Ciprut, Jose V., Editor (2008) *The Future of Citizenship*, Cambridge, MA: The MIT Press.

Cooper, Thomas W., and Clifford G. Christians (2008) "On the Need and the Requirements for a Global Ethic of Communication," in Jose V. Ciprut, Editor, *Ethics, Politics, and Democracy*, Cambridge, MA: The MIT Press.

D'Anieri, Paul (2006) "Explaining the Success and Failure of Post-Communist Revolutions," *Communist and Post-Communist Studies*, 39(3) (September):331–350.

Forbig, Joerg, and Pavol Demeš, Editors (2007) *Reclaiming Democracy—Civil Society and Electoral Change in Central and Eastern Europe*, Washington, DC: The German Marshall Fund of the United States (GMFUS/ERSTE Foundation).

Friedman, Edward (2007) "Living Without Freedom in China," *Footnotes*, The Newsletter of FPRI's Marvin Wachman Fund for International Education, vol. 12, no. 20 (June), Philadelphia: FPRI.

Gutiérrez, David G. (2008) "Citizenship Dispersed: A Third Space Looking for Its Proper Place," in Jose V. Ciprut, Editor, *The Future of Citizenship*, Cambridge, MA: The MIT Press.

Heyd, David, Editor (1996) *Toleration: An Elusive Virtue*, Princeton, NJ: Princeton University Press.

Holt, Robert T., and John E. Turner (1966) *The Political Basis of Economic Development— An Exploration in the Comparative Political Analysis*, Princeton, NJ: Van Nostrand.

Knowledge@Wharton Newsletter (2007) "No Going Back: Russia Today Suggests Stability Instead of Chaos," *Special Report*, April 24, http://knowledge.wharton.upenn.edu/article/1716.cfm.

Kotkin, Stephen (2007) "Russia under Putin: Toward Democracy or Dictatorship?" presented on February 15, 2007, in Philadelphia, cosponsored by FPRI and the Mid-Atlantic–Russia Business Council. Excerpts here reproduced are from FPRI's *E-Note* of March 2007. Copyright © 2001–2007 Foreign Policy Research Institute.

Kuzio, Taras (2006) "Civil Society, Youth and Societal Mobilization in Democratic Revolutions," *Communist and Post-Communist Studies*, 39(3) (September):365–386.

Levitsky, Steven, and Lucan A. Way (2005) "International Linkage and Democratization," *Journal of Democracy*, 16(3) (July):20–34.

Mair, Victor H. (2007) "Classical Chinese Thought and Culture and Early Chinese History," *Footnotes*, vol. 12, no. 3 (April), Philadelphia: FPRI.

Manion, Melanie (2007) "From Mao to Deng and Beyond: The Fate of Policy Oscillations in the Quest for a 'Harmonious Society," *Footnotes*, vol. 12, no. 2 (April), Philadelphia: FPRI.

McFaul, M. (2002) "The Fourth Wave of Democracy and Dictatorship: Noncooperative Transitions in the Postcommunist World," *World Politics*, 54(2):212–244.

—— (2005) "Transitions from Post-Communism," *Journal of Democracy*, 16(3) (July):5–19.

Silitski, Vitali (2005) "Preempting Democracy: The Case of Belarus," *Journal of Democracy*, 16(4) (October):83–97.

Way, Lucan A. (2006) "The Dynamics of Autocratic Coercion After the Cold War," *Communist and Post-Communist Studies*, 39(3) (September):387–410.

2

From Rule of Law to Freedoms to Enlightened Self-Government: Emplacement of Value in Democratization

Charles F. Doran

Democratization is the process of becoming democratic. At the beginning of the twenty-first century, democratization is probably the foremost political process in the world.[1] With the collapse of the Soviet Union, democratization received a large boost, not just because communism, the principal irritant to democratization, succumbed both as an active force opposing democracy and, perhaps more importantly, as a model considered by some to be an alternative to democracy. Almost immediately, a whole cluster of nascent democracies acquired shape in Central Europe and on the periphery of Russia out of the fragments of the empire. But the process of democratization is far from complete, either as an offset to residual autocracy in Asia, Africa, and to some extent South America, or in terms of the struggle to reach a high level of democratic maturity in all of its dimensions among the governments that long have regarded themselves as democracies (such as Japan and the countries of Western Europe and North America).[2] Indeed, the process of democratization is open ended. The process must ever guard against backsliding, protect hard-won gains and seek greater perfection, teach its values to each new generation, and overcome societal rigidities that hinder if not thwart the process with respect to nascent and mature democracies alike. Democratization is a process that will continue to evolve in the twenty-first century.

Law within democracy is institutionalized democratization. Whether law should precede the establishment of democratic institutions[3] or

---

1. "Had we a place to stand on," said Thomas Paine ([1792] 1973, 394) about liberty and reason, paraphrasing Archimedes, "we might raise the world."
2. Democratization, however, is scarcely a neglected topic. Amazon.com lists some 470 books published over the last decade on some aspect of democratization. An excellent annotated review of the subject prior to 1994 is by Doh Chull Shin (1995).
3. Cf. chapter 9 on China by deLisle in this book.

the democratic institutions capable of making law and capable of regulation should precede the presence of an adequate legal structure is itself a debated question (for example, regarding Russia and the former Soviet Republics), but by this definition it is also a moot question. Forward and backward loops connect law and parliaments, for instance. True, a "law-abiding" society will find democratization easier to introduce than will societies unaccustomed to ordering their public and private behavior by established and transparent rules (O'Donnell and Schmitter 1986). To some extent, the ancient Greek ideal of self-limiting behavior (virtue) facilitates the creation of law-making, law-interpreting, and law-enforcing institutions of democracy (Cornford 1945). But in any society, virtue is a scarce good; therefore, democratization and the evolution of a legal foundation for law will tend to go hand in hand.

Despite the difference between the relative lack of law within the international system and the presence of considerable law within the state, both the democratic polity and the decentralized nation-state system have a firm foundation in pluralism. Pluralism and equilibrium, rather than so-called hegemony, characterize world politics, just as democratic pluralism characterizes domestic politics. In a theory of international relations known as *power cycle theory*, I have developed the implications of pluralism for a liberal world order (Doran 1971, 1991, 2003). Introducing the concept of foreign policy role as coequal in significance with power in matters of statecraft, the theory seeks to reconcile realism and idealism in a concept of equilibrium based on reciprocal adjustments to foreign policy role. Similarly, I argue here, the last frontier of democratization employs responsibility, reciprocal accommodation, and the tolerance of diversity to achieve democratic pluralism.

Societal Core Values

Evolution of a legal foundation for democracy, and therefore of the process of democratization itself, emerges historically out of three core values.[4] Aristotle claimed that the primary value was equality. But by equality he did not mean what Marx meant, namely an equality of guaranteed outcomes, but rather equality before the law and equality

---

4. This analysis supports those who believe that values underlie institutions and that, without the proper values in a society, democratization in the form of mere institutions will fail (Huntington 1992; Lipset 1959; Fukuyama 1992). But values do change,, which is the essence of this chapter. Because values change, they can change at different rates

of opportunity. Indeed, for equality of opportunity to exist, equality before the law is presupposed.

The second core value is freedom. Freedom may not be primary in some existential ordering of values—as to which value is the most important—in Aristotelian fashion. Circa 507 B.C.E., Cleisthenes unleashed the power of Athens by enabling the commoner to participate with the aristocrat in some forms of decision making, foreshadowed, for example, by the slow empowerment of the individual as a full participant in the Olympic games and as a citizen. The concept of freedom may not exist (and did not exist in ancient Greece)[5] without the prior existence of the notion of equality or of equality of opportunity. For in the absence of equality of opportunity, Aristotle may be correct that the idea of freedom is meaningless, as the absence of the equality of opportunity enables those with power to abridge freedom whether in terms of institutions as under the medieval church, or of classes as inside the court of Louis XIV, or of rules (notwithstanding seeming meritocracy), as in the ancient Chinese examination system.

But surely in terms of historical time, the origin of freedom tended to precede equality. Man sought political freedom, achieving a modicum of it through the material uplift provided by the Agricultural Revolution, through the political emancipation that followed the clash of religious forces in the Reformation and counter-Reformation, and through the intellectual absolution attained from the verities of science by a man like Galileo. Freedom in any broad-based political sense came first, historically, because it was demanded first and was wrenched from institutions and polities, including absolute monarchy, by resolute men and women.

Finally, tolerance, the laggard societal value, has slowly emerged as a goal of society and as an accepted human value. It is for example almost unbelievable that in a society self-consciously proud of its humanistic record—the United States—adults are alive today who can remember a society that obliged some of its citizens to sit at the back of the bus, that instructed them to use separate washrooms, to attend separate schools, and to live in separate neighborhoods. It is almost unbelievable that, within the memory of these same adults, a young woman operating a labeling machine in an assembly line requiring by

(Inglehart 1997, 267–292). And, because they change at different rates, they can in some cases be assisted to change, and democratization in some cases (as in Poland from 1970 to 1990) can be promoted, although the task is selective and difficult to accomplish (Diamond 1992; Allison and Beschel 1992).

5. See McInerney (2008).

definition everyone to work at the same speed could have been remu-
nerated at a 1 percent lower wage than men working side by side with
her, unabashedly explicitly for the only reason that she was a woman.
Problems of intolerance often deeper and more subtle than in the past
continue to encumber even advanced democratization.

Tolerance in almost every advanced industrial democracy has been
slow in coming and has been uneven in its application. A country like
France, known for its defense of human rights internationally, and
recognized as a society that has been remarkably "color-blind," nonetheless showed an unenviable record toward tolerance during the
Vichy Regime (despite the presence of hugely courageous resistance
fighters during the Nazi occupation[6]) and contends with the issue of
cultural differentiation to this day. As countries like Mozambique and
Rwanda demonstrate, the experience of oppression does not guarantee
tolerance toward the since-displaced minority by the once-benighted
majority now in power.

Indeed, tolerance has been ignored by many political theorists (Voltaire was an exception) as secondary to the battle for political freedom
or secondary to the aspiration for equal opportunity in the workplace.
And maybe tolerance is properly regarded as secondary to these other
values. But what has been neglected by political theory is how relevant
tolerance is to the full achievement of a just society and therefore to
democratization as a more complete and encompassing process.

Historical Evolution of Core Values

Historical evolution of core values across societies globally is thus a
process conspicuous for its exclusivity and biases, not least its disap-
pointments, and its reversals. How, for example, do these societies fit
treatment of native peoples into the overall human rights record? Yet
there has been evolution, albeit from different starting points and at
different rates, for the emplacing of these values into the overall societal
framework of the nation-state. Although there may be great disagreement about the order that these processes of value emplacement
assume, the awareness that societal reform is ongoing and more willing
to accept these core values is hard to deny.

Putting dates on the emplacement of core values across the entire
system of states is even more difficult and speculative than for indi-

---

6. "Special" to *New York Times*, August 24, 1944.

vidual societies. For example, Michael Doyle concludes that democracy as a complex of core values did not begin much before 1700 and then only in a few Swiss cantons and in the northern colonies in America (Doyle 1986). But the analytic reward of attempting to make theoretical generalizations across time and across countries is large. In concept and in practice, the historical emergence of these core values did not proceed in tandem.

Freedom has by far the longest historical record of the three core values. While Spain, Ireland, La Rochelle after the defeat of the Huguenots, most of the Austrian Empire, the Germanies, and all of the remainder of Central Europe and Russia were backwaters of repression, by the beginning of the seventeenth century, pools of freedom were widening in places like the Swiss cantons, the Netherlands, parts of England, and the colonies of the New World, especially in New England and along the banks of the Chesapeake. William Penn's battle for what came to be known as 'habeas corpus' in the Penn-Meade trial was as monumental as any act in the New World and with equal consequence there. It was not surprising that Thomas Jefferson attributed to William Penn the title, "the greatest law-giver the world has produced." Ironically, although much of this expansion of freedom came as an attempt to escape religious bigotry, bigotry was hard to escape.[7] For example, in Salem or in Jamestown or toward the Quakers, and what resulted instead often was political freedom, particularly the right of exit.

Long before the political revolutions of the late eighteenth and mid-nineteenth centuries, political freedom in Western Europe and North America and a few other parts of the world was well advanced. That the majority of the people of the world still did not know freedom of any decisive sort is not the point. Political freedom for white, male property owners (and eventually religious freedom between sects and governments and even inside some sects) was spreading like a spilled can of paint throughout the Western Hemisphere, if more slowly elsewhere.

Equality of opportunity in a sense first emerged among the guilds, more with respect to the guilds vis-à-vis governments and employers than for the individual members of the guilds vis-à-vis the guild organization itself, however. Not surprisingly, freedom of opportunity flourished as early as the twelfth century: when cathedrals required

---

7. See Sheldon Hackney (2008), "Shades of Freedom in America," in Jose V. Ciprut, Editor, *Freedom: Reassessments and Rephrasings*, Cambridge, MA: The MIT Press.

skilled craftsmen; or during the labor shortages after the Plague, or the religious wars; or much later, in periods of boom during canal building; or during early industrialization, when factories demanded labor from the farms; or, as in the New World, from abroad. A rising tide in terms of economic growth or even inflation raised many boats, starting with the most expensive.

But in general, equality of opportunity in any more than a very narrow sense was a product of the industrial revolution. Production increased demand for labor. Demand for labor increased not only the need for labor itself but the wages paid to labor; and this latter demand broke the bonds of convention on immigration, work outside the home, and employment outside the caste, sect, or local community. However, equality of opportunity could often ironically also sometimes be equated with abuse, child labor, and neglect of the workplace. All was not progress, of course. One is reminded of the woman in Stalinist Russia who said that Russian women do not want any more "equality of opportunity," for they cannot stand any more shoveling of cement.

Prior to the 1920s, the only job a respectable middle-class woman in Europe or North America could find was that of teacher or nurse. Despite unequal pay for equal work and "glass ceilings," demand for woman-power during the two great wars opened up the job market. Yet equality of opportunity, even for men, scarcely predated the historic beginnings of the larger migrations to the New World in the late eighteenth century.

Civil tolerance has the shortest historical record. In the broad-based civic sense, tolerance did not much predate the twentieth century. It is true that pockets of tolerance—religious, tribal, personal—existed even in primitive societies. Nor does everything outside the democracies (e.g., in the Third World) equate with intolerance. Caste-ridden India appeared to mimic colonial intolerance even while demanding British-style self-government. Side by side with acts of rather gross intolerance toward women and children stood acts of magnanimity and considerable tolerance, for instance, in terms of willingness to adopt children from outside the sect or community. Demolishing any sense of progress were the monumental cases of intolerance in Nazi Germany and against others by Imperial Japan and by the totalitarian societies of the Soviet Union and of China.

Of course, the democracies themselves were scarcely free of intolerance within their own societies, as slavery prior to the American Civil

War shockingly reminds, and as segregation until 1960 appallingly records. Intolerance inside the democracies was often masked and differed from that experienced elsewhere in the world largely in terms of quantity rather than quality.

Thus, nondemocracies are not inherently "inferior" to democracies socially, culturally, or intellectually, nor are they somehow "contemptible" on the basis of some tenet of universal human rights (despite the empirical findings in Kincaid's chapter in this book [chapter 5]). On the contrary, just as love, human dignity, the capacity for responsibility and courage, and the ability to cope with and find meaning in death may receive superior sensibility in primitive society vis-à-vis life in Third World society today, so may these important aspects of life receive more compassionate understanding at least in some places in the Third World today than in some advanced industrial countries.

Indeed, what is shocking to modern ears is how often intolerance coexists, in supposedly sophisticated society and in the brilliant mind (Ezra Pound), with otherwise generous instincts and creative ability. Although Benjamin Franklin, third only in the popular mind to Washington and Jefferson as architect of U.S. American independence, eventually favored the emancipation of slaves, he and many of his contemporaries spoke pejoratively of the Mediterranean peoples and other "races." "Why should Pennsylvania, founded by the English, become a colony of aliens, who will shortly be so numerous as to Germanize us, instead of [our] Anglifying them?"[8] Apparently, he forgot how even George I, of German stock (Hanover), spoke English badly and "Anglified" slowly and how slowly assimilation occurs. In contrast, the more remarkable were the enlightened views of men like George Washington and John Adams.

Tolerance was the last value to be etched on Locke's tabula rasa. Morality, of course, must in the Lockean sense be taught, since it is not an "inherited characteristic" (notwithstanding Larmarck[9]) in Darwinian or evolutionary terms, and only when learned can it become the morality of Hume as habit. Underlying all of morality is charity; charity is merely the flip side of tolerance. So if tolerance at base is morality, and morality is learned, it is hard not to conclude that mankind has taken an inordinately long time to internalize tolerance.

---

8. Benjamin Franklin as quoted in Carl van Doren (1938, 218).
9. Known for his zoological philosophy, Jean Baptiste Larmarck's work on evolution was published in 1809.—*Ed.*

The reason in part that humankind has taken so long to learn and assimilate tolerance is that collectives (societies and communities) have not learned what the individual, by personal experience, often already knows. In *Two Solitudes*, MacLennan (1945) observes that when a French Canadian (Quebecer) dislikes the cultural other, it is almost never at the individual level and almost always at the level of the collective. Just as mobs induce what the individual himself would never permit, so collectives for their own purpose have perpetuated intolerance as a way of obtaining control, continuity, and longevity for the leadership, and for the collective itself, at the cost of true civility and rational political purpose. Reinhold Niebuhr (1932), in his classic *Moral Man and Immoral Society*, summed up the problem, but did not offer a solution. No matter how intimidated by the collective, the individual possesses a conscience. But the collective in a society without the proper values, system of law, or institutions knows no such constraint upon its will or ego.[10]

Although it may be correct that, like poverty, intolerance, too, will always be with us, we hope that intolerance, like poverty, will also become increasingly a relative problem. Relative intolerance, though less than ideal, is surely less bad than absolute intolerance, which was pretty much what preceded 1945 in a majority of societies worldwide. It is absolute intolerance (sometimes incited by nationalist elites, and sometimes even in the name of democratization) that is the only thing strong enough to induce the bitter acts of revenge and personal violence that have occurred in places like Kosovo, Chechnya, and Rwanda.

What restrains the nonrational motives of collective enterprise and what channels individual wills into productive and more rational collective endeavor is democratic pluralism. Democratic pluralism harnesses collective purpose and teams it with beneficent individual intent within a proper system of law.

Emplacement of Core Values in Democratization

It is not clear whether "the process of establishing democracy" (democratization) results from the increased generation of core values or

---

10. See David R. Williams (2008), "Ego and Ethos," in Jose V. Ciprut, Editor, *Ethics, Politics, and Democracy: From Primordial Principles to Prospective Practices*, Cambridge, MA: The MIT Press.

follows from the increased realization of those values already present in society but not yet released or actualized for productive purpose.

Hence we will use the term *emplacement* when describing the process of movement from core value to political outcome through the institutionalization of democracy inside a legal framework.

Emplacement involves the translation of value into institution through law. Underlying democratization are three fundamental processes: (1) political participation, representation, and regime stability; (2) economic productivity and growth; and (3) social cohesion.

Each process is essential to the others. Without economic productivity and growth, a polity is unlikely to be able to take advantage of political participation, representation, and stability.[11] The decision of Pisistratus (sixth century B.C.E.) to offer low-interest loans and an olive tree to each Athenian preceded and helped ease the shift toward greater political participation in government by those citizens, whose subsequent prosperity created a responsible and necessary commercial base for democracy. Not always appreciated in the case of the thirteen American colonies is that their experiment in democracy was enormously abetted by robust economic growth across these colonies and across time for decades prior to the decision to declare independence. And even then the fear of being cut off from Britain on the part of many of the colonials was more an economic fear of loss of trade and commerce than a political fear of diplomatic isolation or of the inability to make democracy work apart from Westminster.

Similarly, the economic problems of consistent growth and of continuous increase in economic productivity for countries in Latin America is an important variable often left out of the problems of democratization by political scientists concentrating on civil-military relations and intragovernmental shortcomings (Boylan 2001). Conversely, the economic boom in Japan and in Southeast Asia, notwithstanding interim financial crises, is at least in part responsible for the success of democracy throughout the region, especially in South Korea and Taiwan (Scalapino 1993).

That a modicum of social cohesion is necessary for political development is a given and, until fairly recently, has been assumed to be automatic as democracies matured (Evans 1997). In part for external reasons—the end of the Cold War, which reduced security concerns

---

11. "Without a measure of prosperity a man cannot exercise the good activity which is well-being" (in *Aristotle*, Ross 1923, 1964, 192).

and the emergence of regional trade areas, which held out the promise of unrestricted trade gains after independence—a number of countries with longstanding communal divisions have now faced the prospect of separation by these communities despite the presence of mature democratic institutions and the respect for law and order (Leff 1999). Social cohesion, long assumed to be guaranteed, is in danger of becoming unglued, not in the violent manner that occurred in Lebanon, but possibly instead via a kind of peaceful resignation to the perceived inevitable by governments tired of resisting internal communal defiance that has been quite remorseless.[12] Countries included in this category where social cohesion is fragile include Great Britain, Spain, Canada, Belgium, Northern Italy, Romania, and Hungary. Israel, under quite different circumstances of divergent growth rates of communal populations, could be added to the list. Czechoslovakia succumbed to "velvet divorce" carried out by elites in the face of nagging complaints by the poorer Slovak portion of the country. Upon division, opinion polls in Slovakia revealed that a majority of the population had actually wanted to remain united with the Czech Republic but that expression of democratic preference for unity came too late. Even centrist France faced challenges of separatist sentiment, primarily in Corsica but with lesser effect elsewhere as well.

Undoubtedly the collapse of the Soviet Union and of Yugoslavia, each for different reasons and with very different consequences, had an impact on the propensity of communal groups to seek greater autonomy among many of these established and even advanced industrial democracies. Neither of these countries, however, is a good model of what might happen to the rich democracies. Each consisted internally of something like empire, and each also remained whole even in the best of times only through coercion from the top. Empires, unlike states, are likely to break up eventually because of the lack of voluntary participation in the original and continuing makeup of their constitutions.

The true consequence of these problems of social cohesion is in the end much more significant for many nascent democracies in the Third World than for the advanced industrial democracies per se. Bangladesh, India, and Indonesia are countries with large diverse

---

12. Part of the reason that collapse has occurred in some Third World polities, but not others, is that the state is more than a Hobbesian security community. Either internal or external accountability (equality of opportunity) and sacrifice (tolerance) also exist (Gaubatz 2001/2002).

populations in which many cultural, tribal, and ethnic differences have not been resolved. Civil wars, as the experiences in Sri Lanka, Lebanon, Chechnya, Angola, Kashmir, and Dafur (Sudan) suggest, can be intractable, extremely bloody, and very destructive of civil society. Russia itself, struggling with the legacy of empire and the effort to build democratic institutions on a base that has neither a memory of those institutions nor a tradition of the kind of law that facilitates operation of those institutions, is a prime target for problems that will affect its social cohesion.

Thus the greatest contribution that advanced industrial democracy perhaps can make to the rest of the world is as a model regarding how divided societies can cope and cohere even when communal disparity is large and when ethnic and linguistic differences create tasks of communication and management that more monolithic states may not face. Democracy must be shown to work under adverse conditions of social disharmony. Otherwise, governments facing social division, such as Pakistan or the Philippines, may be quite prone to jettison democracy in favor of more autocratic methods that appear to ease the task of sustaining unity when tensions split the country.

When considering the challenge of deepening democracy in terms of political participation as in Mexico, or in terms of representation as in the new regimes of Central Europe, or in terms of the stability of political party structures even in mature democracies such as Italy and Japan, a foundation of social coherence is essential. Political maturity in the sense of long-established democratic traditions seems no longer sufficient, however, to assure that social cohesion will prevail, at least in societies in which more than a single large, territorially based, ethnolinguistic community shares the political space.

If (1) political participation, representation, and stability, plus (2) economic productivity and growth, plus (3) social coherence characterize the modern democracy, then why is entry into that cluster of privileged societies so difficult? Why, with approximately the same interval of time since colonial independence, are the polities of South America less confident democracies than those thriving in North America (Lehoucq 2000)? Why, with cultures as sophisticated and deep as any in the circle of the advanced industrial democracies, with scientific and technical contributions that have predated the West, with aesthetic and intellectual accomplishment in the arts that surpass much of what the West has accomplished, do countries like Turkey, Russia, and Iran struggle to inculcate the values underlying the processes that constitute democratization (Landes 1998)? The answer to these questions, I believe, is that the path of democratization is not as direct or as simple as some theorists of democracy have long thought (see Aronoff 2008).

Overcoming the Inertia to Mature Democracy

At least one answer is that the route to mature democracy is nonlinear geometric growth.[13] However impressive their rate of arithmetic growth may appear to be in the eyes of the society undergoing such, and no matter how difficult the pursuit of such policies may become, monotonic linear progressions typically are insufficient in overcoming the drag of traditionalism, of autocracy, and of "crony capitalism" that usually characterizes predemocratic societies. This rate of increase promises repeated slippage back into unproductive patterns of decision making. Civil society at this rate of increase in democratization is likely to remain stuck in "old ways" of thinking regarding the fit between technology and institutional change. Arithmetic growth is insufficient to crack the mentality that there exists a traditional approach to government that will equivalently lead to democracy, that there is a "Confucian way" or an "Asian way," which is as reliable a guide to democratization as the generalized path (although a bit slower and more selective in its composition and motivation).[14] Behind vigorous endorsement of the alternative "ways" to democracy, despite claims to the contrary, is often the actual desire not to proceed very far or very fast with democratization.

Yet liberalism that reaches too deeply into personal and communal mores, that is too dogmatic and pompous in its self-righteousness, that allows cultural and ethnic difference just too little room to establish or to maintain self-identity, merely feeds the rejection of democracy by equally absolutist critics in the Third World who vow that democ-

---

13. Pontusson (1995, 495–533) found an inverse relationship between industrial organization and employment structure, on the one hand, and the decline of European social democracy measured in terms of labor movements, on the other. Londregan and Poole (1996, 1–30), after controlling for many other variables, found a positive relationship between income and democracy. And Przeworski and Limongi (1997, 155–183) identified a positive relationship between income and democratic regime stability (although not between income and the probability of transition to democracy). In each case, the fit between income and democratization ought to be tighter over longer time intervals when using nonlinear methods, as democratization itself is a nonlinear process.

14. For a vigorous defense of views regarding this point that are the opposite of those presented here, see Chalmers Johnson (2000, 168–169).

ratization, like globalization, is a Western or an American conspiracy. It is fascinating that so many governments with conceptions of society so very different from that of the United States are at least as spirited in their advocacy of democracy. Women and children (e.g., in Iran) are often the best barometers of latent social and political preference. But the excessive promotion of democratization as "human rights" rather than merely as "good government" tends to undermine the progress of democratization in places where democratization is needed most.

Notwithstanding this qualification about style of advocacy and zeal, democratization as a process must be at least as rapid in its development and maturation as other processes around it such as the growth of population, or the required increase in interpersonal and intercorporate communication.

The rate of increase on each of the principal dimensions of democratization must follow a path of multiplicative growth so as to break the shackles of predemocratic attitude and behavior. Only that momentum across time is sufficient to lift the society out of the circumstances that continually force it back into unconstructive patterns of corruption, lack of transparency, and collusive behavior undermining both the political and the economic dimensions of democratization.

Emplacement of Value as a Multiplicative Process

Underlying each of the principal processes of democratization is the emplacement of value that gives the overall process its momentum over time. In keeping with the voluntarism that underlies democracy itself, example is the best mode of emplacement, as John Quincy Adams well understood.

The logic of the dynamic is as follows. Interaction of at least two of the core values is necessary for progress to gain substance toward democratization. In the absence of such interaction between two or more core values the process stagnates or reverses itself. But as these values interact fully, they release a capacity for growth in the resulting process that rises rapidly, so rapidly that the momentum carries the entire movement of democratization with it, or in any case, that portion of the movement that is particularly associated with the specific process so catalyzed. Malthus was right about the mechanism of the growth dynamic, but he was wrong in his assumptions regarding the effect on agriculture of technological inputs. Indeed, multiplicative (geometric, not arithmetic) evolution is the key to unleashing far-reaching democratization.

Equality of Opportunity × Freedom = Economic Productivity and Growth

Equality of opportunity occurs in all societies when a middle class gains enough power to offset absolutism—either an absolute monarch, a hereditary aristocracy, an authoritarian or totalitarian political party structure, or a clique of families that monopolizes economic opportunity. Gradually, equality of opportunity spreads to all members of society. With the spread of economic opportunity comes the increase in freedom including political freedom.

It is not by chance that a true rural middle class of farmers (freeholders) has been the bulwark of political freedom in most of the Western democracies, including Japan, to the point that by the end of the twentieth century, they have become overrepresented in the center-right Christian Democratic parties of Europe, the Liberal-Democratic Party of Japan, the Liberal Party of Canada, and the Democratic Party in the United States, thus actually skewing economic benefit (state subsidy) in their favor (Midlarsky 1992). But their commitment to staunch political freedom against all potential usurpers can never be in doubt.[15]

Equality of opportunity multiplied by freedom amounts to economic productivity and growth, first in the agricultural sector, then in the towns and cities in terms of industrialization. Equality of opportunity is necessary for entrepreneurs to find and employ risk capital. Freedom is necessary for the movement of labor throughout a polity. Freedom ensures that what is earned, minus a reasonable level of taxes, can be retained. Equal opportunity ensures that all of the potential productive sectors and communities within society are able to participate in economic enterprise thus driving economic growth forward at a maximum pace. Equal opportunity means that there is an equal chance for upward or downward mobility and that there are no artificial stabilizers for an indolent rich group of property owners or hereditary elites. Equal opportunity combined with freedom loosens up resources in an economy such that maximum increase of productivity becomes possible through free and open markets.

---

15. That is why in the 1930s Stalin found it necessary to kill some 3 million Kulaks, or property-owning farmers, in the Soviet Union, and why the tension in present-day China is so serious between the Chinese rural middle class and the Communist Party.

Freedom × Tolerance = Political Participation and Political Representation, Plus Regime Stability

The process of enhanced political participation, political representation, and regime stability is an outgrowth of the intense interaction between freedom and tolerance. In sixth century Greece, until Cleisthenes facilitated the toleration of commoners as active participants in society, greater political representation was unable to occur. But it took this toleration to be accompanied by actual political freedom for increased political participation also to take place. Tolerance of difference is essential to the potential for freedom. Increases of freedom, when accompanied by tolerance, can lead to even greater tolerance through contact and familiarization with difference. Over time, greater tolerance leads to increased freedom; increased freedom at first challenges and then reinforces growing tolerance. Together, freedom and tolerance spur the willingness to participate, the capacity to represent, and the confidence necessary to achieve stable political regimes.

Equality of Opportunity × Tolerance = Social Cohesion of Polity

Social cohesion is dependent on the interplay between tolerance in a society and the equality of opportunity for its members. When communities feel they have not been excluded from opportunity, they tend to support the society as a whole. When tolerance of all of the members of a polity exists, there is far less chance that alienation will spoil social cohesion. Equality of opportunity encourages tolerance because the capable and hardworking members of a society feel rewarded regardless of race, color, or creed. And tolerance of ethnolinguistic difference encourages the extension of equality of opportunity.

In Iraq, the democratic challenge is not so much that democracy was externally imposed (as had occurred in India and in many other places as well) but that during the process of building democratic institutions, a revolution had occurred in which the politically dominant Sunni were replaced by the numerically outweighing Shia. For social cohesion to prevail in Iraq, not only tolerance but equality of opportunity must be emplaced in a unifying setting in which Sunni aspirations are reasonable and Shia power sharing is genuine.

When all the members of the various constituent communities feel the cool breeze of tolerance, social cohesion is difficult to dislodge. When they also prosper, or at least believe they have the chance to prosper no less than the members of other communities (i.e., there is reason to believe in an equal opportunity for prosperity), the sense of togetherness within a polity increases regardless of other differences that may divide the society. Equality of opportunity and tolerance go hand in hand. They reinforce each other. But the presence of one does not guarantee the presence of the other. Indeed, only when both values are present in about equal measure is social cohesion likely to flourish. If only one is present, say equality of economic opportunity is present but political tolerance is not, social cohesion is likely to suffer greatly to the point that under extreme conditions of political or religious intolerance a community will seek to cut itself off (as did Calvinists from Britain in 1612–1620) from the larger polity. Consider also a contemporary situation in which tolerance may occur without equality of economic opportunity.

Although the Shia, the Sunni, and the Kurds in Iraq are mostly Muslim, thus assuring tolerance of Islamic faith and practice, one-sided federalism could present a threat to the Sunni community by placing access to the vast bulk of the oil revenues in the hands of only the Shia or Kurds. Such lack of equality of opportunity can destroy social cohesiveness, notwithstanding the ties of religion. Even in a polity known for its political tolerance, if economic favoritism and obstacles to advancement also abound, the affected members of a territorially based ethnolinguistic community are likely to consider separation.

Thus, optimally, when equal opportunity multiplied by political tolerance exists in a society, that society is likely to be a happy one. Each constituent community is likely to feel content with its inclusion in the polity as a whole.

The Just Society

What qualifies as a just society? Rawls (1999, 3–10) and the Roman Catholic Church, for instance, both agree that justice in a society is measured by how it treats the most unfortunate (meanest) among its members. Plato argued that the just society was the "good" society and that only the presence of a "philosopher king" could assure the possible attainment of the good society. Democratic government has the potential to achieve and oversee a just society. When all of the strands of democratization are combined—(1) political participation, representation, and regime stability; (2) economic productivity and growth; and

(3) social cohesion—the outcome can be just. Conversely, alternative forms of government have less prospect of achieving justice if only because the frailty of mankind is less effectively circumscribed and offset by law and institutions in such governments.

What is new with respect to democratization is the awareness now that society must be minimally cohesive to be just. Even advanced industrial democracy is now subject to this principle. Conversely, a just society as interpreted by all of its citizens and based in the law is also likely to be more socially cohesive. Democratic pluralism is thus relevant to the notion of the just society because it is the component of democratization that has been lacking. Democratization as a process is far from complete, either in terms of the number of polities worldwide encompassed by the democratic form of government or in terms of the maturity and fulfillment of those governments presently declaring themselves to be democratic. Democratic pluralism is the "missing variable" in the model of democratization that leads to the just society.

Democratizations: The Unfinished Array of Projects

Historically, albeit perhaps paradoxically for the political scientist, the economic dimensions of democratizations seem to have made the most progress. Worldwide, economic productivity and growth have advanced further than any of the other measurable dimensions of democratization, especially in the age of the globalized economy (van de Walle 1999, 21–42). Underlying this dimension, freedom is the value with the longest history of concerted observance and equality of opportunity and is the value with the second oldest record of widespread observance. Although highly contested as in the Dickens' chronicles and in Hugo's novels, the second underlying value, equality of opportunity, can be traced back prior to the beginning of the nineteenth century. When these two underlying sources of economic productivity and growth are combined, not surprisingly they yield a degree of achievement not matched by any of the other dimensions. Politics seems to have contributed to economics in a way that is very meaningful for this dimension of democratization. And, in turn, this dimension of democratization has become a cornerstone of democracy.

The dimension of democratization with the second greatest degree of performance is that of political participation, representation, and regime stability. Underlying this dimension is the combination of freedom and tolerance; the value freedom has the longest emplacement, and the value tolerance, the shortest emplacement. This intermediate level of achievement for what is the most political of dimensions of democratization conforms to the global reality of many countries attempting to establish democracy and to implement democratic reforms albeit rather incompletely. At least as many "nascent" democracies exist in the world today as "mature" democracies. The difference between nascent and mature democracy is often measured in terms of democratic forms or democratic institutions, which comprise this dimension. But within the cluster of "mature" democracies, although freedom is experienced at a high level, tolerance is still far from universal, thus contributing to the fragmentary performance of the overall dimension (Spinner-Halev 2008).

Social cohesion, the product of equality of opportunity and of tolerance, is the least developed of the three fundamental dimensions of democratization. Considering the history of the efforts to infuse these underlying values within democracy, the explanation for the rather tardy evolution of social cohesion is now evident. Equality of opportunity only emerged with the onset of full industrialization and the impact of immigration on the labor supply. Tolerance in any very enveloping sense only appeared after World War II and even then only as far from a fully entrenched value within mature democracy, while much less elsewhere.

Social cohesion cannot be experienced to its full extent even among the mature democracies because the combination of tolerance and equality of opportunity is still compromised. Equality of opportunity through laws regulating employment, housing, and education has moved further than the disappearance of discrimination and intolerance, which have deeper psychological origins, and a more tenacious behavioral foothold, in many societies.

Thus the discovery that social cohesion is still not guaranteed in Spain, or in Britain, or in Belgium, or in Canada should come as no greater surprise than the fact that social cohesion is still lacking in states throughout the Third World. Complicating the process of enhancing social cohesion is the reality of societal memory lags—for example, the kind that cause the Chinese to remember acidly that the British burned down the Summer Palace (they also burned down the White House in the War of 1812, but so what!) and the Québecois that, during World War II, francophone soldiers had to receive orders in English; just as the Flemish in Belgium find it hard to forget that conversely, they had

to take orders from the French-speaking Walloon officers whom supposedly they found hard to understand. Such sustained and conve-
niently politicized collective memories are about as useful in effect as
allowing Irish blame of the British for failing to prevent the starvation
of more than a million Irishmen in the famines of the 1840s to interfere
with English-Irish trade and investment today.

These lagging collective memories tend to aggravate any genuine
sense of injury or intolerance that may still persist within society over
foreign or domestic policy shortcomings.[16] The Flemish remember the
time when they were impoverished and subordinate to the Walloons
even though they, the Flemish, are now booming while the Walloons
are stagnant. These contradictory but longstanding "memories" make
the combination of tolerance and equality of opportunity one of
the most subjective and least manageable of the dimensions of
democratization.

Democratic Pluralism

Political scientists and theorists of politics often recommend further
refinements of democratic institutions, greater political participation in
governance, and more stability in regime and party structures. Each of
these recommendations has its place in reform. But as the advocates of
stronger civil society have recognized, many of the reforms associated
with the machinery of democracy have reached diminishing returns
(Dahl 1992, 45–59; Almond and Verba 1963). Each additional reform
seems more difficult to achieve, appearing to yield also a smaller return,
at least among the mature democracies. It has become apparent that
the two other dimensions of democratization—economic growth and
productivity and social cohesiveness—must be given greater attention.
Tolerance is integral to each of these processes.

Democratic pluralism, a concept of democracy that places emphasis
on tolerance across social groupings and communities, while retaining
the focus on individual rights and obligations, has found new credence
at the onset of the twenty-first century (Doran 2001). Democratic pluralism stresses the importance of the third of the dimensions underlying democratization, the need for social cohesion within polities, not

---

16. Similar problems of collective memory are also associated with Corsica and the
Mezzogiorno of Italy, for example, significantly complicating trust and tolerance in these
regions (Putnam 1993).

necessarily through complete assimilation, but surely through the extension of tolerance to the members of all ethnolinguistic communities that comprise the polity.

Within the body of democratic political theory, democratic pluralism and its associated preoccupation with the value of tolerance is the last of the great ideals of democratization to be examined in depth. Regarding the challenge of social cohesion, democratic pluralism is the one great civic lesson that has yet to be learned.

For those who wish to see democratization attain its highest potential, a new focus on democratic pluralism is likely to yield benefits that can more than correspond to the effort that must be invested. And by bringing the third dimension of democratization, the issue of social cohesion, to the forefront of attention regarding the overall developmental process, democracy itself is likely to take the next step for mankind.

Conclusion

The argument made here is that democracy must be constructed on a firm underlying foundation of political value. If democratization is to succeed, it must break the bonds that hold it back in terms of many traditional beliefs about politics—for example, the assumption that freedom is unimportant and can be arbitrarily suspended, or that equality of opportunity is unnecessary, or that intolerance is justifiable. As these values change over time in a society, the prospect for democratization improves. Given this momentum, the level of attainment then will increase as a nonlinear geometric process (concave upward). The "ascendancy" of democratization results from this multiplicative process by which its values are emplaced in the society.

Last among the political values to become implanted in the political culture of the state is tolerance. Lack of tolerance has held back political participation and political representation, as well as the procedures and institutions they serve. At the beginning of the twenty-first century, the value that has made the least progress within and between communities is political, religious, and ethnic toleration. The greatest damage has been to the process of social cohesion. It is in jeopardy, not only in many places in the Third World where violence and civil war may be the outcome but also in a number of the rich, advanced-industrial democracies, as well, that have long thought the problems of unity were behind them. Democratic pluralism is thus, today, a foremost preoccupation for theorist and practitioner alike, as the future of democratizations very much depends on it.

References

Allison, Graham, Jr., and Robert Beschel, Jr. (1992) "Can the United States Promote Democracy?" *Political Science Quarterly*, 107(1) (Spring):81–98.

Almond, Gabriel, and Sidney Verba (1963) *The Civic Culture*, Princeton, NJ: Princeton University Press.

Aronoff, Myron Joel (2008) "Democratizations in Fissured Societies: The Makings of Citizenship," in Jose V. Ciprut, Editor, *The Future of Citizenship*, Cambridge, MA: The MIT Press.

Boylan, Delia M. (2001) "Democratization and Institutional Change in Mexico: The Logic of Partial Insulation," *Comparative Political Studies*, 34(1) (February):3–29.

Cornford, Francis McDonald, Translator (1945, 1963) *The Republic of Plato*, Chapter 14, "The Virtues of the Individual," pp. 139–143, New York: Oxford Press.

Dahl, Robert A. (1992) "The Problems of Civic Competence," *Journal of Democracy*, 3 (October):45–59.

Diamond, Larry (1992) "Economic Development and Democracy Reconsidered," *American Behavioral Scientist*, 35 (May–June):450–499.

Doran, Charles F. (1971) *The Politics of Assimilation: Hegemony and Its Aftermath*, Baltimore, MD: Johns Hopkins University Press.

Doran, Charles F. (1991) *Systems in Crisis: New Imperatives of High Politics at Century's End*, Cambridge, UK: Cambridge University Press.

Doran, Charles F. (2001) *Why Canadian Unity Matters and Why Americans Care: Democratic Pluralism at Risk*, Toronto: University of Toronto Press.

Doran, Charles F. (2003) "Economics, Philosophy of History, and the 'Single Dynamic' of Power Cycle Theory: Expectations, Competition, and Statecraft," *Power Cycle Theory and Global Politics*, special issue of *International Political Science Review*, 24(1):13–49.

Doyle, Michael (1986) "Liberalism and World Politics," *American Political Science Review*, 80 (December):1151–1169.

Evans, Peter (1997) "The Eclipse of the State? Reflections on Stateness in an era of Globalization," *World Politics*, 50(1) (October):62–87.

Fukuyama, Francis (1992) *The End of History and the Last Man*, New York: Free Press.

Gaubatz, Kurt Taylor (2001/2002) "The Hobbesian Problem and the Microfoundations of International Relations Theory," *Security Studies*, 11(2):164–186.

Huntington, Samuel P. (1992) *The Third Wave: Democratization in the Late Twentieth Century*, Norman: University of Oklahoma Press.

Inglehart, Ronald (1997) *Modernization and Postmodernization: Cultural, Economic, and Political Change in 43 Societies*, Princeton, NJ: Princeton University Press.

Johnson, Chalmers (2000) *Blowback: The Costs and Consequences of American Empire*, New York: Holt and Company.

Landes, David S. (1998) *The Wealth and Poverty of Nations: Why Some Are So Rich and Some Are So Poor*, New York: W. W. Norton.

Leff, Carol Skalnik (1999) "Democratization and Disintegration in Multinational States: The Breakup of the Communist Federations," *World Politics*, 51(2) (January):205–235.

Lehoucq, Fabrice Edouard (2000) "Institutionalizing Democracy: Constraint and Ambition in the Politics of Electoral Reform," *Comparative Politics*, 32(4) (July):459–477.

Lipset, Seymour Martin (1959) "Some Social Requisites of Democracy," *American Political Science Review*, 53 (March):69–105.

Londegan, John B., and Keith T. Poole (1996) "Does High Income Promote Democracy?" *World Politics*, 49(1) (October):1–30.

MacLennan, Hugh (1945) *Two Solitudes*, New York: Popular Library.

McInerney, Jeremy (2008) "Freedom and the Free Man," in Jose V. Ciprut, Editor, *Freedom: Reassessments and Rephrasings*, Cambridge, MA: The MIT Press.

Midlarsky, Manus F. (1992) "The Origins of Democracy in Agrarian Society," *Journal of Conflict Resolution*, 36 (September):454–477.

Niebuhr, Reinhold (1932, 1960) *Moral Man and Immoral Society*, New York: Charles Scribner and Sons.

O'Donnell, Guillermo, and Philippe C. Schmitter (1986) *Transitions from Authoritarian Rule: Tentative Conclusions about Uncertain Democracies*, Baltimore, MD: Johns Hopkins University Press.

Paine, Thomas ([1792] 1973) "Introduction," in *Rights of Man*, New York: Doubleday Anchor Book.

Pontusson, James (1995) "Explaining the Decline of European Social Democracy: The Role of Structural Economic Change," *World Politics*, 47(4) (July):495–533.

Przeworski, Adam, and Fernando Limongi (1997) "Modernization: Theories and Facts," *World Politic*, 49(2) (January):155–183.

Putnam, Robert D. (1993) *Making Democracy Work: Civic Traditions in Italy*, Princeton, NJ: Princeton University Press.

Rawls John (1999) *The Law of Peoples*, Cambridge, MA: Harvard University Press.

Ross, David, Sir (1923, 1964) *Aristotle*, New York: Barnes and Noble.

Scalapino, Robert A. (1993) "Democratizing Dragons: South Korea and Taiwan," *Journal of Democracy*, 4 (July):70–83.

Shin, Doh Chull (1995) "On the Third Wave of Democratization: A Synthesis and Evaluation of Recent Theory and Research," *World Politics*, 47(4) (July):495–533.

Spinner-Halev, Jeff (2008) "Exclusion, Fear, and Identity in Emerging Democracies," in Jose V. Ciprut, Editor, *Ethics, Politics, and Democracy: From Primordial Principles to Prospective Practices*, Cambridge, MA: The MIT Press.

van de Walle, Nicolas (1999) "Economic Reform in a Democratizing Africa," *Comparative Politics*, 32(1) (October):21–42.

van Doren, Carl (1938, 1966, 1980) *Benjamin Franklin*, New York: Viking Press.

3   Liberal Democracy: Interrogating the Premises and Inferences

Aryeh Botwinick

In response to the terrorist attacks of September 11, 2001, Philip Wilcox, a former Coordinator for Counterterrorism in the Department of State, had offered the following advice: "We should . . . search for ways to strengthen the common bonds between Western values and Islam to combat the notion of a 'clash of civilizations' and to weaken the Islamist extremist fringe that hates the West and supports terrorist actions." Wilcox (2001, 4) suggested that "redefining national security and counterterrorism in this broader sense is the most promising way to fight the war against terrorism." Wilcox's approach for dealing with terrorism calls attention to how excavating a shared theological and metaphysical backdrop to Western liberalism and to Islam's Quran-based theory and practice of religion and nationhood may well harbor the potential for fostering a sense of community between Islam and the West and for nurturing incentives for peace and rapprochement. In this chapter, I therefore would like to take my cue from Wilcox and utilize as my point of departure for an analysis of liberal democracy—and of the tension-laden relationship between the two halves of the composite notion ('representational' liberalism and 'direct' democracy)—the biblical narrative of the Akeidah (the sacrifice of Abraham's son), an account that looms central in Jewish and Christian as well as Muslim consciousness. Reading the Akeidah in the light of Rabbinic Midrashic[1] exegesis as recapitulated by the central medieval Jewish biblical exegete, Rashi (acronym for Rabbi Shlomo Yitzchaki), and twelfth-century Jewish philosopher Moses Maimonides' commentary on it in *The Guide of the Perplexed* (1963), first, I will exhibit Abraham the patriarch as the paradigmatic negative theological believer. Next, I will illustrate how the logical structure and problematics of skepticism duplicate that of

---

1. *Midrash* in Hebrew refers to a legalistic or homiletic exposition of the underlying significance of a biblical text.

negative theology and how the foundational text of modern philosophical liberalism, Hobbes's *Leviathan*, bears the searing imprint of
both negative theological and skeptical modes of argument. In this
context, I will briefly explore the work of four twentieth-century political philosophers—Michael Oakeshott, Sheldon Wolin, David Walsh,
and John Kekes—so as to highlight the limitations of representational
liberalism and direct participatory democracy taken by them and to
show how the synthesized hybrid of liberal democracy constitutes the
most faithful institutional embodiment of the theological and metaphysical inspirations that rest at the source of liberalism.

Maimonides' Analysis of the Akeidah as a Theological Backdrop to the Doctrine of Philosophical Liberalism

In his analysis of the Akeidah in his *Guide*, Maimonides (1963) prefigures the approach pursued by twentieth-century philosopher
Emmanuel Levinas of having the search for the ultimate, supreme
Other (namely, God) devolve onto reconfigured modes of ethical relationship to human others.[2] In *The Guide*, III:24:500–502,[3] where Maimonides discusses the Akeidah (the binding of Isaac in Jewish tradition;
the binding of Ishmael in Islamic tradition), he says that the command
to slay Isaac comes to Abraham "in a dream and in a vision," which
"in the opinion of the prophet" (namely, Abraham) is "a vision of
prophecy." Abraham has to take ultimate responsibility for classifying
the experience that he is having as a prophetic vision and for the interpretation that he places on it. Apparently, from Maimonides' perspective, negative theology (the approach to monotheistic religion that
Maimonides embraces) debars us (even the most exceptional among
us who harbor prophetic capacities) from explicitly affirming that the
message we are receiving comes directly from God. From a negative
theological vantage point (which emphasizes that we can only say
what God is not, not what He is, and that therefore all ascriptions of
attributes or qualities to God remain irredeemably metaphoric), God
cannot speak in a humanly intelligible sense even to His prophets.
Before there can be consent by the prophet's audience to receive his
teaching as prophetic message, hence, there has to be the prophet's own

---

2. The locus classicus for Levinas's treatment of ethics as "first philosophy" is his book
Totality and Infinity: An Essay on Exteriority (1969).
3. The citation in the text refers to part, chapter, and pages of the *Guide* in the Pines
edition. I will use this nomenclature throughout to identify passages in the *Guide*.

consent to regard his vision as prophetic—consent to the event of prophecy (that what is occurring is the communication of a prophetic message, rather than, say, a hallucination) *and* consent to the very content of the specific prophecy. Because in accordance with the tenets of negative theology, which Maimonides elaborates in *The Guide*, God does not speak the way human beings speak, it is only the acquiescence of the receiver of the message (and of those whom he can persuade) to invest it with Divine authority that gives it such authority. The gap between Divine address and human response cannot be closed any less ambiguously than this.

With this premise in place, we are better able to appreciate the second great lesson Maimonides derives from the Akeidah. Maimonides formulates it as follows: We are "being informed of the limit of the *love* for God, may He be exalted, and *fear* of Him—that is, up to what limit they must reach."[4] Maimonides states this teaching first and the teaching concerning the nature of prophecy second. When considered in the order in which he states his inferences—the teaching concerning the extent to which we need to exhibit the love *and* fear of God first—Maimonides' elucidation of the Akeidah seems to conform also to the Muslim interpretation of it,[5] for requiring us to set aside all forms of competitive love such as for one's family for the sake of focusing exclusively on love of God. However, the second inference that he draws from the Akeidah, relating to the centrality of the prophet in interpreting and taking responsibility for his own prophetic message, forces us to reconfigure the impact of the first teaching Maimonides derives from the Akeidah.

Monotheistic teaching generally confronts the believer with a stark contrast between the two routes to follow when actualizing its content. On the one hand, given the august incomparability of God, it can be viewed as imposing upon its adherents a regimen that requires them to decathect from all of their human attachments for the sake of immersing themselves totally in contemplation of, and communion with, God. On the other hand, although, given God's unbridgeable transcendence (which we can never engage despite all of our exercises of mystical contemplation), we might say that it is only the way we work out our organization of the human spheres that can possibly express our relationship with God. To state the dilemma that Abraham confronts in the

---

4. Maimonides (*Guide*, III:24:500) (italics in original).
5. Al-Jilani and Al-Qadir (1992): Cf. Al-Jilani (1997). I am grateful to Imam Abdur Razzaq Miller for pointing these sources out to me.

Akeidah more succinctly: What is the role of 'human others' in relation to the primal Other connoted by God? Does God nudge out of place all others aside from Himself, or is it mainly in relation to human others that traces of the Supreme Other (in some never fully redeemed metaphoric sense) can be experienced? Maimonides' emphasis on "the opinion of the prophet" in the second half of his analysis does suggest that the Akeidah is a drama centering around the limits of the prophetic vision and vocation, given the fact that "the opinion of the prophet" cannot be avoided. Is there one final burst of deliverance available to him by cradling himself completely in the vision of Divine embrace? Or are the limits affecting his vocation as prophet signalized by the necessity of his "opinion" (or affirmation) of the broader limits residing in the content of those messages mandating the nature of the occasion and the message received, as symptomatic of the accommodation of the "others"—before there can be any negotiation of the Other? We might say that from Maimonides' perspective the Akeidah registers Abraham's wrestling with the limits of the monotheistic prophetic vision[6] and that its story records Abraham's resistance to the allurements of Divine deliverance for the sake of affirming an expanded domain of human freedom and responsibility that is itself supremely (Divinely) grounded in the ethos of negative theology.

Maimonides' reading of the Akeidah is corroborated by how Rashi (following earlier Midrashic formulations) interprets key phrases in the biblical narrative. For example, in chapter 22, verse 2, of the Book of Genesis, the text states: "And He said, Take now thy son, thine only one, whom thou lovest, Isaac, and go into the land of Moriah; and bring him up there for a burnt offering upon one of the mountains which I shall tell thee of." Rashi glosses the phrase "And bring him up" as follows: "He did not say, 'Slay him,' because the Holy One, blessed be He, did not desire that he should slay him, but He told him to bring him up to the mountain to prepare him as a burnt offering. So when he had taken him up, God said to him, 'Bring him down'" (Rosenbaum and Silvermann 1972, 93). One could say that the tacit knowledge undergirding this reading is elaborated upon by Maimonides. Or, alternatively, one could say that Maimonides[7] theological explorations support this particular reading of the biblical text. Or yet, a third route: Maimonides' formulation constitutes simultaneously theological inves-

---

6. Compare Haskelevitch (2008).
7. See Rosenbaum and Silbermann (1972).

tigation and textual exegesis. Rashi's formulation helps us see that Maimonides' statement and its "prooftext" click into place together.

The Akeidah, Maimonides, Hobbes, and Liberalism

Now one may ask: "What does this negative theological reading of a biblical text that is pivotal in shaping the consciousness of Jews, Christians, and Muslims have to do with a clearer historical and theoretical understanding of liberalism?" The answer is based on the central role played by one key text, Thomas Hobbes's *Leviathan* (1946).[8] In clearing the ground and making the classic case for philosophical liberalism,[9] Hobbes subscribes to both an extreme formulation of negative theology and a skeptical idealism in his epistemology. First, his version of negative theology: "For the nature of God is incomprehensible; that is to say, we understand nothing of *what he is*, but only *that he is*; and therefore the attributes we give him, are not to tell one another, *what he is*, nor to signify our opinion of his nature, but our desire to honor him with such names as we conceive most honorable among ourselves. When we say anything is infinite, we signify only that we are not able to conceive the ends, and bounds of the things named; having no conception of the thing, but of our own inability" (chap. 34, p. 257). And therefore the name of God is used, not to make us conceive Him, "for He is incomprehensible; and His greatness, and power are unconceivable; but that we may honor Him" (chap. 3, p. 17).

For both Maimonides and Hobbes, negative theology emphasizes that with regard to God we can never pierce beyond the Name, that we can never be even conceptually in contact on a literal level with what the Name names. All we can ever do in relation to God is to discount the literal import of the constituent terms in our definitions and the realistic signification of our terms of reference. Negative theology both requires and presupposes our being able to sustain an abiding tension between our regular deployment of the God vocabulary and our inability to cash in any of its metaphors.

---

8. Thomas Hobbes (Oakeshott edition, 1946). All references to *Leviathan* in this chapter will be to this edition.

9. Both Michael Oakeshott and Leo Strauss have persuasively argued (albeit through somewhat different patterns of argument) for seeing Hobbes in this light. For example, see Oakeshott's *On Human Conduct* (1975) and *Hobbes on Civil Association* (1975). See also Strauss's *The Political Philosophy of Hobbes: Its Basis and Its Genesis* (1952) and his *Natural Right and History* (1953).

The model of skeptical idealist argument to which Hobbes also adheres is already encapsulated in the position of negative theology. In negative theology, there is a potentially infinite string of names for pinning down an entity, namely God, which can never be literally conceptually delimited. And, analogously, skeptical idealism maintains that all of the words in our regular vocabularies can never be taken to pin down certainly the things or events they ostensibly refer to: those "things" or "events" could be theoretically captured by still other verbal constellations without end. Negative theology and skeptical idealism both posit an unbridgeable conceptual distance between words and the One Absolute Being, or things in general, that they ostensibly refer to.

Hobbes's skeptical idealism is communicated to us not only by his nominalism but also via his theory of truth: "There [is] nothing in the world universal but names; for the things named are every one of them individual and singular. . . . Truth consisteth in the right ordering of names in our affirmations" (chap. 4, pp. 19, 21). There is an implicit tension between Hobbes's nominalistic theory and his theory of truth. In the Hobbesean nominalist perspective, there are no real entities corresponding to universals, although, presumably, there are objects in the world that match our particular statements. Hobbes's theory of truth seems to impugn this reading of his nominalism. It denies that there is anything in the world that corresponds even to 'particulars'. It simply invokes "the right ordering of names" as the appropriate test for truth indiscriminately—yes, even with regard to particulars. It would seem then that for Hobbes, what there 'is' (in terms of universals *and* particulars) depends in a crucial sense on our naming of it. Prior to our naming of things, there exists only an indeterminate flux of experience. For, strictly speaking, there is no objective external world in terms of which individual statements about experience can be either verified or falsified until this "objective world" is constituted by us in acts of speech, that is, of naming.[10]

Very little in this picture changes when one conjoins Hobbes's empiricism to his nominalism: when Hobbes says that "there is no conception in a man's mind, which hath not at first, totally, or by parts, been begotten upon the organs of sense. The rest are derived from that original" (chap. 1, p. 7). I think we are intended to read this passage in the light of his nominalism. Particular sense impressions exert their constraints

---

10. See Krippendorff (2008) and Clark (2008).

upon the body of statements that we regard as correct only within the context of a prior naming process that has led us to divide up the world the better to identify discrete particulars—alas, in such a special manner that discrepancies arise between our statements about sense data and our other statements. The cardinal philosophical principle of liberalism that authority rests upon consent is already insinuated in Hobbes's negative theology and theory of nominalism. If none of the metaphors that we employ to describe God ever can be unpacked except, at best, into a string of further metaphors, then the only rationally accountable way that human communities can be bound to this sort of God who does not speak to, or address, them in any literal fashion and whose "being" is infiltrated by irredeemable metaphors is by *agreeing* to be bound by the set of institutions and practices associated with the symbol of God. And so, analogously, Hobbes's radical nominalism, his deep belief that "truth consisteth in the right ordering of names in our affirmations," then allows him to achieve a kind of 'transcendental deduction' of the categories of authority and consent, and of the proper relationship that should subsist between them in the realm of politics proper.

According to Hobbes, there is, strictly speaking, no objective external world until it is constituted as such by us in the act of speech—in the process of naming. So Hobbes is able philosophically to justify and delimit the role of the sovereign. Without the sovereign, who enjoys, at least in a formalistic sense, a monopoly of force and authority within the state, affirming even by his silence the usages current in the society of his time, no stable or enduring patterns of communication could exist among men. Because the creation of sovereign authority also forms a precondition for the world as we know it, our consent to its formation can be formally, rationally reconstructed.[11]

Negative theology and liberalism are vulnerable to a certain logical problematic that has left its permanent imprint on the design and character of the liberal state. The logical structure of negative theological argument parallels the logical structure of skeptical argument, and hence they arrestingly converge upon agnosticism (in the strictest sense of absence of knowledge). Skepticism and monotheism (construed negatively—theologically) confront common dilemmas of consistency, of self-referentialism. In order to emerge as properly consistent,

---

11. For a path-breaking discussion of the relationship between Hobbes's nominalism and his liberalism, see Watkins (1965).

skeptical doctrine must encompass a reflexive maneuver, whereby skeptical critical canons are turned against the tenets of skepticism themselves, now forcing them into a movement of recoil, and thereby inhibiting their adequate formulation. Analogously, the utter conceptual removal of the monotheistic God (which renders Him unlike anything human) posited by negative theological readings of monotheism requires some kind of grammatical subject regarding whom the continual divestiture of predicates can take place. Skepticism is a doctrine of radical critique that both presupposes *and* denies a stable subject (in a grammatical sense): tenets of skepticism. Monotheism (in negative theological perspective), also, is a doctrine of radical critique that simultaneously presupposes and denies a stable grammatical subject, in this case, God (Botwinick 1997, 7–8).

The self-referentialist dilemmas that stand poised to dismantle both skepticism and monotheism suggest that the most coherent reading of both doctrines takes the form of a generalized agnosticism. And a generalized agnosticism implicitly points to the continued vitality of the questions it is unable to resolve. If skepticism must accommodate a moment of self-questioning of its own doctrine, then perhaps the most defensible version of skepticism emerges as the one that includes skepticism within its own ambit of skeptical interrogation, that is, a generalized agnosticism. Analogously, if under the impact of negative theology, monotheism can no longer literally affirm its own utterly transcendent version of God, in order to remain properly consistent, it has to recognize that neither can it conclusively invalidate God's existence. Negative theology is restricted to the more limited claim that monotheistic argument cannot work to establish the veracity of God's existence. Its writ does not extend to proving logically God's nonexistence. For example, in its extreme rationalism, negative theology might be construed as clearing a path for mystical approaches to God, which defy easy translation into a rationalist or linguistic register.

A Generalized Agnosticism, an Indefinite Openness to the Future, and the Liberal Conception of the Good

A generalized agnosticism carries a further implication that has left its indelible mark on the structure of the liberal state. If the background—theological and metaphysical—understandings that inform the historical articulation of liberalism issue forth in a generalized agnosticism, then this suggests that the future is needed as a useful and continual balancing and corrective mechanism to the past—a kind of institution-alization of a pattern of reverse causation. Thus, every present moment in human existence remains radically incomplete, with later events, occurrences, and discoveries being required in order to render more precise (more filled in with palpable content) our present understand-ings and formulations themselves. A generalized agnosticism estab-lishes the future as an indispensable resource for rendering our statements (in the present) more perspicuous and more objective. This significant implication of a generalized agnosticism is of tremendous historical and theoretical import. Maimonides' own theorizing (of the eternity of the world as having no end in time and of the messianic age as being historical rather than strictly speaking posthistorical in char-acter [as representing the elevation to their highest pitch of normal human tendencies, rather than their total transcendence]) hence yields the indefinite future, which both his negative theology and its allied epistemological assumptions require in order to confer maximum coherence upon our knowledge statements and claims.[12] Analogously, in a steady-state society[13] (in contrast to a stationary society) such as Hobbes's Leviathan-state, the future is continually reinforcing and sta-bilizing the past. In this sense, the arrow of time is pointing backward with the future 'causing' the past, enabling it to assume the shape and configuration that it does. Maimonides' naturalistic conception of the messianic age prefigures the endlessly progressive Hobbesian state and harbors the same reverse-causation motifs.

Hobbes's and Hume's extremely conservative theories of revolution, too, can be conceptually linked with a generalized agnosticism. Both of their views on revolution appear to conform to those advanced by the "de facto" theorists who were polemicists writing at the time of the Puritan Revolution and whose literature includes, according to Quentin Skinner (1972, 109–142), Hobbes's *Leviathan* (1946). The "de facto" theo-rists believed that the only grounds upon which revolution could be justified emerged *after* the event, *if* the disruption the revolution intro-duced into society did not prove permanently divisive. Now this for-mulation, of course, is tantamount to asserting that no theory of revolution can exist in the ordinary sense of a body of doctrine defining in advance the appropriate conditions under which rebellion might be justified. The *de facto theory of revolution* thus is a mere misnomer—

---

12. See the discussion in Botwinick (1997), chap. 3.
13. By this, I mean a society that is stable, and not a stagnant society.

a rationalization after a particular set of events has taken place to the effect that it did not after all prove *too* revolutionary, as continuity with the past had been fairly easily reestablished. Presumably, obedience to the new regime was justified as soon as its capacity to maintain order became evident (which is to say that the justification is inherently circular). From Hume's writings it would seem that a certain interval is needed—say, the three generations that had elapsed between the Glorious Revolution[14] and the writing of Hume's *Political Essays*—before the internal mechanism of allegiance could be regarded as safely transferred to a new regime.

As for Maimonides, for Hobbes, and for Hume, too, there seems to be an important epistemological motif animating their political theorizing. Their skepticism and adherence to negative theology, which can only be sustained as a generalized agnosticism, guide them to postulate a nondisruptive future as a continuing resource for filling in with content a not–fully realized or specified present. Hume's "diffidence" with regard to our "philosophical doubts" and "philosophical convictions"[15] seems to suggest that the future needs almost always to be viewed as constituting a seamless web with the past, with there hardly being or ever emerging any justification for rampant historical discontinuity.

The classical liberal theories of justice and political obligation as personified by Hume in the eighteenth century and by Michael Oakeshott in the twentieth seem also to evoke a vision of the nurturance of horizontal transcendence as the ultimate societal good. Hume's theory of justice is bound up with a stark proceduralism: the rules of justice relate to the stability of possession, the transfer of possessions by consent, and the keeping of promises; the content of justice establishes the framework (i.e., it determines the ground rules) in relation to which individual acquisition plans can be pursued and individual projects for realizing the good can be implemented. Thus, Hume is an important architect of what Judith Shklar and Michael Sandel have called the *procedural republic*, which assigns "priority to fair procedures over particular ends" and seeks to confine the state to providing and enforcing a framework of interaction that "respects persons as free and independent selves, capable of choosing their own values and

---

14. Also called the Bloodless Revolution, the Glorious Revolution in English history refers to the events in 1688–1689 that resulted in the deposition of James II and the accession to the English throne of William III and Mary II.—*Ed.*
15. See Hume (1978, 273).

ends."[16] The state is officially debarred from embracing its own concept of the good but must instead assign priority to individuals' and groups' exercise of their primordial right to elaborate and pursue their own version of the good in the private sphere. As Thomas Nagel and others have argued, however, this subordination of the public to the private sphere is itself grounded in a concept of the good that identifies it with neutrality.[17] Nagel does not elaborate the backdrop conception of the good propelling the liberal state. In metaphysical terms, it could be, however, described as the pursuit of horizontal transcendence opening up to infinity: the liberal state is structured in such a way as to ensure endless deferral of final power balances within society—and this is interconnected with endless deferral of such issues as sovereignty, truth, and justice in a substantive sense. The public sphere officially defers to the private sphere, which in turn has its demands processed by multiple tiers of government that contribute to both dispersing and deferring a concerted stand on any of the overarching issues affecting the life of the community. The diffusion of decision making across generations also contributes to dispersal and deferral. From this vantage point, the normative basis for liberal politics therefore may be conceived as a nurturance of time, to enable the play of contingency to be redeployed again and again without thereby succumbing to either premature abstraction or to closure, or to any under-responding by failing to capitalize on the range of possibilities residing within the extant constellations of forces. Justice and the political, from a Humean and Oakeshottian classical liberal perspective, have to do with keeping the prospect of successive presents endlessly available.

Four Contemporary Critiques of Liberal Society and of Philosophical Liberalism

In this section I turn to four contemporary critiques of liberal society (three right-handed and one left-handed), each of which has capably assessed the significance, weight, and attraction of the hybrid form of liberal democracy and, in so doing, also pointed to its superiority in accommodating the background theoretical understandings that inform the liberalism we have been considering here. Writing in the tradition of Eric Voegelin, David Walsh (1997) conceives of liberalism as a system

---

16. See Sandel (1996, 4).
17. See Nagel (1973).

of ordering. Because it can neither fully articulate its theological and philosophical roots nor shake loose from them, it has given rise to a certain amount of confusion with regard to its fundamental commitments and values. For example, the liberal emphasis placed on human dignity, equality, and freedom needs to be seen (according to Walsh) as both deriving from, and being appropriately completed by, the insights of Christianity.[18] For Walsh, "liberal order is the trace of Christianity in a world from which it has withdrawn" (1997, 20).

Walsh proposes Christianity as the not fully articulated source of the conception of the good-animating liberalism. Christianity for him becomes the premise best capable of explaining "why men and women are all equal and utterly inviolable sources of rights, deserving of the dignity that goes beyond any and all achievements within this world" (Walsh 1997, 247). But it is not just Christianity that conduces to this result; it is the skeptical approaches that call Christianity into question, as well. If we follow the route of the skeptic by admitting that we *can* call our knowledge statements and beliefs into question, then none of us is or can be entitled to accord a higher status to our statements about the world in contrast to those put forward by others, and in a negative sense (because none of us can outdo his fellow human beings in the project of justification), our equality vis-à-vis each other and the need to respect each other's positions is also assured.

Of course, the connection between epistemological and metaphysical skepticism and political liberalism is merely rhetorical and informal in character. In conformity with his own skepticism, the skeptic could not tease out of his premises a particular blueprint concerning how to organize political life. By the same token, however, the connections between Christianity and liberalism also need to be regarded as being informal and rhetorical in character. So, out of the complex weave of theological and historical motifs that goes to constitute Christianity— which for long stretches has attached salience to being assigned to authoritarian governing structures, the more effectively to match the supremeness of Divine rule—the notions of freedom and equality can be extrapolated and even invoked to serve as backdrop to liberalism, but only by way of highlighting an affinity, not by way of underscoring a tight logical, or theoretical, or yet a historical connection.

The juxtaposition of the tenets of skepticism to liberalism rather than the theological postulates of Christianity becomes even more compelling given Walsh's skeptical Voegelian hedgings concerning the notion

---

18. Cf. Haight (2008).

of order itself. Walsh says that "[s]ymbolisms of order are what structure our experience of reality. They provide the context in which analysis and critique of specific issues can be carried on, but they are not themselves amenable to the same kind of objective assessment: only from within the perspective of participating in them, and only in relation to the landmarks disclosed within them can they be evaluated" (Walsh 1997, 261). There are ways of life that are internal to specific symbolic ordering systems, but there is no transcendent external perspective—no set of master symbols to order all the other symbolic systems we use—in terms of which, to contrast the internal coherence, the external validity of a set of symbols might be assessed. But the dilemma that Walsh points to is already implicit in Eric Voegelin's formulation (Dallmayr 1989, 85) that "[a]ll the gods have to live under pressure of a divine Beyond that endows them with their divine life while threatening to let them die from their compactness." Voegelin in his own way interprets Christianity, skeptically and relativistically, as meeting a test of internal coherence while remaining arbitrary from a more externally grounded perspective. Liberalism shares the same fate as Christianity. For it, too, is internally coherent or can be rendered such, by adjusting political practice to reflect and conform to whatever set of components in its core principles one takes to be primary, while not being able to vindicate itself outside the charmed circle created by its own set of preferred postulates. In this regard, Christianity is not ontologically superior to liberalism. Why then use the one to 'complete' the other?

John Kekes (1997, 22) for his part believes that within liberalism, pluralism, freedom, rights, equality, and distributive justice achieve their maximum point and force when grouped around the central value of autonomy. With regard to liberalism's commitment to pluralism, Kekes points to a fundamental issue of consistency. Because liberalism is 'liberal' about everything except about the necessity of maintaining a liberal society, its value allegiances resist consistent formulation. For *pluralism* conjures up the prospect of an antiliberal society as well as of a liberal one. Yet isn't the point of including the term *pluralism* among the litany of liberal values to prevent just such an actualization? The upshot of this analysis is that liberalism must renounce its adherence to either liberalism or pluralism: that it just cannot, consistently, sustain both.

This criticism brings us to the heart of Kekes' argument, and it also helps to isolate the precise juncture at which it goes astray. Kekes is driven to locate autonomy as the central value of liberalism because he is primarily interested in liberalism as ideology, not in liberalism as theory. He is preoccupied with liberalism as a set of organizational principles integral to a particular mode of political being in the world, rather than as a series of reflections that are responsive to some of the deepest questions that human beings have raised about themselves and the world. He arrests his inquiry at the level of ideology, without proceeding to a more broadly theoretical domain. From an enlarged theoretical perspective, we could say that the major value informing liberalism is skepticism, not autonomy. Autonomy itself can be viewed as deriving from skepticism. Liberalism stresses the role of the freely self-directing individual as the sole authentic subject of political deliberation and action because, given the limitations to human knowledge argued by skepticism, it is only a free, self-directing human being who can generate enough relevant data concerning human needs, ends, and wants to satisfy the requirements of political deliberation and action. But, as we have seen, skepticism faces a serious challenge of consistency. For it cannot be formulated without engulfing—and therefore also undermining—itself. The version of skepticism that manages to escape these strictures is a generalized agnosticism—an agnostic approach extended across the whole map of knowledge, beyond the philosophy of religion—which facilitates the cultivation of an indefinite openness toward the future, an endless deferral of final crystallization of responses to supreme questions of life and to the balances that should hold between them. Hence, a mode of liberalism suffused with skepticism, rather than autonomy as its dominant metaphysical value, is thus always poised to calling itself—as well as competing and alternative values—into question. And this suggests that its overriding commitment is to pluralism, rather than to liberalism in any narrow ideological sense.

From a generalized agnostic perspective, redrawing the balance of liberal moral and political values in order to draw swifter, greater attentiveness to the need for "prosperity, order, civility, peace, a healthy environment, security, happiness, and law-abidingness" (Kekes 1997, 210) does not represent a departure from liberalism but rather a further elaboration of its commitment to pluralism. Kekes says at one point that "[r]ealistic principles must be derived from, formulated in response to, and continually revised to fit the changing, shifting, unpredictable contingencies of actual human circumstances" (Kekes 1997, 155). The kind of liberalism the primary theoretical notion of which is skepticism, on an intermediate level of deliberation and decision making, tends to remain open to the pragmatic renegotiation of its distribution of the very values that Kekes envisions.

Michael Oakeshott's own philosophy of conversation (1991), which denigrates the possibility ever of achieving moments of such triumphant incandescence that they simply bring conversation itself to a close, belongs to the same family of terms as do *skepticism* and *generalized agnosticism*, which I have discussed in detail in this chapter. For Oakeshott, a primary sense of the term *conversation* is an ideologically neutral metatheoretical category for capturing the perpetually evolving, unfinished, character of philosophical inquiry and reflection. In addition to serving as a metaphilosophical category, which clarifies the ontological status that Oakeshott indeed assigns to philosophical inquiry and also as a category that captures the most pervasive and fruitful mode of human interaction, Oakeshott's specific conception of conversation can be therefore related to his political theory proper, and in ways evocative of John Rawls (1971, 2001), Bruce Ackerman (1980), and Hobbes, as well.

The notion of conversation enables us to reconstruct the terms under which members of a political society can be appropriately understood as relinquishing a part of their freedom for the sake of establishing government. Oakeshott's conceptions of conversation and the just society are symmetrical. They match each other perfectly. For Oakeshott, 'conversation' does not yield a content either locally or globally, either in terms of individual statements whose content (meaning and reference) has been stably pinned down or in terms of the larger systematic import (or drift) of the individual statements themselves. 'Deconstruction' is part of the activity of conversation itself and affects equally the individual components and the overall structure of conversation. For Oakeshott, the emptiness and absence on the level of conversation get duplicated in the emptiness and absence that characterize the liberal state. The rule-governed societas that Oakeshott favors, and which steadfastly refuses transformation into an enterprise association, follows the pattern of 'conversation' modeling endless deferral of its ultimate substantive identity and commitments.

Terms and categories such as *conversation* and *societas* are but placeholders in Oakeshott's argument—registering emptiness, absence[19]—getting transformed through their built-in metaphoric momentum into

---

19. In Oakeshott's marvelously succinct formulation, "The irony of all theorizing is its propensity to generate, not an understanding, but a not-yet-understood."

visions and justifications of their own, which have the tendency to deflect the theorist himself away from the austere minimalism of his very constructions. If in Oakeshott's conception liberal society is suffused with skepticism, then it, too, marks time (passage) without being able to sustain a hypostatization into something more concrete and specific. If liberalism institutionalizes deferral (our lack of secure knowledge), then it does not precommit its advocates to favor the modalities representative of political organization over more participatory forms of it. Neither does it eternally prejudge the question of the extent to which economic issues have to be kept off the political agenda because of the possible taint of the ground rules of civil association by the ground rules of enterprise association.

On political philosophical grounds, we cannot move beyond the emptiness presaged by a generalized agnosticism. Hence philosophical decontamination should not preclude the liberal state from intervening on pragmatic grounds that are purely interim and fully instrumental in character to ameliorate flagrant economic and social inequalities. In Oakeshott's striking formulation (1993, 153–154): "Political philosophy can provide no principles to be 'followed,' no rules of political conduct to be observed, no ideals of policy or arrangement to be pursued." To invoke an Oakeshottian vocabulary against Oakeshott: not-knowing has to be enacted on this side of a shadow line that prevents its degeneration into a spurious and unsustainable form of knowledge.

In contradistinction to Oakeshott, Wolin (1981, 11) advocates an unmitigated embrace of democracy and containment of liberalism: in "The People's Two Bodies," he suggests that "in the American political tradition, the people has had two 'bodies,' with each standing for a different conception of collective identity, of power, and of the terms of power. In one of the bodies, the people was conceived to be politically active, while in the other it was essentially, though not entirely, passive. The one collectivity was political and democratic and can be called a *body politic*; the other was primarily economic and intentionally antidemocratic . . . it can be called a *political economy*." The American Revolution and the *Articles of Confederation* represent the ascendancy of the body politic. The U.S. Constitution epitomizes the triumph of the political economy of what Wolin calls "the higher social classes and the more powerful economic interests" (Wolin 1981, 13). In order for them to achieve and sustain their hegemony throughout American history, liberal protections of minority rights have had to be mobilized continually against the onslaughts of majority will and sentiment. From the

Supreme Court's interpretation of "due process" during the post–Civil War era until the institutionalization of the New Deal that augmented both the policy goals of Big Business and the structure of Congressional authority, which assigned undue power to both its committees and to its committee chairmen, the whole ethos of liberalism—of sanctioning protection of minority rights, even when the minority was composed of the privileged rather than the persecuted—has frustrated the project of democratic participation, even as it has defeated concrete goals sought by the majority of the electorate.

Wolin carries his campaign against liberalism and his apotheosis of democracy into a critique of ancient Greek modes of theorizing political forms. In an essay published in 1994, he attacks the Greeks for what he calls 'the constitutionalizing of democracy'. He argues that "constitutionalism might be defined as the theory of how best to restrain the politics of democracy while ensuring the predominance of the social groups and classes represented by the 'best men'" (Wolin 1994, 35). In marked contrast to constitutionalism, he finds democracy to be "resistant to the rationalizing conceptions of power and its organization which for centuries have dominated Western thinking and have developed constitutionalism and their legitimating rationale" (Wolin 1994, 37). The Greek fusion of democracy with constitutionalism yields what in modern parlance now is termed 'liberal democracy' where *democracy* refers to rule of the people and *liberal* evokes the whole panoply of constitutional-institutional protections of minority rights.

Just as with Oakeshott, we can appropriately say to Wolin that he has conflated the import of his metaphysical skepticism (evident in such statements as, "The richness of the factual world depends upon the richness of our theories. . . . The world must be supplemented before it can be understood and reflected upon" [Wolin 1972, 52–53]) with a particular political ordering that *he* favors (namely, participatory democracy) without even acknowledging that skepticism can be validly construed to support the set of political values *he* rejects (namely, liberalism and its fusion with democracy—a.k.a. liberal democracy). Skepticism undercuts the claims that an individual or group can set to unquestioned superiority of knowledge (from a negative standpoint, to put forward an incontrovertibly grounded positive claim); indeed, it justifies the inclusion of as many people as possible in any public decision making. And at the same time, because the results reached cannot claim unreserved sanction, liberalism also introduces braking mechanisms that allow existing democratic outcomes to be reconsidered and revised: in short, liberalism encourages second thoughts. As a preoccupation with process—in all the manifold constitutional and institutional senses that we are familiar with in U.S. democracy—liberalism facilitates a continual replenishment and adjustment of democratic content. Plato's emphasis on 'process' as a metaphysical concept in his *Theaetetus* finds itself translated in the course of the history of democratic theory, far more narrowly, into the political notions of liberal democracy, where no public verdict on any issue can be conceived as final. Majority rule is counterbalanced by minority rights, and the content of "rights," in turn, is subject to majority interpretation and redefinition. Under this expansive, metaphysical re-envisioning of the nature of democracy, it is not only "the people" but also "sovereignty," "truth," and "the ultimate telos of human personal and collective life" that are "instituted and sustained" by what Claude Lefort has called "the dissolution of the markers of certainty."[20] In Fred Dallmayr's incisive paraphrase of Lefort, these concepts function as "absent presences," that is, neither as "compact" notions nor as "nullities" in a democracy (Dallmayr 1993, 94), but rather as continually actualized and incompletely realized ideas whose elusive content is pragmatically reinvigorated from all directions, including those of democracy *and* liberalism. A generalized agnosticism impels us ever forward in evolving new configurations of balancing mechanisms. The justice and fidelity to "truth" on the part of liberal society reside in the movement, not in the content. Liberal democracy is a theory of perpetual mistrust and of strategically provoked destabilizations.

References

Ackerman, Bruce A. (1980) *Social Justice in the Liberal State*, New Haven, CT: Yale University Press.

Al-Jilani, and Shaikh Abd Al-Qadir (1992) *The Sublime Revelation: A Collection of Sixty-Two Discourses*, Muhtar Holland, Translator, Houston, TX: Al-Baz Publishing.

——— (1997) *The Removal of Cares: A Collection of Forty-Five Discourses*, Muhtar Holland, Translator, Fort Lauderdale, FL: Al-Baz Publishing.

Botwinick, Aryeh (1997) *Skepticism, Belief, and the Modern: Maimonides to Nietzsche*, Ithaca, NY: Cornell University Press.

Clark, Robin (2008) "Reliable Cribs: Decipherment, Learnability, and Indeterminacy," in Jose V. Ciprut, Editor, *Indeterminacy: The Mapped, the Navigable, and the Uncharted*, Cambridge, MA: The MIT Press.

---

20. See Lefort (1988, 17–19).

Dallmayr, Fred (1989) *Margins of Political Discourse*, Albany: State University of New York Press.

———— (1993) *The Other Heidegger*, Ithaca, NY: Cornell University Press.

Haight, Roger (2008) "Human Freedom: A Christian Understanding of Salvation as Liberation," in Jose V. Ciprut, Editor, *Freedom: Reassessments and Rephrasings*, Cambridge, MA: The MIT Press.

Haskelevitch, Levi Y. (2008) "Liberation and Freedom in Jewish Liturgy and Practice," in Jose V. Ciprut, Editor, *Freedom: Reassessments and Rephrasings*, Cambridge, MA: The MIT Press.

Hobbes, Thomas (1946) *Leviathan*, Michael Oakeshott, Editor, Oxford, UK: Basil Blackwell.

Hume, David (1978) *A Treatise of Human Nature*, 2nd ed., L. A. Selby-Bigge and P. H. Nidditch, Editors, Oxford, UK: Oxford University Press.

Kekes, John (1997) *Against Liberalism*, Ithaca, NY: Cornell University Press.

Krippendorff, Klaus (2008) "Four (In)Determinabilities, Not One," in Jose V. Ciprut, Editor, *Indeterminacy: The Mapped, the Navigable, and the Uncharted*, Cambridge, MA: The MIT Press.

Lefort, Claude (1988) *Democracy and Political Theory*, David Macey, Translator, Minneapolis: University of Minnesota Press.

Levinas, Emmanuel (1969) *Totality and Infinity: An Essay in Exteriority*, Alphonso Lingis, Translator, Pittsburgh: Duquesne University Press.

Maimonides, Moses (1963) *The Guide of the Perplexed*, Shlomo Pines, Translator, Chicago: University of Chicago Press.

Nagel, Thomas (1973) "Review of John Rawls, A Theory of Justice," *Philosophical Review*, 82:220–234.

Oakeshott, Michael (1975) *Hobbes on Civil Association*, Oxford: Blackwell.

———— (1975) *On Human Conduct*, Oxford: Clarendon Press.

———— (1991) "The Voice of Poetry in the Conversation of Mankind," in *Rationalism in Politics and Other Essays*, New and Expanded Edition, pp. 488–541, Indianapolis: Liberty Press.

———— (1993) *Religion, Politics and the Moral Life*, Timothy Fuller, Editor, New Haven, CT: Yale University Press.

Rawls, John (1971) *A Theory of Justice*, Cambridge, MA: Harvard University Press.

———— (2001) *Justice as Fairness: A Restatement*, Erin Kelly, Editor, Cambridge, MA: Harvard University Press.

Rosenbaum, M., and A. M. Silbermann, Translators, in collaboration with A. Blashki and L. Joseph (1972) *Pentateuch and Rashi's Commentary*, Jerusalem, Israel. (No publisher listed.)

Sandel, Michael J. (1996) *Democracy's Discontent*, Cambridge, MA: Harvard University Press.

Skinner, Quentin (1972) "The Context of Hobbes's Theory of Political Obligation," in Maurice Cranston and Richard S. Peters, Editors, *Hobbes and Rousseau: A Collection of Critical Essays*, pp. 109–142, New York: Anchor Books.

Strauss, Leo (1952) *The Political Philosophy of Hobbes: Its Basis and Its Genesis*, Chicago: University of Chicago Press.

Strauss, Leo (1953) *Natural Right and History*, Chicago: University of Chicago Press.

Walsh, David (1997) *The Growth of the Liberal Soul*, Columbia: University of Missouri Press.

Watkins, J. W. N. (1965) *Hobbes's System of Ideas*, London: Hutchinson.

Wilcox, Philip C., Jr. (2001) "The Terror," *New York Review of Books*, September 19, 2001.

Wolin, Sheldon S. (1972) "Political Theory as a Vocation," in Martin Fleisher, Editor, *Machiavelli and the Nature of Political Thought*, pp. 23–75, New York: Atheneum.

——— (1981) "The People's Two Bodies," *Democracy*, 1(1):9–24.

——— (1994) "The Constitutionalizing of Democracy," in J. Peter Euben, John R. Wallach, and Josiah Ober, Editors, *Athenian Political Thought and the Reconstruction of American Democracy*, pp. 29–58, Ithaca, NY: Cornell University Press.

4   Globalizations and Democratizations: Forces, Counterforces

Henry Teune

The dynamics of social development in the modern era yielded both globalizations and democratizations. Globalizations today are marked by the beginnings of their fusion with democratizations into a singular developmental force. The fusion started around the middle of the 1970s. And until it is completed, the complex relationship between democracy and globalization is likely to display both in theory a complicated and in practice a controversial knot of reinforcements and contradictions. Even if that fusion is never completed, linkages between democracy and globalization already have transformed macroprocesses of change from those grounded on subordination through threat or conversion of belief to those based on suasion via co-option or cooperation (Guillen 2002).

Empires of conquest were a mainstay of processes of globalization until the end of the twentieth century. Democracy, everywhere in the world, then took over as a viable alternative to empires, grand obediences, and ideologies, thereby also becoming a threat to some and a promise to others, for being both the keystone of globalization and the source of its own rewards. The alluring promises of the new globalization—peace, prosperity, and freedom—became realizable in the last quarter of the twentieth century. The rewards already had become credible in the 1970s, when world markets had begun to dominate national and local ones and when people in many Third World countries started to perceive at least a glimmer of sustained economic growth.

The linkage between globalization and democracy was strengthened further during the last decades of the twentieth century by the established democracies. Acting in concert, they leveraged the productive potential of markets of scale for democracy. Market globalization pushed open the door for the Second Democratic Revolution. Its promised benefits served as incentives for democratic parties and for groups in nondemocratic countries. Two centuries earlier, in the 1780s, the revolutionary image of globalization offered by the New World had served as a catalyst for the First Democratic Revolution, providing an opportunity for freedom only to those groups or peoples ready to defend their identity and ideals by challenging tyranny or escaping it. In contrast, the Second Democratic Revolution, in the late 1980s, expressed the aspiration of individuals for human development through personal freedom.

My main proposition is that globalizations and democratizations are two sides of the contemporary world's developmental wedge. Although they are often in conflict, they are part of the same underlying forces of change that drive social systems to become greater in scale. These dynamics of change gain momentum on an accumulating foundation of human learning about both the know-how of and the benefits from increasing the scale of human systems and simultaneously from enlarging and solidifying initially group independence, then eventually and especially individual autonomy.

The autonomy of groups in a global system is a function of their social development, which depends on their integration with the global system, not their aloofness from it. Social development, however, gains from the complexity of individuals, specifically from their freedom to create variety, not from the autonomy of groups. Therein lies the basic contradiction of social development: that it generates autonomy with democracy and dependence with globalization. And therein, too, dwells a threat against globalization incentives for groups. The leadership of groups achieves autonomy even as it loses control to individualization. Estonians, Slovenes, Slovaks, and others now can afford European-like statehood. But they are bound to lose their late-born autonomy to the global system as they open up to it. That is why globalization is so ambivalently supported and yet so cynically opposed, all in the name of democracy. Globalization made contemporary democracies possible. Yet it poses a threat to the survival of those groups in whose name a democracy might have been established. Those supporting democracy know this, so they are conflicted between celebrating this certainty and inevitably depending on a complex and indeterminate global system. The price paid is a consequent weakening of the older identities of birth, place, and belief—those very foundations of community in the local and national democratic institutions of the past.

Affirmative Forces: Cooperation/Convergence Despite Internal Conflicts

The relationships between globalization and democracy as social development can be presented from several theoretical and interpretative perspectives. I propose to pursue three theoretical viewpoints in this chapter: (1) globalization and democracy as 'development', which leads to the integration of diversity, necessarily breaks the limits—abolishes those hindrances to diversity set by hierarchies and by the objectives on which they are based; (2) globalization and democracy as 'learning', in which collective learning that seeks to minimize the costs and maximize the value of access occurs; and (3) globalization and democracy as 'history', of the evolving legitimacy of political systems—legitimacy being essential for political stability in political systems and for sustainable pursuits of globalization.

Globalization and Democratization as Development

The logic of development is the integration of diversity. In sum, development depends on variety, on the distribution among components of that variety as diversity, and on the integration of that diversity to enhance the probability of producing even more variety. Put differently, the logic of development requires a quest for variety, by importing, or generating, or yet inventing it. But to accomplish that, the system's components must be strongly interconnected. They must not only link up with as many components as possible but also extend their connections to every potential offered by each of these and other components. This has been referred to as the *three dimensions of integration*: strength, inclusion, and extension (Teune and Mlinar 1978, 2000). This means that components of a system come together systemically, that more and more components are brought together on an equal basis, and that more of each component's characteristics go to enriching the system by growingly shared linkages. "Perfectly" integrated systems are those in which any change in any characteristic of any component most certainly affects all of the characteristics of every other component, and instantaneously so. No social system is "perfectly integrated" for all physical or social systems are subject to entropy (decay). And human systems especially are open to influences from other systems. As each of the three dimensions (strength, inclusion, and extension) is a co-process of integration in any social system, it is, as such, in explicit conflict with the other two. This is why failure to proceed together in harmony can lead to system breakdowns.

First, buttressing the strength of relationships between and among the components of a system will prohibit or inhibit components from acquiring new, fully exclusive characteristics of their own. The social prototype of this system is a closed, hierarchical system in which most of the components have a minimum amount of variety, and the control centers—the higher-level nodes to which components converge— discourage lower-level acquisitions of new variety, lest subordinates become uncontrollable. Evidently, hierarchies are control systems, not developmental ones. That is why all hierarchies are adverse to change or resistant to innovation. The search for equilibrium is their dominant dynamic. But hierarchies can be used purposefully, to force integration by bringing together disparate components of a system. And this may jump-start the developmental process of a country. The authoritarian "tigers" of East Asia, especially South Korea and Singapore, where development was more or less successfully forced from the top, prove good examples.

Second, the equal inclusion of each and every component of a system requires loose association with minimum control. The societal proto- type of this system is an anarchic association endowed merely with self-identification rules of membership and the prerogative to defect. Such associations generally have little impact on their members, and even when they do, they engage a very limited range of activities. Their main problem is acquiring more members and then leaving them alone. A diminution in the level of effective collective action often seems to be the price for integrating countries regionally, in some economic union.

Third, a system may attempt an extension of all that it commands within its boundaries. The political prototype is a totalitarian system, where components are in lock step and the system is rigid, leaving no space for slack. Components cannot acquire new dimensions, facets, or characteristics, as individuality would threaten the all-pervasiveness of the tyranny. The main problem here is the gap between the levels of asserted and actual control. All such systems eventually lose out to their "undergrounds"—be they parallel economies or, say, subversive political agencies—usually unavoidably sacrificing their authority to their limitations. They are inherently run-down systems, essentially antithetical to development.

Highly integrated, "closed" social systems reject variety. And because development is a variety-driven process, such systems rarely develop. Integration and diversification exhibit conflicting dynamics within "closed" systems. Diversity is achieved by fuller outward openness to new variety and broader inward distribution, necessitating optimal system slack. The greater the slack, the more the bulk of new variety is likely to slow the pace of systemic integration. And, integrating new variety—whether adopting a new airplane, replacing trains by cars, or computerizing manual accounting systems—is always disturbing. It takes more time to integrate variety than to produce it. Integrative processes occur in continual linear fashion and need more time than it takes for variety to appear. New variety occurs in a discrete discontinuous mode. As a system develops, its internal interactions between integration and diversification occur in zigzags, from introduced variety to distributed diversity on to integrated value. In hindsight, societal transformations from agrarian to industrial modes were a huge revolutionary process made up of billions of actions and thousands of small crises generated by myriad changes in technologies, human skills, settlement patterns, and livelihood problems. Societal transformations from industrially driven to service-led modes were even more complicated.

Development as globalization derives from the expansive process of integrating diversity and continuing to do so until all components are integrated at the highest level of diversity: the world as a total system. The process of globalization logically cannot end before all human societies, encompassing all present and potential variety, become integral to a global system within which maximal social diversity for quantifiably optimal variety obtains as every single component freely differentiates itself from its aggregate(s). The process thus involves nothing less than the creative liberation of individuals. The logic of the world as a system of freedom for individuals builds on the premise of the destruction of all-intermediate level nodes and hierarchies. The theoretical endpoint of social development is when all individuals are equal participants in collectivities of their choice, able to exercise[1] their inalienable right of affiliation or withdrawal from any subsystem. Collectivities would become more or less durable associations of mutual convenience. And that would constitute a world of anarchic

---

1. See Urban (2008).

democracy.[2] Individualization, on the other hand, is a real and necessary part of globalization as development.

Development drives the distribution of ideas as well as of material objects. It educates, but also conciliates differences among, groups and individuals. It is, admittedly, a slow process. The immediate impact on a society, at low levels of development, is substantial inequality among groups, classes, and individuals. It takes a long time for development to generate and to distribute variety, because diversity is likely to exacerbate inequality and to elicit radical opposition. Ironically here, inequality is a necessary ingredient in developmental environments that encourage new variety. Where every component holds the same kind and number of properties, there can be no diversity and no development. Such a system would be as poor and stagnant as the hundreds of thousands of rural villages in China, India, and Africa are today, where equality is achieved by the lowest common denominator. Communism comes to mind.

Development and its attendant inequalities generally ratchet up the aspirations of each and all. It is via development that societies come to shun the mentalities and moralities that institutionalize poverty. In the process they become also politically mature. And as they emancipate, their individuality emerges. Members of these societies develop a keener sense of the options and the possible courses of actions. As the global system develops and penetrates localities,[3] individual persons become consciously attached to the global system. Hesitantly or not, they gain freedom from parochial and provincial modes of power, to the dismay of the latter. Direct electronic one-on-one or chat-group linkages among individuals throughout the world via the Internet have noticeably loosened the grip of even the more traditionally dominant formations: country, community, congregation, and, yes, family, among them.

The development-individualization nexus can also be explained by the law of attractiveness of variety (Teune and Mlinar 1978), according to which those system components (groups or individuals) with the most variety tend to latch onto systems with even greater variety at the

2. This is taken from James Chowning Davies (1977). All theories of social and political systems have a basis in human nature. Here it is an explicit statement of human nature as human development and of the implications of those developments on political systems. See also Ciprut's chapter 14 (especially his translation from the French of Guizot's thoughts on anarchic democracy, which remain valid still today).
3. See Ciprut's chapter 14 for the notion of democratizations as localizations of globalizations.

highest possible levels of aggregation. The most educated villager first gravitates toward a city, then to the capital or to some cosmopolitan center. Alas, as ascending individuals seek to maximize their individual capacities, development not only empties the villages and towns but also drains the brainpower of less developed societies. Today, paradoxically, the most complex among those individuals who work and reside in the most developed subsets of the global system can be a very active part of the world without even leaving their city, sometimes even their home office.

Globalization and Democracy as Learning

A less abstract theoretical perspective on the practical linkages between globalization and democracy (Teune and Mlinar 2000) is perhaps the logic of efficient rational learning: organizations, groups, and individuals seek out linkages with others in some order of preferences. The basic dynamic by which democracy and globalization reinforce and complement each other derives from the simple fact that globalization is the logic of each and every component becoming integrated with every other component in a given system, through the fewest possible linkages. Imagine an inclusive global network comprising 10 billion humans with a minimum of six, maximum of ten, nodes of reference for each individual. In such a system, it should be possible for the greater extent of variety to be readily absorbed by the human capacities of 90 percent of all persons, regardless of individual aptitudes to connect, comprehend, or contribute.

These processes of slow learning and connecting, which have moved people from nomadic spaces to villages, to cities, to countries, and of late to transnational regions and to the world at large, can be viewed as ecological, evolutionary processes.[4] They have already occasioned the radical shrinking of distances through random processes of invention and ensuing purposeful innovations. The domestication of animals, the wheel, the sea-going vessel, the compass, the steam and combustion engines, and a long line of other novelties over the past few thousand years have led to an exponential decrease in the cost of bridging distances by moving people, products, services, and ideas ever farther, ever more quickly and cheaply. It is also this type of ecological

---

4. A learning/ecological approach echoes the legacy of Darwinian rationality. The main theoretical thrust is evolutionary and as such gives wide latitude to random events and rational adaptations to them (Boulding 1978).

processes that has led to the technologies that have enabled humanity to overcome the pessimistic Malthusian predictions and today still help to free individuals from a lifelong dependency on subsistence economies.

This process by which the human self gains increasing access to the domain of others at diminishing costs contributes to democratizations by leveling hierarchy, boosting choice, and allowing individual autonomy to blossom. As hierarchies dissolve, intermediate groups weaken, and old structures reorganize into hubs and spokes, individuals begin to seek out other individuals or nodes best equipped to uphold their preferences and values of the moment. If and when all individuals are linked through networks exacting not more than the marginal cost bearable for a minimum number of nodes, it should become possible for individuals to exit at will from the control of any group or hierarchy. Individuals generally will always seek to acquire added value from the formations they choose to join. And the overarching rationality of complexity through democracy unfolds in networks with maximum connections through minimum linkages, propelling the diversification processes of globalization to integrative ends. That individual search and the consequent emergence of networks diminishing the control of hierarchies move the world to an alignment of policies and actions (by collectivities) that also satisfy the values of individuals. The world order hence tends to become one made of thousands of little democracies, many more of which form continually and become globally interconnected across physical and cultural distances.

In explaining globalizations, this theory of rational learning does not need to go to the unattractive theoretical abstractions of persons alienated from groups of affection or purpose in a global system. But it does produce a messy global social system in which even small groups of individuals gain voice in a world of overlapping affiliations, despite unequal individual relations among and within the groups themselves. It augurs a world of decentralized anarchy with substantial freedom that could nonetheless be inclusive, peaceful, and prosperous.

Globalization and Democracy as History

The third theoretical perspective is down to earth. It is tied to measurable variables that examine empirical relationships in the course of the past decade or two. It seeks to capture specific major historical events

in a "cause-and-effect" mode.[5] It does not explain why and how globalizations occurred—if they happened at all—or in what sense the
ones occurring now differ from taking place during the expansion of
empires or in sporadic past intensifications of trade or migration. It
merely requires plausible empirical assertions as to the relationships of
globalizations to democratizations: first, the relevant effect of globalizations on democratizations and then, as has been suggested in this
chapter, a reversal of that relationship, whereby democratizations
extend and strengthen globalizations. It is a combination of events, of
basic relationships, of actions and mistakes, by individuals as well as
organizations. As such, it depends greatly on the credibility of extant
interpretations. It requires contingent structures of social change and
scenario modes of analysis. It has the virtue of offering many readings
of change and shows the potential to establish empirically verifiable
relationships. It also has the vice of inviting belief that everything is
ultimately happenstance, accidental, which, of course, is a denial of the
possibility of knowing anything at all.

As in most historical explanatory accounts, "main events" are events
selected for "good reason." Three such events clearly helped define the
conditions for the Second Democratic Revolution of 1989: the spurt in
market globalization that followed the oil crises of the Yom Kippur War
in 1973, the opening of China during 1979–1984, and the lengthy collapse of communism in Central and Eastern Europe as of 1989. The first
of these events moved massive amounts of financial assets to the
oil-producing countries. These monies were then recycled as loans to
poorer countries, offering many of them entry to the global market
economy. The second event opened the world to China, once the
world's wealthiest empire, and potentially one of the largest economies
in a global political environment. It made possible the emergence of
East Asia as a significant part of today's world economy. The third
major event not only opened up a number of command systems to the
world market but also, and more importantly perhaps, removed a
major source of hindrance to the emergence of a global political
economy, which has swiftly obtained since.

Whether any of these hypothesized conditions were sufficient for
globalizations or necessary for their linkage to democratizations in the
last decades of the twentieth century is still debatable. What did happen
is that centralized, governmentally directed national economies lost

---

5. For this kind of time-bound analytic perspective, see Geddes (1999).

their legitimacy as institutions of purported prosperity, popularity, and social justice. Their collapse like a row of dominos eliminated the main ideological opposition to Western democracies, ending its use to prevent or retard the spread of Western democratic institutions in Third World countries. Promptly gone, too, were the opportunistic arguments by petty dictatorships, regardless of the ideology or rationale they used to justify the control and closure of their boundaries. During this period, established democratic countries undertook major initiatives to promote democracy, first in Southern Europe and Latin America, and later in the former communist countries and even in parts of Africa. Direct intervention to promote political shifts to democracy quickly followed on a global scale.

The virtual links between globalizations and democratizations would seem to have come about via political legitimacy and stability. When no other pedestal was left for governments to stand on, democracy became a password. Many manipulative countries boasted democratic institutions merely as a facade; others stumbled along. These hollow emulations of change were referred to as *democratic transformation, transition*, even *institutionalization*, and *consolidation*. Such real and unreal processes continued for over a decade, with no serious reversal. And the virulent challenges to democracy by the political right and left in the former communist countries lost their voice to the repeated electoral victories of a democratic middle. By the end of the 1990s, only very few countries among major ones still entertained authoritarian forms of nondemocratic political systems. Among those, Indonesia and Thailand gave way first. What remains today, outside of the world's "communities of democracy," are a few military governments and outlaw countries that have yet to participate fully in the global political economy.

In historical explanations of the links between globalizations and democratizations, local conditions are all important, as are the decisions by key actors. For instance, the fortuitous concomitance of international pressures and certain indigenous events together led South Africa to declare itself ready to envision some decent prospects for democratic development. The long-term efforts of the major Western European political parties, especially the right-of-center Christian Democratic Parties, nurtured the emergence of democracy in Southern Europe. The efforts by several countries to reduce the political effects of the societal implosions triggered by a series of economic collapses in Southeastern Asia brought to power more democratic governments in that region. Yet each of these democratic events rests on explanations that remain open to debate and revision.

Examining countries and sectors within them to identify and establish the dynamics shared today by globalizations and democracies could produce the following rationale: as the main initial force in our epoch, globalization began in the last decades of the twentieth century and spread everywhere, without the benefit of the political controls once wielded by the European empires of the late nineteenth and early twentieth centuries, although the percentage share in gross national product of the terms of trade for trend-setting countries was not much larger in the twentieth century than it had been in the 1800s. It is the different kinds of exchanges—taking place across huge communication networks of production through complex flows of goods, services, and personnel within large global corporations today—that make comparisons with the past so very difficult.

Close analysis of what happened globally, by using a few simple variables (say, foreign direct investment, the number of electoral victories of a coalition of the political "middle," and activities in international organizations), does make it possible to conclude that somewhere around the second half of the 1990s democratic forces were stronger than those of globalizations, reversing the dominance of globalizations as the driving force of change in general and of changes affecting democratizations in particular. Processes of globalization require of all systems and subsystems an openness and penetrability by higher level systems. 'Openness' is clearly understood theoretically as well as empirically today. It is related to economic growth, or at least to the promise of it, either explanation having become a requisite for stabilizing the processes of democratization. Democratic governments are strongly biased in favor of market economies, and openness to others has become the very criterion on which must rest the legitimacy of a system of global democratic governance. Globalizations, however, also entail destabilizations, disruptions, and local opposition. And this is why it cannot succeed without an appropriately optimal measure of transparence.

Democracy leads to stable growth, which attracts foreign investment and domestic savings, which in turn jointly enhance economic development and political stability. There are today many techniques and tools for studying these relationships, though modern social science research is yet to untangle these highly correlated, surrogate-dependent variables. Two shortcomings to "explaining" relationships between democratizations and globalizations promise to endure. First, most of the thinking and much of the data on which measures of these variables obtain refer to a period in history when many of the democratizing countries were seeing a rapid loss in their control not only of events from within but also of intrusions from without. Second, in the final analysis, empirically grounded variables have a way of becoming descriptive enough to elicit skepticism as to whether any applicable macrolevel laws of change and development really exist, let alone apply.

Countervailing Forces: Contentions, Contradictions, and Outward Conflicts

Two types of dialectic and three kinds of conflict-theoretical counter-forces opposed to globalization are of interest here. Some of these inhere in any form of change, but necessarily so in processes of developmental change, namely in the integration of diversity. First is the dialectic of change across levels of human organization. If a system is developing, its further development always takes place initially at higher levels of aggregation within it. It absorbs variety from the lower levels, which lose out. The second dialectic is animated by the different rates of change. It occurs between the two fundamental processes of development, the creation of variety, and the integration of it. Recall that variety appears discretely but integration proceeds continually in time, albeit at a pace slower than the speed at which variety is generated.

These two basic dialectics result in three kinds of conflict which articulate particular, often very real and intense, political contentions that may derive from all kinds of imposed changes but which stand sharply in opposition to the processes of developmental change.

The first type of conflict arises among regions and localities within particular systems. Development cannot happen everywhere or all at once, but occurs in certain places and at particular times, wherever and whenever the highest levels of integrated diversity are attainable. Developmental spaces are those that can most readily attract what is new or can be easily penetrated from without. They range from world cities to places undisturbed by what the modern world has produced or diffused.

The second type of conflict cuts across localities and regions. It is inherent in developmental classes, differentiated in the past by their level of monetized income and wealth, created by the industrial- and service-level economic revolutions of the nineteenth and twentieth centuries and today by democratized abilities to access variety in the global system. This type of conflict thrives especially where those engaged in development and globalizations face those whose stance is passive or inimical to these processes.

The third conflict is between the old and the new elite—those cling- ing to local risk-avoiding privileges and those involved in global risk- taking developmental processes. In established democracies, this type of conflict is commonplace between elected representatives of tradi- tional agriculture and aging industries, who oppose reductions in pro- tective tariffs and favor closure, and those elites who favor regulation at a global level and demand openness. As developmental processes configure a stronger global system, these tough political pockets of resistance seek to transform their nation's political leaders into nation- alists, trying in last recourse to harden the crumbling remnants of the political and territorial ramparts of the past.

Dialectics

The Dialectic across Levels
According to the law of attractiveness of variety (Teune and Mlinar 1978), levels with the highest variety are likely to value novelty even more[6] because they can use such in combinations with extant variety to produce cutting-edge innovations. That same logic explains why villagers who display the lowest variety, or are the least educated, are likely to stay on; those with a measure of greater complexity, especially those newly educated, are likely to move out; and those with vested interests, usually reflected in simple wealth, will stay put if only to preserve what they possess. This is but one side of the conflict: localized self-perpetuation versus globalizing self-development.

The second side of this conflict engages much higher levels of orga- nized aggregation—corporations or interest groups—actively seeking locations in order to establish a local base for their wider activities. Penetrations of lower level localities by higher levels of aggregation will disturb the local if only because such penetration will tend to be

6. It should be noted that this involves not only components with the most variety at the local level seeking higher levels but also components at the higher levels seeking variety at the lower levels. This push and pull is one of the underlying dynamics of hierarchies.

singular in its dimensions and implications. Higher level organization typically has more variety than its lower level homologue. The presence of a multinational corporation in a rather modest town for purposes of production, administration, or research is likely to create adverse local reverberations and not merely for placing new pressures on the demand and supply of a special range of local skills and services. Cognitively, the "international company" or its world headquarters remain cognitively global, beyond any country, above any region. This is the new politics of locations: from the local, to the national, and now to the global political environment.

The traditional advantage of the local has been its physically embedded infrastructure: housing stocks around factories, large carbon-burning steel mills, integrated factory assembly lines, and retailing points in buildings smack at city centers, each and all connected by hardened roads and perhaps even steel rails of the industrial era. The productive processes of modern integrated manufacture can be farmed out and/or brought together across great distances. And services can be located throughout a system of connections rather than in any one site. The consequences are the decay of the industrial cities, the sprawl of settlements, and the threat of capital and labor movements in and out of localities.

A historically well-accepted principle of effective and stable democracy is familiarity. Whether a stable democratic order can be built on impersonal and vicarious relationships, or rather depend on personal contacts that create the trust necessary for iterative bargaining over issues requiring full compliance with authoritative decisions, is still an unsettled issue. The polemic parlance that blames globalization for destroying community also carries part of the secret to the perceived conflict between globalizations and democratizations. Two sources of threat seem to persist. First, the remote center of some inexplicable global decision with local impact cannot be held locally accountable. Second, in addition to being locally uncontrollable, decisions taken by global entities, or resulting from globalizations, seem more often than not insensitive, sanctimonious, and even offensive to local interests. Both of these perceived aggressions are integral to long-standing local reticence, when dealing with higher level authorities or accommodating foreign interests.

These relational aspects of the conflicts between the global and the local aside, there are significant structural differences that also easily lead to conflicts and to overt efforts to defeat, evade, or avoid their consequences. Ironically, globalization has become the source of new clashes in which the local embodies the old. This is where the hate in Luddite responses originates. Both the global and the local are aware of this. But the global can disguise its local maneuvers. It can co-opt local elites, bribe the local community, and even threaten to withdraw. The local can only fight through legal and political processes. It can organize protests or violence and escape the consequences by erecting barriers of all kinds. It can also fake its compliance and wait for the arrogant to move out.

None of these measures offers long-term solutions. All global actors have potential local allies whom they amply reward. Nonetheless, globalization does engage the politics of a local ecology of games among groups within localities as well as between higher levels and the local. These can shift or evade responsibilities, distort information, and even sabotage the intruders (Long 1958; Teune 1979). The advantage of the local is self-knowledge and ways to use it for subverting the global. The advantage of the global resides in its capacity to withdraw and relocate.

The Dialectic among Rates of Change

One of the persistent dimensions of change likely to generate potential destabilization is the difference in rates of change among a system's components. In anthropology, this dimension is called *cultural lag*. It suggests that changes in the values and habits of one sample population are slower than, and possibly incompatible with, those of another whose rate of change is faster. This concept of differential rates of change can be applied widely to developmental processes.

What distinguish the conflicts generated by developmental rates of change are the differences inherent in the occurrence of diversity and in the processes of its integration. This is the real threat to the stability of a system. Nowadays, instability can be attributed much more easily to "globalization"—an impersonal force—than to any other, more specific, foreign influence. What usually happens is that some new item is imported or generated and distributed. The ensuing impact spawns divisions and cleavages, some of which may ignite group conflicts. One example is the automobile. Its erstwhile introduction disrupted other modes of transportation, had an impact on neighborhood organization, altered the supply of goods, and created visible distinctions between those who could and could not afford it. Those disruptions aside, roads had to be built, parking had to be provided, repair stations positioned, and life would never be the same.

New variety has and always will spread at uneven rates throughout a population. Systems entering development from a relatively low or weak starting level run a significantly higher risk of destabilization from development. This explains their political endeavors to control the rate of change, thus perchance to deter novel ideas and items from entering their territory. But systems at very low levels of development also have sparse internal relationships. Destroying one or more components does little harm to a disjointed system that displays low connectedness, poor diversity, and meager integration. In contrast, multiple links, manifold alternative choices, and redundancies abound in highly developed social systems. Hence, even when they are distributed at different rates, new variety exercises little overall impact on such societies, which have the wherewithal to avert deep disruptions.

But development, when spurred by one category of globalization or another, does cause stresses, especially if novel products and ideas are not simply new but also creations of "foreign" origin. Whereas change and difference are valued in highly developed societies, they continue to be frowned upon in more traditional societies. For most countries today, what is both new and alien or global represents a challenge that stimulates a politics of rejection. It is not surprising then that some political systems reject globalism and revert to closure in the name of sustainable development. Even the less developed sectors and regions inside highly developed countries support initiatives by their political representatives to close borders, increase tariffs, and protect their own. The voices that find expression in anti-immigration politics almost always arise in those areas that are least developed and experience only a low presence of immigrants. Immigration and the commingling of peoples are concomitants of globalizations. But the rates of absorption differ radically from one developing system to another and also from region to region inside the developed systems, depending on level of development.

Conflicts

Conflicts among Regions
Economic growth has generated massive inequalities among parts of the world and regions inside nations. Although spatial inequalities

may be the fundamental moral challenge of our times, they do not generate or perpetrate conflicts unless the more developed regions abandon or, worse still, pillage the poorer regions. Globalizations provide alternatives to accessing wealth through political transfers (grants and aid) or in direct investment and trade.

The conflicts generated by regional inequalities within, between, and among countries often pivot on moral claims against democracy for its failures to deliver on the promises of equality. Those failures can be used to justify subversive conduct, even petty lawless behavior by those left behind. Moral claims mixed with fears of unrest have provided cause for arranging income transfers among regions and between rich and poor within the wealthier countries, through public and private welfare programs. None of the established democracies are without welfare and regional development policies, however ineffective these may be. Some level of equality, or at least some perceptible reduction in economic inequalities, is necessary for democratic stability if the democratic assertion of the equal moral worth of all individuals is to be credible.

The direction of improvement has remained positive in all parts of Asia, save those few that have opted out of the global process. In Africa, the structures and dynamics of inequality is perhaps the primary challenge. Here, weather and disease play a part that is difficult for science alone to address. The problems of Africa, however, are not a major impediment to globalization or democratization (see Brown and Kaiser, chap. 10 in this book).

Conflicts among Economic and Social Strata

The revolution that never happened is the uprising the working poor have yet to wage against the rich. Differences among the wealthy and the poor have radically increased with industrialization. They rose once again with the emergence of services. And with the advent of the information economy, differences widened some more. Further widening is to be expected with the imminent emergence of new energy technologies. But each "new economy" holds out promises of betterment even for those worst off. And the economic changes that so far have ensued actually did deliver on those general promises, even if not as quickly or as lavishly as could have been expected. The data on income and welfare, a regular product of research in wealthier countries, and now regularly compiled by international agencies, are politically laden in that they are meant to serve political purposes. And their overall impact has been neither revolutionary nor significant in the delegitimization of globalizations or democratizations.

Yet modern globalization does create conditions for discontent, and dissatisfactions can be mobilized against it. But the sources of discontent from globalization remain diffused and are no longer easily identifiable with a single country. Globalizations do not only diffuse goods, services, and information, but in so doing seem also to reduce the relative position of any one global actor. The United States, for instance, has had a diminishing percentage of the world's total output each year for the past two decades or so. Its share will have dropped from about 50 percent of world output after World War II to about 20 percent in the next few years.

Conflicts between the Old and New Elites

The contradictions between old and new elites are the main source of conflict in the wars waged against globalizations. The new elites of modernization and their political instrument of control, the state, have long displaced the traditional elites of yesterday. Yet two arenas of conflict between the new and old elites do linger. One is international or global in reach; the other, of local societal consequence well inside national boundaries.

The old elites of nationalism and communism have lost their wars. Those that retain control in a few odd places such as Burma, Cuba, and North Korea govern in ways ever more obviously harmful to their populations. The international conflicts fueled by these anachronic entities are likely to continue. Some of these conflicts will intensify, as the losing groups perceive that the forces for modernization in their communities and countries are gaining a strong, if not invincible, ally in the wave of globalizations.

The opening years of the twenty-first century saw the beginnings of the first protracted global war. Just as democratic values and institutions had almost totally triumphed over the secular communalisms of socialism, nazism, fascism, and communism, the militant religious communalisms of a more distant past undertook attacks on some of the most visible symbols of global power in the United States. These rear-guard attacks devoid of vision and incapable of victory are conducted from the lands of a few retarded states in rejection of modernity based on religious militancy.

The main source of political conflict generated by globalizations today plays significantly into the hands of elites, old and new, within countries that are just about to enter the global era. The nationally based elites are becoming marginalized. They are not poor. They remain obsessively connected with a waning era of early modernity. And having attended universities, knowing about international travel, engaging in electronic communications, thus quite unlike the peasants and small-town residents who live in the hope of a better future, they find themselves to be existentially threatened. Their newest material acquisitions are becoming quickly obsolete, and their older parochial beliefs are facing increasingly tough challenges.

To these dying elites in newly globalizing countries can be added those elected representatives and political leaders in long-established democracies whose constituencies are territorially entrenched and whose interests are land- and place-specific. They are all for family-based agriculture; they fight to sustain the economic viability of small-scale production; they support manufacturers heavily vested in a particular area as they are desperate for new investments; they also cater to labor unions representing skills locally organized and easily replaced when employment ends or moves. These elites and their constituencies may well continue actively to protect their interests against the forces of globalization to the bitter end, even if at times only nominally so.

Neither the traditional cliques tied to newly established states nor the residual elites inside countries with a venerable history of indus-trialization can prevail in the long run. The war is over, but the first battles of the postwar globalization era necessarily seem likely to continue to comprise protracted confrontations on battlegrounds still awaiting to be defined (Ciprut 2000), engaging the very technologies that sealed globalization's threat, and victory, against the old order.

A Concluding Comment

Globalizations continue to create many uncertainties for some just as democratizations continue to carry much ambiguity for others. The principal question is whether on balance they have been forces for human betterment or human misery, vectors of good, or conduits of evil. Any dispassionate examination of globalizations and democrati-zations cannot but conclude that separately and together they stand as great achievements. Their most important joint virtue resides in their future-oriented challenge that, in conferring rights and privileges for all, they also demand responsibility from each.

References

Boulding, Kenneth E. (1978) *Ecodynamics: A New Theory of Societal Evolution*, Beverly Hills, CA: Sage Publications.

Ciprut, Jose V., Editor (2000). *Of Fears and Foes: Security and Insecurity in an Evolving Global Political Economy*, Westport, CT: Praeger.

Davies, James Chowning (1977) "The Priorities of Human Needs and the Stages of Political Development," in J. Roland Pennock and John Chapman, Editors, *Human Nature in Politics*, New York: New York University Press.

Geddes, Barbara (1999) "What Do We Know About Democracy after Twenty Years?" *Annual Review of Political Science*, 2:115–144.

Guillen, Mario F. (2002) "Is Globalization Civilizing, Destructive, or Feeble: A Critique of Five Key Debates in the Social Science Literature," *Annual Review of Sociology*, 27:235–260.

Long, Norton (1958) "The Local Community as an Ecology of Games," *American Journal of Sociology*, 64:251–261.

Teune, Henry (1979) "Information, Control, and Territorial Political Systems," *Studies in Comparative International Development*, 14:77–89.

Teune, Henry, and Zdravko Mlinar (1978) *The Developmental Logic of Social Systems*, Beverly Hills, CA: Sage Publications.

—— (2000) "The Developmental Logic of Globalization," in Jose V. Ciprut, Editor, *The Art of the Feud: Reconceptualizing International Relations*, Westport, CT: Praeger.

Urban, Greg (2008) "Citizenship as a Mode of Belonging by Choice," in Jose V. Ciprut, Editor, *The Future of Citizenship*, Cambridge, MA: The MIT Press.

5

Federalism: The Highest Stage of Democracy?

John Kincaid

Relationships between federalism and democracy can be examined empirically and theoretically; that is, how democratic are federal systems compared to other political systems, and is federal democracy, in theory, more democratic than nonfederal democracy? This chapter explores both perspectives, concluding that, empirically, federal polities compare well with nonfederal systems on democracy and rights protection, although in close competition with decentralized unitary systems, but better than other systems on quality of life.[1] Theoretically, however, federal democracy is more democratic than nonfederal democracy.

Federal polities are defined broadly here as polities having constitutionally recognized constituent political communities that exercise exclusive and concurrent powers of self-government through legislative powers of their own and are also represented in the federation's legislature. The following twenty-five polities are thus classified as federal: Argentina, Australia, Austria, Belgium, Bosnia and Herzegovina, Brazil, Canada, Comoros, Ethiopia, Germany, India, Malaysia, Mexico, Micronesia, Nigeria, Pakistan, Russia, St. Kitts and Nevis, South Africa, Spain, Switzerland, United Arab Emirates, United States of America, Venezuela, and Yugoslavia. Another thirty-five polities are classified as decentralized unitary systems (derived from Derbyshire and Derbyshire 1999, I, 23). These include, for example, Bolivia, Denmark, France, Indonesia, Israel, People's Republic of China, Philippines, Poland, Senegal, Solomon Islands, Sudan, Ukraine, United Kingdom, and Zambia. An additional 131 countries (e.g., Cambodia, Egypt, Ghana, New Zealand, Turkey, Sweden, and Uruguay) are treated as having other forms of unitary government.

---

1. I thank Christiane Conn, a student at Lafayette College, for her assistance in compiling data for this analysis.

Historical and Empirical Perspectives

Since the fall of Portugal's dictatorship in 1974, and especially since the fall of the Berlin Wall in 1989, many reformers have linked democracy rhetorically to decentralization and to federalism (Diamond 1999; Kincaid 1995). Such links have been made partly in reaction against the suppressions of democracy and freedom perpetrated by so many centralized, authoritarian regimes during the twentieth century. Many reformers have pitted democracy against authoritarianism and federalism/decentralization against centralization. The link also reflects what Daniel J. Elazar termed "a dual political interest" of the contemporary modern era: "first, in creating more viable units of government . . . to undertake vast new responsibilities and, second, in enhancing citizen participation in government to foster democracy" (Elazar 1987, 114). Ronald L. Watts also identifies two interests in federalism: (1) a "desire for smaller, self-governing political units, more responsive to the individual citizen" and (2) a "desire to give expression to primary group attachments: linguistic and cultural ties, religious connections, historical traditions, and social practices" (Watts 2002, 1). Others hold a dimmer view: "Federalism seems to be creeping insidiously onto the democratization agenda," notes Philippe C. Schmitter (2000, 40). Still others, seeing threats to democracy from globalization, envision a need to extend federalism globally in order to protect democracy locally. David Held asserts that "democracy can result from, and only from, a nucleus, or federation, of democratic states and societies" (1992, 11; see also Teune, chap. 4 in this book).

Links between federalism and democracy, however, were present in all three waves of democratization that followed the advent of the nation-state. The first wave, which "led to the triumph of democracy in some thirty countries" (Huntington 1997, 4), not all of which survived, produced four of the world's five major and successful federal democracies: the United States of America in 1789, Switzerland in 1848, Canada in 1867, and Australia in 1901. The second, short wave of democratization after World War II brought the number of democracies back up to more than thirty, including creation of the world's fifth major and successful federal democracy, Germany in 1949, along with India in 1950, Austria in 1955, and Nigeria in 1960. The third wave increased the number of electoral democracies, as well as federal polities—democratic and nondemocratic. As a result, today 39.0 percent of the world's population lives in the twenty-five federal polities identified above (compared to 34.1 percent living in the thirty-five decentralized unitary polities and 26.9 percent in the 131 other polities).

Federalism in the Third Wave of Democratization

An interesting facet of the third wave has been the actual, or at least attempted, democratization of long-standing federal systems—such as Argentina, Brazil, Mexico, Russia, and Venezuela—that had succumbed to military rule or authoritarian one-party rule during or after the previous eras of democratization. Nigeria also recently returned to democratic governance, although its democracy is threatened by corruption and ethnoreligious violence. For the most part, federal systems that were established during previous eras, and which survived for at least 50 years, still exist (Elazar 1987). Thus democratization or redemocratization in such countries has involved reinvigoration rather than abandonment of federalism. At the same time, a few federations experienced dissolution (i.e., Czechoslovakia) or partial dissolution (i.e., the Union of Soviet Socialist Republics [USSR] and Yugoslavia). The USSR was the only modern federation to collapse after lasting more than fifty years.

Democracy's third wave has also given rise to centrifugal federalization as opposed to traditional centripetal federalization. Instead of forming a federal union through the constitutional unification of separate political communities, a federation can be formed through the constitutional decentralization of unitary states, as in Spain, so as to restore what are often regarded to be the ancient self-governing autonomies of the nation-state's previously suppressed political communities (e.g., Basques and Catalans). The Federal Republic of Germany is the first model of centrifugal federalization. Federalism was a component of de-Nazification intended to inhibit tyrannical recentralization, and the *Grundgesetz* partially restored West Germany's historic political communities as constituent *Länder* and created new ones as well.

The third wave of democratization has also spawned asymmetrical federalism. Typically, federal polities founded during the first and second waves of democratization were symmetrical; that is, all of the constituent political communities were equal with respect to constitutional powers of self-government and relations with the federal government. Asymmetrical federalism awards different levels of constitutional self-governance to different constituent political communities and allows for differential federal-constituent relations, as in

Canada, the European Union (EU) (see Heinemann-Grüder, chap. 6 in this book), Russia (see Shlapentokh, chap. 8 in this book), and Spain. Asymmetry may be established by differential constitutional delegations or reservations of powers to constituent political communities (e.g., Spain) and/or by general constitutional or treaty provisions that allow constituent political communities to opt out of certain rules (the European Union, for instance).

The third wave of democratization also has been associated with what might be called "creeping international treaty federalism" entailing, perhaps, a paradigm shift from statism to federalism—a "shift from a world of states . . . to a world of diminished state sovereignty and increased interstate linkages of a constitutionalized federal character" (Elazar 1995, 5). One can say "creeping" because the process is slow, and there is opposition to it from nation-state sovereigntists, for whom federalism is the F-word of international integration. Although this international or interstate federalism is treaty based, one of its emerging characteristics is the quasi-constitutionalization of treaties—most notably in the European Union, a federated entity that originated during the second wave of democratization but has been deepened and broadened during the third wave, producing an almost-but-not-quite constitutionalized federal polity (Kincaid 1999; Nicolaidis and Howse 2001) that is likely to remain in that status for the foreseeable future since voters in France and the Netherlands rejected the proposed EU constitution in 2005.

Both the second and third waves of democratization have been characterized, as well, by the predominant influence of the world's oldest federal democracy, the United States. Unlike its isolationism after World War I, the United States engaged the world after World War II, fostering democracy and federalism in Germany and Austria, democracy and decentralization in Japan, the federalistic unification of Western Europe, and the establishment of confederal-like international institutions such as the United Nations, World Bank, International Monetary Fund, and North Atlantic Treaty Organization, even while guarding its own sovereignty jealously.

Federalism was an element of U.S. democratization policy during the second wave of democratization but was not a noticeable element of U.S. democratization policy during the third wave until President George W. Bush embarked on the wars in Afghanistan and Iraq and made federalism a key feature of efforts to democratize those countries, especially Iraq. Otherwise, the role of promoting federalism had been assumed by Canada, Germany, and Switzerland, all three of which promote themselves as models of federal democracy. In 1998, the government of Canada funded the establishment of an international Forum of Federations. The Forum's first major international conference, held in Canada, was addressed by Prime Minister Jean Chrétien and Presidents Bill Clinton and Ernesto Zedillo (Addresses 1999). Since the birth of the virtually federal Spanish state of the autonomies (Agranoff and Gallarin 1997; Moreno 2001), Spain also has served as a federal model, especially for Latin America, even though Madrid eschews the word "federal."

Democratic and Rights Performance

How, then, do federal polities perform compared to other systems? Table 5.1 indicates that federal polities perform comparatively well on measures of freedom, democracy, and rights. However, there is little performance difference between federal polities and decentralized unitary polities. To the extent there is a difference, the thirty-five decentralized unitary polities have a very slight edge over the twenty-five federal polities. Both federal and decentralized unitary systems perform much better on these measures, however, than do other, unitary political systems. Put differently, of the 143 polities classified as free or partly free by Freedom House in 2000–2001, 16.1 percent were federal, 21.6 percent were decentralized unitary systems, and 62.2 percent had other

Table 5.1
Freedom, democracy, rights, and corruption in federal and nonfederal polities

	Free (%)	Electoral democracy (%)	Mean political rights	Mean civil liberties	Mean corruption index
Federal (N =)	52.0 (13)	76.0 (19)	2.7 (25)	3.0 (25)	5.2 (19)
Decentralized unitary (N =)	54.2 (19)	80.0 (28)	2.6 (35)	3.0 (35)	4.3 (22)
Other unitary (N =)	40.4 (53)	55.7 (73)	3.8 (131)	3.8 (131)	4.3 (59)

Sources: Columns 1–4 computed from Karatnycky et al. (2001, 655–663); column 5, from Transparency International at www.transparency.org/policy_research/surveys_indices/cpi/2001.
Notes: For political rights and civil liberties, 1.0 = high, 7.0 = low rights protection. For corruption, 1.0 = high, 9.0 = low corruption. Numbersvary in the columns of this and subsequent tables as data were not available for all countries on every measure.

systems.[2] Of all 191 polities, 7.3 percent were free and federal, 10.5 percent were free and decentralized unitary, and 27.7 percent were free with other forms of unitary government.

Interestingly, on average, federal polities are less corrupt than both decentralized unitary polities and other polities, although the federal category includes Nigeria, the world's second most corrupt country (after Bangladesh) according to Transparency International, along with India, Pakistan, Russia, and Venezuela, all five of which, together, have a mean score of 2.2. The five major federal democracies—Australia, Canada, Germany, Switzerland, and the United States—have a mean corruption score of 8.2.

These findings might seem counterintuitive because, given the greater self-governing regional and local autonomy in federations, one might expect more corruption because (1) regional and local officials are not under close control by national officials, (2) they are more likely to be less well paid and less professionalized, and (3) they have more freedom than nationally supervised officials to extract bribes and pay off clients. Apparently, this is not the case. On the contrary, the explanation, perhaps, lies precisely in regional and local self-government. That is, because elected regional and local officials in a federation are more likely to be tied to and held accountable to regional and local voters and taxpayers rather than to distant national officials, they might be held to a stricter regimen of propriety and accountability than would be the case without autonomy (Bennett 1990; Shah and Huther 1999). The possibility of such accountability has often been regarded as one of the values of federalism, a possibility supported although not confirmed by this finding.

Otherwise, the seeming closeness of federal polities ($N = 25$) and decentralized unitary polities ($N = 35$) on the measures of democracy, freedom, and rights protection would suggest that a crucial underlying dimension of these findings is noncentralization or decentralization. It is apparently the lack of centralization in both systems that brings them so close together and distinguishes them from the world's other, unitary polities (see also Diamond 1999). This closeness is also produced by varying degrees of noncentralization among federal systems. Some federal polities, including the United States, are centralized in many

---

2. Freedom House defines "free" as protection of a broad range of political rights and civil liberties, "partly free" as protection of only a limited range of rights and liberties, and "not free" as the denial of basic rights and liberties.

respects; others, such as Belgium, Canada, and Switzerland, are substantially noncentralized. A federal form of government does not always result in noncentralized governance, as was the case, for example, in Mexico during some 70 years of rule by the Partido Revolucionario Institucional (Rodriquez 1998; see also Massey and Pérez, chap. 11 in this book). Thus, these findings lend support to claims made by democratic reformers about the links between democratization and decentralization.

Whether there is, indeed, a causal link between democratization and decentralization is difficult to determine (see Ciprut, chap. 1 in this book). Democracy can exist without decentralization (e.g., Chile and Norway), and decentralization can exist without democracy (e.g., China and Sudan). Democratization can foster decentralization because the unleashing of electoral freedom and political rights can generate citizen demands for administrative discretion and self-government in their own locales. Decentralization can foster democratization because the granting of administrative discretion and some governing autonomy to regions and localities can produce regional and local resistance to national government limits on discretion and autonomy and, thus, generate demands for democratization.

Economic and Quality-of-Life Performance

Federalism is not simply an end in itself. In addition to protecting political rights and civil liberties, a federal polity, especially a federal democracy, should produce economic results and a high quality of life. The data presented in table 5.2 suggest that this is the case. Unlike the results in most of table 5.1, in table 5.2, the federal polities stand apart from all other political systems on all four performance measures. The federal polities display the highest average level of economic freedom. Real GDP per capita is 74.2 percent higher in the twenty-five federal polities than in the thirty-five decentralized unitary polities and 100.8 percent higher than in world's 131 other polities. The United Nations' Human Development score is 10.0 percent higher in federal polities than in decentralized unitary polities and 16.7 percent higher than in all other systems. Although, again, the decentralized unitary polities perform better than the other unitary systems, their performance is second best to the federal polities.

These findings are somewhat puzzling, partly because one might expect decentralization to be an underlying dimension here, too. One

Table 5.2
Economic and quality-of-life performance of federal and nonfederal polities

	Economic freedom	Real GDP per capita	Human development	Life expectancy	Capitalist or mixed capitalist (%)
Federal (N =)	2.8 (22)	$12,550 (22)	0.77 (20)	69.4 (25)	60.0 (25)
Decentralized unitary (N =)	3.0 (27)	7,204 (31)	0.70 (28)	67.2 (34)	54.3 (35)
Other unitary (N =)	3.1 (105)	6,249 (120)	0.66 (112)	64.6 (128)	39.7 (131)

Sources: Column 1 from O'Driscoll, Holmes, and O'Grady (2002); columns 2, 4, and 5 from Karatnycky et al. (2001); column 3 from United Nations (2001).
Notes: For economic freedom, 1.0 = high, 5.0 = low. For human development, 0.939 = high, 0.258 = low.

might also expect greater fragmentation and less policy coherence in federal systems and, thus, weaker performance on the above measures. A recent study of federal and nonfederal systems in the developing world concluded that "federal institutional arrangements negatively affect the capacity of national governments to implement macroeconomic reforms. The result is a tendency toward macroeconomic fragility, volatility, and crisis" (Wibbels 2000, 698). Such problems have been recognized by students of federalism; however, Wibbels' study is problematic because the thirty-one nonfederal countries in his study's sample include many small, substantially homogeneous nations (e.g., Malta and Morocco) as well as countries arguably not in the developing category (e.g., Israel). Furthermore, whereas 75 percent of the federal countries in his sample were electoral democracies, only 68 percent of the nonfederal countries were electoral democracies.

It is likely that some problems experienced by developing countries are aggravated by federalism, especially in the federations established to govern large territories and comprising significant religious, linguistic, racial, ethnic, and/or other geographically based communities that frequently oppose the national government and resist national unity. However, as table 5.2 indicates, the federal polities nevertheless perform better than all other political systems. These findings suggest that a well-structured and well-functioning federal system has quality-of-life benefits, perhaps for several reasons. For one, deconcentrating power and allowing greater self-governing regional and local autonomy is likely to be accompanied by economic liberalization, as in India and China, and to stimulate more entrepreneurial regional and local economic development. In turn, development may yield more investment in human capital (i.e., health, education, and welfare). Greater regional and local self-government may also reduce political tensions, especially in multicultural federations, as various cultural communities feel freer to pursue their destinies and have less reason to accuse the national government of discrimination.

At the same time, most federations delegate monetary policy-making exclusively or substantially to the national government, whereas fiscal policy-making is usually a concurrent or shared power. To the extent that regional and local governments are extended fiscal autonomy and responsibility, more fiscal discipline and accountability are likely to be imposed on regional and local officials by voters and taxpayers than might be the case without autonomy. Generally, accountability requires a close connection between taxing and spending; that is, any politician who enjoys spending tax money should first experience the pain of extracting it from the taxpayers. Absent such pain, usually, politicians are tempted to spend with abandon. Likewise, borrowing and paying down debt require a watertight connection; otherwise, national government bail-outs of overextended regional and local governments create a moral hazard that encourages regional and local governments to borrow excessively.

The alternative is strict regulation by the national government, but such regulation reduces regional and local autonomy. In the United States, for example, the federal government has no obligation to bail out state or local governments; they must swim or sink on their own. Fiscal discipline and accountability are imposed on state and local governments by voters themselves (through their state constitutions, municipal charters, statutes, and elections) and also by the bond market. As the data in table 5.2 suggest, therefore, a well-structured federal system can create a monetary and fiscal climate conducive to economic growth and improved living conditions (Kincaid 2001).

At the same time, federal polities are the most likely to have a capitalist or mixed capitalist economy as defined by Freedom House[3]

---

3. Freedom House identifies seven economy types: traditional or preindustrial, capitalist, mixed capitalist, capitalist-statist, mixed capitalist-statist, statist, and mixed statist. A capitalist economy has a modern market sector; a mixed capitalist economy combines "predominantly private enterprise with substantial government involvement in the economy for social welfare purposes" (Karatnycky et al. 2001, 37).

(table 5.2). Fully 60.0 percent of federal polities have such economies compared to 54.3 percent of decentralized unitary polities and only 39.7 percent of other systems. It is possible that the combination of federalism and capitalism substantially explains the superior performance of federal polities in wealth creation and quality of life.

Is federalism, then, the handmaiden of capitalism, or vice versa? Given that the U.S. Declaration of Independence was issued in 1776, the same year in which Adam Smith published his *Wealth of Nations*, one could say that modern federalism and capitalism were invented simultaneously. They then developed hand in hand in the world's first federal democracy. Although capitalism did not begin to flourish in the United States until the 1840s, there are affinities between federalism and capitalism. For one, the federal republic forged by the framers of the U.S. Constitution was rooted in the liberal proto-capitalist tradition of John Locke, the republican tradition of Machiavelli, and the federal theology of Reformed Protestantism. Second, a federal system is constitutionally noncentralized; a capitalist market is inherently noncentralized. Both federalism and capitalism have characteristics of spontaneous organization. Third, like capitalist markets, federal systems too are animated, in part, by competition—interjurisdictional and intergovernmental competition in federations—and by contractual cooperation; and both federalism and capitalism strike balances between anarchy and monopoly (Kenyon and Kincaid 1991).

Fourth, capitalism requires liberty and self-governing autonomy, as does a federal democracy, along with a reliable rule of law and disinterested governance to enforce contracts and property rights. A federal democracy is also a covenantal or contractual arrangement that requires a reliable rule of law and disinterested governance to enforce the covenant and to protect what Albert Breton has termed "the ownership rights regarding constitutional powers" (2000, 15) in a federal system. This ownership, argues Breton, fundamentally distinguishes federalism from decentralized unitarism. In a decentralized unitary polity, "all powers are owned by the national government" (Breton 2000, 4), which can repossess decentralized powers and, thus, function as a monopolist (see also Elazar 1987, on the distinction between noncentralization and decentralization). In a federal polity, the ownership of powers is dispersed, much like a capitalist market, such that "some powers are owned by the federal government, while others are owned by the *Länder*, provinces, republics, or states" (Breton 2000, 4). The ownership of those powers is constitutionally guaranteed and protected by the rule of law. A key objective for Breton is maintenance of competition, such that a well-functioning federal system will not succumb to monopoly any more than would a well-functioning market.

In addition, capitalism requires free trade, expansive markets, and mobility of capital, labor, and goods. Federalism lowers trade barriers between jurisdictions, facilitates interjurisdictional mobility, and establishes expansive common markets. Finally, federalism may be conducive to capitalism because, given the noncentralized dispersal of powers in a federation, no government possesses sufficient authority or power to command the national economy. Yet a federal polity also can mitigate the ravages of capitalism through dual (national and regional) fiscal policy-making and economic regulation, as well as through redistribution, such as fiscal equalization, which operates in most federations.

Demographic Bases of Federal and Nonfederal Polities

Beginning with the first wave of democratization, two principal rationales for federalism have been needs (1) to govern territorially large polities democratically rather than imperially and (2) to accommodate religious, linguistic, racial, ethnic, and/or other organic cultural heterogeneity, especially geographically based diversity (e.g., French-speaking Quebec), by establishing unity while preserving diversity. The average population (table 5.3) of the twenty-five federal polities is 94.9 million, which is 59.8 percent larger than the 59.4 million average population of decentralized unitary polities and 659.2 percent larger than the mere 12.5 million mean population of all other polities. Additionally, the average land area of the federal countries is more than four times larger than that of all other countries (table 5.3). Indeed, seven of

Table 5.3
Demographic bases of federal and nonfederal polities

	Mean population (millions)	Mean land area (million km²)	Degree of cultural homogeneity (%)
Federal (N =)	94.9 (25)	2.7 (25)	67.3 (22)
Decentralized unitary (N =)	59.4 (35)	0.6 (35)	76.1 (27)
Other unitary (N =)	12.5 (131)	0.3 (131)	72.5 (114)

Source: Computed from Karatnycky et al. (2001).

the world's eight territorially largest nations—Argentina, Australia, Brazil, Canada, India, Russia, and the United States—are formally democratic federal polities. Only China is nonfederal, although some observers (Montinola, Qian, and Weingast 1995; Davis 1999) argue that China has become virtually federal (cf. deLisle, chap. 9 in this book). Together, the twenty-five federal polities account for 50.6 percent of the land area of all 191 countries.

Federal polities are also the most culturally diverse, either in a bicultural manner like Belgium or in a highly heterogeneous manner like Nigeria. The measure used in table 5.3 (column 3) is from Freedom House, which lists for most countries the percentages of the total population accounted for by various racial and ethnoreligious groups. The percentage for each country's largest group was recorded for this study as a measure of cultural homogeneity. The United States, for example, was classified as 73 percent white. For Nigeria, the largest group was the Hausa and Fulani at merely 29 percent. Admittedly, this measure is rough and also somewhat questionable for some countries: the classification of the United States as 73 percent white, for example, masks its population's ethnoreligious diversity. Nevertheless, the measure is revealing. On average, the largest cultural group in federal polities constitutes 67.3 percent of the national population. By contrast, the largest cultural group in decentralized unitary polities constitutes, on average, 76.1 percent of the national population.

Although these data do not confirm that a federal system is a political necessity for large, multicultural countries, they do suggest that federalism may be almost a political necessity for achieving peaceful national unity among diverse cultural groups, especially when those groups are geographically based and insist on maintaining their identities. Cultural cleavages and intergroup mistrust may be too deep to establish a unitary polity without resorting to authoritarianism. In less heterogeneous polities, it may be more feasible to establish a decentralized unitary polity because, at the 76.1 percent average for the twenty-seven decentralized countries, one group is sufficiently dominant to establish a unitary system and then to decentralize power without major risks of opening cultural fissures. This may also explain why the federal polities and decentralized unitary polities scored so closely together on the governmental and political measures in table 5.1.

The remaining 114 "other unitary" polities are less culturally homogeneous than "decentralized unitary" polities but more so than federal

Table 5.4

Cultural homogeneity and freedom

	Mean percent of most numerous cultural community in total national population		
	Free (%)	Partly free (%)	Not free (%)
Federal ($N =$)	75.0 (13)	54.8 (8)	N.A. (2)
Decentralized unitary ($N =$)	80.0 (13)	70.9 (10)	76.8 (4)
Other unitary ($N =$)	78.4 (46)	68.6 (31)	68.3 (37)

Sources: See tables 5.1–5.3 for sources.
Note: "Free" = the combined average of 1.0–2.5; "Partly free" = 3.0–5.5; and "Not free" = 5.6–7.0, on Freedom House's political rights and civil liberties ratings.

polities. These other polities, however, are quite small in both population and land area; hence, neither federalism nor indeed decentralization may be a necessity or probability for them. Cultural diversity can be accommodated democratically in virtue of proportional representation, constitutional rights protections, and other devices, although in small polities having deep cultural cleavages, federalism or decentralization might still be preferable or necessary, as in the tiny bicommunal entity of Cyprus, possibly (Bahçeli 2000; Theophanus 2000). Bicommunal federations, however, are usually unsuccessful (Duchacek 1988). There was hope that a bicommunal Cyprus within the EU might be successful, but the Greek Cypriots voted against the federal plan that was to bring a Greek-Turkish Cyprus into the EU.

Alternately, diversity simply can be suppressed by authoritarian rule. Indeed, as shown in table 5.4, among the other unitary countries, the most numerous cultural community in those classified as "free" by Freedom House constituted, on average, 78.4 percent of the national population ($N = 46$). Among those classified as "partly free," however, the most numerous group constituted, on average, 68.8 percent of the total national population ($N = 31$), whereas among those classified as "not free," the most numerous group, on average, constituted 68.3 percent of the population ($N = 37$). Thus, it appears to be easier to establish a free electoral democracy in a more homogeneous polity than it is in a more heterogeneous polity.

These findings suggest a striking conclusion: that the most heterogeneous polities, by far, are the partly free federal polities. The next most heterogeneous polities are the unfree other unitary polities, followed by the partly free other unitary polities. Put differently, among the world's free and partly free federal polities, the most numerous cultural group constitutes 67.3 percent of the national population (table 5.3); likewise, among the world's partly free and not free other, unitary polities, the most numerous group constitutes 68.8 percent and 68.3 percent of the population, respectively. Thus, heterogeneity fares rather well in terms of freedom under federalism, while faring less well in terms of freedom in unitary polities. All of the other polities of the world are less heterogeneous. However, as the data in table 5.4 indicate, cultural diversity is problematic also for federal polities. In the thirteen free federal polities, the most numerous cultural community constitutes fully three quarters of the national population; in the eight partly free federal polities, the most numerous cultural community constitutes only 54.8 percent of the national population. (Data were not available for the two not-free federations, Pakistan and the United Arab Emirates.) Thus, it also appears to be easier to establish a free federal democracy in a less heterogeneous society.

In summary, the above empirical analysis suggests that federalism might very well be the highest stage of democracy. Although, on average, the world's federal polities perform no better than the world's decentralized unitary polities on democracy, freedom, and rights protection, the federal polities achieve this performance under more adverse conditions than decentralized unitary polities, namely, much larger population, larger territorial size, and greater cultural heterogeneity. At the same time, federal polities outperform all other political systems by having the lowest level of corruption, highest level of economic freedom, highest GDP per capita, highest human-development score, and longest citizen life expectancy.

Theoretical and Normative Perspectives

Given that six of the world's federal polities are not electoral democracies (i.e., Bosnia-Herzegovina, Comoros, Ethiopia, Malaysia, Pakistan, and the United Arab Emirates), a federal system does not, in itself, establish or guarantee democracy. However, it is not evident that federalism is an effective tool or enhancement of nondemocratic governance. Nondemocratic federations tend to be ruled either by an authoritarian party or by a military junta that prefers to override de jure federalism to impose de facto unitarism. The USSR was the classic example of a constitutionally federal polity ruled despotically by a single party. Federalism does, however, seem to be an effective tool and enhancement of democratic governance.

Territorial Scope and Security

It can be argued that federalism is, indeed, the highest stage of democracy insofar as it made democracy globally viable for the first time in history by forging a mode of democratic governance for large, culturally heterogeneous political systems. Such systems had been imperial empires or leagues of feudal principalities or warlords prior to the 1780s. Small republics and leagues of free city-states, such as the Hanseatic League, usually had unstable lives cut short by internal strife or external conquest. As Alexis de Tocqueville (1969) suggested in the 1830s, modern federal democracy remedied these problems by combining the advantages of large republics (e.g., a common defense and common market) with the advantages of small republics (e.g., local self-government) while minimizing the disadvantages of each. In principle, moreover, there is no limit to the territorial size of a federation, nor must the constituent communities all be territorially contiguous (Alaska and Hawaii in the United States, for instance). A decentralized unitary democracy faces territorial limits beyond which it is likely to become no longer viable.

Although Great Britain, a union rather than a federation, played a seminal role in the rise of modern democracy, the United Kingdom's small size and distance from the European mainland rendered it more intellectually than practically influential outside of its imperial reach. The British, however, fostered federal democracy in many of their former colonies (Australia, Canada, India, Nigeria, and the United States). Both as a superpower during the second and third waves of democratization and as the world's first federal democracy, the United States has played a major role in forging the military security and political stability needed for federal and nonfederal democracies to emerge and endure since 1945. The end of the Cold War accelerated democracy's third wave, partly because the United States had often supported undemocratic anti-communist regimes during the Cold War. Although the United States still does support some undemocratic regimes, its strategic incentives since 1989 have shifted toward supporting democratization. Furthermore, the world's largest current experiment in federal democracy, the EU, would be unimaginable without the sixty years of U.S. support and security guarantees behind it.

Democracy and Concurrent Consent

A federation is fundamentally democratic insofar as it is founded on the concurrent consent of the constituent peoples and/or their governments. Federations formed wholly or partly by conquest, such as the former USSR, have poor records of success because federalism ultimately requires a voluntary will to live together. In the absence of such a will, constituent communities exit, or seek to exit, the federation, or an authoritarian regime imposes unity. In many culturally heterogeneous societies, the practical political alternative to federalism is not unitary democracy but rather unitary authoritarianism because the cultural communities, or "nations," within the nation-state do not conceptualize themselves as one nation. This is a common problem in Africa (see Brown and Kaiser, chap. 10 in this book) where diverse nations, or tribes, have been compelled to live within despotic unitary states. The desire of so many cultural communities to territorialize their identity in statist form confronts many nation-states with a stark choice between consent and conquest, either federal or consociational democracy or authoritarian rule. The maladies of democracy in such federations as India (Aronoff 2008; Spinner-Halev 2008), Malaysia, and Nigeria cannot necessarily be solved; therefore, by decentralized unitary democracy, the will for unity is weak in the first place.

Although many critics argue that federalism is less democratic, even anti-democratic, because it frustrates simple majority rule and legitimates far too many veto points to make democratic governance effective, the empirical findings suggest that this is not necessarily the case. Instead, it can be argued that federalism is more democratic—even super-democratic—precisely because it frustrates tyranny by the majority, empowers constituent political communities to become and to act as veto points, and requires national decision making to be more consensual rather than majoritarian precisely to win over those veto points and thus not only to prevent majority tyranny but also to ensure more equitable and politically legitimate governance.

A fundamental flaw of majoritarian democratic theory is the Rousseauian assumption that a polity's demos is, or should be, fundamentally homogeneous. No demos of the sort exists anywhere, and efforts to establish that kind of demos can degenerate into Jacobin terror. It is not without reason that the Jacobins sought to persecute federalists in their drive to amalgamate France's diverse residents into a homogeneous demos. Only recently, under France's Fifth (and second longest-living) Republic (1958 to the present) and decentralization (Bernier 1992; see also Ciprut, chap. 14 in this book), have France's constituent communities begun tentatively to reassert ancient identities.

Unlike Rousseau's General Will, the federal democratic principle does not "lead to the disappearance of countless atomized individuals in a collectivist ant heap" (Kinsky 1995, 8) but rather to the personal empowerment of the autonomous individual within self-governing communities able to reinforce the individual's autonomy and identity, mediate between the individual and the whole polity (see Botwinick, chap. 3 in this book), enhance the individual's voice, serve as a school of democracy for the individual, and attend to the individual's life necessities. According to Henri Brugmans (as quoted in Kinsky 1995, 9), a great concern of the antitotalitarian federalists of the mid-twentieth century was "that the individualism inspired by the Jacobins led logically towards an atomization of society, which . . . would bring out the absolute state as the counterpart of this disintegration."

Since the collapse of fascism and of the Soviet Union, fear of this type of totalitarianism has been replaced by fear of global-capitalist and American-style individualism, which, while promoting democracy, has perhaps already turned traditional national cultures into endangered species (e.g., Declaration 1999) by threatening to denude individuals worldwide of their historic identities and reduce citizens to atomized consumers. Consequently, in many federal democracies, such as Canada, and in every federal democracy within the orbit of the EU, constituent political communities have obtained enhanced constitutional guarantees of self-government and of participation in international and EU negotiations. These constituent communities also pressed for creation of the EU's Committee of the Regions. Likewise, anarcho-federalists and "small-is-beautiful" advocates see in local self-governance a key bastion of communitarian and individual liberty against global capitalism.

Individual and Communitarian Identity and Liberty

A federal democracy seeks to balance individual and communitarian identities and liberties. Historically, federalism aimed first to protect communitarian liberty, namely, the right of the constituent communities, such as the Swiss cantons and U.S. states, to govern themselves in all matters of local relevance and to maintain their ways of life. Protecting communitarian liberty indirectly protects individual liberty, as well, by preventing one group from unilaterally imposing costs on individuals of another group or robbing those individuals of their lives, rights, property, or historic identity. A Christian minority might not wish to be ruled by a Muslim majority, and vice versa. At the same time, federalism creates a national democratic community of limited power and protects certain rights of all individuals within that community. Furthermore, insofar as the national and constituent political communities can check and balance each other, or function as a concurrent or double majority as in Switzerland, they can guard against usurpations of power by each other and, as James Madison argued in *Federalist No. 51* (Cooke 1961), provide securities for individual rights that might not be available in a unitary democracy. This is another attribute that makes the federal principle potentially applicable on a global scale where the desires and rights of individuals to act globally must be balanced with the self-governing rights of more than 191 nation-states and thousands of regional and local communities within those nation-states. A global demos able to construct a benign Jacobin democracy seems neither possible nor desirable (see passages on Guizot in Ciprut, chap. 14 in this book).

There are, however, significant challenges to this balance in modernizing societies and in a globalizing world where some communities still perpetuate appalling deprivations of individual rights, such as the 2002 death-by-stoning sentence, later overturned on appeal, of Amina Lawal for alleged adultery under Shariah (Islamic law) in northern Nigeria. The constitutional and moral authority of the federal entity as representative of the national, regional, or global community to intervene in the affairs of the constituent communities to protect or enhance the rights of individuals in those communities is controversial. This was true even with the EU's rather mild sanctions against Austria. Such interventions can also spill over into authoritarianism, as with the Congress party's repeated use of president's rule over states in India primarily for political rather than democratic or human rights purposes (Ray and Kincaid 1988).

The United States experienced such challenges when southern states claimed states' rights to maintain slavery and, then, racial segregation. The abolition of slavery required a civil war (1861–1865) in which the northern union states defeated the southern confederate states. The abolition of racial segregation in the mid-twentieth century required enormous national political, judicial, and fiscal pressure, including occasional uses of federal troops and marshals, to enforce desegregation in recalcitrant states.

As suggested by table 5.1, however, decentralized unitary systems do not provide significantly better rights protection than federal polities, even though they have less of the cultural heterogeneity that creates tensions between communitarian and individual liberty. In decentralized unitary polities, individual-rights protection is either high or low for everyone, depending on how much majority support can be mustered for protection or how far the regime desires to extend protection. In a federal polity, the presence of self-governing constituent communities creates not only the possibility but also the actuality of various communities providing more rights protection than the national norm and pioneering protections that can be disseminated nationwide. The history of federal democracies is replete with constituent governments advancing rights protections, such as women's suffrage, well before their national dissemination or adoption. Although the United States, for example, is often viewed as a nation of uniform rights, the U.S. Supreme Court and the Congress establish only minimum, national, rights protections; the states, under their state constitutions, grant higher rights protections, including protections that contradict U.S. Supreme Court rulings, so long as the states do not fall below the floor of federal rights. Thus, diverse rights protections exist among the fifty states. Perhaps the tensions between individual and communitarian liberty as well as between the constituent and national political communities are creative ones that produce consensus building that in turn ratchets up individual rights protections more rapidly and effectively than in unitary democracies where a ruling majority might be less disposed to increase protections (especially) for minorities.

Furthermore, if rights protections are low in a unitary polity, there is nowhere to flee for better protection unless one exits the country—a difficult, often impossible, option for most people. A key federal liberty is mobility. The ability to move between self-governing constituent communities (i.e., to vote with one's feet) allows migration to jurisdictions that offer rights protections—as well as economic opportunities, taxes, services, and qualities of life—more compatible with one's interests. Although language and cultural barriers may limit such mobility in culturally heterogeneous federal polities, interjurisdictional mobility is still more viable than emigrating or fleeing abroad as a refugee.

Federal Democracy and Justice

Given that justice is, ultimately, what people believe is fair, equitable, and/or morally right, understandably in democratic theory, justice must rest on consent. In this respect, federal democracy is, in principle, superior for several reasons. For one, federal democracy limits the ability of a majority to impose rules of justice that may be unjust to minorities. This is a critical matter in all polities, but even more so in culturally heterogeneous polities where there are many different conceptions of justice often rooted in ancient customs, traditions, and religions. Given requirements for broader-based or concurrent consent, rather than simple majority consent, in a federal democracy, rules of justice derived from consent are likely to be comparatively benign and to enjoy considerable legitimacy. Because powers are both shared and divided in a federal democracy, there are also multiple forums of justice anchored in multiple forums of consent, and many rules of justice can vary justly among those forums according to socioeconomic and cultural conditions and to public preferences. In turn, multiple forums offer citizens multiple points of access to public power and thus an ability to appeal to other forums or governments when one of them is unresponsive. Forum shopping is common in federal democracies. Multiple governments also provide citizens with competing sources of information, and that enhances political transparency and helps counteract propaganda.

Advocates of universal rights and justice seek uniformity; and yet human beings have fundamental, and often rationally legitimate, disagreements about what is just, beginning with disagreements about negative versus positive rights. Abortion, animal rights, cloning, firearms, capital punishment, child care, conscientious objection, disabilities, education, euthanasia, gender, health care, homosexuality, imprisonment, marriage, pornography, privacy, and welfare are only a few issues of justice about which humans disagree profoundly. Furthermore, some questions of justice have no obviously right answer. A federal democracy accommodates such disagreement by agreeing to disagree on some matters. Rules of justice embedded in the federal constitution and applicable uniformly reflect what is politically achievable for the whole polity, while diversity endures among the constituent political communities on matters of disagreement and ensures that justice issues remain dynamic rather than static. Federalism also allows constituent communities to be laboratories of democracy by experimenting with policies having justice implications without harming the nation in the event of failure. In the United States, for instance, physician-assisted suicide is permitted only in Oregon, and the U.S. Supreme Court refused to strike down the laws of the forty-nine states that prohibit it, in part because it recognized that Americans are deeply divided on this issue. The Court left the issue to be addressed by the federal democratic process, which will likely lead some other states to authorize physician-assisted suicide if Oregon's experience is judged to be benign. Some years from now, individuals desiring such suicide might move to states that permit it.

Justice is also a matter of matching private burdens and public benefits. In a federal democracy where most domestic services are financed and provided by constituent governments, benefits can be matched to burdens. Citizens get what they pay for, rather than paying for what they do not want, need, or get, thus matching public services with public preferences. Furthermore, given that different services have different economies of scale, that federal, regional, and local officials responsible for services are elected by the people of the various jurisdictions, and that interjurisdictional mobility spurs competition between jurisdictions, a federal democracy is likely to enhance service efficiency and effectiveness and to have a high rate of policy innovation and innovation dissemination.

Governance and service provision in a federal democracy require substantial intergovernmental and interjurisdictional cooperation, as the latter promotes efficiency and equity. Cooperation also contributes to bridge building and to mutual aid among the constituent political communities and thus to polity building and justice enhancement—all matters of heightened importance in culturally heterogeneous polities. At the same time, every federal democracy redistributes wealth among places and/or persons. Some, such as the United States, stress redistribution among persons, in part to enhance personal self-governance and promote mobility. Most federal democracies, including Canada and Germany, emphasize redistribution among places, in part to ensure that each constituent jurisdiction can provide a minimum level of services to citizens. Redistribution may reflect a cooperative will to live together, a social welfare consensus, or even a price to be paid for union, as exhibited by the ability of certain constituent communities to extort payments from the federal polity in return for unity. Extortion is not the noblest rationale for redistribution, but it is usually preferable to conquest or fragmentation. Hence, Anglophone Canada pays off

Francophone Quebec, the Western German *Länder* pay off the Eastern *Länder*, and the EU pays off its poorer member states. A salutary outcome, though, is that every federal democracy mythologizes this extortion as a just social compact. Thus, the EU's structural funds enjoy considerable legitimacy as a matter of community justice and are embedded in Title XIV of the *Maastricht Treaty*, appropriately entitled "Economic and Social Cohesion."

It has also been argued that an ideal federal democracy would constitutionally authorize secession, as in Ethiopia's federal constitution, because "[s]ecession, or the threat thereof, represents the only means through which the ultimate powers of the central government might be held in check. Absent the secession prospect, the federal government may, by overstepping its constitutionally assigned limits, extract surplus value from the citizenry almost at will, because there would exist no effective means of escape" (Buchanan 1995, 21–22). This exit option is implicit in all federal arrangements and thus serves as leverage in the pursuit of justice by the constituent political communities and their citizens.

Finally, rooting justice in consent recognizes that justice is also a matter of self-defense, a fundamental right exercised not only by access to courts and other government institutions but, more importantly, by opportunities to vote, hold elected office, and participate in political life in a myriad of ways. A federal democracy vastly increases opportunities for participation by multiplying the number of participatory forums and by making more elected offices and governments accessible to ordinary citizens. In the United States, for example, 537 elected officials and nine unelected justices preside over a federal government encompassing a huge territory inhabited by some 296 million people, but more than 497,000 other elected officials have substantial, constitutionalized self-governing powers in the fifty states and 87,849 localities. In turn, the self-governing responsibilities of the constituent political communities and their localities enhance the self-governing capacities of individuals and their ability to attend to their own needs and to the needs of their community rather than waiting supinely for state intervention.

Conclusion

Arguably, federalism is already the highest stage of political organization because federal polities encompass 39 percent of the world's population. If one adds the EU and China as de facto federal polities, then federalism encompasses more than 60 percent of the world's population. If one also counts such international institutions as the United Nations as federal, then federalism encompasses the world's population. This, of course, stretches the concept. Nevertheless, just as the federal principle, in its various manifestations, appears to be the only nonimperial basis for organizing political life on large scales, so does federalism seem to be the only basis for organizing democratic governance on large scales. The unitary principle can snap when stretched across too much territory, even with decentralization. More importantly, the demos essential for unitary democracy fragments when stretched across human heterogeneity. True, the consociational principle based on elite accommodation can be stretched across territory and heterogeneity, but only up to a point, beyond which it experiences serious democratic deficits, as faced in the EU and in all international political organizations. Although federalism itself does not guarantee democracy, it appears to be the most viable framework for democratization across large territories and human heterogeneity, especially under conditions of freedom. A federal democracy is the highest stage of democracy insofar as it combines unity and diversity, bases both unity and diversity on popular consent, and thereby allows people to have their cake and eat it too: enjoy large-scale democratic governance for the things that large-scale governance is necessary for while also enjoying small-scale democratic self-governance for the things that make life most worth living.

References

Addresses (1999) Jean Chrétien, Ernesto Zedillo Ponce de León, and William Jefferson Clinton, *Publius: The Journal of Federalism*, 29 (Fall):11–32.

Agranoff, Robert, and Juan Antonio Ramos Gallarin (1997) "Toward Federal Democracy in Spain: An Examination of Intergovernmental Relations," *Publius: The Journal of Federalism*, 27 (Fall):1–38.

Aronoff, Myron J. (2008) "Democratizations in Fissured Societies: The Makings of Citizenship," in Jose V. Ciprut, Editor, *The Future of Citizenship*, Cambridge, MA: The MIT Press.

Bahçeli, Tosun (2000) "Searching for a Cyprus Settlement: Considering Options for Creating a Federation, a Confederation, or Two Independent States," *Publius: The Journal of Federalism*, 30 (Winter/Spring):203–216.

Bennett, Robert J. (1990) *Decentralization, Local Governments and Markets: Towards a Post-Welfare Agenda*, Oxford and New York: Clarendon Press.

Bernier, Lynne Louise (1992) "Socialist Intergovernmental Policy During the Mitterrand Era," *Publius: The Journal of Federalism*, 22 (Fall):47–66.

Breton, Albert (2000) "Federalism and Decentralization: Ownership Rights and the Superiority of Federalism," *Publius: The Journal of Federalism*, 30 (Spring):1–16.

Buchanan, James M. (1995) "Federalism as an Ideal Political Order and an Objective for Constitutional Reform," *Publius: The Journal of Federalism*, 25 (Spring):19–27.

Cooke, Jacob E. (1961) *The Federalist*, Middletown, CT: Wesleyan University Press.

Davis, Michael C. (1999) "The Case for Chinese Federalism," *Journal of Democracy*, 10 (April):124–137.

Declaration (1999) *Declaration of the Government du Quebec Respecting Quebec's Participation in International Forums Dealing with Education, Language, Culture and Identity*, Pamphlet, 24 March.

Derbyshire, Denis J., and Ian Derbyshire (1999) *Political Systems of the World*, 2 vols., Oxford, UK: Helicon.

Diamond, Larry (1999) *Developing Democracy: Toward Consolidation*, Baltimore, MD: Johns Hopkins University Press.

Duchacek, Ivo D., Editor (1988) "Bicommunal Societies and Polities," *Publius: The Journal of Federalism*, 18 (Spring) (entire issue).

Elazar, Daniel J. (1987) *Exploring Federalism*, Tuscaloosa: University of Alabama Press.

——— (1995) "From Statism to Federalism: A Paradigm Shift," *Publius: The Journal of Federalism*, 25 (Spring):5–18.

Held, David (1992) "Democracy: From City-States to a Cosmopolitan Order?" *Political Studies*, 40:10–38.

Huntington, Samuel P. (1997) "After Twenty Years: The Future of the Third Wave," *Journal of Democracy*, 8 (October):3–12.

Karatnycky, Adrian, et al., Editors (2001) *Freedom in the World: The Annual Survey of Political Rights and Civil Liberties, 2000–2001*, New York: Freedom House and Transaction.

Kenyon, Daphne A., and John Kincaid, Editors (1991) *Competition among States and Local Governments: Efficiency and Equity in American Federalism*, Washington, DC: Urban Institute Press.

Kincaid, John (1995) "Values and Value Tradeoffs in Federalism," *Publius: The Journal of Federalism*, 25 (Winter):29–44.

——— (1999) "Confederal Federalism and Citizen Representation in the European Union," *West European Politics*, 22 (April):34–58.

——— (2001) "Economic Policy-Making: Advantages and Disadvantages of the Federal Model," *International Social Science Journal*, 167 (March):85–92.

Kinsky, Ferdinand (1995) *Federalism—A Global Theory: The Impact of Proudhon and the Personalist Movement on Federalism*, Nice: Presses D'Europe.

Montinola, Gabriella, Yingyi Qian, and Barry Weingast (1995) "Federalism, Chinese Style: The Political Basis for Economic Success in China," *World Politics*, 48 (October):50–81.

Moreno, Luis (2001) *The Federalization of Spain*, London: Frank Cass.

Nicolaidis, Kalypso, and Robert Howse, Editors (2001) *The Federal Vision: Legitimacy and Levels of Governance in the US and EU*, Oxford, UK: Oxford University Press.

O'Driscoll, Gerald P., Jr., Kim R. Holmes, and Mary Anastasia O'Grady (2002) *2002 Index of Economic Freedom*, Washington, DC: The Heritage Foundation and *Wall Street Journal*.

Ray, Amal, and John Kincaid (1988) "Politics, Economic Development, and Second-Generation Strain in India's Federal System," *Publius: The Journal of Federalism*, 18 (Spring):147–167.

Rodriquez, Victoria E. (1998) "Recasting Federalism in Mexico," *Publius: The Journal of Federalism*, 28 (Winter):235–254.

Schmitter, Philippe C. (2000) "Federalism and the Euro-Polity," *Journal of Democracy*, 11 (January):40–46.

Shah, Anwar, and Jeffrey Huther (1999) "Applying a Simple Measure of Good Governance to the Debate Fiscal Decentralization," World Bank Policy Research Working Paper No. 1894, Washington, DC: The World Bank. Available from Social Science Research Network at http://ssrn.com/abstract=620584.

Spinner-Halev, Jeff (2008) "Exclusion, Fear and Identity in Emerging Democracies," in Jose V. Ciprut, Editor, *Ethics, Politics, and Democracy*, Cambridge, MA: The MIT Press.

Theophanus, Andreas (2000) "Prospects for Solving the Cyprus Problem and the Role of the European Union," *Publius: The Journal of Federalism*, 30 (Winter/Spring):217–241.

Tocqueville, Alexis de (1969) *Democracy in America*, J. P. Mayer, Editor, George Lawrence, Translator, Garden City, NY: Doubleday Anchor Books.

United Nations Development Programme (2001) *Human Development Report, 2001*, Oxford, UK: Oxford University Press.

Watts, Ronald L. (2002) "The Relevance Today of the Federal Idea," Keynote Address at Pre-Conference for the Internationale Föderalismuskonferenz 2002, Glion, Switzerland (14 February).

Wibbels, Erik (2000) "Federalism and the Politics of Macroeconomic Policy and Performance," *American Journal of Political Science*, 44 (October):687–702.

6

Democratizing the European Union: With or without Popular Sovereignty?

Andreas Heinemann-Grüder

Missing: The Prerequisites for the Daily Practice of Democracy

Even in a minimalist version, the modern concept of democracy harbors, at its core, free and fair universal election of those who will govern by those who will be governed (Dahl 2000). This model is by and large based at least on four prerequisites: a popular sovereign that embodies some politico-cultural identity (a demos), an existing statehood, a state bureaucracy, and constitutionalism. Conceptions of constitutionalism vary, of course, but the existence of constituent powers, of some fundamental norms underlying the political regime, and of some limits to the exercise of power seem to rest at the heart of constitutionalism. Although the European Union (EU) represents an effective political apparatus for the execution of collectively binding institutions, the 'collective self' for political self-determination is not defined, the citizenry cannot be mobilized for political will-formation for a common European good, and there is no transborder social solidarity (Habermas 2003). The executive branch of the EU is neither directly nor indirectly elected by the European constituencies. But one clearly necessary if evidently insufficient 'prerequisite' for democratic rule is alive and well: an ample European bureaucracy. So far, the EU lacks almost all characteristics of and prerequisites for a national democracy.

For those who view democracy as a 'bounded whole', obviously, the EU does not qualify as one (Collier and Levitsky 1997, 430–451). A gradualist concept of democracy, however, could qualify the EU, by building on and aligning to its existing as well as missing properties. In this case, the EU could provide a fit to the concept at least on several accounts. It is, after all, a territorial span governed by democratic regimes in twenty-five member states, each of which enjoys political participatory rights, civic freedoms, liberal values, rule of law, and a market economy to boot. According to the still-dominant specific deficits, too, the EU could be described as a 'democracy'—albeit an "exclusive democracy"—with serious deficits in vertical (bottom-up) legitimization and control of the EU's executive power. And in regard to the weakness of the European Parliament vis-à-vis the EU Commission,[1] the fusion of lawmaking and executive capacities in the Commission, and the improper mechanisms of control and accountability to the European Parliament, between elections, one could keep a straight face when referring to the EU as a *delegative democracy* as well: nationally elected governments make decisions on the European level on matters that did not become a subject of scrutiny during domestic electoral campaigns. As the effective decision making in the Commission rests with nonelected officials, the EU might be characterized as an 'enclave democracy', too, of course. The recognition of the uncontrived description and the appropriateness of these terms would be of itself a tacit acknowledgment of one's perception of the EU as an impoverished subcategory of the general concept of democracy. However, the EU lacks a property that even diminished subcategories would share: meaningful elections.

The EU was, and in many respects still is, an international intergovernmental organization. One therefore may ask why political science should concern itself at all with something the EU does not represent, may never embody, and indeed may not even come to need at all: a democratic form of governance (Dahl 1999, 19–36). But in contrast to its post–World War II and post–Cold War appeal, more continent-wide integrative expansion is no longer welcome, erstwhile diffuse support for the grand idea is vanishing, and issue-specific backing is scarce and only instrumental. On the one hand, the EU may contribute to the 'democratization' of the postsocialist and/or authoritarian regimes of Eastern and Southern Europe; yet, on the other hand, the EU does not just lack democratic credentials, it may also undermine democratic achievements among its member states. For, in the final analysis, as a whole, the EU does exert a major impact on its parts and more particularly on the perceptions, the institutions, and the practices of democracy within the borders of each member state.

---

1. The European Commission consists of the President and twenty-four Commissioners responsible for the implementation of specific policy spheres of the Union. The President of the Commission is chosen by the Council of Europe for a five-year term; the Commissioners are appointed by their national governments, and the Commission as a whole must be confirmed by the European Parliament.

The Altering Purposes of the European Union

European integration began with the so-called 'Monnet method', named after Jean Monnet (1888–1979). That 'method' featured a mix of incrementalism, intergovernmental consensus, and the integration of trades and economies, supposedly able to 'spill over' into other functional areas. Beginning with the Single European Act of 1986, its confirmation by the Treaties of Maastricht (1992), Amsterdam (1997), and Nice (2000) and continuing with the introduction of the Euro— now the monetary unit of twelve EU member states—and the further, farther, and quicker expansion of the EU toward Eastern and Southern Europe, the 'Monnet method'[2] began to confront some very serious limitations. Over time, three modes of European governance came to coexist in varied policy fields: (1) intergovernmentalism, (2) centralized supranationalism, and (3) the so-called 'community method', whereby supranational and national actors codecide. Apart from the already existing supremacy, and thus direct effects, of the EU law over national laws, the Treaty of Maastricht introduced two fundamentally new elements: the European Economic and Monetary Union and the concept of EU 'citizenship' for all nationals of the EU's member states.

Understandably, national-level executives had much enjoyed the intergovernmental 'Monnet method' because of the unmatched autonomy it bestowed on decision–making. For Europe's sake, far-reaching decisions could be taken, thereby increasingly affecting structural and financial policies, the rules for investment, as well as social coherence and also helping to curb the division of power enshrined for so long in each member-state's democracy. While preserving the idea of national sovereignty and the vague concept of subsidiarity and continuing to

---

2. As a syncresis of Jean Monnet's sayings and Robert Schuman's siftings, the logic of the method resided in the need for concrete achievements that, after creating a de facto solidarity, would have warranted limited transfer of national sovereignty to a closer-knit compact on a European level. One of the distinctive characteristics of the Monnet approach was the ambiguity of the final stage; it involved building a united Europe through a series of concrete projects, each supposedly leading to the next. Monnet hoped that this would allow him to achieve his goal without public debate, which he distrusted. As the original idea of limited transfer cannot now be construed into what it never was—a principled intent to create one body, under one constitution—the vagueness in foundational principles and the ambiguity in procedural guidelines, end up making of systemic Europeanization in general and of European democratization in particular an open-ended process.

claim that only the national governments retain ultimate say, the costs of opting out in practice began to increase enormously. Once a member, the costs of exiting the EU had to be weighed against the benefits of belonging to it.

Among the many self-assigned ideals of the EU, 'democracy' is mostly but a means to yet another end—a way of 'authorizing' the decision makers to continue to do what they do best: for 'them', the central issue here appears to be one of legitimization rather than democracy as such. At the turn of the twentieth century into the twenty-first, Tony Blair of the United Kingdom, Joschka Fischer of Germany, Alain Jospin of France, and the then-President of the Commission, Romano Prodi of Italy delivered eloquent speeches on the burning issue of Europe's final destination, yet none of them could offer more than a few catchy phrases.

Some politicians and many observers began to take the language of an 'ever-closer union' to mean a vision of a European federation as the final outcome. This notion turned into a deterrent instead of an inviting prospect, however. The "federal" prospect was suspected and feared to downplay dominance by the larger powers, particularly France and Germany; more centralization at the expense of national and regional competencies; and a departure from the consociational mode of commonplace decision making. Before the end of 2001, this blurry federal vision was sharpened by the promise that the euro currency, to be introduced in January 2002, somehow magically would unify Europe and the Europeans. Well, the euro did not become the 'golden calf' around which Europe's citizenries would begin dancing and bonding with each other in their newfound unity.

For as long as the integration of Europe was nigh exclusively grounded on intergovernmentalism—at first as a "plan" for coal and steel and successively thereafter as EEC (*a* European Economic Community), as *the* European Community, and as the European *Union*—the study of European affairs for long seemed to belong to the social science field of International Relations. Originally, the member states did not even strive together to constitute a new polity or a novel political community. And because the EU represented a limited regulatory form of governance, the transfer of national legitimacy and sovereignty remained limited to economic liberalism and very marginal in the classic spheres of statehood. For as long as this view prevailed, the legitimatizing power of elections, the division and control of powers, and the realms of state politics—including foreign policy, security policy, distributional policies, public services and welfare—remained largely within the national purview. Consequently, no need ever was felt for a European Constitution.

The desire to devise a mode for legitimizing the EU originated from vacillations between ambitions for an institutional framework, qualified to assure peace among the member states, and aspirations for an economic arrangement, capable of fostering a larger European market, on the one hand, and, on the other hand, between explorations of ways to pool powers in international relations vis-à-vis the balancing power wielded by the United States, and excavations for a mechanism capable of transforming postsocialist Eastern Europe and the Balkans into capitalist democracies. The EU was also portrayed as a utensil, for increasing the member states' competitiveness; as a framework, for creating a pan-European sociopolitical identity; or as a tool, for preserving heterogeneous cultures. Some still see in the EU a device of sorts for the protection of 'European' social welfare criteria and standards, while others more simply perceive it as a serendipitous mode of institutionalizing 'globalization' in homogenizing ways.

The approaches to legitimizations of the EU actually appeal to highly contradictory values. To begin with, one still cannot find a single joint-European model for Social Policy but only an array of coexisting models. The diversity in traditions of Catholic social policy, social standards, social liberalism, trade unionism, public services able to guarantee welfare, acute ecological awareness, and specific human rights standards were all expected to function as European answers to the negative impacts of globalization. But the discrepancies already brought with enlargement and 'harmonization' would require either radical social asset stripping in countries such as Germany or enormous transfers that no one would be willing to pay for. Some politicians—the former German federal president Johannes Rau (2001), among them—appealed to the European sense of 'self-preservation' in the face of media globalization, fundamentalism, and fierce modes of market liberalization. The prevailing model of globalization calls for humans to act as rational homini economici, as also for the reduction of the state into a service agency, and for deregulation, however. And the EU happens to be an embodiment of just this kind of globalization; due to the mobility of capital, it exposes national labor markets to barely restrained pan-European competition. More recently, two new concepts of legitimization came to be added: the EU as a 'stabilizer' and 'democratizer' among applicant countries and the EU as 'a community of states', one sagaciously unified in the prevention of a 'clash of civilizations' between 'the West' and 'the Muslim world'.

Against the backdrop of these vectors that pull the European project into disparate directions, Euro-politicians are concerned about low approval rates. The mantra that 'the European journey' itself 'already constitutes its own destination' simply does not resonate far, any longer. The hitherto passive acquiescence of the European publics to greater and greater supranational institution building and enlargement from originally six to now twenty-five members has begun to erode good-will, trust, and patience. The ratification process over the Maastricht Treaty already had revealed how distant the EU's legal provisions and institutions were from the European populations' preferences (Plattner 2003). Not only are any putative profits from further integration questioned among the more substantial constituencies, but both the far-right and the far-left parties have begun to mobilize voters on anti-European sentiments. The shared themes of these anticampaigns are fears of crime, of wage dumping, of erosion of social standards, and of the perceived menace of a loss of identity should Turkey be allowed to join.

The So-Called Democratic Deficit

Since the late 1980s, much academic debate of the 'democratic deficit' ("demdef") has flourished. Although viewed from different angles, there in principle grew a wide agreement on the existence of real demo-cratic deficiencies in the EU. The 'demdef' has been identified on different levels. There has been the growing fear that European gover-nance would undermine national-level democratic traditions and social standards, entailing a quest for compensating the loss of national par-liaments by increasing democracy across the EU. Whereas the decision-making autonomy of the member states, of their parliaments, of their parties, and of their citizens declined with increasing integration, no greater corresponding empowerment or augmentation in protection mechanisms occurred on the European level. And their marginalization turned national parliaments into rubber stamps for legislation already adopted in Brussels. Although the Amsterdam Treaty did mildly strengthen the consultation process among national parliaments in European decision making, legislative initiative still rests with the Commission.[3] Neither prohibited by powerful parties nor inhibited by

---

3. A functional link to the content of the Treaty of Amsterdam can be accessed at: www.eurotreaties.com/amsterdamtreaty.pdf.

citizens' ballots, the Council of the EU (the Council of Ministers),[4] and the Commission itself, continue to make autonomous decisions. The Brussels-based Commission enjoys combined executive and legislative functions and acts (serves) as the EU's bureaucracy.

An essential 'demdef' concerns the evident lack of an explicit or coherent mandate for EU policies. It prevents transparency and also a clear delineation of competencies and accountability. This deficiency pertains to the weak constraints on expanding the policy fields of the EU. The EU Treaties and the practices of their main actors—including the European Court of Justice—incrementally did absorb policy areas that had been long the purview of national constitutions, but without receiving a clear and direct mandate to that end, from the popular sovereigns.[5] The evolutionary shift from intergovernmentalism, based on manifest and specific consensus over the marginalization of the member-state governments, to the touted 'community method' lacks the 'diffuse support' of the 'populace'.

'Under-parliamentarization', too, has been pointed out to be a democratic deficit: the European Parliament is unaccountable to its voters, at once nontransparent and feeble. Not a parliament in the common sense, it performs mostly as a convenient 'fig leaf', even if its powers in budgetary affairs, its clout in holding to account the Commission, and its role in the appointment of commissioners has increased. Also, a lack of direct democracy has been voiced by some authors who reproach the absence of direct access and direct input channels for the citizenry (Abromeit 1998a, 1998b). Finally, a lack of constitutionalism,

---

4. The Council is the EU's main decision-making body. The Council represents the member states; its meetings are attended by one minister from each of the EU's national governments. Which ministers attend which of the meetings depends on what subjects are on the agenda. The Presidency of the Council is held for six months by each member state on a rotational basis; it has as its primary responsibility to organize and chair all meetings of the Council. The Council is assisted by the Committee of Permanent Representatives (COREPER), which consists of the ambassadors of the member states to the EU. COREPER prepares the Council's agenda, negotiates noncontroversial matters, leaving controversial issues for discussion and formal agreement by the Council. Working below COREPER, civil servants from the member states negotiate in Council Working Groups, often reaching de facto agreements that then are merely formalized through COREPER and the Council of Ministers.

5. The notion of popular sovereign refers to the community of citizens who are endowed with unalienable rights and who lay down limits to the exercise of power by governments in a kind of social compact. Popular sovereignty is the notion that no law or rule is legitimate unless it rests directly or indirectly on the consent of the individuals concerned.

were it of a symbolic constitutional founding document, is also lamented, among the many other jeremiads to date.

Nevertheless, two principal objections remain: the first has questioned whether the 'demdef' actually is at the heart of popular disappointment with the EU. Hanns W. Maull (2005), for one, claims that "concern about the democratic deficit of the EU as a source of the present malaise is mostly rubbish" and that "if there is anyone to blame," surely "it is member governments." He might not be wrong in suggesting that the greatest concern of the voters is not with the 'demdef' per se as with their detecting a vacuum in political leadership, their seeing only opaque direction and contradictory content, and their developing a rather unsettling feeling about the implications of a simultaneously deepening and widening EU. The second objection concerns not so much the 'demdef' but rather the generally purported 'proactive antidemocratic impact' of the EU. Philippe Schmitter (2003:80f), for one, has remonstrated by stating that intergovernmentalism may not necessarily strengthen the national executives at the expense of the national parliaments because participation in intergovernmental bargaining sets its own price. National executives and electoral candidates would in turn anticipate negative domestic repercussions to their behavior on the European level; national judiciaries would be strengthened by their empowerment to question the compatibility of national legislation with the quasi-Constitution of the EU; national firms, citizens, associations, and movements might develop capacities to coalesce across national boundaries, even as subnational governments found ways of influencing EU institutions. One can agree that there exist constraints to the infringements by the EU as well as opportunities for pan-European deliberative politics, but one can hardly doubt that the EU is not yet a democracy, or that it critically affects the configuration of actors and institutions in the member states.

Depending on the school of thought academics subscribe to, the democratic deficit is treated as incurable, negligible, or something that could be overcome over time. Some authors, like Paul Kirchhoff (1998) and Dieter Grimm (1995), argue in a communitarian vein that democracy would require a pre-existing 'community of communication' displaying a strong sense of solidarity, a shared fate and a common responsibility, emotional-cultural bounds, identical myths, and at least some social cohesion—in sum, a 'people'. Put succinctly: 'no demos, no democracy'! Respect for majority decisions is expected usually only where faith in community precedes state formation. The EU lacks such collective identity; hence, minorities have no reason to accept majority decisions. The German Constitutional Court, in its famous ruling on the Maastricht Treaty, consequently has argued that the nation-state should retain supremacy vis-à-vis any further European integration (Bundesverfassungsgericht 1993). But, in this perspective, integration without a European demos implies a process of de-democratization.

Intergovernmentalists, such as Giandomenico Majone or Fritz Scharpf, do not neglect the democratic deficit, either; but they claim European integration to be sufficiently legitimized by the democratic character of the member states, by the autonomy of the functional subsystems, and also by the economic output of the EU (Majone 1999; Scharpf 1998). Given the EU's heterogeneity and lack of social legitimacy, European integration, according to this view, could be legitimized only by its efficiency in problem solving. The key concern for intergovernmentalists never was with the democratic deficit but rather with 'efficiency', which in turn depends on the ability to prevent politicization. Acquiescence, not agreement, is the underlying concept here. Yet another argument entertained is that, in themselves, the Treaties are already tantamount to a form of constitution. Intergovernmentalists see a sound solution to the democratic deficit in the re-empowerment of national parliaments. Yet a return to powerful national parliaments seems unlikely in the EU at this juncture.

In the republican view, most prominently expressed by Jürgen Habermas, the social bearer of democracy, the demos as such, is a historically and politically constructed order. Assuming that the sharing of group interests, loyalty to parties, and social milieus, as well as the priority of national interests, is diffusing among the EU's member states in some way or another, it was argued that public deliberation on the common European values and networks of social interest groups could lead to pan-European civil society and pan-European constitutional patriotism. Thus, constitution building was deemed crucial for creating social legitimacy, a feat that both communitarians and intergovernmentalists saw as an insurmountable barrier (Habermas 1999). In a similar vein, the prospects for an emerging European public were hailed, and the developing European 'networks' considered by some as an adequate form of transnational democracy (Kohler-Koch 2000). Beyond academic talk, the political debates about 'constitutionalizing' Europe began for real only when the 'beast' came to be seen as capable of encroaching on national living standards, social welfare, and democratic participation.

Looking for a Lifeline and Holding unto the
European Constitution

What were the reasons for the EU Council meeting in Laeken, in December 2001, calling for a European Convention tasked to develop a European Constitution? I submit that the need for a constitution was informed by five 'driving' motives, only one of which could be traced to the exigencies of the much-touted 'democratic deficit'.

First, the normative grounds on which European integration was to be justified seemed no longer firm. With the brusque evaporation of 'socialism' in Eastern Europe—the sudden disappearance of one's 'defining other'—and given the established conviction that Germany is now safely and stably anchored, Europe's own future normative and cultural bounds came into question. Left with an even farther-spread sense of disempowerment, politicians now began a desperate search for some diffuse support for the EU idea itself.

Second, there came to be sensed a need for greater solidarity as a result of the EU's enlargement toward Eastern Europe. In the past, it had befallen Germany and France in greater part to balance the give-and-take of structural, mostly agricultural, policy. But why and how should such solidarity function in a Europe about to be enlarged to include ten highly heterogeneous Eastern and Southern European countries? Unmistakable inequalities did increase, in turn raising the question of whether Europeans were ready and willing to accept income differences hitherto admitted to exist between Europe and less developed nondemocratic countries but not so obviously among the European nation-states themselves. Should then European integration proceed with the liberalization of the internal market, or should it rather promote employment, social policy, and financial equalization, thereby affecting European taxes, thus also having an impact on the core competencies of the EU member states? In Eastern Europe, particularly, people began to question why they should abandon the sovereignty rights they acquired only a decade before (see Wiatr, chap. 7 in this book). Hence, it became clear that the willingness to accept majority decisions would largely depend on anticipated benefits. As long as the EU offered economic growth, people could sacrifice on legitimacy, but with inequalities among the current and prospective member states growing, the EU would have to come up with some extra social-economic policies, lest protectionist instincts set in quite precipitously.

A third quest for an EU Constitution resulted from problems and considerations of collective action. A Europe of twenty-five nations could no more function as once had a Europe of six, twelve, or fifteen. How could an enlarged EU secure institutional efficiency? With the prospect of enlargement, one could no longer escape the efficiency-versus-legitimacy dilemma or the problems linked with consensual-versus-'binding majority' modes of decision making. To retain its functionality, the EU would have to prolong the reach of majority decisions.

Fourth, there was an unmistakable demand for a new delineation of competencies, of joint or divided authorities, instead of the EU's predilection for 'mission creep'. The EU formally did discern between 'community competencies' and intergovernmentalism, but the lines of demarcation gradually grew so blurred that at a certain point even professional Eurocrats themselves no longer knew where exactly the competencies were being allocated (Prodi 2001).

Fifth and final, the experience of the Balkan wars, especially in Kosovo, demonstrated how weak the EU was, not in global politics abroad but on its very own continent, as well. With the security engagement of the United States for Europe in decline, the EU's continental states sensed the need to overcome the disarray demonstrated during the Balkan wars.

The Constitutional Convention

The Constitutional Convention, working on a draft constitution in 2002 and 2003, held great expectations for adding legitimacy. It was believed that a Constitutional Treaty somehow would succeed in constituting the EU in a simpler, more intelligibly consistent, and thus more widely acceptable, participatory, efficient, and therefore ultimately more democratic manner. That accomplishment was supposed to put a halt to incrementalism and to end chronic mission creep, while also increasing transparency, accountability, credibility, and legal certainty. It was hoped that it would improve access to justice, facilitate legal recourse, provide more concrete levels of control over Union acts, and bring about change via deliberation. These represented the starting positions of the member states. And although the EU already possessed a quasi-constitutional order, it was hoped that the Constitutional Treaty would come in the form of an ultimate 'democratic baptism' for a new-born supranational mode of governance (Weale 1995).

For the first time, the Constitutional Convention transgressed the academic debates on reform, even creating a semblance of public sphere that did not merely comment on, but was truly connected with, EU decision-making procedures. The Convention itself allowed for a mode of participation far broader than any practiced in the past, by reserving room for inputs to treaty formulation, beyond the say of heads of governments and the provisos of the EU Commission. The process of elaborating the draft of the Constitutional Treaty was a deliberative process, publicly accessible to everyone interested. And many civil society associations and Internet forums did provide comments on options and recommendations made during the Convention.

Ratifying the Constitutional Treaty, it was assumed, would make of the voters themselves a party integral to the constituting power (*pouvoir constituant*) of the EU. But already the title *Constitutional Treaty* itself carried a caveat—in the form of an advance warning: a supranational state with a constitution resembling the known national templates was not, and could not be, the intended product. In legal terms, the Constitutional Treaty was "nothing more than a treaty of international public law" (Abromeit and Wolf 2005).

The Convention was a collective attempt to 'finalize' the form of governance the EU would adopt; it was not yet another repetition of tentative approaches tried in the past, but rather recognition that the earlier methods of preparing new treaties by the European Council could no longer work. The Constitutional Convention had too many burdens and expectations, and tackling the democratic deficit was but only one of them. The Convention was not supposed to create a 'new' EU but one to be determined in light of what had remained in existence over the last fifty years (Crossick 2003).

What then was the novelty of the Constitutional Convention? The formal setup of the Convention reflected the triple nature of the EU: an entity that was at once a Union of States, a Union of Peoples, and a Union of Citizens. Some interpreted this Convention to be just another stage in an evolutionary process of deliberation and, more particularly, a mechanism for 'socializing' applicant countries (Maurer 2003). Perhaps more noteworthy was the fact that the deliberations in the Convention focused in greater part on institutional design, not on federal or intergovernmental democratic principles or policy content. The Convention's attention was invested in institutional reform, in the hope that the thereby emboldened institutions would provide both greater efficacy and a more complete mode of democracy. Paradoxically, all institutions were seen to be in urgent need of emboldening—the Presidency, the European Parliament, and the Commission, as if no zero-sum game would ensue and only mutual gains would result. And as no clear-cut decision could be made, the aging model ended up being modified.

Early consensus among the participants of the Convention had been to create a constitution for a Union that embodied a single legal personality, to include a Charter of Fundamental Rights, not to add substantial novel competencies to the Union, to strengthen both subsidiarity and proportionality, and to state the Union's economic and social objectives in the Constitutional Treaty.[6] The competencies were to be categorized by their exclusive, shared, and supportive character and tenor. There existed also an early general agreement on simplification—a reduction in the number of decision-making instruments—and one on reducing the instances of Council voting that depended on unanimity.

On the surface, there have been two distinct competing avenues of approach to the future construction of the EU: a federalist and an intergovernmental one. Some countries, the United Kingdom for instance, are traditionally antifederalist, whereas France and Germany prefer a "federation of nation-states." But during the debates at the Convention, 'federal' versus 'intergovernmental' stands often were less principled than expected. The label *federal* was used in lieu of *supranationalism* instead of being guided by fundamentally authentic federalist concerns (see Kincaid, chap. 5 in this book).

In theoretical terms, the experience that the Constitutional Convention offered does not allow for generalizable conclusions. Neorealists and intergovernmentalists may find some support in the observation that both larger and smaller states vividly reached for certainty and for relative gains wherever they saw areas of key importance to their national interests. Where vague values clashed with vital national interests, expected concrete national gains did prevail over abstract benefits from 'European' values. But it would be difficult to support the intergovernmentalists' claim that the Convention's deliberations

---

6. Subsidiarity is the idea that matters should be handled by the lowest competent authority. According to this principle, the EU may act only where member states agree that action of individual governments or regions is insufficient. The proportionality principle provides that EU measures must be no more than are necessary to achieve the desired end; it may also be relied on in challenging disproportionately harsh national laws that lead to an infringement of EU Treaty provisions.

were driven inordinately or primarily by economic interests. Remarkably, states did not behave as unitary actors, and nonstate actors played a substantial role. Disputes over the Constitution cut across countries, even across the usual left-right cleavages. Hence, the Convention turned into a forum of its own, governments sought for compromise, and output proved to be dependent on process, not only on input. Preferences were not pre-set: they emerged as a result of interaction and process. The Convention's 'method' was praised as a promising first exercise in multinational deliberative democracy.

The single document, signed by the heads of member governments in Rome in October 2004, consists of four sections: constitutional provisions, the Charter of Fundamental Rights, the Union's policies, and their implementation and final clauses. The EU's Constitutional Treaty was supposed to replace the existing treaties, but it had to be ratified by all member states. The Constitutional Treaty somehow ended up becoming a convoluted 500-page version of all previous EU treaties combined into one, now supplemented by some new features: a permanent Presidency of the European Council, a Foreign Ministry, an increase in the powers of the European Parliament, and notably the elimination of single-country vetoes on basic EU legislation.

As of now, the 'first pillar' of the EU consists of matters pertaining to the Single Market, the 'four freedoms'—free movement of persons, goods, services, and capital across borders—matters related to agriculture, the environment, competitiveness, and trade policy as well as cooperation in fiscal and monetary issues, that is, the Economic and Monetary Union. The 'second pillar' consists of the Common Foreign and Security Policy (CFSP). A 'third pillar' comprises police cooperation and cooperation in areas of criminal law. For the 'first pillar', a Qualified Majority Voting (QMV) rule applies, whereas for the 'second pillar' and the 'third pillar', unanimous voting[7] is required.

---

7. The Council of Europe has to take its decisions either unanimously via majority vote or by qualified majority vote. Qualified majority vote means that a decision cannot be taken unless a specified minimal number of votes is cast in favor. The number of votes that each EU country can cast roughly reflects the relative size of its population (Germany, France, Italy, UK: twenty-nine votes; Spain and Poland: twenty-seven; Netherlands: thirteen; Belgium, Czech Republic, Greece, Hungary, and Portugal: twelve; Austria and Sweden: ten; Denmark, Ireland, Lithuania, Slovakia, and Finland: seven; Cyprus, Estonia, Latvia, Luxembourg, and Slovenia: four; Malta: three (a total of 321). A minimum of 232 votes (72.3 percent) will be required to reach a qualified majority. In addition, a majority of member states (in some cases, two-thirds) must approve the decision, and any member state can ask for confirmation that the votes cast in favor represent at least 62 percent of the EU's total population.

In the Constitutional Treaty, the codecision procedure was supposed to become the general rule through the extended Qualified Majority Voting used in the Council. The new rules for QMV would allow a law or regulation to pass if 55 percent of the member states were in favor, so long as they jointly represented 65 percent of the EU's total population. The QMV's applicability thus was extended. In contrast, the different types of secondary legislation were to be reduced to European Laws and to European Framework Laws.[8]

The European Parliament did acquire additional rights vis-à-vis the Council of Ministers in some cases: now it may elect, not select, the President of the Commission, and henceforth it also may censure the Commission. The Constitutional Treaty introduced a new nomenclature of exclusive and shared competencies with 'supporting, coordinating, or complementary action' in a typology that leaves practically no field of action in the exclusive purview of a member state. Ultimately, the Convention preferred to reject the idea of a clear 'catalogue of competencies' because this would have proven to be 'antagonistic' to the fancied model of 'multilevel governance'.

A closer look at the final document, however, would reveal that progress in the anticipated direction was quite modest in effect, the power and decision-making procedures now being neither simpler nor any clearer than before. The allocation of competencies left very few of those at the national level. The delimitations of the spheres of power remain highly imprecise, while they clear the road to further 'harmonization' and centralization. Participatory rights were strengthened, as were the right to petition and the right to apply to the Ombudsman. Individuals and associations may initiate legal action against the Union, but this now-extended possibility of instituting legal proceedings applies to European regulations and to European decisions only. The Constitutional Treaty also reinforced the concept of EU 'citizenship' by placing fundamental rights at the heart of the Constitution, thus providing a guideline for the future accession of the Balkan countries

---

8. EU laws (*les acquis communautaires*) are of three types: (1) primary legislation includes the Treaties and other agreements, which are subject to ratification by the national parliaments or by referenda; (2) secondary legislation comprises (a) *regulations* directly applicable and binding in all member states; (b) *directives*, which bind member states but leave to the national authorities the choice of form and the means for implementation; (c) *decisions*, which are binding in all of their aspects and do not require national-level implementing legislation; (d) *recommendations* and *opinions* that are not binding; and (3) case law that includes judgments of the European Court of Justice and of the European Court of First Instance.

and of Turkey. But it did not provide content for the Common Foreign and Security Policy or add anything of substance to the 'fundamental rights' enshrined in the Charter of Fundamental Rights passed in 2000. And despite the original expectations, the Constitutional Treaty did not instill an enhanced sense of ownership by citizens.

Regardless of its invocations of the subsidiarity principle, the Constitutional Treaty could not provide a mechanism to prevent supranationalism from cutting deeply into and through the national regulatory policies, taxation policies, subsidies, and governmental social policies. Against the far-reaching deregulatory implications of market liberalization, the call for a joint social policy seemed best left alone. And hence the Convention did not seriously address this issue. In any event, the Constitutional Treaty would not have been able to resolve the problems awaiting integration, including the socioeconomic discrepancies, the matter of unequal subsidies for farmers, let alone the increasingly serious immigration issues.

The governments of all twenty-five member countries now have signed the Constitutional Treaty, but it could not take effect unless ratified by each member state separately. Of a total of twenty-five member countries, ten chose to hold referenda, and the others, rather, a ratification by their national parliament. By fall 2005, fourteen member states had ratified the constitution, either by referendum or by parliamentary ratification.[9] Following the negative results of the French and Dutch referenda, Britain, Denmark, Ireland, Poland, Portugal, and Sweden chose to postpone their own popular referenda indefinitely. The crushing "no" that the French and Dutch populations opposed to the European constitution in the spring of 2005 sufficed to bring the intended process of 'vote by acclamation' to a grinding halt. As a result, in its present form, the Constitutional Treaty seems defunct. In order to prevent such an outcome, some countries had favored a simple and quiet parliamentary approval from the outset. The EU elites were not prepared for a "no" vote by the citizenry. Some observers were quick to claim that the "no" votes had nothing to do with Europe per se, only with national agendas—nothing else than a firm "no" to French president Chirac and nothing more than a mere identity crisis in the Netherlands. Others claimed that it was just a communication problem.

---

9. For details of the ratification process, please see www.euractiv.com.

A study on the French referendum came to the conclusion that the main motivation for the "yes" vote lay in the perception of the indispensability of European construction and in the long-standing support for the EU, otherwise. The reasons for "no" votes were much more diversely explicable: 31 percent attributable to the negative effects of the Constitution on issues of employment, 26 percent to France's poor economic situation, 19 percent to the perception of the Constitution as an economically much too liberal document, and 18 percent admitted voting "no" out of personal opposition to their president, Jacques Chirac (European Commission 2005).

In the Netherlands, the "no" voters explained their opposition by attributing their rejection to the enlargement of Europe, to the complexity of the wording of the Constitutional Treaty, to their lack of trust in the development of the EU, and to their own fear of Turkey's eventual adhesion as a EU member (Maurer 2005, 46).

No matter what their underlying reasons might have been, the resounding "no's" helped bring some powerful undercurrents to the surface. This many-faced crisis was looming, foreseeable, and maybe inevitable (Pfaff 2005). Unintentionally, the referenda became the conduit for expressing past frustrations over the lack of popular voice in the EU. The motivations for Euroskepticism were diffuse. The "no" vote was against the political class of Eurocrats, against the depoliticized, elitist, technocratic patterns of bureaucratic transfer of greater and greater competencies from state governments to the EU—in sum, a warning call for taking time off to digest the adhesion of the EU's ten new members, although probably also a vote in nostalgic defense of an increasingly anachronistic nation-state. The "no" votes were symptomatic of the alienation felt by salient constituencies; they were also an affirmation of national identity and sovereignty opposed to much further concentration of executive powers at the Capital of Europe. The Constitutional Treaty, although intended to alleviate parts of the decision-making malaise, became the "slapping boy" of national governments disillusioned with waning social cohesion, fearful of domestic alienation by huge waves of newcomers, and reluctant to abandon practicing a high-browed style of governance. The referenda were but an anticlimax to a top-down, elitist, bureaucratic process of decision making.

The negative results of the French and Dutch referenda pointed to a crisis by expansion: the sense of "Europeanness" does not, as of yet,

embrace a Europe of twenty-five. The referenda helped pool the scattered disappointment over the implications of an ever-wider Union.
Though Eastern Europeans may have had their own moral 'right of
return' to Europe, the distance between most old and new members is
considerable. After the "big bang" that expanded the EU by ten new
members in 2004, skepticism and fear prevailed. And with more knocks
at the EU's doors, by Turkey, Croatia, other Western Balkan states,
Ukraine, Georgia, and future applicants even farther away, the yet-
untested territorial, political, and societal limits to the EU's absorptive
power may harbor some scary prospects of its own.

The failed referenda revealed a crisis of legitimacy, as well. Postwar
reconciliation, shared anticommunism, the transformation of poor
postauthoritarian countries such as Greece, Spain, and Portugal, and
now Eastern Europe are no longer a rallying cry. The voters in the
EU's member states are divided along their national interests. The
French complain about the inexistence of a 'social Europe', the British
complain about 'red tape', the Spanish and Portuguese extol the benefits of the agricultural subsidies, the Dutch grumble about the costs,
while the Eastern Europeans cannot help but wonder how so very
quickly their model organization could fall into such total disarray
(Kurpas 2005).

One can only speculate about the long-term consequences of the
"no" votes in the referenda. The attempt to organize 'from above' a
general mandate for further broadening and deepening, by means of a
plebiscite with a single anticipated answer (a "yes") did not quite work
out. Although some had once argued that referenda should be the most
democratic form of legitimizing the Constitutional Treaty, now others
warn that referenda are likely to prove too risky, absent a European
public space (Jopp and Kuhle 2005). For several years, there likely will
be a pause on the Constitutional Treaty, and the Treaty itself might
prove beyond rescue. One should not overstate the EU's crisis, however.
The French and Dutch votes against the European Constitutional Treaty
do not signal the end for the EU, nor are they the forerunners of the
biggest reversal for Europe in fifty years, much less an omen for the
EU's lurch into nationalism. Bellamy may be right in saying that "no
European constitution can claim to promote a European popular will
or express a consensus on the shape of a European polity" (Bellamy
2004). Perhaps it is not a fixed constitution but rather an evolutionary,
continuous, open-ended process of constitutionalization that might
prove to be the very best outcome the EU could hope for.

Anti-Americanism Will Not Alleviate the Legitimacy Crisis

During the Iraq war, the EU evidenced deeply divided interests in face of the United States' resolve to oust the Iraqi regime. This in turn occasioned a lack of intra-EU communication and coordination. The governments were disjoined. Due to the poor institutionalization of the Common Foreign and Security Policy (CFSP), compared to the EU's common economic policy, there were no central mechanisms in place for constraining or sanctioning individual behavior. The diverging attitudes to the United States/British-led war in Iraq have raised pressing questions regarding a common ground for a foreign and security policy in the EU. Harsh critics have written off the CFSP. Others argue that there nevertheless exists a European consensus over 90 percent of external issues. The EU speaks with one voice on the International Criminal Court, on the Kyoto Protocol, on the Balkans policy, vis-à-vis Russia, or regarding the Arab-Israeli conflict; and 70 to 85 percent of the EU public was against the war in Iraq, including the residents of countries whose governments sided with the Bush Administration (Cameron 2003). According to opinion polls, there exists overwhelming public support for the further strengthening of the CFSP. But the direction to be adopted in non-European conflicts and in response to U.S. foreign and security policies remains to be defined. Even after the dust settles in the Middle East, the query will live on as to what kind of EU behavior U.S. hegemony is likely to provoke or to stimulate. Has Europe developed 'truly global' or merely regional interests and 'responsibilities'? Some EU members seem to favor multilateralism, multipolarity, a balancing function, and an avant-garde role by France and Germany. Others, particularly Eastern Europeans and the UK, favor bandwagoning with the United States.

The extent to which the EU may play a role independent of that of the United States, be it in conflict prevention, in conflict management, or in military intervention, is likely to be determined by two very distinct, opposite approaches: either balancing the United States hegemony, or bandwagoning with the United States. Are there some clear determinants to these patterns? Secondary European states, in particular those in Eastern Europe, but also states wary of an overly intimate French-German axis, are likely to bandwagon with the United States, as entertaining a special friendship with the United States would be a proper mechanism for balancing French-German aspirations. Unable to afford the means to invest in NATO and in the EU's CFSP, the newer (especially Eastern European) NATO members favor NATO and transatlantic ties over those with the EU's CFSP. For EU members with a secondary status, siding with the United States may at times also function as a means for settling scores inside the EU.

The lessons learned from the Cold War vary for the United States and the Central Eastern European states on one hand and especially for Germany and France on the other. Germany, Austria, France, and the Scandinavian countries (except Denmark) have been deeply shaped by the philosophy of détente—containment and change via rapprochement instead of military rollback. Poland, Romania, and Bulgaria on the other hand, having been suspicious for very long of the philosophy of détente, almost automatically choose to team up with the United States. Clearly, differences with U.S. foreign and security policies are, by themselves, unlikely to help constitute Europe.

The dictum 'no success like success, no failure like failure' applies to U.S. allies in Europe, as well. Those that bandwagoned with the United States during the war in Iraq placed their bets on success. Those that stayed aloof, like Germany and France, feared the costs and risks involved, particularly in the face of unfinished business in the Balkans and in Afghanistan. Once the Iraq war was perceived as too costly, those initially bandwagoning with the United States disengaged; but it would not be sagacious to expect a lasting balancing stance against U.S. hegemony by the EU. One would be correct, however, in expecting some kind of opting out, on a case-by-case basis. If the Europeans cannot prevent the United States from acting independently of the UN Security Council and of NATO, the United States, in turn, may not expect from the Europeans mentionable supportive participation in postwar management, whether in feeding, financing, or administrating roles.

The CFSP probably will be confined to areas of prime concern, say, the fringes of the EU, specifically the Balkans, the Mediterranean, the Middle East, and increasingly the Caucasus and Central Asia as well. Following the EU's failure to adopt the Constitutional Treaty, the CFSP is likely to fall behind. Neither a defensive retreat nor a self-righteous critique by the EU of U.S. foreign policy would prove helpful or effective, however, in any practical sense for long. Europeans have to face the challenge of the 'democratic peace' thesis: no long-term peace and stability is possible, absent democratic regimes. Due to the large presence of Islamic communities in the Western European countries, the EU will have to engage Islamic countries and local Muslim communities in a dialogue. Against all odds and warnings, the Council of Ministers of the EU decided at long last in favor of (prolonged) accession talks with Turkey. Prominent politicians and intellectuals have warned that this would destroy the EU, mostly on the ill-disguised fear from an alleged basic Christian-Muslim incompatibility (Wehler 2004). Yet the perspective of a Turkish EU membership may not only testify to the adaptability of Islam to democracy but also help in supporting and stabilizing further democratic and economic reforms in Turkey, in promoting minority rights and gender equality there, also in ensuring against a regression into radical Islamism, and in easing the integration of ever-segregated or still self-contained Turkish communities inside the EU (Kramer 2004).

The integration of Eastern Europe since 1989/1990 is a major feat and a potential template for further expanding the territories governed by liberal and democratic values. In the course of their process of accession, former socialist countries had to learn and come to be seen to respect fundamental human rights, to protect their minorities, to abolish the death penalty, to fight corruption, and to democratize their civilian-military relations. To develop a forward-looking EU strategy in support of democratization, at least in the OSCE area, would depend on a sense of urgency and on extant leadership skills. Unfortunately, at this time there is neither such a sense of urgency nor the requisite European leadership.

Conclusion

The disparate nature of the EU obtains from the multiplicity of nation-states, the variety of regions, and the great heterogeneity of the peoples it encompasses, but is also due in part to the lingering discrepancies among its extant multilevel institutions. The EU is, and will likely remain, a union of governments and, to a lesser extent perhaps, also a union of peoples cooperating on their shared objectives, as such common purposes arise. What the EU is not, and does not even strive to become, is a nation-state. The now twenty-five–member EU does not constitute a popular sovereign. As the second war in Iraq, the de facto division of Cyprus with no regard for its EU membership, or the absence of a European policy for the Balkans amply demonstrate, the EU's CFSP describes at best an ambition, an aspiration, not a reality. There are—if we stretched the concept—only elements for a constitution.

There is at best a very poor and much underdeveloped European public space. For freely associating citizens to govern their lives democratically, a 'joint communication sphere' is key: one that can accommodate a developed sense of common concerns, the citizenry's shared interest in public affairs, their forums, town meetings, and the media's public discussions, too. Some pan-European issues—such as the introduction of the euro currency, mad cow disease, the "Haider Affair" in Austria, the EU's enlargement by Turkey, or the referenda on the Constitutional Treaty—began dominating the media in the member states at the same time (Eder and Kantner 2002; Risse, van de Steeg, and Rauer 2003). National politicians have taken to externalizing their domestic failures by pointing their blaming finger toward Brussels. Public concerns still do find ways of Europeanizing, albeit only upon the appearance of outstanding events. Otherwise, the everyday coverage by the member-state media of European decision making and European institutions is miserably low, notwithstanding the direct significance of their de facto impact. A Eurobarometer study in 2004 confirmed, for example, that a mere 45 percent of Europeans had ever heard about the Constitutional Convention (Novy 2004). Today, Europeans are still segmented according to their language, ethnic, and political communities. Apart from a few TV channels such as Arte or Eurosport, the mass media are national or subnational but not pan-European.

In principle, the 'democratic deficit' of the EU could be tackled by an array of practical strategies, such as strengthening the national voice, widening co-decision making, using "reserved powers,"[10] providing for select veto positions or opt-out clauses for member states, or strengthening democracy across the EU, for example, by way of true parliamentarization or via direct elections of the executive branch. An institutional incentive for the emergence of pan-European social entities would be pan-European laws for pan-European elections and referenda. This would undermine the control of outcomes by national politicians, however.

---

10. Powers not granted to the EU would be reserved to the member states, the regions, or the citizenry. All would be retained that have not been explicitly surrendered. The idea of reserved powers is also at the heart of Tenth Amendment of the U.S. Constitution.

Authors such as Ulrich Beck and Edgar Grande boldly call for more direct democracy and for a pan-European movement 'from below' in order to create the missing intermediary organizations and civil society (Beck and Grande 2005). They do not say, however, why, how, and from where the very movement should emerge. An increase of civil participation would depend, above all else, on pan-European associations and parties that do not exist. What do exist are well-formed business organizations. After the disappointment over the referenda in France and the Netherlands, the Euro-elites will think twice before embarking on yet another round of popular voting, for the agendas of direct democracy hardly can be kept under control.

A true parliamentarization of the European Parliament seems to offer a more robust panacea—people would not have to pool all of their anger into one referendum, and parties could prepare policy options, arrange for structural cleavages, and maybe even provide labels for clear choices.

Intensified cooperation among the segmented coalitions of the willing, veto positions for minority groups among member states, and the reservation of significant areas of consociationalism for decision making are among the most likely outcomes of the numbness now reigning. A 'way out' seems to comprise opt-out clauses and areas where 'enhanced cooperation' is allowed for, implying that subgroups of member states willing to integrate more closely than others will be allowed to do so, regardless of the fact that the Constitutional Treaty did not even address the issue of asymmetry, electing instead to adhere to the esoteric ritual chant for, yes, an 'ever-closer Union'.

The current halt to institutional 'deepening' will probably affect the widening as well. Bulgaria and Romania's adhesion in January 2007 is likely to be followed by Croatia's entry. But the pressure to keep the other Western Balkan countries and especially Turkey outside of the EU's borders, for as long as possible, will not decrease. In the meantime, the EU may turn inward and occupy itself with institutional bargaining. The splits between France and Germany on the one hand, and with Britain on the other, over protectionist economic and social policies—and as to transatlantic relations as well—are likely to deepen. It will become harder for the EU to push forward and to proceed with economic liberalization and enlargement concomitantly.

The fate of the Constitutional Treaty merely mirrors the state of the Union. The democratization of Europe "has only just begun and remains a rather remote prospect," wrote Philippe C. Schmitter before the referenda (Schmitter 2003, 71). The overwhelming message of the referenda on the Constitutional Treaty is probably: (1) that people reject both an ever-closer Union and an ever-wider one, (2) that they prefer legitimacy over efficiency, (3) that the extant consociational decision making in the EU is preferred over majority voting, and (4) that the national welfare state needs to be protected over unrestrained market competition. The failure of adopting the Constitutional Treaty eliminates certain options, among them the ideas of a United States of Europe, of a European federation, and of a supranational state. For the time being, the EU will preserve a system of multilevel and polycentric governance instead of a single system of government. The contest between supranationalism and intergovernmentalism is likely to persist, but the gap nonetheless will close. In the end, the balance is likely to shift in favor of more supranationalism and majority voting, with little or no regard for the popular sovereign's—the demos'— attempts to retard the process. Very likely, European-wide democracy will remain brittle.

References

Abromeit, Heidrun (1998a) *Democracy in Europe: Legitimising Politics in a Non-State Polity*, New York, Oxford: Berghahn Books.

———— (1998b) "Ein Vorschlag zur Demokratisierung des europäischen Entscheidungssystems," *Politische Vierteljahresschrift*, No. 1:80–90.

Abromeit, Heidrun, and Sebastian Wolf (2005) "Will the Constitutional Treaty Contribute to the Legitimacy of the European Union?" *European Integration online Papers* (EIoP), vol. 9, no. 11, http://eiop.or.at/eiop/texte/2005-011a.htm.

Beck, Ulrich, and Edgar Grande (2005) "Europas letzte Chance," *Blätter für deutsche und internationale Politik*, 9:1083–1097.

Bellamy, Richard (2004) "Which Constitution for What Kind of Europe? Three Models of European Constitutionalism," paper for the CIDEL Workshop "Constitution-making and Democratic Legitimacy in the EU," London, November 12–13.

Bundesverfassungsgericht (1993) "Judgement on Maastricht Treaty," *Europäische Grundrechte Zeitschrift*, 429 ff.

Cameron, Fraser (2003) "After Iraq—Can There Really Be a Future for CFSP?" European Policy Centre, Brussels, March 18.

Collier, David, and Steven Levitsky (1997) "Democracy with Adjectives: Conceptual Innovation in Comparative Research," *World Politics*, 49 (April):430–451.

Crossick, Stanley (2003) "The Convention on the Future of Europe," European Policy Centre, Brussels, February 18.

Dahl, Robert (1999) "Can International Organizations Be Democratic? A Skeptic's View," in I. Shapiro and C. Hacker-Cordon, Editors, *Democracy's Edges*, pp. 19–36, Cambridge, UK: Cambridge University Press.

—— (2000) *On Democracy*, New Haven, CT and London: Yale University Press.

Eder, Klaus, and Cathleen Kantner (2002) "Interdiskursivität in der europäischen Öffentlichkeit," *Berliner Debatte Initial*, 13(5/6):79–88.

European Commission (2005) *Flash Eurobarometer 171, The European Constitution: Post-referendum Survey in France*, Brussels, June.

Grimm, Dieter (1995) "Braucht Europa eine Verfassung?" *Juristen-Zeitung*, no. 50, pp. 581–632.

Habermas, Jürgen (1999) *Die Einbeziehung des Anderen*, Frankfurt am Main: Suhrkamp.

—— (2001) "Warum braucht Europa eine Verfassung?" Hamburg Die Zeit Lecture, June 26. Available at http://hermes.zeit.de/pdf/archiv/2001/27/200127_verfassung_lang.xml.pdf.

—— (2003) "Nach dem Krieg: Die Wiedergeburt Europas," *Frankfurter Allgemeine Zeitung*, no. 125 (May 31).

Jopp, Mathias, and Gesa-S. Kuhle (2005) "Wege aus der Verfassungskrise—die EU nach den gescheiterten Referendums in Frankreich und den Niederlanden," *Integration*, 3:257–261.

Kirchoff, Paul (1998) "Die Gewaltenbalance zwischen staatlichen und europäischen Organen," paper presented at the Forum Constitutionis of the Walter Hallstein Institute, Humboldt University, Berlin, May 25.

Kohler-Koch, Beate (2000) "Regieren in der europäischen Union: Auf der Suche nach demokratischer Legitimität," *Aus Politik und Zeitgeschichte* B6:30–38.

Kramer, Heinz (2004) "Die Türkei im Prozess der 'Europäisierung,'" *Aus Politik und Zeitgeschichte*, August 9, pp. 9–17.

Kurpas, Sebastian (2005) "When the European Constitution Went National," Centre for European Policy Studies (CEPS), Brussels, May 4. Available at www.ceps.be/Article.php?article_id=421&.

Majone, Giandomenico (1999) "The Regulatory State and Its Legitimacy Problems," *West European Politics*, 222(1):1–24.

Maull, Hanns W. (2005) "The Melt-Down of European Politics," in *Deutsche Aussenpolitik. de*, www.deutsche-aussenpolitik.de/digest/op-ed_inhalt_17.php.

Maurer, Andreas (2005) "Die Ratifikationsverfahren zum EU-Verfassungsvertrag. Wege aus der Krise," Berlin: Stiftung Wissenschaft und Politik," discussion paper, September 8.

Maurer, Andreas Peter (2003) "Less Bargaining—More Deliberation: The Convention Method for Enhancing EU Democracy," in *International Politics and Society*, no. 1, pp. 167–190.

Novy, Leonard (2004) "Vom Schweigen der Union," *Eurozine*, July 21, www.eurozine.com.

Pfaff, William (2005) "What's Left of the Union?"*New York Review of Books*, vol. 52, p. 12, July 14.

Plattner, Marc F. (2003) "Making Sense of the EU: Competing Goals, Conflicting Perspectives," *Journal of Democracy*, 14(4) (October):42–56.

Prodi, Romani (2001) "For a Strong Europe," speech given at the Institut d'Etudes Politiques, Paris, May 29. Available at www.futurum.gov.pl/futurum.nsf/0/ 89E3C36770C7CBD8C1256CAB0028A5EE.

Rau, Johannes (2001) "Plädoyer für eine Europäische Verfassung," speech given at the European Parliament, Straßbourg, April 4. Available at www.dstgb.de/homepage/ europa/aktuell/bundespraesident_rau_vor_dem_europaparlament/plaedoyer_fuer _eine_europaeische_verfassung/index.html

Risse, Thomas, Marianne van de Steeg and Valentin Rauer (2003) "The EU as a Political Community: A Media Analysis of the Haider Debate in the European Union," paper presented at the Annual Meeting of the European Union Studies Association (EUSA), in Nashville, TN: March 27–30.

Scharpf, Fritz (1998) *Regieren in Europa: Effektiv und demokratisch?* Frankfurt am Main: Campus.

Schmitter, Philippe C. (2003) "Democracy in Europe and Europe's Democratization," *Journal of Democracy*, 14(4) (October):71–85.

Weale, Albert (1995) "Democratic Legitimacy and the Constitution of Europe," in R. Bellamy, V. Bufacchi, and D. Castiglione, Editors, *Democracy and the Constitutional Culture in the Union of Europe*, pp. 103–120, London: Lothian Foundation Press.

Wehler, Hans-Ulrich (2004) "Verblendetes Harakiri: Der Türkei-Beitritt zerstört die EU," *Aus Politik und Zeitgeschichte*, 9 (August):6–8.

7

Democratizations in Central Europe: Comparative Perspectives

Jerzy J. Wiatr

What a mere 20 years ago still was but a relatively (for never having been an absolutely) homogeneous bloc of communist states in Eastern and Central Europe presents today an interesting disparate conglomerate of countries whose political systems vary from almost consolidated democracies to unstable authoritarian regimes. Although in the Freedom House Survey, on the comparative measures of freedom (Piano and Puddington 2001), East Central Europe does fare considerably better than the former Soviet republics (the USSR with the exception of Estonia, Latvia, and Lithuania), differences within the region are certainly not negligible, and in many important ways quite considerable.[1] The nature, origins, and consequences of these differences constitute a most fascinating subject for comparative political analysis. It has been difficult for political scientists to compare such a large group of nations, which have departed from a system common to (but not identically shared by) all of them and have done so almost exactly in the same period: from 1989 to 1991.

Why Is East Central Europe Different?

Over the period of more than four decades spent under a regime of communism in the Soviet-controlled part of Europe, non-Soviet communist states always differed from the Soviet model in an array of ways

---

1. Of the former republics of the USSR, only the three Baltic republics were listed as "free"; six (Belarus, Kazakhstan, Kyrgyz Republic, Tajikistan, Türkmenistan, and Uzbekistan) were found to be "not free"; and six (Armenia, Azerbaijan, Georgia, Moldava, Russia, and Ukraine) as "partly free." Among the East Central European post-communist states, none was found to be "not free"; four Balkan republics (Albania, Bosnia-Herzegovina, Macedonia, and Yugoslavia) were classified as "partly free"; and the remaining eight (Bulgaria, Croatia, Czech Republic, Hungary, Poland, Romania, Slovakia, and Slovenia) as "free."

that would escape the gleanings from a purely ideological analytical approach toward understanding them. Paul Shoup (1971) emphasized the need to depart from the earlier tradition of seeing all communist systems as monolithic and postulated the comparative approach to the study of the varieties of the communist polities. Writing in about the same period, Jan Triska (1970, 338) pointed to the systemic differences between the East European communist states and the USSR and linked these differences to the fact that the communist regimes were considerably younger in Eastern Europe than in the USSR. In the 1960s, Polish political scientists were among the first to underline the differences already existing at the time between the communist states, particularly in the extent to which they were or were not totalitarian and the degree to which they showed elements of pluralism (Wiatr and Przeworski 1996). Looking back, it has become quite clear that those who saw the diversity in communist systems were closer to the truth than those for whom all communist states were mere carbon copies of the Soviet model.

There were four main reasons for the difference between the Soviet and the East Central European communist states. First, the communist system was established in the former Russian Empire one full generation earlier than in the non-Soviet European states. By the time the communist systems were coming to their end, the pre-communist past was no longer a part of the life experience even of the older generation of Soviet citizens (except maybe in the Baltic republics of the USSR, forcibly incorporated in 1940), but it was still very much alive in the memories of the older generations of Poles, Hungarians, and Czechs.

Second, a majority of the East Central European states, variedly different from the Soviet republics, had had at least some experience in democracy prior to witnessing the establishment of the communist rule. Several of them, before World War I, were integral to the Hapsburg Empire, with very considerable elemental exposure to political freedoms and to democracy, at least since the constitutional reform of the 1860s. Political democracy existed in almost all of them for parts of the interwar period. In the case of Czechoslovakia, democracy functioned well during the entire period of the First Republic. Memories of the past are important for the formation of political culture: the political cultures of East Central Europeans, while generally speaking less democratic than those extant in Western Europe, have been considerably more democratic than the political culture of Russia and the other parts of the Russian and then-Soviet empire. The case of the three Baltic republics is closer to that of the states of East Central Europe than to that of Russia or any of the other former Soviet republics.

The third difference concerns the pattern of establishment of the communist rule. In Russia, communists came to power on their own—by exploiting the dissatisfaction from the war and skillfully organizing the new state in such an astute way that they were able to defeat their once-powerful adversaries. In East Central Europe, with the exception of Yugoslavia, communist regimes were imposed on the unwilling population by the overwhelming might of a victorious Soviet empire (and, let us face it, with the passive acceptance by the Western powers). Being imposed upon from without, but disposing of a very weak popular base within, the newly communist regimes of East Central Europe were forced to make numerous concessions. This was particularly true about the three most 'Western' nations of the region: Czechoslovakia, Hungary, and Poland.

Finally, the fourth factor was the relatively short duration of the fully totalitarian, Stalinist, stage of the communist system in East Central Europe. In the USSR, a totalitarian system of mass terror was imposed fully, during the forced collectivization of the agriculture (1929–1933), lasting until the death of Joseph Stalin in 1953—that is, for almost a quarter of a century. By contrast, in East Central Europe (with the exception of the two thoroughly totalitarian states, Albania and Romania), totalitarianism in its full form lasted only a few years—approximately from 1948 through 1953. Although it left many scars, its impact on the population and on the elite of the East Central European communist states was by far much weaker than what it had been and what it would be in the USSR.

These historical differences explain most but not all of the contrasting characteristics between East Central European communist states and the Soviet Union prior to the changes in the system. For the beginning of the transition added a new dimension: indeed, the Soviet Union collapsed not only as a communist state but also as a multiethnic empire. With the exception of Yugoslavia, this was not the case in East Central Europe. Even the "Velvet Divorce" in what once was Czechoslovakia took effect smoothly, without major harmful consequences for the emerging new democracies. In Russia, as well as in most of the former Soviet republics (except the three Baltic states), the collapse of the empire was a traumatic experience, in many ways complicating the process of building democracy.

In this sense, the relative success of the new democracies in East Central Europe as compared with the former Soviet Union, can best be explained by holistic reference to the deep historical factors that made those two groups of nations so profoundly different. It should also be noted, however, that the most successful among the new democracies in East Central Europe benefited from the quality of their political leaders—both those who emerged from the ranks of the democratic opposition and those who came to power in the ruling communist parties in the latest period of their rule. They provided wise and strong leadership at a time when such leadership was of paramount importance for the overall success of the emerging democracies. Not all nations in East Central Europe were so lucky. Contrary to Hegel's view, history does not always provide leaders capable of meeting their historical destiny.

Challenges of Democratization

The democratization of an absolutist dictatorship in general and of a communist dictatorship in particular seems to necessitate the advance resolution without delay of four principal problems.

First, democratization requires a break with and a transition from dictatorial rule by a supreme communist party to governance by a democratically elected government. With the exception of Romania, this process was peaceful[2] in all of the formerly communist states of East Central Europe, although it did assume various forms.

The transition began in Poland, following the Round Table negotiations between the ruling bloc and the democratic opposition. It led to the admittedly only partially free parliamentary election won by the democratic opposition and promptly to the formation of the coalition government of Tadeusz Mazowiecki, which would become the very first cabinet in a formerly communist state to be headed by a politician

---

2. The case of Serbia and Montenegro is more complex. The departure from power of Slobodan Milosević and his Serbian Socialist Party was caused by their defeat in presidential and parliamentary elections, but this electoral result was mostly caused by the fact that the outgoing regime had provoked an international crisis over Kosovo and the military intervention of NATO forces in 1999, ended—after three months of bombing—in defeat of the Yugoslav regime. Still, the transfer of power was executed peacefully through election. Political violence (with the assassination of Prime Minister Djindjic as its climax) points to the fact that Serbia is still far from democratic consolidation. Montenegro fares somehow better, but the post-communist regime is being accused of massive corruption.

of the democratic opposition. The Polish pattern of negotiated transition was emulated by other states, particularly by Hungary and two of the republics of Yugoslavia (namely, Croatia and Slovenia) where the ruling communist parties decided to open talks with the rapidly emerging opposition and to allow fully democratic elections (in all three cases, during the spring of 1990). All were carried by the noncommunist opposition except for the presidential election in Slovenia, won by the former leader of the League of Slovenian Communists, Milan Kucan. This pattern of transition can be defined as 'negotiated reform'. Its main characteristics include the cooperation between the main current of democratic opposition and the reformist leadership of the ruling communist party, thereby leading to orderly transition from supreme party rule to democracy.

The transformation of Czechoslovakia and the German Democratic Republic (GDR) in the fall of 1989 assumed a different pattern. In each of these states, the communist regime survived especially by virtue of the military and political umbrella provided them by the USSR. In the GDR, this was the consequence of the artificial nature of the state, created by the USSR on the principal territory of the Soviet zone of occupation. Whereas in the case of Czechoslovakia, it was the outcome of the military intervention of the USSR and of its allies in August 1968, directed against the reformist policies of the "Prague Spring" and resulting in the firm imposition of the collaborationist regime of President Gustav Husak. When, in 1989, the USSR withdrew its support for the East German and Czechoslovak regimes, these were unable to survive the wave of street protests, largely motivated by news of the democratic changes that had taken place in Poland and Hungary. The result was the capitulation of the communist regimes, free elections in 1990, and finally the transfer of power to the political forces arising from within the democratic opposition. In Germany, it also led to 'unification', in fact, the absorption[3] of the GDR by the Federal Republic of Germany (FRG).

In the third group of communist states, the ruling parties abandoned their communist identity, changed their names, and called for free election, which they were able to win, largely because the opposition had too little time to get organized. This was the case in Bulgaria (1990), Albania (1991), and three Yugoslav republics: Serbia, Montenegro, and

---

3. Unlike chemists, social scientists seldom differentiate between *absorption* and *adsorption*—a term, in retrospect, perhaps more appropriate here.—*Ed.*

Macedonia (also in 1990). The case of Serbia is special, because the transformed post-communist party (the Serbian Socialist Party) adopted an aggressive nationalistic program that allowed it to win several consecutive elections and to govern until its defeat in the election of 2000. The (new) Socialist parties in Bulgaria and Albania lost their second electoral campaigns (in 1991 and 1992, respectively), although the Social Democrats of Macedonia remained in power until the election of 1998. In Montenegro, which along with Serbia did remain within the Yugoslav Federation, the Socialist Party split into two distinct parties, and both—the one supporting democratic reforms and the other supporting Montenegrin sovereignty—remain in power.

The fourth group of Central European post-communist states is composed of the three formerly Soviet Baltic republics: Estonia, Latvia, and Lithuania. There, the transition began as part of the Gorbachev reforms, in particular, the basically free elections of the republican Supreme Soviets in 1990. These elections were part of the program of democratization initiated by the last of Soviet General Secretaries and, as of March 1990, President of the USSR, Mikhail Gorbachev. In the context of the Soviet multinational state, free elections to the republican Soviets brought to power advocates for republican independence in Estonia, in Latvia, and in Lithuania. They came to power on the republican level, but it was only in the summer of 1991 following the aborted coup d'état in Moscow that the three republics became independent, soon receiving international diplomatic recognition. Former communists reorganized themselves in new parties of social-democratic persuasion, but only in Lithuania were they able to win both the parliamentary elections (1992 and 2000) and the presidential election (1993), in which their leader Algirdas Brazauskas was elected president of the Republic.

The case of Romania is different from all other East Central European transitions: only in Romania was a communist dictatorship overthrown by force. Following a revolutionary outburst in December 1989, the newly formed Front of National Salvation captured power under the presidency of veteran communist Ion Iliescu, who would be elected President of Romania in the first presidential election of 1991, then lose the presidency in the succeeding national election held in 1996, only to regain it in the third election of 2000.

Bosnia-Herzegovina, too, is a very special case, difficult to interpret. Following the 1992 election and irrevocable secession from Yugoslavia, four years of bloody ethnic war destroyed the very fabric of the Republic. Since the Dayton Peace Agreement, signed in the United States during 1995, Bosnia-Herzegovina has remained de facto divided in two distinct parts: Serbian and Muslim-Croat, both under international supervision. To the extent that anyone could speak of, state power now is in the hands of the nationalistic parties that represent the ethnic communities in conflict with each other.

There are two lessons from this review of the ways in which transition from dictatorship to democracy took place. First, although in all formerly communist states parliamentary elections played a crucial role in the process of transition, the very specific way in which these elections played such a role depended on the relations between the reformists in the ruling parties and the opposition in the latest period of the communist rule. Second, the transfer of power from the ruling communist parties did not automatically ban the successor 'post-communist' parties from returning to power via democratic elections at some later stage. This happened in Albania, Bulgaria, Croatia, Hungary, Lithuania, Poland, and to some degree in Slovakia and Slovenia: in these countries, the post-communist socialist parties became junior partners in governing coalitions.

The second great challenge for these new democracies has been the establishment of the rule of law and of effectively functioning democratic institutions. Experience with and by new democracies in other parts of the world has demonstrated that the rejection of dictatorship constitutes a necessary but not sufficient condition either for consolidating democracy or for establishing the rule of law (Linz and Stepan 1996; Przeworski et al. 1995). In this respect, the East Central European states can be divided into three groups: from the most triumphant to the least successful ones.

The first group is composed by those states in which, during the entire period since departure from the communist rule, popular elections were free, honest, held on constitutionally prescribed dates; citizens' rights were adequately protected; and the level of extra-legal political public protest was low. The Czech Republic, Estonia, Hungary, Lithuania, Poland, and Slovenia, each and all, meet these criteria fully. Were it not for its controversial law on citizenship, which denies most of the ethnic non-Latvians their full citizens' rights, Latvia could have belonged in this group too. The second group consists of those states in which instances of gross violation of democratic rules of governance and of basic citizens' rights have occurred at some recent time, but where the situation has improved sufficiently for these to be defined now as recently consolidated democracies. It is in this second group that Bulgaria, Croatia, Moldova, Romania, Slovakia, and perhaps also the new Federation of Serbia and Montenegro can be placed at this time.

The third, and smallest, category comprises the three Balkan states which, for a long time, have remained in protracted crises either because of the unresolved ethnic conflicts (such as the ones lingering in Bosnia-Herzegovina and Macedonia) or owing to the fragmentation, partly tribal, of the political system (as exhibited by Albania).[4]

The unmistakable general trend in the broader region, however, is toward better-consolidated democratic regimes. In Bulgaria, the parliamentary election of 2001 was free and resulted in an orderly transfer of power without extra-parliamentary pressure that had taken place before. In Croatia, after the death of authoritarian President Franjo Tudjman in 1999 and following the defeat of the ruling nationalistic party in the presidential and parliamentary elections of 2000, the rule of law has been reestablished, and the political life of that nation shows healthy progress in direction of democratic consolidation. In Romania, the return to power of its first President, Iliescu, and of his socialist party, took place in fully democratic fashion. The reinstallation of this administration suggests that it is not likely to repeat the authoritarian blunders of the past. And in neither of these two countries has the return to power of the right-wing parties in the recent elections resulted in any weakening of the democratic trend. In Slovakia, the defeat of Vladimir Meciar's Populist party in the parliamentary elections of 1998 terminated gross abuses of power. In Serbia, the victory of the democratic opposition in 2000 did create initial conditions for building a fully democratic state, although the bitter divisions of the past, still haunting the present, and the ethnic tensions still tormenting Kosovo may complicate the processes of consolidation on which depends so much the fragile future of this nascent democracy.

The larger picture looks reasonably positive, however. East Central Europe has gone much further along the path of democratic consolida-

---

4. In Albania, the parliamentary election of 1996 was flagrantly rigged by the then-ruling Democratic Party, and a situation close to an open civil war resulted a year later. The post-communist Socialist Party won parliamentary elections in 1997, which were called ahead of their constitutionally fixed date (owing to the quasi-total collapse of state power) and described as fair by foreign observers. It ruled the country in a basically democratic way. There did remain strongholds of armed opposition in the North, however, and the overall situation was far from normal. In 2001, the Socialist Party won the next election; but in 2005, it lost (by a small margin) to the Democratic Party.

tion than either Russia or the other republics of the former USSR so far have been able to achieve. Democracy has won or is winning in the whole region, with the notable exception of the more troubled parts of the Balkans.

The third problem of the democratic transition is the reform of the legal system. Compared with the earlier situation even in the most liberal communist states, the present state of law and order looks significantly better. Arbitrary police repression, especially for political reasons, has been stopped or considerably reduced in almost all countries of the region. Capital punishment has been abolished, largely under the impact of the position adopted by the Council of Europe. The human rights of prisoners are now far better protected than they ever could be under former communist rule. Yet, although progress in all these respects seems to be taking place in most of the East Central European post-communist states, even the most successful among them still seem to face serious problems that include but are not limited to the weakness of the administration of law, the continuing shortage of fully qualified specialists, the evident inadequacy of legal rules, the overcrowding of prisons, and the other daily obstacles to the effective administration of law. These ailments were magnified by the fact that the rapid transition to a market economy at the same time as the erstwhile harsh police controls were being abolished had the overall effect of producing unprecedented peaks in unlawful activities, especially of organized crime. These young democracies are not particularly successful in combating these problems; the frustrations they occasion among many of their citizens are not of a nature to favor greater liberalism.

And there are also those aspects of legal order in which the new democracies are perceived by their citizens to be performing worse than their communist predecessors. The principal criticism, expressed in no uncertain terms in surveys, concerns the widespread and growing corruption, seen as tolerated where not supported by the state. "Across post-communist Europe," reports Richard Rose, "barometer surveys find that an average of 72 percent believe that their new regime is more corrupt than its predecessor, 23 percent believe that the level of corruption is much the same as before; and only 6 percent believe that corruption has been reduced by political change" (Rose 2001, 101). Rose concludes that "corruption is the greatest obstacle to progress in post-communist countries" (p. 105). It has become evident that corruption results from the weakness of institutions, from all too rapidly emerging great social inequalities, and from the attitudes of many state officials who see politics as a game of spoils rather than public service. It also may be true that present-day corruption reflects continuity in hidden corrupt practices from communist times. The question here is not whether corruption, indeed, is more widespread now than it used to be under communist governments but whether the citizenries tend to believe that this is the case. Popular trust in democracy might, rightly or wrongly, depend on such preliminary public perceptions.

A special aspect of the legal system in all new democracies is the application of what is called *retroactive justice.* How should a democratic state treat those held responsible for past dictatorial rule and particularly for violations of law during that dictatorial rule? The problem offers three main aspects. First, those guilty of having violated the laws valid at the time, if they could be put on trial, should respond for their crimes in a way consistent with the rules of law. Torturing or killing prisoners were crimes against the laws that existed even under the communist system. Punishing those guilty in such instances does not violate the standard rule of jurisprudence: *lex retro non agit.* However, the passage of time creates practical problems for conducting fair trials. Witnesses die, or their memory is impaired by the passage of time. Documents often seem to have been lost or deliberately destroyed in the last days of communist rule. Although in principle there is no opposition to this aspect of retroactive justice, one way of dealing with this problem is the passage of laws that lift the statute of limitation for political crimes committed by functionaries of these communist regimes. And this, indeed, has been the way axes have been grinded in a number of states of the area.

A more complicated, second, aspect of the problem at hand is the responsibility of communist politicians for the actions of the state that, although based on the then-existing laws, now can be seen to have been undemocratic. And, indeed, in several post-communist states, politicians of the old regime were put under investigation and sometimes even on trial for such acts. In Germany, several leaders of the GDR were sentenced to jail terms for their role in imposing highly repressive rules on the use of firepower against individuals trying to escape to the West. In the Czech Republic, investigations were launched against some communist politicians known to have been involved in collaboration with the Soviet-imposed regime following the incidents of 1968. In Bulgaria, a number of leading communists, including the renowned sociologist and formerly reformist secretary of the Central Committee of the

Communist Party, Stoian Mikhailov, were briefly put in jail, although charges against them ultimately were dropped. In Albania, too, following the elevation to power of the Democratic Party, the former Prime Minister and leader of the Socialist Party Fatos Nano was sentenced to a long term in prison on fabricated charges.[5] The collapse of the corrupt government of President Sali Berisha in 1997 allowed Nano to regain his freedom and to return to the leadership of the Socialist party.

And in Poland, after the elections in 1991, the parliamentary Commission on Constitutional Accountability spent more than four years investigating charges against General Wojciech Jaruzelski and his subordinates, accused of having acted against the Constitution by the imposition of martial law in 1981. The case resulted in a fundamental debate on the historical context of this act and on the constitutionality of the decision (Wiatr 1996). Finally, in 1996, the Parliament decided to drop all charges, even though the subject remains controversial. The majority of Poles, according to public opinion surveys, support the decision, but there are also those who believe that the authors of the martial law should be put on trial. The matter has been reviewed at length by the American journalist Tina Rosenberg (1995), who clarified the difficulties of confronting those who attempt to resolve complex political issues by appealing to criminal justice. The Austrian political scientist Anton Pelinka (1999) argued convincingly in defense of General Jaruzelski's past action, by basing it on 'the principle of lesser evil'.

The third aspect of the preoccupation with retroactive justice concerns the laws that take away or severely reduce the political rights of former communist leaders or activists not so much for any specific action taken by them in the past but for their membership and position in the former regime, particularly in the leadership structures of the Communist Party. The so-called 'de-communization' reflects desire for revenge and has little in common with justice. It has been rejected in most of the post-communist states but not without heated controversies (Bartkowski 1993). Considering the degree of public support for politicians with a communist past in many of the post-communist states,[6] it should seem evident that such de-communization would

---

5. The Nano case was described fully in several reports by the Committee on Human Rights of Parliamentarians of the Inter-Parliamentary Union. It constitutes the most flagrant case of political vengeance against a former communist leader.
6. Algirdas Brazauskas, former President and presently the Prime Minister of Lithuania; Guyla Horn, former Prime Minister of Hungary; Milan Kucan, former President of

mean depriving many citizens of their right to choose the leaders of their republic, and that would be clearly incompatible with even the elementary principles of democracy.

The fourth problem facing the new democracies in former East Central Europe is the formation of viable party systems. At the very outset, in some of these post-communist countries, leaders of the democratic opposition somehow seemed to believe that it should be possible to do without political parties and that broadly based movements of democratic opposition would serve the noble goals of democracy even better.[7]

Parties in the post-communist states are still quite weak and unstable. Comparative research conducted in several countries of the region has demonstrated that the main weaknesses are manifold. First, their membership is relatively small, probably as a result of widespread frustration with mass party politics of the communist era. Second, in terms of programs, most parties lack a clear vision of the future, tending to substitute electoral platforms for long-terms programs (Kitschelt et al. 1999). Third, their social base often remains undefined, largely owing to the confused pattern of social cleavages in post-communist states (Lawson, Roemmele, and Karasimeonov 1999). Fourth, post-communist citizens are distrustful of all political parties (Barnes and Janos 1998). Fifth, party politicians cultivate weak commitment to their respective parties, tending to exhibit high propensity to jump ship rather than face their difficulties.[8] Probably because they have not yet

Slovenia; Ion Iliescu, former President of Romania; Aleksander Kwasniewski and Leszek Miller, respectively President (1995–2005) and former Prime Minister of Poland; Grigorij Parvanov, the President of Bulgaria; and Victor Woronov, the President of Moldova, are the best examples of former communist politicians who have been returned to power as a result of democratic elections.

7. In Poland, the Solidarity Union, founded in 1980, operating in the underground after the imposition of the martial law in December 1981, and legalized again in 1989, served as a comprehensive democratic movement during the founding election of June 1989; but in the following year, the Solidarity-based bloc suffered many splits although it has been reunited since then. In former Czechoslovakia, the Citizens Forum (in the Czech Republic) and The Public Against the Violence (in Slovakia), too, were comprehensive democratic movements in the initial stage of the transition; both subdivided eventually into several parties. In Lithuania, the movement for national independence, *Sujudis*, transformed itself into the Conservative Party and lost its once-unique position as the comprehensive bloc of democratic and proindependence forces. This was also true in other countries where such movements emerged in the early stage of the transition.

8. The case of Poland's Center-Right parties in the 2001 elections illustrates this point extremely well. On the eve of the parliamentary election, the then-ruling Electoral Action Solidarity was subdivided toward the creation of three formations: Citizens' Platform,

completely freed themselves from their past, but also owing to the pattern of socialization they perceive in their leaders, post-communist parties seem to have remained somewhat more impervious to the challenges of the present. And this advantage seems to have helped them exploit successfully the frailties of rivals.

The weakness shown by political parties in almost all of East Central Europe's post-communist states is sometimes explained away as resulting from the relative short period of time during which they have been able to function. It must, however, be remembered that more than ten years have elapsed since East Central Europe's divorce from communism. Political parties have had plenty of time to mature. And if they did not, it is probably because of the very deep and lasting influence of the communist indoctrination, which prevented the citizenries from developing a political culture of democratic dispute and competition. In this, the shadow of the past is a factor of importance that should not be ignored.

Confronting Social Malaise

The post-communist societies of East Central Europe are quite frustrated with the social results of their precipitous transition from the communist system. Whereas only a minority of East Central Europeans would like to see a return to the past, many of them do express their discontent with the economic and social realities of the post-communist era.

Upon surveying post-communist citizens in East Central Europe, Laszlo Bruszt found that most of them did demonstrate much patience in the early days of transformation (Barnes and Janos 1998, 165–194) and that their patience is now long gone, at least in most of the East Central European states. After more than a decade, it is all but

---

Law and Order, and the League of Polish Families. The Union of Freedom, which until May 2000 was the junior partner in the ruling coalition, was weakened by the desertion of dissatisfied politicians who cofounded the Citizens Platform. Consequently, neither the Electoral Action Solidarity nor the Freedom Union passed the threshold required to enter the Parliament. The three new formations won enough votes to enter the Parliament but far too few to form the majority. And during the four years (2001–2005) that the Alliance of Democratic Left was in power, its political position weakened considerably, owing to a losing combination of unfulfilled electoral promises and widespread corruption. The parliamentary elections in September 2005 served to switch the balance once again in favor of the right-wing parties. On Polish democracy, cf. Raciborski and Wiatr (2005).

impossible for the citizenries of the post-communist states to believe that things can or will be any better in the near future. Such social malaise finds its complex roots in the economics of the transition as well as in the psyche of post-communist citizenries.

The economy of each and every post-communist state has faced serious problems. All of them have registered a deep slump in the level of their GNP, mainly owing to the many difficulties they came to face in the rapid restructuring of their economy, but also due to the collapse of the international markets of the former COMECON.[9] The slump was, however, uneven. The economic report presented by a group of Polish economists (Lubinski et al. 1998, 28–39) pointed to the marked differences between the post-communist states. The report revealed that the economic situation was much worse in Russia, in the Commonwealth of Independent States, and in the Baltic republics than in East Central Europe. In 1997, all of these countries had a level of GDP considerably lower than what it had been in 1990, and since then they have not been able to regain their ability to grow, let alone to develop. As of the end of 2000, Russia seems to have been doing better somehow, as a result of the more aggressive economic policy pursued by President Vladimir Putin,[10] although the distance between Russia and Central Europe remains quite significant.

Within East Central Europe, the Polish report emphasizes the differences between the more successful and the less successful groups of countries. The first group includes the Czech Republic, Hungary, Poland, Slovenia, and Slovakia, each of which by 1997 had already registered some growth in their GDP, after several years of decline. In 1997, Poland was the first of the five to register a GDP higher than its level in 1989. The other four countries passed their 1989 levels of GNP in the years after 1997. The second group of post-communist countries, comprising Albania, Bulgaria, Croatia, Estonia, Latvia, Lithuania, and

---

9. COMECON, an economic organization emulating the U.S. Marshall Plan for West Europe, lasted from 1949 to 1991. As the economic complement of its predecessor, the Warsaw Pact, it cross-linked the USSR with its ideological satellites: Bulgaria, Czechoslovakia, Hungary, Poland, Romania, but also with Albania (1949–1961, until its adoption of Maoism), with the German Democratic Republic (1950–1990), Mongolia (1962–1991), Cuba (1972–1991), and also Vietnam (1978–1991). Marshall Tito's Yugoslavia had been an associate member. In 1987, COMECON established official relations with a European Economic Community by then seeking to rename itself European Community. Only a very short time after deciding to adopt a free-market outlook in 1990, it decided to scuttle itself.—*Ed.*

10. For the USSR's transition to 'Russia', see Shlapentokh, chap. 8 in this book.

Romania, suffered an economic slump deeper than the one faced in the first group, and "the process of turning their economies around has been subject to delays and made slow progress." However, since the first appearance of this report, the Baltic republics, especially Estonia, have been making visible progress in improving their economies. The other four countries of the second group remain in a rather precarious economic situation. The analysis did not include the Balkan states,— Bosnia-Herzegovina, Macedonia, and Yugoslavia—whose disastrous economic situation was caused by prolonged wars on the territories of the former Yugoslav Federation.

The economic and social transformations in the post-communist states have created widespread frustration for three main reasons. First, because of the intense and well-deserved criticism of the communist command economy, the population of East Central Europe expected rapid improvement in its living conditions, promptly after the replacement of the communist system by market economics. Yet in some countries such expectations were magnified by overly optimistic prognoses offered by the economic reformers at a very early stage of the transformation. In Poland, for instance, the chief reformer of the economy, Deputy Prime Minister Leszek Balcerowicz, foresaw the first glimmers of evident improvement to appear by 1990, after just six months of sacrifices. In reality, the improvement began only in 1994. Whether such official optimism was a deliberate ploy, a tactic aimed at building support for reforms, or a genuine human blunder in forecasting is irrelevant here. The significant fact is that such optimistic prognoses led to massive dissatisfaction, once it became clear that the improvement was late in coming and by far less impressive than what had been suggested it would be.

The second reason for popular dissatisfaction is unemployment. The citizens of communist countries were used to various forms of deprivations such as low wages and shortages of even low-quality goods on the marketplace. One thing they were unused to was unemployment. For almost fifty years finding a job was the easiest thing. All surveys suggest now that it is the lack of job security that is perceived to be the main negative consequence of the economic transformation.

The third source of frustration is the rapidly growing social inequality. Differences in income in the East and Central European post-communist states are greater than in Western Europe, although not as great as in Russia and in the other Commonwealth of Independent States (CIS) countries. There is a class of new poor—those who cannot satisfy even their elementary needs and have to exist in poverty. When this abject human penury takes place alongside conspicuous consumption by the new bourgeois, it creates the feeling of injustice, leading to the belief that the state has been stolen from ordinary people by the privileged elite.

The social malaise is the strongest in those countries where expectations were the highest. Poland's overall economic record for last twelve years is reasonably good, a temporary deterioration during 1999–2001 notwithstanding. But Poles show their frustration with their economic and social condition at least as strongly as the citizens of those post-communist countries the economic prowess of which leaves much more to demand. The psychology of frustration is easy to understand. It reflects the subjective distance that is created between wishful expectations and factual reality, more than the traits actually deployed by a socioeconomic situation as such.

Such social malaise has political repercussions. Frustrated citizens withdraw from politics and withhold their participation. Many of them do not even vote—not because they have lost interest in politics but because they do not believe that voting can change anything in their life. In most of the Polish electoral campaigns after 1989, less than 50 percent of potential voters cared to cast a ballot. Many of those who do vote demonstrate their frustration by voting against the party in power, even if this now means voting for the very people they voted in the last election. And yet others switch to the radical populist parties, either to show their disappointment with the old established parties or because they genuinely believe in the miracle solutions offered by the radicals.

From the very beginnings of the post-communist transformation, it has been recognized that social malaise can raise questions that may place the very survival of new democracies under interrogation. In 1991, Adam Przeworski compared the changes in Eastern Europe and in Latin America, sadly to conclude that "the East has become the South" (1991, 191). In his analysis of the Polish case, he stressed the importance of reducing unemployment—the single most dangerous consequence of economic reforms—and warned that "the technocratic policy style inevitably leads to a moment when the political choice becomes one of beating a retreat or risking a political explosion" (Przeworski 1993, 183). In the mid-1990s, I wrote about the danger of intensifying social conflicts and unleashing serious political consequences for new democracies in post-communist states, going on to propose four responses to the growing social tensions: revising the strategy of transformation in the direction of a more equitable distribution of its social burdens; introducing a policy of "social accord"; including left-wing parties into the process of governing; recognizing the existence of social conflicts and strengthening the political mechanism of compromise-building (Wiatr 1995).[11]

The fact that social malaise has not led to political upheaval can be explained in terms of the corrective mechanism that exists in the political systems of the new democracies. Elections now give people their chance to say "no" in an orderly and peaceful way. The fact that a social-democratic left now does exist and even plays an important role in most of the European post-communist states is of critical importance in this respect. The governments of the left introduce policies intended to reduce the burdens of reforms for the poorer strata. The assurance that they now have an alternative reduces voters' propensity to resort to violent means of protest. But there is no guarantee that the social peace will last forever. The years nearest/next to the present are crucial. Several East Central European post-communist states have joined the European Union in 2004, and others are in the process of negotiations, which should lead to their admission in the next few years. The enlargement of the European Union is surely in the long-term interest of the post-communist European states, but the process of further enlargement, with its inevitable costs for all, tends to increase social tensions not least also in some of the post-communist states themselves.[12] The leaders of these face the ingrate task of building an acceptable compromise in their long negotiations with Brussels, while at the same time securing steady domestic public support for the coveted enlargement on the one hand and for the Constitutional Treaty on the other, increasingly skeptical populations notwithstanding. Resolving this problem will determine the future of East Central Europe for generations to

---

11. In 1988, Guillermo O'Donnell, then-president of the International Political Science Association, invited Adam Przeworski and me to convene a group of comparativists from Europe, Asia, and Latin America to conduct a comparative analysis of reforms of democratization and marketization. The rapid change in formerly communist states offered us an interesting possibility to compare them with countries of the South (Mediterranean Europe and Latin America) and the East (Asia). In the final report, the group expressed its critical assessment of reforms that, by ignoring the social aspects of economic change, potentially also endangered the stability of new democracies (Przeworski et al. 1995).

12. See Heinemann-Grüder, chap. 6 in this book, for the view from the vantage point of the European Union.

come. It is therefore of the greatest importance that democratizations and economic reforms are seen realistically as the most complex but vitally important changes these societies have been confronting in their recent history.

References

Barnes, Samuel H., and Simon Janos (1998) *The Postcommunist Citizen*, Budapest: Erasmus Foundation for Democracy and Institute for Political Science of the Hungarian Academy of Sciences.

Bartkowski, Jerzy (1993) "Public Opinion and 'Decommunization' in Poland, in Jerzy J. Wiatr, Editor, *The Politics of Democratic Transformation: Poland After 1989*, pp. 80–107, Warsaw: Scholar Agency.

Kitschelt Herbert, Zdenka Mansfeldova, Radoslav Markowski, and Toka Gabor (1999) *Post-Communist Party Systems: Competition, Representation, and Inner-Party Cooperation*, Cambridge, UK: Cambridge University Press.

Lawson, Kay, Andrea Roemmele, and Georgi Karasimeonov, Editors (1999) *Cleavages, Parties, and Voters: Studies from Bulgaria, the Czech Republic, Hungary, Poland, and Romania*, Westport, MD and London: Praeger.

Linz, Juan J., and Alfred Stepan (1996) *Problems of Democratic Transition and Consolidation: Southern Europe, South America, and Postcommunist Europe*, Baltimore, MD, and London: Johns Hopkins University Press.

Lubinski, Marek, et al. (1998) *Poland: International Economic Report, 1997/1998*, Warsaw: Warsaw School of Economics.

Pelinka, Anton (1999) *Politics of the Lesser Evil: Leadership, Democracy and Jaruzelski's Poland*, New Brunswick, NJ, and London: Transaction Publishers.

Piano, Aili, and Arch Puddington (2001) "Gains Offset Losses," *Journal of Democracy*, 12(1):87–92.

Przeworski, Adam (1991) *Democracy and the Market: Political and Economic Reforms in Eastern Europe and Latin America*, Cambridge, UK: Cambridge University Press.

——— (1993) "Economic Reforms, Public Opinion, and Political Institutions: Poland in the Eastern European Perspective," in Carlos Luiz, Bresser Pereira, Jose Maria Maravall, and Adam Przeworski, Editors, *Economic Reforms in New Democracies: A Social-Democratic Approach*, pp. 132–198, Cambridge, UK: Cambridge University Press.

Przeworski, Adam, et al. (1995) *Sustainable Democracy*, Cambridge, UK: Cambridge University Press.

Raciborski, Jacek, and Jerzy J. Wiatr (2005) *Demokratie in Polen: Elemente des politischen Systems*, Opladen: Verlag Barbara Budrich.

Rose, Richard (2001) "A Diverging Europe," *Journal of Democracy*, 12(1):93–106.

Rosenberg, Tina (1995) *The Haunted Land: Facing Europe's Ghosts after Communism*, New York: Random House.

Shoup, Paul (1971) "Comparing Communist Nations: Prospects for an Empirical Approach," in Roger Kanet et al., Editors, *The Behavioral Revolution and Communist Studies*, pp. 15–47, New York: Free Press.

Triska, Jan (1970) "Some Reflections in Conclusion," in R. Barry Farrell, Editor, *Political Leadership in Eastern Europe and the Soviet Union*, pp. 337–348, Chicago: Aldine.

Wiatr, Jerzy J. (1995) "Social Conflicts and Democratic Stability: Poland in Comparative Perspective," in Jahn Egbert and Rudolf Wildenmann, Editors, *Stability in East Central Europe?* pp. 124–140, Baden-Baden: Nomos Verlagsgesellschaft.

—— (1996) "Constitutional Accountability in Poland after 1989," *East European Constitutional Review*, 5(1):42–45.

Wiatr, Jerzy J., and Adam Przeworski (1996) "Control without Opposition," *Government and Opposition*, 13(1):227–239.

8 Russian Civil Society: Elite Versus Mass Attitudes to the Democratization of Russia

Vladimir Shlapentokh

Twenty years after the collapse of the Soviet Empire and only just into the first decade of the twenty-first century, political processes in Russia remain important to the world, because Russia has immense oil and gas resources as well as a vast arsenal of nuclear weapons. The West's foreign policy thus continues to depend on assumptions and predictions over the present and future state of Russia's political system. A *Washington Post* editorial argued that "the preservation of democracy in Russia is more than an ideal; it is a crucial U.S. interest" (Editorial 2003).

U.S. concern over Russian democracy in the 1990s looked much like the attention Soviet leaders paid to the Marxist revolution in the aftermath of World War I, with one difference: Washington hoped that a democratic Russia now would be a reliable ally in helping to make the world safe and stable; Moscow, on the other hand, had hoped that a revolutionary Germany would make a great Soviet ally and assist it in destabilizing the world through global war and world revolution.

Moscow and Washington, each in its own time, saw their hopes shattered. The crushing of the Hamburg insurrection in Germany in 1923 meant that the Kremlin should forget its geopolitical visions of a Marxist Germany as one more Soviet nation. And by 2004–2005, the White House had to revise its expectation of Russia's becoming a new member of the world democratic community. The causes of the failure of the German revolution have been studied by many. In this chapter, I would like to make a modest contribution to a new area of research by examining why Russian democracy has failed and which of the political actors assume primary responsibility. To that end, I target two agents of change: the masses and the elites in Russia.

Soviet Russia and America as Self-Appointed Beacons for the World

The focal role reserved for Russian democracy in contemporary American minds, particularly in the U.S. ruling elite's perceptions of the world, should be linked directly to the fact that in the twentieth century the United States and Russia each positioned itself as the standard bearer of ideals for all mankind. Note that both the American and the Russian intellectual classes had made much of a special calling—evoking an exceptionalism said to propel their country, even well before the twentieth century.[1] After World War I, Soviet Russia became much more aggressive than the United States in disseminating its universal ideals for mankind.[2] But after World War II, with its life-and-death confrontation with the USSR still fresh in its mind, the United States had to boost its ideological activity in the struggle for influence in the world, using an array of means for intensifying the propagation of the ideals of liberal capitalism against Marxist ideology (Brzezinski 1989; Gaddis 2005).

Belief in the universalism of the American model grew inside the United States after victory in the Cold War (McFaul 2005). But as war against international terrorism and Islamic fundamentalism evolved, views of the United States as savior of the world, or as "benevolent empire" (Kagan 1998), were confined mainly to Washington, DC (Kolodziej and Kanet 2007; Nye 2002; Ferguson 2004; Fukuyama 2006; Krauthammer 2004; Lieven 2004; Mandelbaum 2002, 2005). Publications about the missionary role of the United States as world champion of democracy began to appear during this last decade, impacted by neoconservative ideology (Chua 2003; Steyn 2006; Sharansky and Dermer 2006; Hobsbawm 2005). But it was Fukuyama's article "The End of History" (1989) and then his book *The End of History and the Last Man* (1992) that opened the way for triumphalist publications (Sen 1999).

In most of the publications celebrating the U.S. victory in the Cold War, Russia took an honorable place as the most important object of liberal transformation along the American model. The end result of

---

1. For more on American exceptionalism and the missionary role of America, see Ignatieff (2005) and Madsen (1998).

2. Even after the fall of the Soviet Union, the torrent of books on the role of the USSR in spreading socialist ideas and fomenting world revolution did not subside (Shlapentokh 2001a; James and Robert 1986; Reissner 1974).

liberal reforms in Russia after the fall of the USSR was of utmost importance in debates about the future of democracy in the world and the validity of keeping faith in its victory. The belief that Russian democracy was being built on American standards was dominant in Russia in the 1990s among liberals, if particularly also among their foes: communists and nationalists (Ivanov 1998).

The Triumph of Structuralists[3] in Post-Soviet Russia in the 1990s

Insiders' Belief in the Victory of Democracy and in Civil Society

In the 1990s, Russia was a state whose move toward democracy was beyond doubt. The comfort derived from the irreversible demise of the centralized planning system was great; the confidence gained from the privatization of state property, even greater. The future of democracy, the chances for Russia's return to an authoritarian (or even totalitarian) order remained hotly debated by scholars and by ordinary people; but only a minute minority of leftist radicals could imagine the abolishment of private property in the country.

In the early 1990s, the Russian people witnessed the birth of democratic institutions that could only have been dreamt of during Soviet times: an elected head of state, an independent parliament, real political parties, an autonomous judicial system, the Office of Prosecutor General, freedom of speech, a free media, the right of free movement inside and outside the country, private property ownership, and unbridled freedom in economic enterprise.

As of the 1990s, Russians could clearly distinguish between "electoral democracy" and liberalism, focusing on various freedoms (political, economic, and religious). They enjoyed their newfound freedoms more than their automatic rights to take part in the governance of their country. Not surprisingly, when Yeltsin died, the Russians who paid tribute described him as a champion, not of democracy, but of freedom.[4]

---

3. Of the two schools of thought, each of which claims to explain the human mind and human behavior, the structuralists (who usually are also universalists) focus on present social, economic, and political structures, whereas culturologists focus on traditional patterns of behavior and on ways of thinking inherited from the past. Universalists hold the belief that all societies tend to have the same structures.

4. "Yeltsin led Russia from unfreedom to freedom" (Chubais 2007).

Outsiders' Views on the Victory of Democracy and in Civil Society

In the 1990s, Western scholars hailed Russia's political progress almost unconditionally. In 1995, it was even argued that "the problems Russia faces in the transition to democracy are not sui generis," that "Russia may . . . indeed be considered a democracy" (Loewenhardt 1995). Enthusiasm over democratic progress continued even in 1999, a year before Putin's appearance, when it was stated that "relative to the élite, the ordinary people in Russia and Ukraine exhibited more coherence of (democratic) beliefs than is usually found in Western democracies" and that "a substantial majority of the élite and the masses prefer democratic to authoritarian values" (Miller, Hesli, and Reisinger 1994, 187). Moderate optimism for Russia's democracy was shown by many authors in the late 1990s, even as political developments began to look less promising than they had been much earlier in that decade.[5]

It was typical during this period (just as Alexander Dalin had done in 1993)[6] to mock views that Russia's long-held traditions were a powerful factor capable of determining the fate of Russian democracy in the decades to come. Also in 1994, William Riesinger (1994, 274), not without sarcasm, announced that the debate about the role of Russian political culture "is faring poorly," that this subject no longer retained much interest. Political scientists such as Harry Eckstein (1988, 801) who, as democratic triumphalism began to accelerate, cautioned that contextual factors could not overcome long-term cultural patterns were looked down upon. Nevertheless, Robert Brym (1996), Graeme Gill and Roger Markwick (2000) in the West, and Lev Gudkov (2000) among the Russian scholars, remained exceptionally stubborn supporters of the view that Russian cultural traditions would be playing a very important role in the country's political developments (Dubin 2006).

Vladimir Putin's Counter-Democratic Perestroika

The structuralists celebrated the victory of Russian democracy throughout the decade, paying little attention to the authoritarian tendencies that began to grow in 1992–1993. By 2005–2007, Russian society could be seen as mostly authoritarian. President Putin had concentrated more

---

5. For democratic processes in post-Soviet Russia, see Finifter and Mickiewicz (1992); Gibson, Duch, and Tedin (1992); Miller, Hesli, and Reisinger (1994); and McFaul (1999).
6. For a typical argument against the pessimists on Russian democracy see Dalin (1993, 132).

power than could any of the Soviet leaders since 1953. In three years, he eliminated all traces of any division of powers. He turned the Duma (parliament) into a puppet institution, not unlike the Soviet Supreme Council now of the past. The judicial system became as compliant to Putin as it had been servile to the Soviet masters of the Kremlin. Putin turned the election process into a sham that could guarantee voting outcomes at all levels. He eliminated voting procedures for individual candidates in national and local parliamentary elections. Now people had to choose between the lists of candidates offered by the parties that received access to the election. Thus, in many cases, opposition parties could not participate in the local elections.

Putin banned the popular election of governors, depriving the people of influencing local executive power. He also abolished the rule that invalidated election results should a minimal number of registered voters not vote. This action guaranteed the success of any election, notwithstanding the level of voter disinterest. Putin wiped from the ballot the 'against everybody' option that had been the only means for dissenters to voice their protest of pro-Kremlin parties (Borodin 2007). In March 2007, both independent analysts and opposition parties almost unanimously denounced as dishonest the local elections held in thirteen regions (Rudneva and Lebedeva 2007).

A special target of Putin's offensive was the nascent civil society. Putin significantly reduced freedom of the media.[7] In 2006, fearing a 'color revolution' of the kind that brought regime change in the Ukraine and Georgia, Putin launched a direct offensive against non-governmental organizations (NGOs) by asserting that many of these organizations acted as fronts for the West, trying to undermine Russia's political stability even as they claimed to promote democracy (Politov 2006). In March–April 2007, demonstrators and protestors in Moscow, St. Petersburg, and Nizhnii Novgorod were brutally attacked by the police. These demonstrators had wanted only to express disapproval of official crackdowns on Russian democracy (Chelysheva 2007; Zudin 2007; Veretennikova 2007).

To assess realistically the relative merits of day-to-day political practices in Russia under Putin today, suffice it to note that on Freedom House's scale for "non-free" countries in 2007 (where 1 = best and 7 = worst), Russia received a 6 in a group of countries that included Algeria, Angola, Azerbaijan, Cambodia, Egypt, Iran, Kazakhstan, and

---

7. See Kramer (2007) on the extinction of free media in Russia.

Pakistan, and where conditions were reported to be somewhat worse only in Uzbekistan, Turkmenistan, Syria, Saudi Arabia, and North Korea.

The case of Khodorkovsky, the owner of an oil company called Yukos, who challenged the political regime, was characteristic in this respect (Shlapentokh 2004). In 2006, this man was arrested and sentenced to eight years in prison. The Russian business community and its organizations did not utter a single word in Khodorkovsky's defense. During their meetings with Putin in 2005–2007, none dared to make even an indirect remark in favor of their jailed colleague.

Today, only Putin (in his presidential address to the Duma in April 2007) and his propagandists can describe the political system as a "democracy" based on honest elections. In order to reject any comparison of Russian political reality with those in the West, one of Putin's leading ideologues and a major advocate of Russian-style democracy, Vladislav Surkov invented the term *sovereign democracy* in June 2006 to distinguish the specificity of Russian democracy (Latukhina, Kushin, and Rudneva 2006; Tsipko 2006). Surkov's terminology was adopted by the ruling "The Unity of Russia" (Edïnstvo Rossii) Party as its ideological platform (Samarina and Varshavchik 2006). Pro-Kremlin politicians and experts such as Andronik Migranian, Kirill Privalov, and Gleb Pavlovsky saw in *sovereign democracy* a newly accomplished feat (Tumanov 2006; Migranian 2006; Privalov 2006; Zabrodina 2006). Other pro-Kremlin experts (Markov 2006) more humbly suggested that Russia was still in the process of building that mode. Despite official propaganda, in early 2007, only 30 percent of Russians perceived their country to be democratic (Levada-Tsentr, *Bulletin*, February 15, 2007).

Most analysts inside Russia mocked the official propaganda and the term *sovereign democracy*, dismissing it as a ludicrous intent to flatter the authoritarian regime in the country.[8] Even Dmitry Medvedev, a leading Putin aide, scoffed; he remarked that democracy either exists or it does not, and that such adjectives are redundant.[9]

---

8. For the famed liberal Boris Nemtsov's scolding of this term in his article "'Kakoi khotiat videt' Rossiiu grazhdane strany?" [What kind of country do Russian citizens want Russia to be?] (seen March 7, 2007; online source: http://www.nemtsov .ru/?id=705026&PHPSESSID.=2fe50d058921deff2f24ea06b8e6ed2b).

9. See Gromov (2006); also Dmitrii Medvedev's interview (online source: http://www .newsway.ru/interviews/10/15/010307/13994.html).

Public Attitudes toward Democracy and Liberalism in the 2000s

While power holders' assault on democracy in Russia was by itself a development heinous enough, the Russian masses' support of this offensive was particularly painful for the structuralists as also for those who had begun to believe that Russia was joining the community of democratic nations.

It is not easy to assess Russian attitudes toward democracy, because of the various interpretations of this term by ordinary people.[10] On issues related to democracy, Russian polling firms are often at odds with each other.[11] Despite all these caveats, Putin's policy of dismantling democracy seems to have been supported by the majority of the population.

In a survey conducted by the Levada-Tsentr in February 2007, only 25 percent of the respondents saw in "democracy" a "just system." One-third preferred Soviet rule to democracy (Levada-Tsentr, *Bulletin*, February 15, 2007). Demanding from the state the promulgation of various social values, only 5 percent suggested the necessity to propagate democratic values in 2003.[12] Most Russians (70 percent according to a Romir survey in 2003) rejected the Western model of society and

---

10. The analysis of data on Russian attitudes toward democracy is complicated by the lack of a common interpretation of the term *democracy*, which is a common problem in any society and even in the United States. According to pollsters from the public opinion firm Levada-Tsentr, in 2007, two thirds of Russians "have big problems with the definition of democracy" (Levada-Tsentr, *Bulletin*, February 15, 2007). The Fund of Public Opinion (FOM) found that more than 20 percent of Russians answering an open question about the concept of democracy pointed primarily to the participation of people in the governance of society. Eighty percent of the respondents linked this concept to freedoms, the observation of law, discipline, and social equality. Other data also suggested that Russians were confused by the concept of democracy. In 2005, trying to answer the question, "In Russia, is there too much or too little democracy?" 21 percent thought that "there is too much democracy," 34 percent "too little," 17 percent "exactly what we need," and 28 percent abstained from answering (FOM, *Bulletin*, March 31, 2005). The answers to abstract questions about such things as democracy or freedom are extremely sensitive to the formulation of the questions, to the alternatives offered, to their order of presentation, and also to several other factors. For more about the differences in human reactions to abstract and concrete questions about democracy and freedoms, see Shlapentokh (2001a).
11. In 2006, according to the *Eurasian Barometer*, 50 percent of Russians voted for democracy and 35 percent voted against it [*Evraziiskii Monitor*, Volna IV–otchet (Eurasian Monitor, Wave IV report)]. Only 25 percent of Russians supported democracy, according to Levada-Tsentr data from a practically identical time period (Levada-Tsentr, *Bulletin*, February 2, 2007).
12. Romir http://romir.ru/news/analitika/russian_ch (accessed March 11, 2007).

insisted on "the special road of Russian development." Merely 11 percent voted for a Western-type political order.[13]

Observing the negative or contemptuous popular stances toward democratic institutions, the structuralists consoled themselves by considering the Russians' appreciation for individual freedoms and human rights, as previously discussed. Surveys conducted by various public opinion firms over the last ten years converge on the shared conclusion that most Russians (60–80 percent) highly appreciate individual freedoms such as the right to move around, inside and outside, the country; the right to make choices in their economic activities; the right to own houses and land; and the right to exchange currency freely.[14]

The Counteroffensive of Culturologists in the 2000s

The real developments in Russia since 2000 radically changed the polemics between structuralists and culturologists. The later began an offensive, even as the former took a defensive stance.[15] As evidence for the "authoritarian" trend in Russia began to multiply, many scholars and politicians in search of explanations turned to the "cultural factor." Nikolai Petrov and Darrell Slider (2003, 35) viewed Putin's Russia to be a traditionally authoritarian society, if conceding that it did have some liberal elements. Others deemed the country to be authoritarian and used several surrogate terms such as *Caesar's democratic rule* or *directed democracy*, pointing to that country's antidemocratic traditions as the principal cause of failure for the liberal experiment in Russia.[16] Among this group, Stephen Hedlund (1999) gravitated toward the view that, with the failure of the economic reforms and the emergence of "predatory capitalism," Russia would return to old-style, autocratic rule.

As of 2000, several Russian scholars abandoned the optimists' camp, starting to grasp the crucial role that political traditions and people as bearers of the authoritarian mentality could assume. Among these were political scientist Liliia Shevtsova (2005, 2001), sociologist Yurii Levada (2000a), philosopher L. Poliakov (2000, 173), historians

---

13. Romir http://romir.ru/news/analitika/russian_ch (accessed March 11, 2007).
14. See Fund of Public Opinion, *Bulletin*, No. 399, 1998; Fund of Public Opinion, *Bulletin*, August 28, 2003, Levada-Tsentr, March 9, 2004; and Gorshkov (2000).
15. Some scholars have maintained their strong beliefs in the ultimate victory of democracy in Russia in the years to come (Mendelson 2001).
16. For details, see Ekho Moskvy, "Osoboie mnenie," June 28, 2006.

V. Shelokhaev (2000, 10), V. V. Zhuravlev (2000, 92), V. N. Dakhin (2000, 101), H. G. Sherbinin (2000, 209), and Victor Danilov (2000, 6), and a few other experts of Russian history.

Among the Russian authors focusing on the role of culture as the main explanatory factor for Russia's rejection of democracy were those who insisted on Russia's being a "unique civilization." This group comprised people with varying political views, ranging from pro-Western intellectuals (e.g., Andrei Konchalovsky [2006] and Alexander Akhiezer [1995]) to gradated nationalists (from philosopher V. Fedotova to rabid nationalist Alexander Prokhanov [2007]). Some prominent, but by now politically passive, liberals blamed Russian traditions and popular mentality for the failure of democracy. The journalist Leonid Radzikhovsky, for example, in almost all of his radio talks on Ekho Moskvy, describes prospects for democratization as hopeless, owing to the authoritarian mind of the Russian people. He mocked the participation in the protest march of April 15, 2007, in Moscow, of liberals like Garry Kasparov and Mikhail Kasianov.[17]

Why Does Russia Reject Democracy?

The dominant view among scholars, politicians, and journalists (that the roots of Russia's rejection of democracy are in mindsets Russians nurtured all too long in a deeply authoritarian political culture hostile toward democratic institutions) supposes that this "culture" (a homogeneous assortment of values, beliefs, and patterns of behavior), shaped several centuries ago, predetermines behavior, regardless of changes that keep transforming people's environments.

That some traits of culture sustained by existing political, religious, or economic establishments over a long time will transfer from one generation to the next and influence human behavior is a truism. Because Russians lived for centuries in an authoritarian or totalitarian society, they tend to assume that only a strong state can guarantee "order" in human societies. In reality, however, as soon as other centers of power and influence emerge, the ensuing changes in daily life lead to quick shifts in values and in modes of behavior, and these new patterns occupy the core of the dominant culture. A comparison of Russian attitudes toward their political system before and after 1985 provides a powerful argument for the flexibility of culture and its dependence

---

17. See, for instance, his talk on Ekho Moskvy, "Osoboie mnenie," on April 17, 2007.

on developments in social reality. It should be well worth a brief examination at this stage.

The Dominant Political Culture in Russia by 1985

When Gorbachev began his liberal reforms, the Russian masses viewed
the totalitarian order, with its omnipresent Communist Party and powerful state, to be necessary for the functioning of Russian society. They
had been exposed to no alternative political system in remembered
history. They knew from their own experiences and the experiences of
their ancestors that obedience to one's superior was a necessary and
sufficient condition for survival and prosperity. Even dissidents never
went beyond preaching "socialism with a *human* face" and hardly
ever raised their brows (even in the underground literature, the brave
Samizdat) over the domineering stance of the Communist Party or the
privatization of big industry. As I deduced from my own surveys of
the Soviet people in the 1960s and 1970s, the Russian masses never
went beyond critiquing the local bureaucrats. In my estimates, based
on studies of the adult population in the country, 80 to 90 percent duti-
fully accepted the existing order as the only alternative to chaos. Their
support for the country's foreign policy commanded a 90 to 95 percent
approval (Shlapentokh 1969, 1986, 2001b).

Russia, with its supposedly strong political traditions, does provide
us with data supporting the hypothesis of the flexibility of culture and
the capacity of "reality" to overcome the rigidities created by cultural
traditions. The developments in Russia during Perestroika provide a
perfect example.

The Dominant Tendency toward Democracy (1988–1991)

In a very short period of time (1988–1991), under the impact of a new
course in Soviet leadership, democratic views began to develop quickly
in Russia, despite the total absence of democratic experience in the
country. Gorbachev needed to get several things done in order to
prompt upper-crust Russian intellectuals to believe in the reality of
Glasnost (openness) and to launch their assault against the old
ideology.

With the blessing of the Kremlin, the Russians, with great enthusiasm, participated in the first relatively free election of the Congress of
People's Deputies in 1989. In Leningrad, Kiev, and a few other key

republican and regional centers, thirty-seven Party bosses were defeated in the election. In most cases, insult was added to injury because those who were defeated had run unopposed. They could not garner the required 50 percent of the vote to be elected. In 275 districts (almost one-fifth of all districts), the candidates—most of whom had been nominated by the party apparatus—were ousted. In many cities, thousands of people from many walks of life bravely participated in election meetings to challenge KGB agents and party apparatchiks.[18]

The sessions of the elected Congress of People's Deputies (between May 25 and June 9, 1989) watched the first-ever television broadcast of the work of the Soviet parliament. Overnight, ordinary people became instant connoisseurs of democratic procedures and savvy enough to become furious about the comportment of Gorbachev who, in their opinion, blatantly had "violated" these procedures.[19]

The emergence of the first parliament with a democratic face triggered a serious strike by miners in Kuzbass in June 1989. Next, other regions began to impose political demands (Lopatin, Gordon, and Kudelin 1998; Borisov 2001). The gradual expansion of democratic processes emboldened a series of mass demonstrations in support of democratic slogans, with Boris Yeltsin as leader of the democrats.

Official data indicated that between January 1 and February 23, 1990, 6.4 million people participated in similar meetings across the country. Attendance at mass meetings peaked on February 24–25, and then in March when, despite the Kremlin's frenzied opposition, more than one million people traveled to join meetings and demonstrations. In the end, the Kremlin could only watch these popular movements—waves that the daily *Pravda* characterized as not only "dangerous and destructive" but "destabilizing and explosive."

These meetings were followed by the brilliant success of the democratic forces in the election of the parliament of the Russian Federation on March 4, 1990. Two famous democrats, Gavriil Popov and Anatolii Sobchak, were elected mayors of Russia's two biggest cities, Moscow and Leningrad. But it was Yeltsin's election to the presidency of the

---

18. One such memorable meeting occurred in Zhitomir, where Alla Yaroshinskaia, an unknown journalist of a local newspaper, ran against Kovtun, the First Secretary of the Congress of People's Deputies, and won the support of ordinary people. Online source: http://www.rightlivelihood.org/recip/alla.htm.

19. When I arrived in Moscow at the time, I was amazed to see how ungrateful the Russians were toward Gorbachev, evidenced by their discontent with his demeanor as chairman of the sessions.

Russian Federation in June 1991 (all attempts by Gorbachev to the contrary notwithstanding) that provided the clear and eloquent evidence of Russians' devotion to democratic ideals.

During this period of democratic euphoria, the people flocked to political parties and movements (although they would come to shun them only a few years later). Thousands of informal organizations pursuing various goals—human rights, democratic freedoms, national autonomy and environmental protection—emerged in 1988, multiplying as of 1989 (Pechenev 1990; Sedaitis and Butterfield 1991; Smith 1991; Tolz 1990; Babosov 1990; McFaul and Petrov 1998; Danilov and Zasorin 1991; No Author 1991).

The democratic media became extremely popular. The liberal program *Vzgliad* (Outlook), airing on the main Soviet TV channel, attracted several million viewers every Friday. The weekly journals *Moskovskie Novosti* (Moscow News) and *Ogoniok* (A Little Fire) beat all records in popularity among the publications of this type. The anti-Stalinist novel *Children of Arbat*, by Anatolii Rybakov (1988), became an unprecedented bestseller in the country. Movies critical of the Soviet system, such as Tengis Abuladze's *Repentance* (1987), drew millions of spectators. Economists like Larisa Piasheva (1989, 1990) became as popular as movie stars, in the period from 1987 to 1991, for their commendation of liberal capitalism.

Sociological data on the developments in 1988–1991 are rather scanty, because free polling did not begin until 1988. The quality of these polls was not impeccable, maybe also because many ordinary people were still afraid to speak openly with pollsters. Among the twelve events mentioned in the survey of the All Union Center of Public Studies (VTSIOM) in 1989, ten had democratic overtones: the lifting of restrictions for subscribing to newspapers and journals, the rehabilitation of Andrei Sakharov, the beginning of political reforms, among others (Levada 1990, 30). Also remarkable was the reaction of respondents in the same survey to the question, "What should be done to change the country for the better?": 66 percent were in favor of peasants being allowed to own private property, 44 percent wanted a drastic increase in local self-government, 33 percent said that private entrepreneurship should be encouraged, and only 29 percent favored forms of stronger order (Levada 1990, 70). In 2007, Alexander Zipko, an ardent nationalist, a fierce enemy of Perestroika, and a foe of the liberals, had to concede that by the early 1990s "even the 'genuine ethnic Russians'. . . followed not 'the patriots' (the adversaries of Western democracy) . . .

but 'democratic Russia' and its pro-Western leaders, such as Gavriil Popov, Elena Bonner, Andrei Sakharov, and Galina Starovoitova" (Tsipko 2007).

The Growth of Anti-Democratic Mass Attitudes after 1992–1993

After 1992, Russia's mood quickly moved from high political activity and support for democratic ideals to political passivity and a negative stance toward liberal, political, and economic reforms. The democratic backslide began. Between 1989 and 1992, the percentage of people partaking in political activities decreased by 4 times (from 13 percent to 3 percent). The number of people who believed that at last they had an opportunity to be politically active declined by 20 times (from 11 percent in 1988 to 0.5 percent in 1992). The number of people who said they were disappointed in politics increased by 1.5 times (from 12 percent to 16 percent), and the number of people who said they are "not interested in politics" grew by almost 2.5 times (from 11 percent to 25 percent). The evolution of attitudes toward Gorbachev, the living symbol of these liberal reforms, was not less indicative. In 1988, 51 percent of Russians had voted him "man of the year" (versus 44 percent in 1989), but that percentage dropped to 16 percent in 1990 and to 1 percent in 1992. The change in attitudes toward Yeltsin, who, for a time, seemed to be a good democratic alternative to Gorbachev, was also characteristic. In 1990, he garnered 44 percent to become "man of the year," like his rival before him, but after the ominous developments in 1993, his rating drastically declined to 17 percent (Levada 2000a).

During the 1990s, Russians uniformly moved from supporting liberal ideas to outright rejecting them. In November 1991, less than half the population (41 percent) thought education should be free; by 1993, 58 percent supported this idea, and in 1996, the figure rose to 74 percent. The corresponding data for medical services were 22 percent, 46 percent, and 60 percent, respectively for 1991, 1993, and 1996 (VTSIOM *Bulletin* No. 3, 1996).

Respect for Stalin, which had been high in Soviet society, declined in the late 1980s but then grew again in the mid 1990s. In 1989, only 12 percent of Russians saw Stalin as an eminent personality of history; by 1999, the percentage had risen to 35 percent. And in 2003, two thirds of Russians, despite the enormous amount of information about the terror in Stalin's time, saw the dictator in a positive light, compared to one third who condemned him (Levada-Tsentr, *Press–vypusk*, March 13,

2003; Dubin 2006, 25). Practically the same levels of positive and negative assessments of Stalin were detected in polling data gathered by another firm, in 2006 (Fund of Public Opinion, *Bulletin*, February 23, 2006).

The fact that there was rapid and radical change in people's views on vital issues of social life refutes the hypothesis that the old political culture dominates the mind of the Russians and their attitudes toward "democracy." The most important factor that triggered change in Russians' attitudes toward democracy was the new material realities of the 1990s.

Why then did Russians turn their back on their fledgling democracy? I reject the assumption that they suddenly came to their senses and returned to their old political culture or to their deep-rooted sympathies for authoritarianism. In my opinion, three major developments during the period of liberal reforms and of praise for democracy in the public ideology account for this shift. And all of them happen to engage the material side of life: (1) the collapse of the standard of living and the growing disorder in Russia, (2) the crude violations of democracy by reformers themselves, and (3) crime and corruption.

Collapse of the Standard of Living, and Disorder, in the 1990s

A major factor accounting for the surge in the antidemocratic mood in Russia was the development of a "present time" mentality: that only events in the post-Communist period count and that events in the eras of Ivan the Terrible or even Stalin do not. The events that account most for the shift in the public mind occurred in the 1990s. The impact of the 1990s influenced the decade that followed and will probably continue to affect people's thinking for the next twenty years. Although the half-life in people's minds of the impressions occasioned by big events remains debatable, not many would contest that such developments as 'collectivization', the 'great purges', and the 'wars' people have had to live through in their generation have continued to condition Russians for decades thereafter.[20]

Americans vividly remembered the Great Depression of the 1930s for at least three more decades. Why would Russians tend to forget the

---

20. In 1995, during a meeting at the American Association of Advanced Slavic Studies in Washington, DC, intensive polemics erupted among Russian sociologists over the role of the historical memory for Russians. Some, like Boris Grushin, insisted that the influence of this memory is close to zero, while Vladimir Shubkin and I upheld the opposite view (Shlapentokh 1997).

developments of the 1990s within a much shorter period of time? Since the end of Perestroika and throughout the 1990s, Russians found themselves pursuing their liberal reforms in a country with a high degree of disorder. Disorder across the country, combined with catastrophic decline in the standard of living, engendered palpable correlations in citizens' minds. By 2000, the Russian standard of living had decreased twofold from its level in 1990. In 1993, the number of Russians who did not receive their salaries on time was never lower than 37 percent; and in 1994, it never fell below 58 percent.[21] In 1992, in addition to delays in payments to workers, the Russian government was unable to pay retiree pensions on time. Millions of retirees rose at dawn to stand in line, hoping to draw their belated meager pensions from the banks. But by the end of 1992, astronomical inflation ate 70 percent of pensioners' purchasing power, according to official data.[22] In 1992, 82 percent of Russians saw their major problems not in political issues but in unemployment and in the pauperization of the population (Levada 2000b). The 1990s also saw an immense increase in corruption and criminality across the country. And according to General Alexander Gurov (2003), chairman of the Duma's committee on security, one out of four Russian adults would fall victim to some form of criminal action in 2001.

In this context, Russians began returning to their old belief: that in Russian society only an authoritarian ruler can maintain country-wide order and guarantee satisfactory supply of basic needs for the majority of the people. Russians witnessed the strengthening of the police force and the increasing recourse to outmoded authoritarian methods in the fight against street crimes and corrupt petty state bureaucrats, and they concluded that these were the only remedies left for solving their daily problems. Although the question "What is more important, order or democracy?" is awkward, and hard to answer, it has had its uses in exploring Russian reactions: In the 1990s, 80 percent of the Russians approached with the question chose "order" first.

In the early 2000s, from among the ten most popular values in a list of twenty-four (from which respondents could choose no more than five), four of the chosen values related directly to order: security (43 percent), human rights (34 percent), law (31 percent), stability (25

---

21. See VTSIOM, 1995, No. 1, *Ekonomicheskie i Soitsial'nyiie Peremeny* [Economic and social changes], p. 28.
22. See Rossiiskaia Federatsiia v 1992 godu [Russian Federation in 1992]. Moscow: Respublikanskii Informatsionno-izdatel'skii Tsentr [Republican Information Publishing Center], 1993, p. 156.

percent), and order (21 percent). In contrast, the values of family garnered 46 percent and wealth 37 percent (Petrova 2003). People's benign
attitudes toward the security police and FSB[23] (in 2003, 64 percent
wanted to strengthen it) were further evidence of Russia's concern with
order (Zorkaia 2003, 42).

Social order is a universal value that is highly respected in all societies (Inglehart 2002). The choice between democracy and order is not a
test for Russia only. Many authors in the West recognize that order and
democracy are often in conflict and that people in many societies prefer
the first value over the second, should they have to choose between
them (Stiglitz 2002). It is suggested that democracy can emerge only
when law and order obtain. In 2007, David Brooks argued that the idea
that "security leads to freedom" was the dominant paradigm for our
time and that only people "with a secure base" can build up a "better
life" (Brooks 2007). Examples abound.

It is surprising that so many researchers have overlooked the material developments and the disorder of the 1990s in their quests to
explain the failure of Russian democracy. In his research, Neil Munro
(2006), a British scholar, investigated the roots of "nostalgia for the
past" in contemporary Russia. Although he came up with a number of
hypotheses (values of the old culture, dissatisfaction with the political
activity of the regime, dissatisfaction with the economic activity of the
regime, lack of knowledge), he did not analyze the objective data about
the evolution of the standard of living in the 1990s, even though "size
of city" did figure in his correlation analysis.

Crude Violations of Democracy by Reformers in the 1990s

In the 1990s, Russians not only experienced the collapse of the standard of living in a chaotic society but also saw how the liberals tram-
pled on the very democratic principles they had celebrated. Whatever
the valid reasons for the Kremlin's fatal decision to shell the parliament in October 1993, it signaled firm retreat from the giddy days of
nascent Russian democracy. Since the bloody showdown with the
parliament, Yeltsin's regime inexorably moved away from democratic
principles, while still profiting from the full direct and indirect support
of Gaidar and his friends. And the fraudulent referendum on the constitution, endorsed in December 1993, provided the Russian president

---

23. Like its predecessor, the Soviet KGB, the FSB is Russia's federal security agency.

with powers similar to those of a monarch. The two presidential elections after 1991 (in 1996 and 2000) were deeply flawed. Since 1996, the regional elections were also in most cases dishonest and unfair. The elections for the Moscow Duma, the election of the heads of the republics in places such as Bashkortostan, Kabardino-Balkaria, and Mordovia, the ballot count for governors of the Orel and of other regions all guaranteed "landslide" triumphs for the incumbents whose Soviet-style majority wins naturally boasted some 90 percent of all votes counted (Petrov 2000).

Not surprisingly, Russians mistrust Russia's new democratic institutions. According to the Levada-Tsentr, in 2005, three "pure" democratic institutions (the lower chamber of the parliament, the upper chamber, and the political parties) earned the trust of a mere 5 to 10 percent of the Russians. Among the seventy-nine countries included in the *World Values Survey* in 1999–2001, Russia was ranked sixty-ninth as to the popular trust that its parliament generates (Inglehart 2002).

Crimes by, and Corruption of, the Leaders of Democratization

The third major cause of the rejection of democracy by Russians is their deep disillusionment with the leaders of Russian "democracy." They angrily condemned those who ideated and applied the liberal reforms and ruled the country for a full first decade. Various polls have converged on the finding that leaders such as Yeltsin, Gaidar, and Chubais, who publicly presented themselves as democrats, are responsible for the gloomy developments. And I am inclined to agree with the Russian people, not out of principle (*vox populi vox dei*) but because various data support this verdict.

The Russian reformers and champions of democracy not only brought misery to the Russian people but also illegally enriched themselves in the process. The ordinary Russian was furious about the huge wealth amassed by the "oligarchs" who made their gigantic fortunes overnight with the help of Yeltsin and liberal reformers.

However, liberal officials were not the only ones who enjoyed a luxurious life and large bank accounts in foreign countries. The armada of servants on TV and other media also enriched themselves enormously, defending democracy and flying to London on weekends to play a game of tennis, as did Evgenii Kisilev, a leading journalist working for Gusinsky's TV station. The arrogance of the new elites, who encouraged TV shows about their conspicuous consumption, could turn even the most dedicated democrat into an enemy of democracy in this country with poor folk yet huge oil and natural gas reserves.

None of the liberals in power criticized Yeltsin's political actions. None of them were critical of the fraudulent referendum on the constitution in 1993, the election campaigns in the parliament in 1995 and particularly in 1999, or the presidential elections in 1996 and 2000. Resignation as a form of protest against policies or in response to personal humiliation was very rare in Yeltsin's time and even later. One Moscow journalist compared Russian liberals in the 1990s to "small dogs who forget the insults of their masters and return to them jumping with joy as soon as they are called back" (Kalinina 1999). Moreover, all leading liberals did actively participate in Yeltsin's political machinations.[24] Even now, many years later, none of the liberals or oligarchs of the 1990s who tried to cancel[25] the presidential election of 1996 are inclined to maybe recant their involvement in the de-democratization of Russia. Rather, they position themselves as the victims of this process (Gaidar 1999).

The Russian public had an accurate image of the political and economic elite of the 1990s. In April 1999, 45 percent of Russians polled believed that "real power" belongs to "big business and oligarchs," 23 percent placed it in the hands of the president and the government, 8 percent dared say Mafia, and 4 percent pointed at the State Duma (Milekhin and Popov 2000, 27). Most people see those who rule Russia as dishonest and corrupt. The Russians ascribe the fortunes made in the country to "dishonesty" (76 percent), "connections" (88 percent), and only partially to "hard work" (39 percent) (VTSIOM, *Bulletin*, No. 2, 1997). The Russian public greeted the prosecutions of Russian officials and oligarchs in the West.[26] In fact, during the 1990s and 2000s, they did not have any positive role models for their youth—

---

24. Anatolii Chubais, a leading liberal during Yeltsin's presidential election campaign, was linked to a scandal over several large photocopy paper cartons filled with $500,000, which were illegally used in the election campaign.

25. See the famous letter of thirteen oligarchs in June 1996 who tried to persuade Yeltsin to drop the presidential election in Butrin (2006).

26. A survey by the Fund of Public Opinion found that 59 percent of Russians supported the arrest of Pavel Borodin by the American authorities; among people with higher educations, two-thirds supported it. Only 10 percent of the respondents used Borodin's arrest as an occasion to voice their negative feelings toward the West; yet less than 2 percent denounced America (Fund of Public Opinion, *Internet Bulletin*, January 27 and February 1, 2001).

a stark contrast to the 1960s, when the Soviet people honored several dozen honest and brave intellectuals, as old surveys report (Shlapentokh 1969).

However, even if ordinary Russians were highly disappointed with Russia's democratic institutions and liberal reforms, they were not—and cannot be held—accountable for the dismantling of democracy in Russia.

Russia's Ruling Elite as the Motor of Antidemocratic Tendencies

In my opinion, it was the Russian ruling elites under both the Yeltsin and Putin regimes that intentionally sacrificed democracy. Along with Dmitry Travin, I remain strongly against opposing the two regimes, Yeltsin's and Putin's. They were both deeply inimical toward democracy (Travin 2006). The question is, why? Perhaps one may suggest that the elites fell victim to the old political culture and chose to behave accordingly. I would not think so. The ruling elites define the political processes in a society. Elite decisions about the political course to be adopted are usually made with only minimal consideration for the stances of the masses or that of the dominant political culture.

Of course, I would not deny that the masses are important and that the elites are aware of them. Like other elite groups elsewhere, Russian elites have always tried to pull the masses to their side, particularly when these elites were in a struggle for power or when the country was in danger from foreign enemies. For instance, during World War II, Stalin ordered the abandonment of socialist phraseology, including the slogan "Proletarians of all countries unite" in the media, and made Russian nationalism, which was thought to be more appealing to the masses, the crux of the official propaganda.

During Perestroika, Gorbachev appealed to the people's hatred of local bureaucracy and even tried to direct their anger against the provincial party apparatchiks. He instigated the masses against bureaucracy during the election process of the Congress of People's Deputies in 1989, when dozens of party secretaries fell victim to the Kremlin's propaganda.

Yeltsin, when he started his new political career in 1987–1988, chose his own target inside the Russian psyche—the astute idea of egalitarianism—and he began to pose, ironically, as an adversary of all privileges. Yeltsin did not miss the opportunity to play with Russian nationalistic feelings, either. In 1990–1991, he described the country as an oppressed nation caught inside the USSR and went on to demand its sovereignty.

What was the impact of the dominant political culture on the ruling elite? There is no doubt that remarkable influence did occur during the period of socialization when the media was controlled by the same elite. In some cases, members of the elite became victims of their own propaganda and particularly of its language (Bukovsky 1995, 616).

However, the influence of the old political culture on elites was much weaker than its influence on the behavior of the masses.[27] The political elites, along with the cultural elites who served them, were the providers of ideology, whereas the masses were only consumers. The elites imparted concrete content to the political culture and, in particular, shaped the dominant ideology in each given period of history.[28]

When the attitudes of the masses conflicted with the ideology of the elites, the stance of the majority of people was practically ignored. An example from Soviet times would serve us well here. In the aftermath of the revolution, the Bolsheviks were so assertive in their behavior that they defied the deep elements of the old political culture, including religion, private property, Russian nationalism, and anti-Semitism, among others.[29] The ruling liberal elites of the early 1990s were as self-confident as the Bolsheviks. They challenged seemingly deep-rooted Russian values such as patriotism, the geopolitical status of the country, the army, public property, collectivism, egalitarianism, atheism, among others.[30]

In fact, the de-democratization of the country began in 1992–1993, when no one was talking about an antidemocratic shift inside Russian

---

27. In some ways, this view is inspired by the idea that there are radical differences between active and passive people in social life, between people who tend to be commanders (leaders) and those who would rather prefer to be obedient (followers), an idea developed by Theodore Adorno and his coauthors (1950), as well as by Eric Fromm and other representatives of the Frankfurt School (Arendt 1976; Fromm 1967).

28. For the interaction between the elites and the masses, see Shlapentokh (2006).

29. The transformation of the Russians as religious people into an atheistic nation is particularly remarkable. Studying the Soviet people's religious views in 1989, Levada (1993, 216–218) concludes that "mass nonbelief in God surpasses belief in God," and "it is possible to speak about the non-religiosity of Soviet society."

30. The case of the public's high respect for the army in Soviet times, as well as in pre-revolutionary times, is quite characteristic. After the very strong ideological campaign launched in 1987 by the liberal media and then continued by the new rulers of the country after 1991, the attitudes of the population toward the army changed drastically. According to a 1997 survey, only 18 percent of young Russians wanted to serve in the army (see the survey of the Independent Institute of Social and National Issues, *Moskovskii Komsomolets*, February 2, 1998).

society. It would be against common sense to assert that Yeltsin's policy was affected by the political attitudes of the masses. In 1992, Yeltsin waged war against the parliament and was ready to gas the parliament if it decided to impeach him (Korzhakov 1997). He continued the process of de-democratization, full-scale in 1993, when he ordered the shelling of the freely elected leftist parliament.

The Influence of the Changing Public Ideology

Having moved against democratic institutions, the ruling elite started to change the public ideology with the goal of transforming popular attitudes. Already by the mid-1990s, the ruling elite began shifting the tenor of the public ideology. While continuing to talk about democracy, the leadership turned away from its praise of the Western model and started to focus on the primordial importance of Russian statehood and on the centrality of national interests.[31]

A decisive change in ideology occurred with Putin's arrival to power in 2000. The Kremlin managed to change the public ideology. It identified as being of major value those elements that praised the state; it consolidated the idea of state intervention in almost all spheres of social life; it stressed the importance of Russia's high geopolitical status; and it showed open hostility toward the West. The new public ideology expressed regret about the collapse of the Soviet Union and nostalgia for the Soviet empire; it also included in its roster of values Russian nationalism, xenophobia, Orthodox religion, and the dream of restoring the Soviet Union, even if only selectively. The new ideology praised the glorious past of Russia and particularly those Russian and Soviet leaders who strengthened the state and the empire.

A series of movies, which praised Stalin and denigrated his opponents, appeared on official TV channels in 2006–2007, revealing the essence of Putin's public ideology. In 2007, a state television station showed a forty-part series on Stalin in which the dictator was praised beyond imagination and even shown to be a deeply religious man (Kazhdaia 2007). In a TV movie that was released the same year, Trotsky was described as an agent of Western powers, while Stalin once again looked like an angel. The same technique was used for a movie about Khrushchev (2007), who was derogated, while Stalin was praised.[32]

---

31. The shift in the composition and ideology of the elites started already in 1996–1997 (see Shlapentokh 1998a, 1998b).
32. For Stalin's popularity on TV, in the movies and on stage, Bordiugov (2007) is a good source.

The efficiency of Putin's public ideology was remarkably high. And Russian attitudes toward foreign countries (the United States, the Ukraine, Georgia, or Belorussia) in 2000–2007 strengthen this viewpoint. The Kremlin could easily regulate the temperature of public attitudes toward these countries by starting an acrimonious campaign against them, or by suggesting that a particular country is almost a good friend. The people's negative attitudes toward democracy were not a cause but a product of the official propaganda.

Why Did the Elites Need or Want an Authoritative Regime?

If we discard the old political culture as the major factor that pushed the ruling elites toward de-democratization, what then were the causes of it? The answer lies in the radical changes in property relations after 1989–1991, when the new Russian political elites, in collusion with the oligarchs, acquired large fortunes through mostly illegal means. With Putin's arrival to power, the Yeltsin elites were joined by a new group of elites who received a gigantic chunk of national wealth through a new phase, inaugurated in privatization and in the redistribution of property. The very legitimization of this gratuitously possessed private property was a major determinant in the political processes under both regimes.

Under Putin, when the country was ruled by a network of former KGB and army generals, the focus on private property and wealth evolved into a sort of corporative ideology, as Andrei Illarionov (2006) has suggested. In fact, the need to protect their wealth in the long term against a redistribution or confiscation by some new regime directly affected Putin's domestic and international policy. The legitimization of their wealth in the eyes of the Russians and under foreign law is the dream of the political and economic elites (Inozemtsev 2007). In 2007, the fact that two-thirds of the Russian population still had not recognized the legality of the origin and size of the big fortunes in the country provides fertile ground for an Orange Revolution: "It happened in Ukraine, in 2004; why not in Russia?" The people have good cause to fear some members of the Putin regime. The ruling elite's obsession with their personal private property is crucial for understanding why the offensive against democratic institutions started in 1992 and continued full scale under Putin. Russian elites suspect that the preservation of their property is unlikely should an independent parliament empowered to investigate the sources of elite wealth emerge. The same precautions apply in matters of having an independent judicial system and letting it launch open investigations at the request of the parliament. A free media, too, could uncover and question the roots of elite fortunes. The elites' obsession with the task of protecting their property is behind the Kremlin's policy toward presidential change in 2008 (Belokovskii 2007). It is noteworthy that at the core of the new (The Patriots of Russia) political party's program resides the "deprivatization" of numerous major companies that belong to 720 Russian billionaires. Gennadii Semigin, a well-known politician, proposed implementing such deprivatization by legal means, through the judicial system. Not less than two-thirds of Russian voters and of the Russian population would support the proposed program, if it somehow were put in place (Ponomarev 2007).

The critical roles that private property and personal wealth play in determining the political elite's ideological agenda offer a counterargument strong enough to debunk the hypothesis that it is the old Russian political culture that plays the greater role as a crucial stimulus for Russia's de-democratization. Is it not ironic that traditional Russian political culture and Orthodox religion were both always hostile toward the extremely rich. Since the times of Alexander Radishchev, not many Russian writers have lauded wealth and the privileged lifestyle, and neither had Gogol, Turgenev, Dostoevsky, Tolstoy, let alone Maxim Gorky, for that matter (Shlapentokh 1999).

The views developed here hence take a position against the idea that the evident trend toward autocracy in Russia is determined by "objective" economic processes. A hypothesis by Russian economists Victor Polterovich and Vladimir Popov suggests that autocracy in Russia is a reaction to sustained economic growth under conditions of low order and weak state institutions. The hypothesis completely denies any role by the material interests of the ruling elites.[33]

Conclusion

As is often the case, two major schools attempted to explain the political processes in Russia; both are right, and both are wrong. The structuralists (or universalists) are right because the changes in economic

---

33. See Polterovich and Popov (2007) and also their online article, "Appropriate Economic Policies at Different Stages of Development" at www.nes.ru/english/research/pdf/2005/PopovPolterovich.pdf (accessed April 28, 2007).

structure—especially the changes in property relations—in Russia have changed the political and social order, making it impossible to return to the old totalitarian society. The new property structures had many political and social implications. As subsequent developments did show, the anti-communist revolution in 1991 was essentially similar to the French Revolution, which also created a new class of property owners who (several decades after The Restoration in 1815) still worried about the legitimacy of their ownership of property. The French historian, Hippolyte Taine (1895, 200–230) wrote in the mid-nineteenth century that "whatever the grand words adorning the revolution . . . it was a transformation of property, which made up its historical meaning." Taine came to this conclusion by observing how those who had acquired property during the French revolution kept worrying about its preservation and legitimization after the restoration of the monarchy in 1815.

Yet, at the same time, the structuralists were wrong, if only for ignoring the specific character of the Russian reality and the particular character of the Russian elites. The confluence of some factors (including a yearning for enrichment by all means necessary and a conviction in the inability of ordinary Russians to behave as rational democratic citizens[34]) brought greedy, cynical people to the summit of Russian political life. These people believe in crass power and in wealth's proven privileged capacity to buy off anyone and everything, to any end deemed timely convenient for a price.

Ultimately, the problems of Russian democracy can be traced to the absence of people at the top echelons of society who are devoted to democracy, minimally altruistic, and optimally selfless enough to want to make Russia a modern democratic society. Years ago, in 1975, a Frenchman authored a book titled, *La Trahison des Clercs* (The Betrayal of the Intellectuals) (Benda 2006). Today, Russia's tragedy consists of the betrayal of its liberal elites and of its intelligentsia—namely, the very people who wanted to see democracy in the country in the first place.

Here is where my views differ with those of Dimitry Travin, one of the best analysts in Russia, who sees the de-democratization in Russia to be an outcome of the authoritarian mentality of the people. First, in

---

34. Cf. Jefferson's insightful perspective, philosophical mindset, and personal stance, thoughts, and utterances from an American Founding Father's perspective, on this very issue, as paraphrased for the reader in this book's preface by Ciprut.

his opinion, this mentality accounts for the lack of civil society in the country and in the people's inability to resist the authoritarianism of the Kremlin (Travin 2006). Second, in his perception, the victory of oligarchic capitalism in 1990 was inevitable. It is not easy to imagine how different Russian history might have been if Gorbachev had not been an idealistic communist or if Yeltsin, indeed, had been a greedy, power-hungry individual.

As history teaches us, however, civil society cannot emerge spontaneously in a country. It needs to be nurtured over decades and fostered over centuries by the ruling elites. Civil society is unlikely to emerge simply because disposable income has ballooned, as suggested by Andrei Shleifer and Daniel Treisman (2004), who invented the formula "middle income middle democracy" and insinuated by Egor Gaidar (2005), too, who still clings to the tenets of economic determinism.

The fact that the anti-communist revolution could not advance an ascetic politician is the curse of Russian history. Almost every prominent person could partake in the nation's wild privatization and get awfully rich awfully quickly. It is sad that Russian society could not muster even one leading politician who could serve as a model of integrity.

Those who are responsible for Western foreign policy have to understand that genuine democracy has hardly any chance of being established in Russia over the next decades. The American vision of democracy has failed in Russia in the early twenty-first century, just as the utopia of a world revolution failed in Germany in the 1920s.

References

Adorno, T. W., E. Frenkel-Brunswik, D. Levinson, and D. Sanford (1950) *The Authoritarian Personality*, New York: Harper.

Akhiezer, Aleksander (1995) "Rossiia: Nekotorye problemy sotsial'no-kul'turnoi dinamiki" [Russia: Some problems of sociocultural dynamics], *Mir Rossii*, no. 1.

Arendt, Hanna (1976) *The Origin of Totalitarianism*, New York: Harcourt, Brace.

Babosov, Evgenii (1990) *Chelovek i perestroika: Sotsiologicheskii analiz* [A person and perestroika: A sociological analysis], Minsk: Nauka i Tekhnika.

Belokovskii, Stanislav (2007) Interview with Ekho Moskvy, April 6.

Benda, Julien (2006) *The Treason of the Intellectuals* [*La Trahison des clercs* (1975), Paris: B. Grasset], New Brunswick, NJ: Transaction Publishers.

Bordiugov, Gennadii (2007) "Stalin s nami. Stalin v nas." [Stalin is with us. Stalin is in us], *Moskovskie Novosti* (Moscow News), no. 4 (February 2).

Borisov, Vadim (2001) *Zabastovki v ugol'noi promyshlennosti, analiz shakhterskogo dvizheniia za 1989–1998* [Strikes in coal industry, the analysis of movement of miners during 1989–1998], Moscow: ISITO.

Borodin, Vladimir (2007) Interview with the radio program "Osoboie mnenie" [Special opinion], Ekho Moskvy, March 3.

Brooks, David (2007) "No U-Turns," *New York Times*, March 29.

Brym, Robert J. (1996) "Re-evaluating Mass Support for Political and Political and Economic Change in Russia," *Europe-Asia Studies* 48(5):751–765.

Brzezinski, Zbigniew (1989) *The Grand Failure: The Birth and Death of Communism in the Twentieth Century*, New York: Scribner.

Bukovsky, Vladimir (1995) *Jugement à Moscou*, Paris: Robert Laffont.

Butrin, Dmitri (2006) "Nizhepodpisavshiesia" [Those who have signed below], *Kommersant'–Vlast,'* April 24.

Chelysheva, Oksana (2007) "Russia's Great Leap Backwards," *Guardian*, April 20.

Chua, Amy (2003) *World on Fire: How Exporting Free Market Democracy Breeds Ethnic Hatred and Global Instability*, New York: Doubleday.

Chubais, Anatolii (2007) "El'tsin privel nas iz nesvobody k svobode" [Yeltsyn led us from unfreedom to freedom], *IAREGNUM*, April 23.

Dakhin, V. N. (2000) "Nekotorye voprosy analiza rossiiskoi vlasti" [Some questions of analysis of Russian government], in T. I. Zaslavskaia, Editor, *Kuda idet Rossiia. Vlast,' Obshchestvo. Lichnost'* [Where is Russia headed. Power. Society. Individual] Moscow: Vysshaia shkola sotsial'nykh i ekonomicheskikh nauk [Higher School of Social and Economic Sciences].

Dalin, Alexander (1993) "The Uses and Abuses of Russian History," in Frederick Fleron and Eric Hoffman, Editors, *Post Communist Studies and Political Science: Methodology and Empirical Theory in Sovietology*, Boulder, CO: Westview.

Danilov, A., and S. Zasorin (1991) *Novye politicheskie partii I dvizheniia Rossiiskoi Federatsii* [New political parties and movements of Russian Federation], Moscow: Obschestvo "Znanie."

Danilov, V. P. (2000) "Rossiiskaia vlast' v 20 veke" [Russian government in the 20th century], in T. Z. Zaslavskaia, Editor, *Kuda idet Rossiia. Vlast.' Obshchestvo. Lichnost.'* [Where is Russia headed. Power. Society. Individual], Moscow: Vysshaia shkola sotsial'nykh ekonomicheskikh nauk.

Dubin, Boris (2006) "Dve daty i eshche odna" [Two dates and one more], *Vestniki Obshchestvennogo Mneniia* [Bulletins of Public Opinion], no. 5.

Eckstein, Harry (1988) "Culturalist Theory of Political Changes," *American Political Science Review*, 82:801.

Editorial (2003) "Pedaling Backward," *Washington Post*, October 28.

Fedotova, Valentina (1997) *Modernizatsiia Drugoi Europy*, Moscow: IF Iran.

Ferguson, Niall (2004) *Colossus: The Price of America's Empire*, New York: Penguin.

Finifter, Ada, and Ellen Mickiewicz (1992) "Redefining the Political System of the USSR: Mass Support and Political Changes," *American Political Science Review*, 86:857–874.

Fromm, Erich (1967) *Escape from Freedom*, New York: Avon Books.

Fukuyama, Francis (1989) "The End of History?" *National Interest*, 16 (Summer):3–18.

——— (1992) *The End of History and the Last Man*, New York: Free Press.

——— (2006) *America at the Crossroads: Democracy, Power, and the Neoconservative Legacy*, New Haven, CT: Yale University Press.

Gaddis, John Lewis (2005) *The Cold War: A New History*, New York: Penguin Press.

Gaidar, Yegor (1999) *Dni porazhenii i pobed* [Days of defeats and victories], Seattle: University of Washington Press.

——— (2005) *Dolgoe vremia, Rossiia v mire: Ocherki ekonomicheskoi istorii* [Long time. Russia in the world: Articles on economic history], Moscow: Delo.

Gibson, James, Raymond Duch, and Kent Tedin (1992) "Democratic Values and the Transformation of the Soviet Union," *Journal of Politics*, 54:329–371.

Gill, Graeme, and Roger D. Markwick (2000) *Russia's Stillborn Democracy: From Gorbachev to Yeltsin*, Oxford, UK, and New York: Oxford University Press.

Gorshkov, Mikhail (2000) *Rossiiskoe obshchestvo v usloviakh transformatsii: Sotsiologicheskii analiz* [Russian society in the conditions of transformation: A sociological analysis], Moscow: ROSSPEN-Pub.

Gromov, Andrei (2006) "Glaz odinokogo Surkova" [Eye of lonely Surkov], *Expert*, April 9.

Gudkov, Lev (2000) "Negativnaia identifikatsia" [Negative identification], *Monitoring Obshchestvennogo Mneniia*, [Monitoring of Public Opinion], no. 5.

Gurov, Alexander (2003) "Vchera reket, segodnia kompromat" [Racketeering yesterday, the compromising evidence today], *Argumenty i Fakty* [Arguments and Facts], no. 19, pp. 1–2.

Hedlund, Stephen (1999) *Russia's Market Economy: A Bad Case of Predatory Capitalism*, London: University College London Press.

Hobsbawm, Eric (2005) "The Dangers of Exporting Democracy: Bush's Crusade Is Based on a Dangerous Illusion and Will Fail," *The Guardian*, January 22.

Ignatieff, Michael, Editor (2005) *American Exceptionalism and Human Rights*, Princeton, NJ: Princeton University Press.

Illarionov, Andrei (2006) "Drugaia strana" [The other country], *Kommersant*, January 23.

Inglehart, Ronald (2002) *World Values Surveys and European Values Surveys*. Ann Arbor, MI: Institute for Social Research.

Inozemtsev, Vladislav (2007) "Vverkh po lestnitse" [Up the stairs], *Svoboda Mysli* (Freedom of Thought), 2.

Ivanov, Nikolai (1998) "Dozhivem do demokratii?" [Will we live to see democracy?], *Segodnia* (Today), September, 8.

James, Cyril, and Lionel Robert (1986) State Capitalism and World Revolution, Chicago: Charles H. Kerr.

Kagan, Robert (1998) "U.S. Dominance: Is It Good for the World? The Benevolent Empire," *Foreign Policy*, 11 (Summer):24–34.

Kalinina, Yulia (1999) "Kazat'sia gordoi ne khvatilo sil" [There was no strength to look proud], *Moskovskii Komsomolets* [Moscow Komsomolets] August 21.

Kazhdaia, Valerii (2007) "Stalin za steklom" [Stalin behind the Glass], *Moskovskie Novosti*, March 8.

Kisilev, Evgenii (2004) "Itogi" [Conclusions], *Moskovskie Novosti*, June 4.

Kolodziej, Edward A., and Roger E. Kanet, Editors (2007) *From Superpower to Besieged Global Power: Implications for American Foreign Policy and Global Order*, Athens: University of Georgia Press.

Konchalovsky, Andrei (2006) "Verit' ili razmyshliat'" [To believe or to reflect], *Moskovskie Novosti*, July 13.

Korzhakov, Aleksandr (1997) *Boris Yeltsin: Oot rassveta do zakata* [Boris Yeltsyn: From dawn to sunset], Moscow: Interbuk.

Kramer, Andrew (2007) "50% Good News Is the Bad News in Russia Radio," *New York Times*, April 22.

Krauthammer, Charles (2004) *Democratic Realism: An American Foreign Policy for a Unipolar World*, Washington, DC: American Enterprise Institute for Public Policy Research.

Latukhina Kira, Vasilii Kashin, and Elena Rudneva (2006) "Surkov vyshel iz teni" [Surkov came out of the shadow], *Vedomosti* [Register], June 29.

Levada, Yurii, Editor (1990) *Est' mnenie* [There is an opinion], Moscow: Progress.

Levada, Yurii (1993) *Sovetskii prostoi chelovek* [A Soviet ordinary man], Moscow: Intertsentr.

——— (2000a) "Obshchestvennoe mnenie i obshchestvo na pereput'iakh 1999 goda" [Public opinion and society on the crossroads of the year of 1999], in T. I. Zaslavskaia, Editor, *Kuda idet Rossiia. Vlast'. Obshchestvo. Lichnost'* [Where is Russia headed. Power. Society. Individual], Moscow: Vysshaia shkola sotsial'nykh i ekonomicheskikh nauk [Higher School of Social and Economic Science].

——— (2000b) *Ot mnenii k ponimaniiu, Sotsiologicheskie ocherki 1993–2000* [From opinions to understanding, Sociological articles 1993–2000], Moscow: Moskovskaia shkola politicheskikh issledovanii [Moscow School of Political Studies].

Lieven, Anatol (2004) *America Right or Wrong: An Anatomy of American Nationalism*, New York: Oxford University Press.

Loewenhardt, John (1995) *The Reincarnation of Russia*, Durham, NC: Duke University Press.

Lopatin, Leonid, Leonid Gordon, and Aleksandr Kudelin, Editors (1998) *Rabochee dvizhenie Kuzbassa v vospominaniiakh ego uchastnikov i ochevidtsev (1989–1998)* [Workers' movement in Kuzbass in memoirs of its participants and witnesses (1989–1998)], Moscow: In-t mirovoi ekonomiki i mezhdunarodnykh otnoshenii Rossiiskoi akademii nauk [Institute of World Economy and International Relations of Russian Academy of Science].

Madsen, Deborah (1998) *American Exceptionalism*, Jackson: University Press of Mississippi.

Mandelbaum, Michael (2002) *The Ideas That Conquered the World: Peace, Democracy, and Free Markets in the Twenty-First Century*, New York: Public Affairs.

—— (2005) *The Case for Goliath: How America Acts as the World's Government in the 21st Century*, New York: Public Affairs.

Markov, Sergei (2006) "Interview with *Argumenty i Fakty*: "Chto takoe suverennaia demokratiia?" [What is sovereign democracy?], *Argumenty i Fakty*, September 6.

McFaul, Michael (1999) "Getting Russia Right," *Foreign Policy*, 117 (Winter):58–73.

—— (2005) "Democracy as a World Value," *The Washington Quarterly*, Winter: 147–163.

McFaul, M., and I. Petrov (1998) *Politicheskii Almanakh Rossii 1997, Tom 1: Vybory i politicheskoie razvitie* [Political Almanac of Russia 1997, vol. 1: Elections and political development], Moscow: Moskovskii Tsentr Karnegi.

Mendelson, Sarah E. (2001) "Democracy Assistance and Political Transition in Russia: Between Success and Failure," *International Security*, 25(4):68–106.

Migranian, Andranik (2006) "Zachem Rossii kontseptsiia 'suverennoi demokratii'?" [What does Russia need the concept of sovereign democracy for?], *Izvestiia*, July 27.

Milekhin, A., and N. Popov (2000) *Obshchestvennoe mnenie Rossii* [Russian public opinion], Moscow: ARPI.

Miller, Arthur H., Vicki L. Hesli, and William M. Reisinger (1994) "Political Values in Russia, Ukraine and Lithuania: Sources and Implications for Democracy. Conceptions of Democracy among Mass and Elite in Post-Soviet Societies," *British Journal of Political Science*, 24:183–223.

Munro, Neil (2006) "Russia's Persistent Communist Leagacy: Nostalgia, Reaction, and Reactionary Expectations," *Post-Soviet Affairs*, 22 (4):289–313.

No Author (1991) *Soviet Events of 1989–1990 as Reported by the Express Chronicle*, New York: Center for Democracy in the USSR.

Nye, Joseph S., Jr. (2002) *The Paradox of American Power: Why the World's Only Superpower Can't Go It Alone*, New York: Oxford University Press.

Pechenev, Vadim, Editor (1990) *Neformaly. Kto oni? Kuda zovut?* [Neformaly. Who are they? Where do they call us?], Moscow: Politizdat.

Petrov, Nikolai (2000) "Prezidentskie vybory 2000 goda: Kontes publichnoi politiki?" [Presidential elections of 2000: The end of public politics?], *Moskovskii Tsent Karnegi*, 3 (March).

Petrov, Nikolai, and Darrell Slider (2003) "Putin and Regions," in Dale Herspring, Editor, *Putin's Russia, Past Imperfect, Future Uncertain*, Lanham, MD: Rowman & Littlefield.

Petrova, A. (2003) "Tsennostnye orientatsii rossiian" [Value orientations of Russians], *Fund of Public Opinion*, August 28.

Piasheva, Larisa (1989) "Kontury radikal'noi sotsial'noi reformy" [The contours of radical social reform], in Fridrikh Borodkin, Editor, *Postizhenie* [Comprehension], Moscow: Progress.

——— (1990) "Umom poniat' Rossiiu" [To comprehend Russia], *Ogonek* [Spark], no. 44 (October).

Poliakov, L. V. (2000) "Rossiiskii avtoritarnyi sindrom: Anamnez i epikriz" (ANAMNEZ I IPIKRIZ) [Russian authoritarian syndrome: Anamnesis and epikrisis], in T. I. Zaslavskaia, Editor, *Kuda idet Rossiia, Vlast' Obshchestvo Lichnost'* [Where is Russia headed. Power. Society. Individual], Moscow: Vysshaia shkola sotsial'nykh i ekonomicheskikh nauk [Higher School of Social and Economic Science].

Politov, Yurii (2006) "Bit' v nuzhnuiu tochku, po vsem peshcheram. Vladimr Putin otsenil rabotu chekistov protiv terroristov I shpionov" [To hit the correct place, all the caves. Vladimir Putin evaluated the work of chekists against terrorists and spies], *Izvestiia*, February 8.

Polterovich, Viktor, and Vladimir Popov (2007) "Demokratizatsiia, kachestvo institutov i ekonomicheskii rost" [Democratization, the quality of institutions and economic growth], in *Obshchestvennye nauki i sovremennost'* [Social sciences and the present], 2:13–27.

Ponomarev, Aleksander (2007) "Privatizatsiia ne ulitsa s odnostoronnim dvizheniem" [Privatization is not a one-way street], *Komsomol'skaia Pravda*, no. 59, April 24.

Privalov, Kirill (2006) "Narod Rossii—samostoiatel'nyi sub'ekt Istorii" [The Russian people is an independent subject of history], *Izvestiia* July 12.

Prokhanov, Aleksandr (2007) "Rossiia—imperiia sveta" [Russia—the empire of light], *Zavtra*, 1.

Reisinger, William (1994) "Conclusion: Mass Public Opinion and the Studies of Post Soviet Society," in Arthur H. Miller, Vicki L. Hesli, and William M. Reisinger, Editors, *Public Opinion and the Regime Change: The New Politics of Post Soviet Societies*, pp. 26–56, Boulder, CO: Westview Press.

Reissner, William, Editor (1974) *Dynamics of World Revolution Today*, New York: Pathfinder Press.

Rudneva, Elena, and Oksana Lebedeva (2007) "Ne tak poshchitali" [Did not count right], *Vedomosti*, March 16.

Samarina, Aleksandra, and Sergei Varshavchik (2006) "Suverennuiu demokratiiu— kazhdomu" [Sovereign democracy for everyone], *Nezavisimaia Gazeta*, August 31.

Schleifer, Andrei, and Daniel Treisman (2004) "A Normal Country," *Foreign Affairs*, 83(2) (March/April):20–38.

Sedaitis, Judith B., and Jim Butterfield, Editors (1991) *Perestroika from Below: Social Movements in the Soviet Union*, Boulder, CO: Westview.

Sen, Amartya (1999) "Democracy as a Universal Value," *Journal of Democracy*, 10 (3):3–17.

Sharansky, Natan, and Ron Dermer (2006) *Case for Democracy: The Power of Freedom to Overcome Tyranny and Terror*, New York: Public Affairs.

Shelokhaev, V. (2000) "Osobennosti otnoshenii vlasti i obshchestva v Rossii: istoriia i sovremennost'" [Peculiarities of relations of government and society in Russia: History and the present], in T. I. Zaslavskaia, Editor, *Kuda idet Rossiia. Vlast'. Obshchestvo. Lichnost'* [Where is Russia headed. Power. Society. Individual], Moscow: Vysshaia shkola sotsial'nykh i ekonomicheskikh nauk [Higher School of Social and Economic Science].

Sherbinin, H. G. (2000) "Chelovek vo vlasti (regional'nye politicheskie elity v sovremennom izbiratel'nom protsesse" [A person in government (Regional and political elites in contemporary election process)], in T. I. Zaslavskaia, Editor, *Kuda idet Rossiia, Vlast', Obshchestvo, Lichnost'"* [Where is Russia headed. Power. Society. Individual], Moscow: Vysshaia shkola sotsial'nykh i ekonomicheskikh nauk [Higher School of Social and Economic Science].

Shevtsova, Liliia (2001) "From Yeltsin to Putin: The Evolution of Presidential power," in A. Brown and L. Shevstova, Editors, *Gorbachev, Yeltsin, and Putin: Political Leadership in Russia's Transition*, Washington, DC: Carnegie Endowment for International Peace.

——— (2005) *Putin's Russia*, Washington, DC: Carnegie Endowment for International Peace.

Shlapentokh, Vladimir (1969) *Chitatel' i Gazeta: Chitateli Izvestii i Literaturnoi* Gazety [The reader and the newspaper: Readers of Izvestiia and Literaturnaia Gazeta], Moscow: Institut Konkretnykh Issledovanii [Institute of Concrete Studies].

——— (1986) *Soviet Public Opinion and Ideology: The Interaction between Mythology and Pragmatism.* New York: Praeger

——— (1997) "Catastrophism on the Eve of 2000: Apocalyptic Ideology between Russia's Past and Future,"*Demokratizatsia*, 5 (Winter).

——— (1998a) "'Old,' 'New' and 'Post' Liberal Attitudes toward the West: From Love to Hate," *Communist and Post Communist Studies*, 31(3):119–216.

——— (1998b) "The Changing Russian View of the West: From Admiration in the Early 1990s to Hostility in the Late 1990s," in Tom Casier and Katlijn Malfliet, Editors, *Is Russia a European Power?* Leuven: Leuven University Press

——— (1999) "Social Inequality in Post-Communist Russia: The Attitudes of the Political Elite and the Masses (1991–1998)," *Europe-Asia Studies*, 51(7):1167–1181.

——— (2001a) *A Normal Totalitarian Society: How the Soviet Union Functioned and How It Collapsed*, Armonk, NY: M.E. Sharpe.

——— (2001b) Russian Attitudes Toward America: Split between the Ruling Class and the Masses. *World Affairs*, Summer (1).

——— (2004) "Wealth Versus Political Power: The Russian Case," *Communist and Post-Communist Studies*, 37(2):135–160.

——— (2006) *Fear in Contemporary Society: Its Positive and Negative Effects*, New York: Palgrave.

Smith, Hedrick (1991) *The New Russians*, New York: Random House.

Steyn, Mark (2006) *Why America Will Have to Fight Alone in the Battle for Western Civilization*, Washington, DC: Regnery.

Stiglitz, Joseph (2002) *Globalization and Its Discontents*, London: Allen Lane.

Taine, Hippolyte (1895) *L'origine de la France contemporraine*, Paris: Hachette.

Tolz, Vera (1990) *The USSR's Emerging Multiparty System*, Washington, DC: Center for Strategic and International Studies.

Travin, Dmitrii (2006) "Putinskaia Rossia: Segodnia i v perspektive" [Putin's Russia: Today and in perspective], *Neva*, 11.

Tsipko, Aleksandr (2006) "Ideologiia suverennoi demokratii" [Ideology of sovereign democracy], *Izvestiia*, April 21.

———— (2007) "Russkaia ideia ili Russkii mif?" [Russian idea or Russian myth?], in *Literaturnaia Gazeta*, February 28.

Tumanov, Boris (2006) "Na proshloi nedele. Kak obustroit'" [Last Week. How to Improve], in *Novoe Vremia*, September 10.

Veretennikova, Kseniia (2007) "Marsh-marsh levoi', marsh-marsh pravoi" [March with the left foot, march with the right foot], *Vremia Novostei*, no. 49 (March 22).

Yampol'skaia, Elena (2006) "V posteli so Stalinym" [In bed with Stalin], *Izvestiia*, December 21.

Zabrodina, Ekaterina (2006) "Parad suverennykh demokratii" [The parade of sovereign democracies], *Moskovskie Novosti* (September 7).

Zhuravlev, V. V. (2000) "Lichnost' kak zalozhnitsa gosudrastva i obshchestva" [The individual as a hostage of the government and the society], in T. I. Zaslavskaia, Editor, *Kuda idet Rossiia. Vlast', Obshchestvo, Lichnost'* [Where is Russia headed. Power. Society. Individual], Moscow: Vysshaia shkola sotsial'nykh i ekonomicheskikh nauk [Higher School and Social and Economic Science].

Zorkaia, Natalia, Editor (2003) *Obshchestvennoe Mnenie, Ezhegodnik* [Public opinion, annual], *2003*, Moscow: VTSIOM.

Zudin, Aleksei (2007) "Grazhdan bit' nel'zia: Vse li sdelalivyvody?" [It is forbidden to hit citizens: Did everyone make notes?], *Moskovskie Novosti*, no. 15 (April 20).

9

Development without Democratization? China, Law, and the East Asian Model

Jacques deLisle

The People's Republic of China (PRC) poses the greatest contemporary challenge to conventional wisdom upon which East Asia has long cast doubt: development, democracy, and legality go hand in hand. More precisely, capitalist, market-oriented development, liberal electoral democracy and the rule of law—or at least rule by law—are mutually dependent or, failing that, positively correlated, at least over long periods and across widely separated points on the spectrum.

This vision, strongly espoused in the United States, emerged in the 1960s, amid the postwar era's peculiar optimism that all good things go together and pessimism that much of the world faced a struggle in which the survival of liberal economics, politics, and legality was at stake (Packenham 1973). A similar worldview ascended with post–Cold War triumphalism, the global spread of market-based economies and democratic political structures, and newly (re)constructed legal systems (Fukuyama 1992; deLisle 1999a, 2002; Windsor 2002; Siegle, Weinstein, and Halperin 2004).

The attacks on September 11, 2001, and Islamist radicalism more broadly, illustrated the dangers of backlash. Wall Street's bursting bubble and corporate scandals suggested weaknesses in the model's disproportionately American economic pillar. And the popularity of illiberal parties in newly democratizing states offered another cautionary tale. So too did the survival of some repressive regimes and the backsliding of some new democracies. Such developments chastened the apostles of the new trinity but did not shake their fundamental beliefs. In U.S. policy and some observers' views, it became more urgent to build markets, democracy, and legality to secure prosperity and stability internationally (Perlez, Sanger, and Shanker 2001; Haas 2002; Sanger 2004).

The designers of China's reforms have rejected this paradigm. Pursuing the "four modernizations" and building a "socialist market economy" while preserving "socialism with Chinese characteristics" and the "four basic principles of communist rule," the PRC regime has attained much development without democracy or robust rule of law. This seemingly echoes the East Asian model analysts derived from Japan, South Korea, Taiwan, Singapore, and Hong Kong during their periods of industrialization.

Reform-era China and these other cases do not, however, pose the monolithic, thoroughgoing challenge to the conventional wisdom that the recently battered East Asian model once appeared to support. The PRC "model" departs from the East Asian model, which itself is less homogenous than the label suggests, particularly with respect to the roles of law. China's approach during the post-Mao decades implies a distinctive thesis about achieving development without democracy, partly through relying on law (but not full-fledged rule of law) to support development and forestall democratization.

China's recipe might fail. Reasons for skepticism arise more particularly from the East Asian model's cracking during nearly two decades of democratization (besieged in Hong Kong, rapid and sustained in Taiwan and Korea, more measured and from higher baselines in Japan) and years of economic setbacks (the Asian Financial Crisis of the 1990s, export-crippling recessions of the 2000s, SARS scares in 2003, and post-bubble stagnation in Japan). Doubts stem not least from the possibilities that the post–Cold War revived conventional wisdom may be right and that the Chinese state may lack the capacity and will to implement its implicit model. Still, "success" is relative and can be claimed by transitional solutions. By these standards, the contemporary Chinese challenge remains potentially viable and undeniably intriguing. Indeed, some see the emergence of a "Beijing Consensus" that takes contemporary China's experience with undemocratic development as the basis for a distinctive model (Ramo 2004)—one that could supersede or supplement the East Asian model.

Development without Democracy in China and East Asia

The model of rapid economic development with reliance on markets and without democratization that emerged from East Asia has paralleled and partly inspired elite Chinese reformers' agendas. The model did not seem impossibly remote for China. Three of the "tiger" economies underpinning the model—Taiwan, Hong Kong, and Singapore—culturally are Chinese. In the PRC's view, the first two are part of China, and a fourth member (South Korea) as well as the model's avatar (Japan) reflect Chinese civilizational influence. Many characterize Korea as especially steeped in Confucianism. As earlier Chinese elites (and others) saw it, Japan's success since the mid-nineteenth century was a case of the pupil surpassing his master.

True, some of the model's features ill fit reform-era China. It was assertedly rooted in a traditional culture that the PRC regime long attacked. Its principal instantiations were smaller, already more developed entities. Still, the East Asian model was less alien than the Soviet model that China's communist leadership once embraced, let alone the liberal-democratic, capitalist-market, and rule-of-law prescriptions that Western triumphalists and radical Chinese reformers now proffered.

The East Asian Model

Accounts of the East Asian model of development disagree about its contours and admit intramural variation (and strain to accommodate Hong Kong's relatively laissez-faire and free trade policies). Still, some elements are generally accepted (Johnson 1982, 1995; Vogel 1979, 1991; Hofheinz and Calder 1982; Wade 1990; Haggard 1990; Berger and Hsiao 1988). East Asian model countries rapidly transform from preindustrial economies (agricultural in most instances, entrepôts in Singapore and Hong Kong) to high-growth industrial economies and onward to advanced industrial and service-based economies. They do so by adopting policies that are ultimately market conforming. Behind these policies lie strategies of export-led growth with specialization according to evolving international comparative advantage. As a corollary, domestic prices cannot depart too far for too long from international prices. Partly as another corollary, restrictions on imports and foreign investment face foreseeable long-term pressure for liberalization.

The policies resulting from this market-consistent strategy can be far from laissez-faire or free market in practice. The state often adopts a heavy guiding hand over enterprises and extensive domestic industrial principles, along with neomercantilist external policies. Interventions abound: from public funding for infrastructure (including industrial development zones) and human capital, to state-subsidized, state-controlled, or state-mobilized capital (and land), to measures protecting domestic industries (especially infant industries) from foreign and domestic competition, to actually assisting in the capture of export markets. Such state interventions can be industry neutral, although they often target state-identified 'strategic', 'potential', 'winner', and 'pioneer' industries, sometimes to the extent of favoring certain specific firms over others in the same sector.

The state also acts to overcome market failures, shape the national economy's comparative advantage, reduce uncertainty-related risks, and promote flows of resources to long-term highest uses. Policies harder to square with market norms, import-substitution industrialization for instance, are deployed as transitional means, used in moderation, or abandoned when they become too costly.

Thus, while aims are consistent with long-term market dictates, methods are those of a particular type of activist developmental state. The state is highly competent and technocratic, staffed by the nation's best and brightest, whether concentrated among a ruling political elite or a professional bureaucracy over which political leaders reign but do not micromanage. The state achieves cooperation from social sectors, especially controllers of enterprises vital to economic policy aims. The state obtains needed leverage through state ownership or management, control of access to (domestic, foreign, or subsidized) capital, taxes, fiscal incentives, and economic ministries' collaborative informal relationships with, or guidance of, key firms. The state is insulated from capture, especially by labor and narrow business elites. The state thus enjoys autonomy to pursue national economic interests.

Politics is undemocratic (although postwar Japan here strains the model's coherence). This can take many forms, including military dictatorship (Korea, arguably Taiwan under martial law), colonial rule (Hong Kong, early Singapore), or nominally democratic regimes dominated by single parties (Singapore, Korea before military rule, Taiwan under the Kuomintang,[1] Japan during Liberal Democratic Party hegemony). And, typically, corruption (see Kincaid, chap. 5 in this book) remains low or fleeting by developing country standards.[2]

On many accounts, such politics, the model's economic elements, and sociocultural contexts are interconnected. Undemocratic politics

---

1. The Kuomintang, the Nationalist Party of the Republic of China, remained in power in Taiwan from 1949, the date of its retreat from Mainland, until 2000, the date of its presidential electoral defeat in the ROC, and retook the presidency in 2008.

2. For accounts of the East Asian model's political dimension and its exemplars, see Johnson (1995); Haggard (1990); Miners (1995); Chan (1994); Gold (1986); Régnier (1991); Clifford (1998).

is viable because structures of corporate finance and organization of labor undercut political clout and independence of economic actors, or because institutional mechanisms for pressing popular will or interest group agendas are absent or preempted, or because state and economic elites share interests and values, or because citizens have dissent-inhibiting perceptions that their country is highly vulnerable, or simply because democracy is alien to these culturally homogenous, group-oriented, hierarchical societies that covet harmony and order. In such contexts, absence of democracy contributes to state autonomy and capacity that are vital to the model's developmentalist strategy, and development need not generate divergent interests or preferences and, in turn, stability-undermining and growth-threatening politics of redistribution or, indeed, pressure for democratization.

China

In many ways, the path of reform-era China resonates with the East Asian model. Slogans of the early post-Mao years (when reforms that continue to unfold today were adumbrated) superficially suggested something different: China would pursue socialist modernization and socialist democracy. But the agenda was development without democracy. Socialist modernization evolved into a "socialist commodity economy" and then a "socialist market economy" in which *socialist* had ever-thinner meaning. Socialist democracy, however, meant much that was "socialist"—specifically, the Party's monopoly of power—and little that was "democratic."[3] Seeking more accurate alternatives to official formulations, observers offered labels: *market-Leninism, bureaucratic capitalism,* or *market-Stalinism* (Kristoff and WuDunn 1995, 431–440; Meisner 1999, 474–478; Blecher 1997, 226–227).

Chinese developmentalist policies embraced market-oriented structures.[4] Early 1980s reforms replaced collective farming with "production responsibility systems" that allocated land to peasant households

---

3. Such terms are staples of official proclamations, including *Communiqué of the Third Plenum of the Eleventh Central Committee* (1978), Party General Secretary Zhao Ziyang's *Address to the Thirteenth Party Congress* (1987), *Decision of the Central Committee on Issues Concerning the Establishment of a Socialist Market Economic Structure* (1993), Jiang Zemin's "Hold High the Great Banner of Deng Xiaoping Theory" (1997), and *Reports of the Fifteenth and Sixteenth Party Congresses* (1997, 2002).
4. For overviews of these policies and their impact, see Chai (1997); Wang (2000); Liu (1988); Dernberger (1999).

for periods sufficient to encourage investment. Farmers enjoyed new autonomy in choosing what to grow, to whom to sell, what to do with proceeds from sales at less-controlled prices, and when and from what sources to deploy capital. Many tens of millions of peasants left agriculture for industry and services, with official tolerance or encouragement. Central and local authorities' initiatives and acquiescence allowed rural enterprises to take many forms, which included leased-out enterprises that had been established under the old system, truly private firms founded by local entrepreneurs, and hybrid entities with varied entanglements with local governments. All of these enterprises faced environments increasingly shaped by markets for products, inputs, capital, and even ownership.

In the cities, early reforms dismantled the planned economy and gave state-owned and collective (often local state-owned) enterprises expanded autonomy in production, marketing, employment, and investment. Firms sold outputs and acquired inputs increasingly through voluntary transactions at market prices. Laws, policies, and ad hoc deals rewrote fiscal relationships between state-owned enterprises and the state, moving from remission of profits to the state, to partial retention of profits by enterprises, to a "tax-for-profit" system of semi-negotiated tax rates, to contract responsibility systems (modeled on rural reforms) and profit-contracting systems, on to more rule-governed taxes on enterprises' income and transactions. By the late 1980s, the specter of bankruptcy, forced merger, or privatization haunted floundering state enterprises. During the 1990s, experiments with issuing shares spawned equities markets that mobilized capital and generated nascent capital market discipline and markets for corporate control. In the late 1990s and 2000s, the agenda turned to widespread selling off of state companies ("grasping the large, letting go the small"), bank reform (attempting to free dangerously weak principal providers of credit from politically mandated loans that kept inefficient state firms afloat), and corporate governance (to address opacity and corruption that facilitated insiders' asset stripping and dampened private investors' interest).

State-owned enterprises' share of industry shrank markedly as local government-owned, private, hybrid, and foreign-invested firms expanded rapidly. From the start, these enterprises operated in more market-regulated environments. Increasingly, market-oriented rules in principle applied broadly, regardless of ownership type, with uniform tax and contract laws emerging in the 1990s and more unified and comprehensive regimes for property rights and bankruptcy as foci for the 2000s.

The turn to markets, the developmentalist agenda, the notion that the state properly plays large economic roles, and the coexistence of established, large, state-linked, and politically influential firms with smaller, newer, and more purely market firms resemble features of several East Asian model exemplars. Still, much in China's agenda was different, partly due to different starting points. Working from Maoist baselines and facing tasks of state retrenchment and market creation on a scale unknown to the East Asian model, China's leadership focused on building more market-oriented economic entities that could outgrow and surround the residuum of the planned and collectively or state-owned economy (Naughton 1995; Shirk 1993).

The PRC's circumstances and policy choices made some elements of East Asian model economic policy unavailable. Many of China's largest firms were among the economy's more revanchist entities and principal targets of reforms and were in no position to become Chinese *chaebol* or *zaibatsu*,[5] or stalwarts of a PRC Keidanren, or focal points of Chinese *keiretsu*, or even counterparts to Taiwan's or Singapore's state-owned companies. Enterprises' proliferation of business lines and branches to seek new revenue in a half-reformed economy, political impediments to state firms' exit from employment-providing declining sectors, and regime policies to create industrial groups and shotgun marriages to salvage weaker firms threatened to push some of China's largest economic entities toward the structural problems featured

---

5. In South Korea, the *chaebol* (literally "business associations") are large, conglomerate, family-owned, family-controlled firms that enjoy the strongest ties with government agencies. Although family-owned enterprises did exist in Korea even before 1961, this formal category of state-corporate alliance arose into its latter-day importance first with the regime of Park Chung Hee (1961–1979), who had modeled this arrangement on Japan's Meiji-era *zaibatsu* system. Among the most important differences between the *chaebol* and the *zaibatsu*, however, is the crucial fact that the *zaibatsu* could afford big-bank capital, whereas the *chaebol* never were allowed to own a bank: a significant source of power for the Park regime resided in his having nationalized his country's banks, the better to direct much sought-after capital to favored industries or to those few deemed indispensable to the nation's (i.e., the state's) foremost interests and longer-term objectives. *Keidanren* (Japan Federation of Economic Organization) brings together all of Japan's major companies and industry associations and is not to be confused with MITI (Japan's Ministry of International Trade and Industry). The *zaibatsu* were formally dissolved after World War II, but as now-individual conglomerates, former elements continued to recognize and favor each other in the new "system" or "series" that ensued: the *keiretsu*. Each of these interlocking giants employs thousands of actual and potential voters.—*Ed.*

by Korea's conglomerates and Hong Kong's family-based business empires.

PRC party and state organs, still staffed partly on bases of political loyalty and personal connections, and with too few members trained in economics and related fields, were unable (or unwilling) to replicate East Asian model bureaucracies. Expertise deficits and noneconomic agendas precluded emulation of East Asia's industrial policy crafters, Singapore's state managers of enterprises, Taiwan's and Singapore's technocrats, Hong Kong's free market-oriented civil servants, or Japan's providers of informal "administrative guidance" to industry and brokers of cooperation among business interests. China's poverty and vastness, the leadership's reliance on hard-to-reverse political decentralization to achieve reform's first waves, and cadres' corruption and indiscipline produced weak implementation capacity.

This left China well short of East Asian model exemplars' ability to wield complex regulatory tools, for example, Taiwan's targeted tax incentives, Singapore's wage and employment policies, or Japan's structural adjustment measures. China's state revenue shortfalls, exacerbated by troubled fiscal, banking, and state-enterprise reforms and decentralized control over economic resources, left the regime unable to imitate the East Asian model's targeted largesse to key sectors and firms, whether state owned as sometimes was the case in Taiwan or Singapore, or state favored as was typical in Korea and Japan. This was perhaps just as well, given the PRC regime's still-limited technical skill, severe and worsening corruption, and sensible rejection of post-Soviet-style shock privatization.

The other core developmentalist strategy of China's reform era, opening to the outside world, seemed more nearly to parallel the East Asian model. China abandoned near-autarky, reconceptualizing trade as more than just exporting to pay for necessary imports and foreign investment as not merely a means for foreigners to exploit or corrupt China. Foreigner-friendly and export-oriented Special Economic Zones, with enhanced physical and regulatory infrastructures, were positioned near Hong Kong, Macao, and Taiwan in 1979 (Ciprut 2000). A similar model was adopted for fourteen cities in 1984. It spread with variations and augmentations to much of China in the decades that followed. Sectoral restrictions on foreign investment waned, with requirements that projects earn foreign exchange, transfer advanced technology, and enter specified sectors replaced by provisions that now sheltered security-sensitive, newly emerging, or declining industries from both foreign competition and alien acquisition. Although the state still played discretionary gate-keeping roles, investment options for foreigners proliferated to include flexible joint ventures, wholly foreign-owned entities, portfolio investment, and mergers and acquisitions.

Openness to trade increased. Central state monopolies yielded to countless enterprises of all types that came to enjoy foreign trading rights. Tariffs fell sharply, and many nontariff barriers were phased out. Once-severe foreign exchange restrictions were replaced by full convertibility in the current account. China's accession in 2001 to the World Trade Organization (WTO) followed from changes already effectuated, and it committed China to even further liberalization of trade and investment (Lardy 2002). These reforms sought to foster specialization consistent with China's comparative advantage (initially, primarily labor-intensive manufacturing) to put PRC exporters in competition in global markets, to expose firms to challenges and opportunities presented by both foreign rivals and coventurers in China, to attract foreign technology and capital to improve China's human and physical capital, and to move China's economy toward higher-end goods and services. Much here echoes the East Asian model, including moves to engage world markets largely on their own terms, to follow a "flying geese" model of exploiting initial advantages in old technology exports while developing one's competitiveness in more advanced sectors, to utilize foreign capital and know-how, and to retain significant state control over trade and investment.

Such 'fit' is somewhat unremarkable, given the East Asian model's capaciousness. China's openness to foreign investment conforms to a model that ranges from Hong Kong and Singapore's emphasis on external capital, to Korea's greater dependence on foreign borrowing, to Japan's greater reliance on domestic capital. The Chinese state's role as powerful but liberalizing gatekeeper to foreign investment fits a model that stretches from Hong Kong's light regulation to more closed environments in Korea, Taiwan, and Japan during their high growth phases. China's rapid if incomplete liberalization of its trade rules falls inside a spectrum that extends from the openness pursued by Hong Kong and Singapore to the protectionism practiced by Korea and Japan even after their industrialization exceeded China's current high levels. Still, similarities to the East Asian model are significant. China's reforms made it more closely resemble its neighbors' developmentalist pasts. Although reports of near-double-digit growth rates were sometimes exaggerated, the PRC's economy did expand rapidly and has transformed structurally. Agriculture's share declined from nearly one third to one sixth, while industrial production soared both in volume and in technological sophistication. Service sectors expanded still more quickly. Foreign trade and investment have grown more rapidly than the economy, with China ranking among the world's top trading states and recipients of foreign capital.

Connections among development, market-oriented reforms, and international openness are perhaps clearest in the profile of firms that have contributed disproportionately to development. As the more traditional state-owned enterprises' portion of a rapidly expanding industrial economy dropped (to well under half), private and foreign-invested companies burgeoned from near-zero levels to become large, advanced sectors. The foreign-invested and export-oriented sectors greatly overlap and include many of China's most dynamic and efficient companies.

While pursuing development through markets and via international engagement, the Chinese regime has sought to evade democracy. Instead, China has moved toward East Asian model–style authoritarianism, away from totalitarian features and institutional chaos of Mao's final years. Among elites, conflicts over power and policy ceased being the mortal struggles they often were under Mao. The top leader's power has waned from Mao to Deng to Jiang Zemin to Hu Jintao. Proponents of divergent visions of reform survived in top echelons, as evidenced by struggles throughout the 1980s and early 1990s between Deng Xiaoping's followers and less innovative rivals around Chen Yun, later skirmishes that pitted Premier Zhu Rongji and his supporters against less market-minded, more chaos-fearing critics, and more recent frictions between President Hu and Premier Wen Jiabao—who at least rhetorically endorse greater openness and attention to reform's losers— and Jiang Zemin protégés, who seemingly favor greater continuity.[6]

Institutional pluralism arose and something akin to corporatism emerged. To an extent previously unacceptable, now ministries and provinces press distinct interests. It has become commonplace to refer to inland and northeastern provinces, old-line industrial ministries, and the military as bastions of relative conservatism, and to describe southeastern and coastal provinces, light industry, international trade bureaucracies, and proreform commissions as proponents of change.

---

6. On elite politics, see Baum (1994); Fewsmith (1994, 2003); Lam (1999); Nathan and Gilley (2003); Li (2005).

Recruiting and training gave reform-supporting and economics-focused bureaucracies more technical talent and clout. Often, these institutional actors have social constituencies: imperiled workers in state-owned enterprises and rust-belt industries, functionaries in state planning bureaus and Party ideological organs, leaders of rural industries, peasants with rising or falling fortunes, employees of foreign-invested and globally trading firms, and members of new business elites and white-collar classes among them. Some of these interests sometimes found a forum in the National People's Congress, China's nominally democratic legislature, which became a platform for criticism of top elite-endorsed policies and an institution that could force reconsideration of legislation backed by ministries and powerful leaders. In the later 1990s, even the Party reconsidered its social base and began to embrace entrepreneurs under Jiang's "three represents" policy.[7]

Elections have been implemented for local posts, albeit ones with little power. In 1980, balloting for county-level people's congresses saw some yeasty contests and opposition victories. In the 1990s, village-level elections spread across China, complete with some of the successful candidates' sometimes criticizing incumbents and making promises or leveling charges in manners familiar to local politicians in established democracies. Extension of grassroots elections to cities and higher levels in the countryside became issues for the 2000s (Nathan 1985; McCormick 1990; O'Brien and Li 2000; Kennedy 2002).

None of this made politics democratic: China's rulers still are unaccountable to any electorate. Chinese-style institutional pluralism reflects leaders' deployment of institutions as power bases, and not simply institutions' representation of their social bases (see Wiatr, chap. 7 on central Europe; Heinemann-Grüder, chap. 6 on the EU; Shlapentokh, chap. 8 on Russia; and Brown and Kaiser, chap. 10 on Africa, all in this book). The NPC's power and political leanings, for example, at least partly reflect its unmistakably having been headed by relatively conservative top elite members. Social groups lack autonomous institutionalized channels for aggregating or articulating interests. The electoral openness of 1980 has not recurred. After years of village elections, voting has only begun to reach the most local formal units of government and remains vulnerable to manipulation, fraud, or even

---

7. On institutional, regional, and social constituency issues, see Lieberthal and Lampton (1992); Shirk (1993); Lieberthal and Oksenberg (1988); Tanner (1999); Solinger (1993).

illegal suspension. Jiang's "three represents"[8] is more cooptation than democratization (Dickson 2003). Talk of intra-Party democratization, and greater transparency and accountability, marked the beginning of the post-Jiang era but brought little innovation and has coexisted with new strictures on discussion of constitutional and political-systemic reform. Elite reformers with nonradical agendas and solid political connections have accomplished little. The "socialist democracy," articulated by Deng-favorite Liao Gailong in 1980 faded quickly with only an abortive revival in 1986. Well-connected intellectuals Yan Jiaqi, Bao Tong, Su Shaozhi, and others faced jail or exile for activities in the 1980s that had begun with tacit approval from senior leaders. In the 1990s and 2000s, a few intellectuals with both access and influence offered proposals for democratizing reform (with the most radical ones including multiparty systems and sharper separation of Party and government). But, in most assessments, the Hu era brought a mixed climate for intellectual freedom and embraced nothing more transformative than democracy that remained merely consultative, "intra-party," non-Western-style or something for the distant future (deLisle 2008).

Top leaders deemed too soft on "democracy movements" (including Hu Yaobang in 1987 and Zhao Ziyang in 1989) have fallen. Some sympathizers of, or participants in, such movements have fared worse. From Democracy Wall in 1978–1979, to the Democracy Movement that included the tragic Tiananmen protests in 1989, to the China Democracy Party (and arguably Falun Gong) in the 1990s, to diffuse Internet-based critics in the 2000s, each decade of the reform era has seen proponents of change encounter unyielding repression. By the early 2000s, the U.S. State Department human rights reports—accurately—concluded that dissent in China was effectively silenced.

Such politics broadly resembles elements of the East Asian model: an authoritarian system, leaders wielding noninstitutionalized power, institutional pluralism, quasi-corporatism, limited elections amid

---

8. A new party-building theory, first articulated in February 2000, by Jiang Zemin in his presidential capacity, then elaborated by him also as general secretary of the Central Committee of the Chinese Communist Party, on July 1, 2001, on the occasion of the Party's eightieth anniversary: "Three Represents" claims that the CPC *represents* "the development requirements of China's advanced social productive forces," "the progressive course of China's advanced culture," and "the fundamental interests *of the majority* of the Chinese people." Promulgated as a development of Deng's Theory, the "Three represents" was meant to serve as basic guideline for the CPC in the twenty-first century. (Editor's italics: cf. Doran, Botwinick, Kincaid, and Teune elsewhere in this book for other theories of fair and just *representative* governance.)—*Ed.*

formal democracy, and repression of dissent. But the contrasts are important. PRC authoritarianism—residually Leninist and nominally Marxist—seems harder to square with East Asian model economics than do other forms of East Asian undemocratic rule (despite vestigial socialism or statist solidarity in Taiwanese or Singaporean rhetoric during eras of rapid development). China's leaders have been less accepting of elections and civil liberties than were several regimes that underpin the model, including Japan in the 1920s and postwar decades, Singapore under People's Action Party rule, and Hong Kong under a colonial government that routinely consulted local elites and answered to Parliament.

China's regime also has had a more ambivalent commitment to a technocratic developmentalist vision. Although bounded by a broad reformist consensus, institutional bargaining and elite in-fighting in China have entailed tensions and trade-offs among economic and political concerns, with the latter including residually socialist ideology and conceptions of political stability less purely identified with economic progress than in most East Asian model cases. Despite economic accomplishments and amid rising corruption and social tensions, the PRC regime's claim to be uniquely able to deliver order and prosperity may not match the classic East Asian model regime's success in securing acceptance of its methods as indispensable means to developmentalist ends.

Nonetheless, the notion that market-consistent development can be achieved without democracy is a fundamental feature of the East Asian model that the reform-era PRC approach shares. Like the East Asian model, the implicit PRC model embraces the first but not the second element in the trinity of "markets, democracy, and law." The third element is a more complicated matter.

Law and Development without Democracy

Law in the East Asian Model

The East Asian model accords law famously little role. Economic regulation by informal negotiation between state and industry, or by administrative fiat from state to bureaucrat-entrepreneurs or state-appointed managers, marginalizes legal rules. It clashes with rule-of-law ideals of general, neutral rules that bind rulers and ruled and are applied effectively and predictably, preferably by independent institutions. Rights-asserting litigiousness chafes against the model's purported cultural norms. A lawsuit constitutes an inescapable admission of a breakdown of harmony between parties and signals that the complainant seeks or concedes some equality with the defendant.

Practices typifying the model's exemplars downplay law. In standard accounts of Japan, ministries openly pursue informal resolution of controversies and proffer informal administrative guidance (under sparse, vague statutes) to regulated actors, even where this entails short-term compromises of state aims. This preserves the bureaucratic discretion and insulation from rights claims on which the system depends. Standards for judicial review of administrative action discourage litigation by making plaintiffs' victories unlikely and nearly valueless. Substantive laws and litigation procedures encourage settlement by making awards predictably small and slow (Haley 1991; Young 1984; Upham 1987). Assessments of the Taiwanese and Korean versions describe little role for law in development strategies that relied on ad hoc policies, or directives to state-owned enterprise managers (especially in Taiwan), or opaque interactions between the state and private firms (especially in Korea).

Under martial law in Taiwan and military rule in Korea, there was little government under law and no rule of law to protect rights of dissent, as bloody suppressions of protests at Kaohsiung and Kwangju illustrated. Singapore and Hong Kong had only limited rule of law in the political sphere, with Hong Kong marked (until the twilight of colonial rule) by troublingly uncertain foundations for its liberal civil liberties regime, and with Singapore guided for decades by a founding ruler who derided Western rights-consciousness (see the interview dated 2005, in this book's epigraph) and litigiousness, and who wielded criminal and civil laws against political opponents.

But central features of Hong Kong's and Singapore's experiences strikingly ill fit the East Asian model's supposed alegality. Hong Kong and Singapore have widely recognized rule-of-law regimes, particularly in economic affairs. Although much of East Asian model rhetoric slights the point, these city-states' ability to attract foreign investment, human capital, and the regional headquarters of multinational corporations depended on laws and legal institutions that met international standards for predictability, neutrality, and efficacy. Whether seen as a benevolent British colonial legacy or a sensible response to former entrepôts' international situations and to the demands of their development strategies, the rule of law figures prominently in plausible accounts of the East Asian model's two smallest exemplars. Although one must look to more subtle aspects of other East Asian model countries' legal development to understand fully the roles of law, law has played a far greater role in Japan and its former colonies than simplistic foreign accounts—and even orthodox indigenous ones—typically admit.

Law and China's "Model"

Law's place in reform-era China's pursuit of development without democratization does not neatly parallel any of the variants of the East Asian model. "Socialist legality" has stood alongside "socialist modernization" and alongside "socialist democracy" at the forefront of PRC ideology from the reform era's founding charter (that proclaimed there should be more laws and that they should be strictly followed and enforced), to a key slogan of the early Jiang Zemin era (calling for ruling the country by law), to a blizzard of prolegality pronouncements accompanying China's entry into the WTO (amid sweeping commitments to conform Chinese laws and practices to international standards), to Hu Jintao's call for further development of law, of the legal system, and of the constitution.

Although such rhetoric says little about a regime that has been wildly uneven in pursuing officially proclaimed aims, in practice, China's turn to law falls between its welcoming of market-oriented developmentalism and its shunning of democracy. Law was energetically, if ambivalently and very unevenly, pursued precisely because of its perceived instrumental value in promoting development and forestalling democratization. In the implicit reform-era model, law is to serve these ends in three ways that diverge both from the alegality often associated with the East Asian model and from the practices of its variant exemplars.[9]

First, law is intended to help build frameworks for market-oriented growth on the problematic foundations of a formerly planned, and still developing, economy. For promoting prosperity in that way, law is crucial to the regime's implicit social contract: if the Party-state provides increasing material well-being, the people will not challenge authority or demand vastly larger roles in their own governance.

---

9. For overviews of legal developments, see Lubman (1996; 1999); Potter (1994); Leung and Chiu (1985); Peerenboom (2002); Du and Zhang (1990); *Zhongguo Falu Nianjian* (annual). For a discussion of issues this section addresses, see deLisle (2003a).

Manifesting this role for law, development-promoting reform policies have been cast heavily in legal form: the Economic Contract Law, the Unified Contract Law superseding it nearly two decades later, and other laws provided for the engagement of economic actors in market-based transactions with a widened universe of partners. China's laws on enterprise taxation and profit allocation delineated increasingly arm's-length and rule-governed fiscal relationships between firms and the state. Laws authorized economic actors to pursue self-defined goals and to respond to market signals. For the chiefs of state-owned companies, laws proclaimed autonomy of management and insulation from meddling on the part of government supervisory departments. Laws set forth the propriety and powers of new, more market-regarding entities, such as township and village enterprises, partnership organizations, private firms, and foreign-invested companies. Laws also promised owners expanding rights to control management. China's Company Law, other business organizations laws, and laws governing issuance and trading of shares and sale of enterprises ratified or encouraged diverse ownership forms and emergent modes for transferring control. Laws on bankruptcy, security interests, banks, and securities and futures markets directed promarket reforms for credit and capital.

Efforts to strengthen the legal profession and legal institutions partly sought similar ends. More, better-trained lawyers were to help enterprises and regulators implement policies reflected in promarket laws. Lawyers, courts, arbitration commissions, and laws promoting formal dispute resolution promised means for protecting economic rights that substantive laws formally conferred. At a crisp pace, China produced market-friendly laws on Chinese-foreign equity joint ventures; on contractual joint ventures; on wholly foreign-owned enterprises; on foreign ownership of shares in, or acquisition of, PRC companies; on foreign trade, foreign exchange and related matters, the better to attract development-fueling international capital and trade. Other laws addressed resolution of disputes arising from the expanded foreign economic presence, offering access to Chinese courts, even to litigation outside China, and to specialized arbitration organs. The idea was straightforward: foreigners required legal frameworks with relatively familiar content and reliable implementation as a condition for providing technology, capital, goods, training, and competitors and collaborators for Chinese enterprises.

Law's market-supporting roles extend beyond the problematic enforcement of the law on the books. Amid China's relatively weak legal institutions and traditions, and recalcitrant, inefficient, or corrupt functionaries, market-friendly laws also served to signal the regime's political commitment to market-oriented development and thus invited economic actors to seek enforcement of legal commitments by informal political means. Such signaling also warned officials of the risks of resistance.

Second, law is to fulfill development-sustaining monitoring and control functions that democratic politics sometimes perform. China's rulers have recognized that corruption, parochialism, favoritism, and failure to avoid or correct badly designed or executed economic policies can imperil development. Reform-era China's approach accepts that some discipline, transparency, and accountability in governance are economically important and that law might help to provide them.

Reforms have favored litigation, and dispute resolution in the shadow of the law, to check market-subverting activities by Party-state functionaries and those acting with their protection. Contract suits in rural areas during reform's early years were brought by peasants who had successfully managed assets leased from the collective and faced attempts to extort larger payments or nullify agreements. Other disputes have involved challenges to contracts that smacked of self-dealing and insider trading, where cadres or their relatives obtained rights to collectively owned economic assets on favorable terms. Contract litigation by industrial and commercial enterprises often has involved breaches stemming from official lawlessness, such as misdeeds by the governmental "owners" of enterprises. Sometimes the problem has been state actors' extortion of enterprise revenues or issuance of orders preventing enterprises from fulfilling obligations or in effect compelling them simply to refuse to perform their contractual duties. Sometimes the problem has been enterprises' expectation of protection by supervisory authorities (sometimes to the point of influencing the courts) so that the enterprises can avoid the consequences of their opportunistic behavior. In handling these cases, courts and other organs have assumed their conventional roles of upholding parties' rights. They also have played policy-implementing roles of explicating the law-embodied policies and commitments to promarket directives of the higher authorities.[10]

---

10. For accounts and examples of these developments, see Zweig et al. (1987); Ross (1990); Clarke (1991); Zhong and Yu (1999); Ding (2000); *Renmin fayuan anli xuan (minshi juan shang, xia)* [Selected Cases of the People's Courts, Administrative volume] (1997).

Similar patterns characterize the foreign-linked sector, where parties generally are more willing and able to seek and assert legal rights. In general laws and policies, sector- or zone-specific incentives, and individual project approvals, Chinese authorities promised foreign investors extensive ownership and operational rights. Foreign-owned private property received constitutional entrenchment before Chinese-owned private property did. Formal mechanisms for resolving economic disputes with a foreign element are widely seen as more neutral and law-regarding than are their domestic analogues.

Here, too, law's role has lain partly outside implementation and enforcement of legal rules. Where those wielding Party-state authority threaten rights promised by law, victims sometimes invoke legal norms informally. Enterprise managers, entrepreneurs, or peasants who face market-subverting pressures from officials now turn to bureaucratic patrons or to higher authorities to protect the policy commitments embedded in laws, by bringing Leninist (or at least Weberian) discipline to bear on recalcitrant functionaries. Wary of Chinese courts, concerned about problems in enforcing judicial or arbitral awards, and confident of their clout, foreign investors, too, pursue informal or political resolution of conflicts with uncooperative or exploitative officials.

At times, the law on the books has seemed to invite such informal means, mandating economic rights without explicit legal remedy. For example, officials encouraged the use of contract forms in the rural economy before most such agreements were covered by contract law. Property rights achieved constitutional status while a long-pending statute detailing rights and underpinning remedies languished. State-owned enterprise laws authorized managers to reject improper exactions or reallocation of funds by governmental departments-in-charge, while other statutes similarly directed government functionaries not to engage in market-infringing activities, before Chinese administrative law fully authorized litigation challenging state action.

As this suggests, public law has included pledges to check official behavior inimical to developmentalist and reformist economic policies. By the 1990s, citizens sometimes won administrative lawsuits reviewing government decisions that improperly granted or denied business licenses or permissions to use economic assets, or unlawfully imposed fines or fees on economic activities. Throughout the reform era and especially (though still inadequately) in the post-Deng years, administrative penalties and criminal sanctions were deployed against cadres who engaged in market-subverting activities such as bribe-taking, extortion, intrusion on enterprises' operational rights, and improper impositions of taxes or fees.[11]

The leadership also adopted laws and law-like rules to regulate selection, recruitment, and discipline of Party and state cadres and to allocate institutional authority to make and implement law and policy, much of which concerns economic matters. Examples include Party admission and promotion rules, civil service laws, organic laws for government institutions, laws governing the legislative process and the hierarchy and forms of laws and regulations, as well as a much anticipated administrative procedure law to govern rule making. Like many private law reforms, these changes in the content of public law sought to increase the likelihood that reformist principles and technical expertise shape both formulation and execution of economic policies and laws, that parochial interests, bureaucratic ineptness, and partisan resistance do not undermine economic reform and national interests, and that diverse actors benefit from institutionalized opportunities for exposing development-threatening policy errors.

Third, law is to channel or slake popular demand for democracy that might arise as China develops and changes. Law is to help fulfill the regime's side of a reform-era tacit political bargain: subjects receive greatly expanded freedom from Party-state intrusion and from demands for political conformity, via some constraints on corrupt or abusive officials, and new mechanisms that take public preferences and interests into account when formulating policy. In return, citizens are to forego "bourgeois" electoral democracy, organized challenges to the Party's monopoly of power, and order-threatening mass action.

Several laws have embodied promises of greater negative liberties or "freedoms from" a pervasive, disruptive, or unpredictable state. Even though substantive criminal law has remained draconian and procedural protections weak, greater transparency, predictability, and (for some behaviors) leniency were incorporated (at least for nonpolitical cases) in the first full criminal law and criminal procedure law (in 1979), in revised versions of those laws (enacted in the mid-1990s to alter provisions that looked like "thought crimes," to mandate some limits on police and prosecutors and greater procedural rights for defendants), and in laws permitting administrative, technically

---

11. For descriptions, assessments and examples, see Clarke (1992); Corne (1997); Pei (1997); *Renmin fayuan anli xuan (xingzheng juan)* [Selected Cases of the People's Courts, Administrative volume] (1997).

noncriminal detentions (amended to provide shorter, more definite terms; narrower ranges of covered behavior; and broader judicial review). Administrative laws allowed suits—albeit with high risk of failure and some risks to plaintiffs—challenging official acts infringing citizens' legal rights, including noneconomic ones. The 2000s brought fragile but rather striking potential harbingers of judicial enforcement of constitutional provisions, including liberal articles on individual liberties. Informal invocations of legal norms offered prospects of occasionally enlisting higher officials to protect citizens from abusive cadres.

Legal changes also promised citizens limited positive liberty or "freedoms to"[12] affect their governance. Although they did not allow suits challenging rules for failing to follow statutory or constitutional dictates, reform-era laws authorized citizens to affect state actions by suing over concrete administrative acts for nonconformity to legal requirements, by seeking rescission, reconsideration, or even forms of compensation. Complaints from citizens and the press have been allowed to prod criminal prosecution or lead to the administrative punishment of misbehaving officials. Legislative and administrative procedure laws promise modest formal rights to submit comments to authorities who have been free to decide without regularized input from interested constituencies.

Laws and rules addressing the authority of Party and state organs have tolerated increased (though limited) quasi-corporatist input into policy- and law-making processes. Such measures accepted virtual or indirect representation of social groups' interests via the central ministries, the NPC, or the provincial and local party committees, governments, and quasi-representative organs. To the regime, they were acceptable because they did not go much further down the path of democratization and because they promised to promote better informed, better monitored, and potentially more popularly legitimate Party-state institutions.

Such legal and law-related measures seek to divert complaints about, or attempts to influence, the regime into safely mediated institutional channels or atomistic, unorganized forms.[13] In this respect, they are of

---

12. For a detailed theoretical discussion of positive and negative freedoms, see Hirschmann 2008.

13. Some Party-state-mediated participation in China occurs through law-making institutions and arguably resembles corporatism. (On corporatism, see Schmitter 1974; Wiarda 1997). Legal scholars ranging from liberal to radical note law's "atomizing" and

a piece with other elements in the Chinese leadership's repertoire for avoiding democratization: a tool kit that includes informal bureaucratic pluralism and quasi-corporatism of reform-era politics, the system of "letters and visits" whereby citizens make individual complaints to local officials, reportage by muck-raking journalists, and elections at the village level. Such means join their legal cousins as instruments accepted by the regime for their utility in monitoring and revealing official behavior or popular sentiments that can lead to discontent, to demands for democratic participation, to challenges to the regime, and hence to political instability.

This complex agenda for law's roles leaves open the question of whether the implicit reform-era Chinese formula for development without democracy could work—in theory, if fully implemented, and in practice, if marred as it is by imperfection and ambivalence.

China and the East Asian Model

Given the battering the East Asian model has taken in the 1990s and 2000s, the PRC's partial deviation from it might support optimism (that China might avoid the model's pathologies) or pessimism (that China falls short of an inadequate paradigm). Either conclusion is too simplistic, in misreading post–Cold War developments in East Asia and in overlooking factors affecting prospects for development without democracy in China.

(Ir)relevance of the East Asian Model's Failures

Recent years have not been kind to the model once credited with producing the East Asian Economic Miracle. During the Asian Financial Crisis, Korea's exchange rate plummeted and once-mighty firms teetered. Hong Kong's equities markets, growth rates, and employment levels tumbled. Taiwan survived the crisis relatively unscathed but the recessions in developed countries at the turn of the century and the continued limits on economic ties with mainland China brought some previously unthinkable negative growth to that island. The late 1990s and early 2000s left economic policymakers in Singapore and more so in Hong Kong (hit hard by reversion-related fears, the rapid rise of

---

"taming" complaints that might generate autonomous, organized, and potentially radical participation (see Shklar 1986; Unger 1986).

Shanghai, and the Asian Financial Crisis) scrambling—in rivalry with one another—to (re)reinvent the two city-states' roles in the global economy. And well into the 2000s, Japan was still struggling to escape a decade of economic stagnation.

Newly critical (re-)readings of the East Asian model's cardinal economic principles now depicted the model as dangerously out of step with market gospel: industrial policy meant government stifling of market forces and led to pursuing folly more often than to picking winners; close, informal state-enterprise cooperation yielded crony capitalism and impeded healthy capitalism's creative destruction; ostensibly market-compliant or market-supplementing management of external economic relations masked costly protectionism and brought vulnerability to currency speculation.[14]

The East Asian model's undemocratic or weakly democratic politics democratized. Japan's one-party dominance gave way in the 1990s to flashes of a multiparty system and then to a Liberal Democratic Party–led coalition government. Korea democratized during the 1980s, with a former dissident and political prisoner winning the presidency, power peacefully transferred to winners of subsequent elections, and sharp conflict among opposing parties (Kim 2003; Diamond and Kim 2000). Taiwan followed a similar path, as the "outside the party group" fielded candidates to challenge the ruling KMT and then organized as the Democratic Progressive Party, with other opposition parties following. With constitutional reforms of the early 1990s, democratic contests became the norm for Taiwan's increasingly powerful, and highly fractious, legislature. Direct elections for president began in 1996, with the 2000 election bringing the first non-KMT politician to Taiwan's highest office and the 2008 election marking the crucial, democracy-consolidating "second transition" back to the former ruling party (Wachman 1994; Rigger 1999; deLisle 2008). Even in Hong Kong, democratization accelerated when the last British governor introduced reforms to entrench international civil and political rights, expand the legislature's powers, and increase voters' roles in selecting the legislature. Although Beijing overturned or undercut late colonial innovations, postreversion election campaigns and popular protests over antisubversion legislation and the pace of implementing direct

---

14. For critiques of the East Asian model in light of weaknesses assertedly contributing to the Asian Financial Crisis, see Gilpin (2001, 321–333); Krugman (1994).

elections for top posts showed that politics remained more open and democratic than on the mainland or in the East Asian model (deLisle and Lane 1997b; Baum 2000; Cheng 2004).

The East Asian model's antilegalism fared badly too. Western analyses of the Asian Financial Crisis attributed it partly to inadequate legal and regulatory structures that tolerated crony capitalism and opaque financial dealings by major firms, especially in Korea (Pei 1999; Garten 1999; Richter 2000; Hormats 2000; Kim 2005). While the rule of law clearly advanced from martial law-era baselines in Taiwan, weaknesses in the regulatory structure for banks and financial markets (along with legal restrictions on cross-Strait investment) became foci of prescriptions for fixing Taiwan's economy in the 2000s. Outside critiques and indigenous reformers attributed Japan's intractable economic doldrums partly to shortcomings in legal mechanisms for regulating financial institutions and for providing government accountability. On some accounts, neither Hong Kong's nor Singapore's seemingly robust legality had been able to protect these two from economic troubles because their rule of law was less than it had appeared: Hong Kong's rule of law had deteriorated with growing assimilation to China, or Hong Kong's and Singapore's rule of law for the economy had finally faltered due to a lack of democratic institutions or strong rule of law in the political sphere (deLisle and Lane 1997a).

Although resonant with post–Cold War visions of virtuous circles of development, democracy, and legality, this apparent unraveling of the East Asian model may say little about the PRC's prospects, except perhaps in the long run. The model's recent troubles support only limited reassessment of its development magic and do not mean a similar approach cannot work for China. Any sense of failure comes partly from comparisons to the astonishing progress during the preceding decades or the East Asian triumphalism of the 1980s. Economic reversals (which generally have been limited and temporary) came only after attaining levels of development to which the PRC still can only aspire. Democratization did not advance in the East Asian model's exemplars until they were far more developed than China will be for some time to come. And democratization remains uneven today, with Singapore and Hong Kong lagging. East Asian model countries thus may merely confirm venerable political science theories that portend little for China in the near future: development produces demand for democracy, but not until a fairly high level is reached, or a large bourgeoisie or middle class emerges (Huntington 1968; Moore 1966; Lipsett 1980; Huntington and Dominguez 1975, 59–66).[15]

Some of the crises that struck East Asian model countries stemmed from international contagions that are menacing primarily to economies more entwined with the global economy than reform-era China has been. China has not equaled its neighbors' high trade ratios or fully convertible currencies and hence their vulnerability to sudden outflows of capital. On some accounts, the Asian Financial Crisis devastated several economies in part because governments had departed from the East Asian model's neomercantilist and managerial approaches to the international economy and had acquiesced in pressures to adopt more American-style deregulatory approaches—by permitting, say, freer mobility of capital into and (disastrously) out of their economies and/ or by exposing long-protected sectors all too suddenly to international market forces (Wade 2000). Indeed, by the middle 2000s, there was much talk of a "Washington Consensus"–rejecting "Beijing Consensus" that saw in China's partial rejection of neoliberal economics and thoroughgoing free trade a new model for the developing world (Ramo 2004).

If liberal-democratic and other ostensibly alien and potentially system-changing values entered East Asian model societies from abroad, they did so through channels much wider and deeper than those so far established in China, including ones carved by decades of integration with the international economy (in all cases of the East Asian model), influences borne of the American security guarantee and related U.S. military presence (in Japan, Korea, and Taiwan), dependence on U.S. aid in pivotal years (in Korea and in Japan) and U.S. occupation during a transformative period (Japan), education of much of the local elites in the United States (Korea, Taiwan) or in the United Kingdom (Hong Kong, Singapore), or transformative experiences of colonial rule under the United Kingdom (Singapore, Hong Kong).

The Challenges for China's Model

Although the East Asian model's recent difficulties need not augur failure for China's quest for development without democracy, China's approach does face challenges. First, elements of the East Asian model's

---

15. For a somewhat different view, foreseeing relatively near-term democratization in China, see Gilley (2004).

successful phase that reform-era China's approach does parallel may require conditions not replicable in China. Export-led growth cannot occupy as central a role for a nation of 1.3 billion as it did for countries that constitute the East Asian model's principal examples. China's lower levels of development and trade-to-GDP ratios may make China less subject to the disciplining effects of international markets that perhaps did force efficient and market-conforming practices on East Asian model states. Absent such external discipline, illiberal economic policies and undemocratic political regimes that elsewhere supported development may become economically dysfunctional. On the other hand, extensive opening to foreign investment and sharp lowering of barriers to imports—both of which accelerated in association with WTO entry (Lardy 2002)—have limited China's ability to use import substitution policies that many see as playing major roles in the initial economic transformation of states in the East Asian model.

Unlike East Asian model countries when they began eras of rapid development, China has severely and increasingly unequal distribution of wealth. Urbanized Singapore and Hong Kong, occupied (and arguably Meiji) Japan, post–land-reform Taiwan and postwar Korea were, by developing country standards, egalitarian. This may have fostered development by promoting social harmony, or speeding creation of human capital, or sparing the state from capture by wealthy elites or even rebellion by excluded and impoverished masses.

Unlike the East Asian model's exemplars, reform-era China is a major power, free from international vulnerability that, on many accounts, helped create solidarity and willingness to sacrifice for collective ends in Singapore (a tiny island in a vast Malay region), Hong Kong (a small colony adjacent to a hostile China), Taiwan (an object of PRC reunification and a fault line in the Cold War), Korea (a state at the Cold War's front line with a fratricidal neighbor), or Japan (a defeated nation that faced monumental rebuilding and that a century earlier had undertaken development defensively against Western encroachment).

Compared to East Asian model states, China, ironically, may have a deficit of Chinese culture. As many Chinese laments about Chinese society and morals claim, a half century of communist rule and a preceding century of revolutionary tumult may well have undermined "traditional" or Confucian values of reciprocity, harmony, trust, and so on—values that some identify as tenets of the East Asian model.

Second, PRC practice may fall short of what the implicit PRC model demands. Sustaining rapid development may be becoming much harder. Removing irrationalities of state planning and international autarky, shifting to material incentives and profit motives, and transferring a first wave of labor from agriculture to industry largely have been completed, and easy gains thereby exhausted. Although controlled in recent years, overheating and inflation followed by growth-limiting austerity in the 1980s and 1990s illustrated the difficulty of maintaining high growth. While burgeoning foreign investment and trade have fueled economic expansion and transformation, especially since the early 1990s, and have surged since China's accession to the WTO, these too will plateau. Citing wasteful investment and suspect statistics, critics have questioned China's ability to use capital efficiently. Mid-2000s pressure to revalue the *renminbi*[16] and rein in China's trade surpluses imperils aspects of export-led growth strategies.

Future development requires difficult and costly undertakings: investing in infrastructure, restructuring or privatizing debt-ridden state enterprises, funding a social safety net for displaced workers, reforming and strengthening financial sectors, addressing the huge environmental costs of post-growth, and easing adjustment for firms facing formidable competition amid China's WTO-accelerated opening. Ongoing economic reforms surely will—and arguably must—be pursued partly through laws. But these laws are likely to prove more complicated to design, more likely to encounter elite and institutional resistance, more painful to reform's losers, and more difficult to implement than the predecessor laws had been. Many earlier laws were themselves notoriously hard to adopt and even harder to render effective. Consider the still-unfinished agenda: decade-long struggles for fair and efficient enterprise taxation; much-delayed and troubled drives to commercialize and to marketize the banking sector; endeavors to phase out "policy lending" to money-pit state enterprises; protracted efforts to create institutions to regulate China's "Wild East" financial markets; epic wrangling over reforming bankruptcy law to reduce state organs' power to stymie creditors and to prevent transfers of ownership; and the odyssey of crafting an administrative procedure act, to increase regularity, transparency, and public input in processes by which most Chinese law is made.

Addressing intranational legal variation and fragmentation is another daunting task, vital to reaping developmental benefits of an integrated

---

16. *Renminbi* (RMB)—literally "the People's Currency"—is the official currency of the PRC.—*Ed.*

national economy and urgent because of WTO obligations. A major preoccupation of Premier Zhu Rongji's later years was getting provincial and local governments to change laws and practices in a manner to comply with China's WTO commitments. As this implies, poor implementation of national laws has been a festering problem. Local protectionism and disregard for central directives have been chronic. The Hu-Wen leadership received an early reminder of the continuing perils of lawless localism when lower officials covered up SARS and erected roadblocks to keep outsiders (and disease) from entering (deLisle 2003b). Foreign investors routinely characterize China as plagued by corruption, bureaucracy, and weak legality. Economic actors complain about functionaries who are ignorant of the laws or unwilling (except perhaps at a price) to follow them. Courts concededly suffer from incompetence, corruption, and local bias, partly because they depend on same-level governments for funding and Party authorities for appointment. Judges and other interpreters of laws sometimes broker or impose compromises in economic cases. Winning parties often cannot enforce judgments, especially against powerful defendants (Cheng and Rosett 1991; Clarke 1996; Lubman 1999).

Such phenomena also indicate that Chinese practices may fail to fulfill the second function expected of law—limiting economically harmful behavior by those wielding Party-state authority. So too do other signs of official illegality. The 1990s and 2000s brought with them recurrent anticorruption campaigns that never seemed to obviate the need for another. High-profile corruption cases—former Beijing mayor Chen Xitong in 1995, leaders in the coastal boomtown of Xiamen in 2000–2001, Shanghai Party chief Chen Liangyu in 2006, and several wealthy and well-connected individuals (among them, one designated to bring Chinese-style open door policies to North Korea)—are relatively rare, disconnected from institutionalized criminal justice, and widely perceived as befalling defendants who lost political conflicts.

Sharp criticism and embarrassing exposés, but at best emergent systematic reforms, target insider deals and fire-sale prices for entrenched managers and well-connected actors engaged in privatization or restructuring of state-owned enterprises. Protests have become more common and violent, among peasants who object to lawless fees and fines, extortion, and embezzlement by local cadres and also among the many furloughed or unpaid urban workers. More recently, city and rural residents have demonstrated and litigated against seizures of land and houses by local authorities who collaborate with developers and disregard increasingly clear and pointed state policy and legal commitments to property rights. Such unrest has spotlighted regime failures to fulfill economic pledges made partly in legal form (Manion 1996; Ding 2000; Perry 2002; Johnson 2004; Bernstein and Lu 2003).

As this suggests, PRC practice may be inadequate for law to play its third assigned role: substituting for democratic politics. Although reforms have decreased unpredictability and politicization in the sanctioning process, laws' promise to enhance negative liberties has been limited in theory, given the vagueness of laws that prohibit acts endangering "state security" and disclosing "state secrets" and of laws allowing discretionary detention or incarceration without judicial process. The promise has foundered in practice amid continued harsh sentences, disregard for minimal mandated procedural protections, and periodic relaxation of legal constraints during anticrime campaigns, as well as the continuation of politicized justice for those suspected of political offenses.

Pledges that add elements of positive liberty confront similar constraints. Meritorious administrative litigation often fails, and some complainants in such suits and even less formal invocations of legal norms fear official retaliation. Contemplated or adopted legislative and administrative procedure rules are sure to have less democratic effect in China than do similar provisions in states that boast other legal means of popular control over rulemakers and more robust cultures of interest group politics. Even China's modestly democratizing village election laws have been violated or manipulated, while other law-based means for citizen input into law and policy remain anemic.

China's legal reforms and economic growth have not preempted or satisfied demand for more democratization. Most jarring was the 1989 Democracy Movement, linking demands for democratic reforms with calls to address the Party-state's political and legal unaccountability (Goldman 1994; Calhoun 1994; Schell 1994): protesters argued that the leadership must recognize constitutional free speech and press provisions, that China's rulers unconstitutionally imposed martial law without the ostensibly democratic NPC's consent, and that constitution-disregarding and democracy-snubbing Premier Li Peng—and others—step down. The 1989 demonstrations built on antecedents dating to the reform era's dawn, including Democracy Wall (1978–1979), liberal ideas targeted in the Anti-Spiritual Pollution Campaign (1983–1984), "democracy salons," and student protests (1986–1987) (Seymour 1980; Schram 1984; Baum 1994).

Since 1989, the regime has repressed pressures in favor of robust democracy, political accountability, and civil society. Means have included imprisonment and exile of dissidents, the banning of alternative political parties and seemingly innocuous NGOs, drives against underground "house churches" that reject supervision imposed by Chinese law on religious organizations, and a campaign against Falun Gong, precipitated by 10,000 sect adherents' nonviolent gathering outside the top leadership compound to protest authorities' prohibition of their organization (Baum 1994; deLisle 2000; U.S. Department of State 2003–2005; Chang 2004).

Ahead may be looming pressures for democratization that law *and* development may be inadequate to dissipate or divert. The peasantry's energetic participation in rural voting and the protests against local cadre misbehavior indicate rising demand for meaningful elections in the countryside, where most Chinese live. China's cities, like those of most developing countries, may prove more demanding. Chinese democracy movements have been city based. Urbanites manifested enthusiasm for democratic elections in 1980 and when urban district-level elections came onto the agenda in the 2000s. Large, frequent, and violent demonstrations by laid-off workers suggest the potential for mass-based democracy movements, much of the kind the leadership feared when autonomous labor groups formed amid the 1989 protests (Goldman and MacFarquhar 1999, 173–332; Perry 2002; Pei 2002). A resentful and ill-regulated "floating population" of rural migrants that comprises a massive urban underclass could add fuel for this fire. Property rights in city and countryside have become a focus of incipient civil society and of calls for more law-governed and accountable local government.

The "crisis of faith" in the regime has been especially deep in the cities, where disdain for communist ideology has created space for new views and hitherto foreign ideas. As earlier reform-era movements foreshadowed, these can encourage and foster prodemocracy political participation (particularly among rising middle classes), especially because the Party seems to have few alternatives beyond banalities such as "socialist spiritual civilization" and ideology-corroding efforts of cooptation such as the "three represents."

Finally, the purported iron law-du-jour may hold true, at least for now. The most developed and stable countries today have market economies, democratic institutions, and rule-of-law regimes, while the poorest and most troubled nations have weak markets or nonmarket economies, undemocratic politics, and little legality. If development, democracy, and the rule of law are so connected, the contemporary PRC model is, like the classic East Asian model, in long-term trouble. Yet it would be premature to dismiss China's implicit model. As many studies of transitions from authoritarian rule have underscored, moving from an underdeveloped, non–market-based economy, undemocratic politics, and lawlessness may not be linear, smooth, or limited to one pathway or one endpoint (O'Donnell and Schmitter 1986; Haggard and Kaufman 1995; Linz and Stepan 1996; Huntington 1991; Friedman 1994; Lee 2002). The East Asian model and the political transformation of its exemplars suggest that a "sequencing" that puts development (and some legalization) before democratization can produce successful transitions. And it can do so when starting from initial conditions that China partly shares. Problems besetting many chips off the Soviet bloc caution that an opposite sequencing can well mean crisis for those nations proceeding from starting points somewhat similar to pre-reform China.

Can reform-era China's implicit model of "development without democratization" (and with distinctive roles for law) provide a transitional arrangement or evolve into a longer-term solution? As Zhou Enlai, when asked for his opinion on the French Revolution's longer-term effects, is reputed to have replied, here, too, "It is too early to tell." For although the PRC's approach is plagued by serious weaknesses and faces difficult challenges, it has adapted and survived so far, heeding, and provisionally validating Deng's admonition to cross the river by feeling one's way, one stone at a time and without falling in.

References

Baum, Richard (1994) *Burying Mao*, Princeton, NJ: Princeton University Press.

—— (2000) "Democracy Deformed: Hong Kong's 1998 Legislative Elections and Beyond," *China Quarterly*, 126 (June):439–464.

Berger, Peter L., and Michael Hsiao, Editors (1988) *In Search of an East Asian Development Model*, New Brunswick, NJ: Transaction Books.

Bernstein, Thomas P., and Xiaobo Lu (2003) *Taxation without Representation in Contemporary Rural China*, Cambridge, UK: Cambridge University Press.

Blecher, Marc (1997) *China against the Tides*, New York: Pinter.

Calhoun, Craig (1994) *Neither Gods nor Emperors: Students and the Struggle for Democracy in China*, Berkeley: University of California Press.

Chai, Joseph C. H. (1997) *China's Transition to a Market Economy*, Oxford, UK: Clarendon Press.

Chan, Ming K., Editor (1994) *Precarious Balance: Hong Kong between China and Britain, 1842–1992*, Armonk, NY: M.E. Sharpe.

Chang, Maria Hsia (2004) *Falun Gong: The End of Days*, New Haven, CT: Yale University Press.

Cheng, Joseph S. Y. (2004) "The 2003 District Council Elections in Hong Kong," *Asian Survey*, 55(5) (September):734–754.

Cheng, Lucie, and Arthur Rosett (1991) "Contract with a Chinese Face: Socially Embedded Factors in the Transformation from Hierarchy to Market, 1978–1989," *Journal of Chinese Law*, 5:143–244.

"China's Transitional Economy," *China Quarterly*, no. 144, December 1995 (special issue featuring articles by many authors).

Ciprut, Jose V. (2000) "Macau SAR: A Space in Search of Its Place," *East Asian Economic Perspectives*, 11 (March):109–115.

Clarke, Donald C. (1991) "Dispute Resolution in China," *Journal of Chinese Law*, 5:245–296.

—— (1992) "Regulations and Its Discontents: Understanding Economic Law in China," *Stanford Journal of International Law*, 28:283–322.

—— (1996) "Power and Politics in the Chinese Court System: The Enforcement of Civil Judgments," *Columbia Journal of Asian Law*, 10:1–125.

Clifford, Mark L. (1998) *Troubled Tiger: Businessmen, Bureaucrats and Generals in South Korea*, Armonk, NY: M.E. Sharpe.

Corne, Peter H. (1997) *Foreign Investment in China: The Administrative Legal System*, Hong Kong: University of Hong Kong Press.

deLisle, Jacques (1999a) "Lex Americana?" *University of Pennsylvania Journal of International Economic Law*, 19:179–308.

—— (1999b) "Who's Afraid of Falun Gong?" *Foreign Policy Research Institute*, on F.P.R.I.'s website, http://www.fpri.org/enotes/19990805.asia.delisle.delisle .afraidfalungong.html. (Accessed May 19, 2008.)

—— (2000) "The Rule of Law and the Roles of Law in China" (review essay of "The Limits of the Rule of Law in China") in *Sino-Platonic Papers*, Reviews IX, October 2000:1–21.

—— (2002) "The Roles of Law in the Fight against Terrorism," *Orbis*, 46(2) (Spring):301–320.

—— (2003a) "Chasing the God of Wealth while Evading the Goddess of Democracy," in Sunder Ramaswamy and Jeffrey W. Cason, Editors, *Development and Democracy: New Perspectives on an Old Debate*, pp. 252–293, Hanover, NH: University Press of New England.

—— (2003b) "SARS, Greater China, and the Pathologies of Globalization and Transition," *Orbis*, Fall:587–604.

———— (2008) "Legalization without Democratization in China under Hu Jintao," in Cheng Li, Editor, *China's Changing Political Landscape: Prospects for Democracy*, pp. 185–211, Washington, DC: Brookings Institute Press.

deLisle, Jacques, and Kevin P. Lane (1997a) "Cooking the Rice without Cooking the Goose," in Warren I. Cohen and Zhao Li, Editors, *Hong Kong Under Chinese Rule*, pp. 31–70, New York: Cambridge University Press.

———— (1997b) "Hong Kong's Endgame and the Rule of Law" (parts I and II), *University of Pennsylvania Journal of International Economic Law*, 18:195–254, 811–1047.

Dernberger, Robert F. (1999) "The People's Republic of China at 50: The Economy," *China Quarterly*, 159 (September):606–615.

Diamond, Larry, and Byung-kook Kim, Editors (2000) *Consolidating Democracy in South Korea*, Boulder, CO: Lynne Rienner.

Dickson, Bruce J. (2003) *Red Capitalists in China: The Party, Private Entrepreneurs, and Prospects for Political Change*, New York: Cambridge University Press.

Ding, Xueliang (2000) "The Illegal Asset Stripping of Chinese Firms," *China Journal*, 43 (January):1–28.

Du, Xichuan and Lingyuan Zhang (1990) *China's Legal System: A General Survey*, Beijing: New World Press.

Fewsmith, Joseph (1994) *Dilemmas of Reform in China*, Armonk, NY: M.E. Sharpe.

———— (2003) "The Sixteenth Party Congress: Implications for Understanding Chinese Politics," *Chinese Leadership Monitor*, no. 5 (Winter).

Friedman, Edward, Editor (1994) *The Politics of Democratization: Generalizing East Asian Experiences*, Boulder, CO: Westview Press.

Fukuyama, Francis (1992) *The End of History and the Last Man*, New York: Free Press.

Garten, Jeffrey E. (1999) "Lessons for the Next Financial Crisis," *Foreign Affairs*, 8(2) (March/April):76–92.

Gilley, Bruce (2004) *China's Democratic Future*, New York: Columbia University Press.

Gilpin, Robert (2001) "The East Asian Miracle Project," "The East Asian Financial/Economic Crisis," and "The Future of the Developmental State," *Global Political Economy: Understanding the International Economic Order*, Princeton, NJ: Princeton University Press.

Gold, Thomas B. (1986) *State and Society in the Taiwan Miracle*, Armonk, NY: M.E. Sharpe.

Goldman, Merle (1994) *Sowing the Seeds of Democracy in China*, Cambridge, MA: Harvard University Press.

Goldman, Merle, and Roderick MacFarquhar, Editors (1999) *The Paradox of China's Post-Mao Reforms*, Cambridge, MA: Harvard University Press.

Haas, Richard N. (2002) "Ending Islam's Democracy Deficit," *Korea Herald*, January 19.

Haggard, Stephan (1990) *Pathways from the Periphery*, Ithaca, NY: Cornell University Press.

Haggard, Stephan, and Robert R. Kaufman (1995) *The Political Economy of Democratic Transitions*, Princeton, NJ: Princeton University Press.

Haley, John O. (1991) *Authority without Power*, New York: Oxford University Press.

Hirschmann, Nancy J. (2008) "Theorizing Freedom," in Jose V. Ciprut, Editor, *Freedom: Reassessments and Rephrasings*, Cambridge, MA: The MIT Press.

Hofheinz, Roy, Jr., and Kent E. Calder (1982) *The Eastasia Edge*, New York: Basic Books.

Hormats, Robert (2000) "Reflections on the Asian Financial Crisis," *International Lawyer*, Spring:193–199.

Huntington, Samuel P. (1968) *Political Order in Changing Societies*, New Haven, CT: Yale University Press.

––––––– (1991) *The Third Wave: Democratization in the Late Twentieth Century*, Norman: University of Oklahoma Press.

Huntington, Samuel P., and Jorge Dominguez (1975) "Political Development," in Greenstein, Fred I., and Nelson Polsby, Editors, *Macropolitical Theory*, pp. 1–114, Reading, MA: Addison-Wesley.

Johnson, Chalmers A. (1982) *MITI and the Japanese Miracle*, Stanford, CA: Stanford University Press.

––––––– (1995) *Japan: Who Governs? The Rise of the Developmental State*, New York: W.W. Norton.

Johnson, Ian (2004) *Wild Grass: Three Stories of Change in Modern China*, New York: Vintage.

Kennedy, John James (2002) "The Face of Grassroots Democracy in China," *Asian Survey*, 42(3) (May–June):456–482.

Kim, Jung (2005) "The Political Logic of Economic Crisis in South Korea," *Asian Survey*, 45(3) (May–June):453–474.

Kim, Samuel S., Editor (2003) *Korea's Democratization*, New York: Cambridge University Press.

Kristoff, Nicholas D., and Sherryl WuDunn (1995) *China Wakes*, New York: Vintage.

Krugman, Paul R. (1994) "The Myth of Asia's Miracle," *Foreign Affairs*, 73(6) (November–December):62–78.

Lam, Willy Wo-Lap (1999) *The Era of Jiang Zemin*, New York: Prentice Hall.

Lardy, Nicholas R. (2002) *Integrating China into the Global Economy*, Washington, DC: Brookings.

Lee, Junhan (2002) "Primary Causes of Asian Democratization," *Asian Survey*, 42(6) (November–December):821–837.

Leung, Shao-chuan and Hungdah Chiu (1985) *Criminal Justice in Post-Mao China*, Albany: State University of New York.

Li, Cheng (2005) "The New Bipartisanship within the Chinese Communist Party," *Orbis*, 49(3) (Summer):387–400.

Lieberthal, Kenneth G., and David M. Lampton, Editors (1992) *Bureaucracy, Politics and Decision Making in Post-Mao China*, Berkeley: University of California Press.

Lieberthal, Kenneth, and Michel Oksenberg (1988) *Policy Making in China*, Princeton, NJ: Princeton University Press.

Linz, Juan J., and Alfred Stepan (1996) *Problems of Democratic Transition and Consolidation: Southern Europe, South America, and Post-Communist Europe*, Baltimore, MD: Johns Hopkins University Press.

Lipsett, Seymour M. (1980) *Political Man: The Social Bases of Politics*, Baltimore, MD: Johns Hopkins University Press.

Liu Guoguang, Editor (1988) *Zhongguo jingji tizhi gaige de moshi yanjiu* (Research on patterns of reform of China's economic system), Beijing: China Social Sciences Press.

Lubman, Stanley B., Editor (1996) *China's Legal Reforms*, Oxford, UK: Clarendon Press.

———— (1999) *Bird in Cage: Legal Reform in China after Mao*, Stanford, CA: Stanford University Press.

Manion, Melanie (1996) "Corruption by Design: Bribery in Chinese Enterprise Licensing," *Journal of Law, Economics and Organization* 12:167–195.

McCormick, Barrett L. (1990) *Political Reform in Post-Mao China*, Berkeley: University of California Press.

Meisner, Maurice (1999) *Mao's China and After*, 3rd ed., New York: Free Press.

Miners, Norman (1995) *The Government and Politics of Hong Kong*, 5th ed., Hong Kong: Oxford University Press.

Moore, Barrington, Jr. (1966) *The Social Origins of Dictatorship and Democracy*, Boston: Beacon Press.

Nathan, Andrew J. (1985) *Chinese Democracy*, New York: Knopf.

Nathan, Andrew J., and Bruce Gilley (2003) *China's New Rulers: The Secret Files*, New York: New York Review of Books.

Naughton, Barry (1995) *Growing Out of the Plan: Chinese Economic Reform, 1978–1993*, New York: Cambridge University Press.

O'Brien, Kevin J., and Lianjiang Li (2000) "Accommodating 'Democracy' in a One-Party State: Introducing Village Elections in China," *China Quarterly*, 162 (June):465–489.

O'Donnell, Guillermo, and Philippe C. Schmitter (1986) *Transitions from Authoritarian Rule: Tentative Conclusions About Uncertain Democracies*, Baltimore, MD: Johns Hopkins University Press.

Packenham, Robert A. (1973) *Liberal America and the Third World*, Princeton, NJ: Princeton University Press.

Peerenboom, Randall (2002) *China's Long March Toward the Rule of Law*, New York: Cambridge University Press.

Pei, Minxin (1997) "Citizens v. Mandarins: Administrative Litigation in China," *China Quarterly*, 152 (December):832–862.

—— (1999) "Will China Become Another Indonesia?" *Foreign Policy*, 116 (Fall): 94–109.

—— (2002) "China's Governance Crisis," *Foreign Affairs*, 81(5) (September–October): 96–109.

Perlez, Jane, David E. Sanger, and Thom Shanker (2001) "A Nation Challenged," *New York Times*, September 23, p. A1.

Perry, Elizabeth J. (2002) *Challenging the Mandate of Heaven: Social Protest and State Power in China*, Armonk, NY: M.E. Sharpe.

Potter, Pitman B., Editor (1994) *Domestic Law Reforms in Post-Mao China*, Armonk, NY: M.E. Sharpe.

Ramo, Joshua Cooper (2004) *The Beijing Consensus*, London: Foreign Policy Center.

Régnier, Philippe (1991) *Singapore: City-State in Southeast Asia*, Honolulu: University of Hawaii Press.

Renmin fayuan anli xuan (minshi juan shang, xia) (1997) [Selected Cases of the People's Courts, Civil, vols. 1 and 2], Beijing: People's Court Press.

Renmin fayuan anli xuan (xingzheng juan) (1997) [Selected Cases of the People's Courts, Administrative volume], Beijing: People's Court Press.

Richter, Frank-Jurgen, Editor (2000) *The East Asian Development Model: Economic Growth, Institutional Failure and the Aftermath of the Crisis*, New York: St. Martins.

Rigger, Shelley (1999) *Politics in Taiwan: Voting for Democracy*, London: Routledge.

Ross, Lester (1990) "The Changing Profile of Dispute Resolution in Rural China: The Case of Zouping County, Shandong," *Stanford Journal of International Law*, 26:15–66.

Sanger, David E. (2004) "At All Bush Rallies, Message Is Freedom Is on the March," *New York Times*, October 21, p. A1.

Schell, Orville (1994) *Mandate of Heaven*, New York: Touchstone.

Schmitter, Philippe C. (1974) "Still the Century of Corporatism?" in Frederick B. Pike and Thomas Stritch, Editors, *The New Corporatism*, Notre Dame, IN: University of Notre Dame Press.

Schram, Stuart R. (1984) *Ideology and Policy in China since the Third Plenum*, London: School of Oriental and African Studies.

Seymour, James D. (1980) *The Fifth Modernization: China's Human Rights Movement, 1978–1979*, New York: Earl M. Coleman.

Shirk, Susan L. (1993) *The Political Logic of Economic Reform in China*, Berkeley: University of California Press.

Shklar, Judith N. (1986) *Legalism: Law, Morals and Political Trials*, Cambridge, MA: Harvard University Press.

Siegle, Joseph T., Michael M. Weinsten, and Morton H. Halperin (2004) "Why Democracies Excel," *Foreign Affairs*, 83(5) (September–October):57–71.

Solinger, Dorothy J. (1993) *China's Transition from Socialism*, Armonk, NY: M.E. Sharpe.

—— (1999) *Contesting Citizenship in Urban China: Peasant Migrants, the State, and the Logic of the Market*, Berkeley: University of California Press.

Tanner, Murray Scot (1999) *The Politics of Lawmaking in China*, Oxford, UK: Clarendon Press.

Unger, Roberto M. (1986) *The Critical Legal Studies Movement*, Cambridge, MA: Harvard University Press.

Upham, Frank K. (1987) *Law and Social Change in Postwar Japan*, Cambridge, MA: Harvard University Press.

U.S. Department of State (2003) *Human Rights Reports: China* (March 2003).

Vogel, Ezra F. (1979) *Japan as Number One*, New York: Harper and Row.

—— (1991) *The Four Little Dragons: The Spread of Industrialization in East Asia*, Cambridge, MA: Harvard University Press.

Wachman, Alan M. (1994) *Taiwan: National Identity and Democratization*, Armonk, NY: M.E. Sharpe.

Wade, Robert (1990) *Governing the Market*, Princeton, NJ: Princeton University Press.

—— (2000) "National Power, Coercive Liberalism, and 'Global' Finance," in Robert J. Art and Robert Jervis, Editors, *International Politics*, 5th ed., New York: Addison-Wesley.

Wang Mengkui, Editor (2000) *China's Economic Transformation over 20 Years*, Beijing: Foreign Languages Press.

Wiarda, Howard J. (1997) *Corporatism and Comparative Politics: The Other Great "Ism,"* Armonk, NY: M.E. Sharpe.

Windsor, Jennifer L. (2002) "Better Development through Democracy," *New York Times*, July 19, p. A17.

Young, Michael K. (1984) "Judicial Review of Administrative Guidance: Governmentally Encouraged Consensual Dispute Resolution in Japan," *Columbia Law Review*, 84: 923–983.

Zhong, Jianhua, and Guanghua Yu (1999) "China's Uniform Contract Law: Progress and Problems," *UCLA Pacific Basin Law Review*, 17(1) (Summer):1ff.

Zhongguo Falu Nianjian (1985–   ) Beijing: Law Yearbook of China Press, annual.

Zweig, David, Kathleen Hartford, James Feinerman, and Deng Jianxu (1987) "Law, Contracts and Economic Modernization: Lessons from the Recent Chinese Rural Reforms," *Stanford Journal of International Law*, 23:319–364.

10

Democratizations in Africa: Attempts, Hindrances, and Prospects

Stephen Brown and
Paul Kaiser

Experiences vary so widely in Africa that one can only speak of democratizations in the plural.[1] Although most African countries were granted independence under a multiparty system, before long, military rule and one-party states typified African regimes. Some of these countries underwent crippling civil wars (from which a few are only beginning to emerge) and even state collapse. After 1989, however, Africa witnessed a sudden resurgence of democracy. The vast majority of African countries held multiparty elections, albeit of widely divergent quality. In some, dictators peacefully ceded power to elected opposition leaders. In others, the ruling party controlled the process to ensure that its base would not lose power. In a few cases, military coups reversed previous gains. Even if the results were often disappointing or short-lived, in the 1990s the continent was swept by a wave of democratization unseen for a generation. This is a phenomenon that warrants further study.[2]

This chapter analyzes postcolonial democratic experiences in sub-Saharan Africa, concentrating on four carefully selected cases: Botswana, Benin, Kenya, and Burundi. These cases were drawn from each of the four regions of sub-Saharan Africa (West, East, Central, and Southern) and reflect the main colonial legacies (two former British colonies, one French, and one Belgian). First, Botswana has enjoyed decades of uninterrupted multiparty politics (but rule by a dominant, single party), and sustained economic growth. The land-locked country developed a

1. Originally written for this book, this chapter appeared as an article in slightly different form in *Third World Quarterly*, 28(6) (September 2007):1131–1149. The authors thank Jose Ciprut, Stephen Ndegwa, and the late Donald Rothchild for their helpful comments, as well as all parties involved for consenting to its publication in both places.
2. This series of events is part of the worldwide process that Teune (chap. 4 in this book) calls the *Second Democratic Revolution*, also termed, more broadly speaking, the *third wave* of democratization.

political system that mixes Western-style liberal democracy with traditional top-down structures. Second, Benin has democratized rather rapidly and relatively successfully since 1989, after a long period of dictatorial rule. Benin followed a transition process that became a model for the continent's other francophone countries: the convening of all stakeholders in a national conference. Third, Kenya, pressured by the donor community and domestic actors, halfheartedly permitted a multiparty system in 1991, but resisted all further democratization. Despite widespread unpopularity, the ruling party remained in power for more than an extra decade by manipulating (at times violently) the transition process. Finally, Burundi offers an example of a democratic transition process beset by a decade of ethnic and regional violence. After a set of well-run elections in 1993 that resulted in rule by the ethnic Hutu majority for the first time since independence, some members of the ethnic Tutsi-dominated army assassinated the new president. This situation sparked waves of retributional 'ethnic' violence that have recently subsided but have not completely ended despite the peaceful, indirect election of a Hutu president who has attempted to reach out across the ethnic and regional divides.

In order to explore competing explanations for success and failure of these democratizations, we will examine the varying impact of voluntaristic and structural factors. The comparative case study approach, supplemented by these thematic investigations, will provide us with the opportunity to reconsider the extent to which the African continent's grave impediments to democratization might be overcome, as well as to reflect on alternatives to the dominant Western model of liberal democracy.

Experiences with Democracy and Democratization

Some authors, Osabu-Kle (2000) for example, have maintained that precolonial African societies largely were democratic. Although some elements of democracy—such as varying degrees of accountability of the ruler to the ruled—certainly did exist, for one to characterize authoritarian military empires (the Zulu under Shaka, for instance) and decentralized, stateless societies (the Twa in Central Africa, for example) as explicitly democratic entities would require considerable conceptual stretch. It is nonetheless true that colonialism disrupted existing institutions, reducing vertical accountability. Indirect rule in British colonies, for instance, made chiefs subservient to the British, thereby adding a new layer of autocratic rule.

For a century or more, the main purpose of the colonial state in Africa was to extract wealth, which was obtained through domination and imperialism. It was, as Berman reminds us, "an authoritarian bureaucratic apparatus of control and not intended to be a school of democracy" (Berman 1998, 329). The colonial powers did not envisage independence for generations, nor did they intend to give local people a say in how they were governed, because Africans were not considered capable of rational and intelligent deliberation.

Yet, after World War II, Europeans realized they could not maintain control over their colonies much longer. Most African countries, especially the former French and British territories, were hastily granted representative government in the years leading to independence. With the exception of the former Portuguese colonies, "[f]ormal democratic institutions were part of the decolonization pact everywhere" (Young 1999, 16).

Although the "democratic outlook" of independence struggles did confer to them international legitimacy (Young 1999, 17), nationalism, for the most part, was hardly a 'liberal' movement (Chazan 1993, 75). Independence leaders aimed to seize the state more than to reform it or to follow Western political models. These new leaders initially received substantial popular support from the masses in recognition of their anticolonial struggles, but they soon used it to articulate a political vision far more authoritarian than initially presented. In only very few countries, -such as Gambia and Botswana, did multiparty democracy survive more than a handful of years. More typically, soon after independence, almost all of the new governments "decayed" into authoritarianism, often instituting single-party states or being summarily overthrown in military coups. Some countries descended into extreme kleptocracy (such as Mobutu Sese Seko's Zaire), and a few others were decimated by brutal dictatorships (including Idi Amin's Uganda and Jean-Bédel Bokassa's Central African Republic/Empire). This trend toward authoritarianism and political centralization continued until the late 1980s, when changes in the former Soviet Union and Eastern Europe, combined with economic decay, political mismanagement, and a more proactive international community, strengthened the ability of the local opposition to confront incumbent leaders. Only after 1989, did Africa undergo a dramatic democratic renewal. Since then, forty-five out of sub-Saharan Africa's forty-eight countries have held multiparty elections.[3]

Below, we present a synthesis of selected African countries' postcolonial democratic "experiments," to borrow an expression from Bratton and van de Walle (1997). No two countries have identical political trajectories, and there is no "typical" African experience of democratization. However, common patterns do emerge and some experiences can be considered paradigmatic in their own way, allowing for valid, if tentative, generalizations.

A Stable Democracy with Authoritarian Roots: Botswana

The southern African country of Botswana is often cited as one of the continent's "premier" democracies (Holm and Darnloff 2000, 134). The sparsely populated, land-locked country has experienced several decades of stable, competitive multiparty politics, basically on a republican parliamentary model of governance. Unlike most other countries on the continent, Botswana is endowed with valuable mineral deposits that have been considerably well managed by a succession of democratically elected political leaders. These leaders have drawn, maintained, and derived legitimacy from a political system that has been able delicately to balance a sense of modern statecraft born in the West with traditional authoritarian structures that predate the advent of colonialism.[4]

When the former British protectorate of Bechuanaland became independent in 1966, the newly named Botswana was one of the poorest countries in the world. With arable land estimated at 1 percent and thus a topography unsuitable for productive farming, the country faced an uncertain future until large deposits of diamonds and copper-nickel matte were located in 1967 (Morton, Murray, and Ramsey 1989). These discoveries helped to radically restructure the political economy of Botswana, creating a revenue stream that facilitated economic growth and the provision of social services. Valuable natural resources have

---

3. van de Walle (2002, 67) identifies the exceptions of the Democratic Republic of Congo, Eritrea, Rwanda, Somalia, Swaziland, and Uganda. However, since his article was published, D.R. Congo, Rwanda, and Uganda have held multiparty elections. As a result of political liberalization, between 1989 and 2003, the proportion of Africans living in "not free" countries (using the Freedom House classification) fell from 54 percent to 29 percent, according to Chege (2005, 273).

4. For a more sanguine perspective, see Kenneth Goode (2005).

not always resulted in stability and growth on the continent, as is the case in Nigeria and the Democratic Republic of Congo (formerly Zaire). Successive military and democratically elected governments in Nigeria have squandered billions of dollars through mismanagement and corruption, and President Mobutu of Zaire accomplished the same feat during three decades of predatory rule. A close look at the structure of government in Botswana would reveal some important insights into the reasons this newfound wealth resulted in relative prosperity and stability in lieu of endemic corruption and political disintegration.

The country's primary architect of independence, and Botswana's first president, Seretse Khama is largely responsible for setting the precedent of managing the country's mineral wealth in a transparent and nationally advantageous manner. When he died in 1980, his sitting vice-president assumed the presidency and was reelected several times before retiring in 1998 and providing the opportunity for *his* vice president, Festus Gontebanye Mogae, to assume the office through elections. Although Botswana sometimes is characterized as a de facto one-party system, the 2004 elections in which Mogae was reelected help demonstrate the extent of existing competition. The ruling Botswana Democratic Party (BDP) received 52 percent of the popular vote, while two other major parties received 26 percent (Botswana National Front, or BNF) and 17 percent (Botswana Congress Party, or BCP) of the total votes cast.[5]

In addition to the National Assembly, the bicameral parliament is composed of the House of Chiefs, which is a fifteen-member advisory body consisting of chiefs from the eight primary ethnic groups in the country, four elected subchiefs, and three additional representatives chosen by the chiefs and subchiefs. This institutional and somewhat symbolic recognition of the importance of traditional authority is supplemented at the local level by the oft-cited *kgotla*, namely the village council system (Ngcongco 1990, 46; Somolekae and Lekorwe 1998). According to Holm and Darnolf, since gaining independence, government ministries have been using this traditional network of local councils headed by a local authority to "communicate with local communities on development projects." Whereas civil servants often set the agendas for *kgotla* gatherings, the *kgotla* "provides an opportunity for citizens to voice their concerns about proposed programs or to criticize [the]

---

5. See http://en.wikipedia.org/wiki/Politics_of_Botswana. See also
http://africanelections.tripod.com/bw.html for additional information.

functioning one" (Holm and Darnolf 2000, 134). Given the largesse of the public sector, the implicit importance of this power should not be underestimated. Overall, the "willingness to reflect traditional political and juridical structure—through the Kgotla and the chiefs [serving in the House of Chiefs] . . . established the critical organic links between the institutions of the modern state and a still-traditional society" (N'Diaye 2001, 84).

Despite the seeming success of this traditional/modern balancing act, Sklar offers a necessary cautionary note, citing "evidence of political domination by . . . elite and prosperous civil servants who have co-opted the traditional authorities of Tswana society and rule in conjunction with the leaders of the dominant political party" (Sklar 1999, 166). In addition, this "dominant political party" has remained in power since independence, making of parties such as the BNF and BCP a permanent opposition. Given the absence of alternation in political leadership, therefore, Africa's "premier" democracy has yet to demonstrate its ability to withstand the challenges of genuine political change. Although the contradictory notions of "democracy" and the bottom-up assertion of popular will, countered by distinctly nondemocratic tendencies of top-down traditional authority and single-party control of the government, have coexisted harmoniously since Botswana's independence, there remains potential for future leaders with explicit nondemocratic agendas to upset this delicate balance.

Democratization and the "National Conference" Model: Benin

Although it is a small country in West Africa, the relevance of Benin's experience extends to the whole continent. The country faces problems shared by much of Africa, such as economic dependency and sharp ethnoregional cleavages, and "according to the usual indicators of democratic success, Benin was not a good democratic prospect" (Magnusson 2005, 75). Nonetheless, its transition to democracy, in particular its "national conference" mechanism, served as a model for a number of other countries. Moreover, it is one of the few African countries to practice a systemic alternation of power.

For its first dozen years of independence, political life in Benin (then known as Dahomey) was extremely volatile. From the late 1950s to the early 1970s, successive governments, often identified with a particular ethnoregional group, endeavored but were unable to achieve stability. They were overthrown by the military, which—for being itself ethnically divided—would soon return power to civilian rule. This cycle, which had produced ten violent changes of government in twelve years (Onadipe 1996, 88), ended in 1972, when military officer Mathieu Kérékou seized power. In a few years, a single-party system was declared. France, Benin's former colonial ruler, remained Benin's principal commercial partner and aid donor. The country's small size and rather feeble resource endowment made it "one of Africa's least economically viable states" (Decalo 1997, 45). Only France's continued financing of the trade deficit kept the country solvent.

In the 1980s, incompetent economic management and ballooning domestic graft, including the draining of funds from parastatals, combined with a continent-wide economic crisis, simply bankrupted the economy. The government turned to the Bretton Woods institutions for support, but these required the implementation of unpopular economic austerity measures. In 1988, France refused to meet the budgetary shortfall, the three main banks—all state owned—collapsed, and the government was unable to pay teachers, civil servants, and soldiers their earned salaries, or students their grants. This crisis caused domestic opposition to mushroom, rendering the country "virtually ungovernable" (Heilbrunn 1993, 285). Both the World Bank (IBRD) and the International Monetary Fund (IMF) refused to provide emergency assistance because of Benin's failure to adhere to prior agreements (Westebbe 1994, 94). Kérékou convened a national conference to discuss the country's future course, bringing together representatives of all the sectors of Beninese society: "teachers, students, the military, government officials, religious authorities, [NGOs] nongovernmental organizations, more than fifty political parties, ex-presidents, labor unions, business interests, farmers, and dozens of local development organizations" (Magnusson 1999, 221).

Kérékou had believed that he could retain control of the 488 delegates. Instead, when it met in February 1990, the convention declared itself sovereign, redefined the powers of the presidency, reducing Kérékou's position to a figurehead role and appointing a former World Bank staff member, Nicéphore Soglo, to act as executive prime minister. In exchange for a full pardon for any crimes he may have committed, Kérékou peacefully ceded power. By March 1991, the Beninese electorate had ratified a new constitution, democratically electing Soglo to be president.

This transition process, inspired by the convening of the *États Généraux* (Estates-General) in France two centuries earlier, provided a model for other francophone countries in Africa—Congo Brazzaville, Niger, Chad, and Madagascar, among them. The outcome of the Beninese conference served as a warning to a number of authoritarian leaders in other countries—Gabon, Togo, and Zaire (as it was still known)—who managed to prevent their own national conventions from ousting them from power (see Robinson 1994).

The first democratic regime in two decades proved profoundly disappointing to many Beninese. President Soglo's structural adjustment policies became deeply unpopular, associated not only with high inflation and high unemployment but also with his autocratic style of leadership characterized by corruption, nepotism, and utter intolerance of dissent. Kérékou made a stunning comeback, defeating Soglo in the 1996 presidential elections.

Thus, in 1996, power in Benin was peacefully transferred from one democratically elected leader to another, thereby meeting the "two-turnover" criterion for democratic consolidation, "a succession test" that serves as a better indicator of democracy than a founding election (Segal 1996). To portray Beninese democracy as consolidated would be patently premature, however. Most striking about the 1991 and 1996 elections was the regional polarization of the electorate: both times the North overwhelmingly supported Kérékou, whereas the South supported Soglo. The 2001 presidential elections, too, pitted Kérékou and Soglo against each other (with several lesser-known contenders). Alleging severe irregularities in the first round of voting, Soglo and the third-ranked candidate withdrew, allowing Kérékou to beat the fourth-place candidate in the run-off without any difficulty. But the 2006 presidential elections marked the beginning of a new era, as both Kérékou and Soglo were ineligible to run because of their age. Characterized by some procedural complaints, the polls nonetheless produced an uncontested winner; a newcomer to politics, Boni Yayi, was elected in the second round with almost 75 percent of the vote (Seely 2007).

Benin thus can boast both a smooth transition to democracy and subsequently an alternation of presidents. Its democratic credentials remain, however, somewhat tarnished by electoral irregularities and also by serious corruption, no matter who takes power. Ethnoregional divisions often threaten the institutionalization of compromise, and the recycling of erstwhile discredited leaders has left voters with few alternatives all too long. Now that power has peacefully passed to a new generation, Benin may once again prove to be a model for the rest of the continent.

Reluctant Democratization: Kenya

For almost thirty years, between 1963 and 1991, Kenya remained a prototypical one-party state. Although Kenya achieved independence from the United Kingdom under a multiparty parliamentary constitution, the leader of the party of independence, Jomo Kenyatta, head of the Kenya African National Union (KANU), soon absorbed the opposition. Kenyatta relied on a "kitchen cabinet" of trusted advisors, drawn mainly from his own Kikuyu ethnic group and repeatedly amended the constitution to centralize power. Kenyatta's successor, Daniel arap Moi, assumed power after a bitter internal struggle and replaced influential Kikuyu with members of the Kalenjin (the ethnic group to which he belongs) and some allied ethnicities, thus further concentrating power in the hands of the presidency (Widner 1992).

Throughout the 1980s, a dramatic rise in autocratic rule and high-level corruption combined with steady economic decline fed internal discontent. Open pressure for political liberalization was exerted principally by the Law Society (the bar association) and the mainstream churches, both of which enjoyed a measure of protection from reprisals due to their professional standing and international contacts. Dissenting former politicians who had left—or had been expelled from— KANU could reenter the political arena only through a return to multipartyism. Inspired by the falling of single-party regimes in Eastern Europe after 1989, these domestic actors became bolder, beginning to draw increasing international attention from human rights organizations and donor countries. Most prominent among these pressure groups was the Forum for the Restoration of Democracy (FORD) (for details, see Throup and Hornsby 1998).

Until 1991, Western aid donors had been steadfast supporters of the Moi regime. In 1989, and once again in 1990, for instance, Kenya received over $1 billion in development assistance, most of it from the United States, the United Kingdom, Japan, Germany, the World Bank (IBRD), and the IMF (Organisation for Economic Co-operation and Development, n.d.). After the demise of the Soviet bloc and the concomitant decrease in the strategic value of Africa, donors tended to become explicitly more concerned with the internal affairs of their African allies. The "maverick" U.S. ambassador to Kenya, Smith Hempstone, played an important role in supporting multiparty advocates. Large popular demonstrations in 1990–1991 drew violent government repression and led to the arrest of prominent activists, and this in turn increased international attention to the issue of democratization in Kenya and, more generally, in Africa as a whole.

Donor pressure grew during this period, and in late 1991 donors suspended all new aid to Kenya (except for humanitarian assistance), pending a number of reforms to be adopted, including the liberalizing of the political arena. Within days, Moi announced that Kenya would return to multipartyism—something he had long maintained was out of the question, arguing that it was not only undesired by Kenyans but also inappropriate for a multiethnic country such as Kenya. Soon after Moi's announcement, the parliament did amend the constitution in a manner to allow opposition parties to function legally. The executive branch nevertheless remained quite powerful.

Since the return to a multiparty system, Kenya has held four elections (in 1992, 1997, 2002, and 2007). The first two times, President Moi was reelected, and KANU managed to retain control of parliament in a process that fell short of the international standards of "free and fair," in large part due to a host of illegitimate strategies, which included skewed distribution of constituencies, gross irregularities in voter registries, partisan media and electoral commission, and also fraudulent vote counts and even ethnic cleansing in key areas. Although ethnic- and personality-based divisions within the opposition facilitated KANU's victory, it is unlikely that those in power would have allowed themselves to be removed through the ballot box. In the 1992 and 1997 elections, donors had sufficient evidence of an uneven playing field and of poll irregularities to contest the legitimacy of the outcomes. However, they chose not to do so, mainly out of concern for stability. In between elections, they virtually ignored issues of democratization (Brown 2001).

The 2002 elections, however, were much more free and fair than the preceding ones, actually removing KANU from power for the first time since independence. Prohibited from running again by term limits, Moi personally had selected Jomo Kenyatta's son Uhuru as the KANU candidate, though Uhuru lacked both political experience and general support. Many high-level KANU loyalists, who resented being passed over, subsequently joined an opposition alliance, decisively crippling KANU. A coalition among most major opposition parties and the KANU defectors thus gained a majority of seats in parliament, and Mwai Kibaki, the coalition's joint candidate, was elected president. His new coalition government contained a number of senior officials that had been KANU stalwarts; therefore, it was reluctant to deal with their past crimes. And, in large part, because it had relied on these tainted politicians to maintain a parliamentary majority, it also did not pursue any major cases of corruption and of human rights abuses (Brown 2004). The Kibaki government reneged on its promise to reduce significantly the extensive powers of the presidency and thereby to broaden and deepen the gains made in democratization since the early 1990s.

Many hoped that the 2007 elections would be another watershed for democracy in Kenya, marking the first time in Kenyan history that a democratically elected leader, having lost an election, would hand over power to another—a rare event in Africa and, for well-wishers, a hallmark of democratic consolidation. However, amid irregularities in the count, an improbable razor-thin majority for Kibaki in the presidential poll led to a national crisis. Anger over "stolen elections" translated into political violence in many parts of the country, causing hundreds of deaths and the displacement of hundreds of thousands of people targeted because of their ethnic group and in consequence of their presumed political affiliation. The government's response was reminiscent of Kenya under Moi: curtailment of freedom of assembly and expression, combined with violent repression by security forces.[6] At the time of finalizing this chapter, American and South African mediators were trying to broker a compromise between Kibaki and Raila Odinga, the opposition's principal presidential candidate, in order to break the deadlock and defuse tensions. The impact of this setback in Kenya's democratization process will be felt for many years to come.[7]

---

6. Parallels with Moi's rule began to be drawn within months of Kibaki's inauguration (Brown, fieldwork, June–July 2003; see also Murunga and Nasong'o 2006).

7. As in Kenya (home to some forty "minority" ethnic groups), elections in African presidential regimes often occasion zero-sum power games among political affiliations that are markers for ethnic or tribal identity. Intolerant rivalries among these suspicion-laden allegiances fuel ambitions to concentrate resources and power in a single tribe or in temporarily convenient coalitions. Regime instability is in-built, in that it is easy for political operators to exacerbate latent ethnic tensions for their own political gain at any given moment. Yet, notwithstanding its multiple porous borders (Ethiopia 861 km, Somalia 682 km, Sudan 232 km, Tanzania 769 km, Uganda 933 km); its manifold segmented society (Kikuyu 22 percent, Luhya 14 percent, Luo 13 percent, Kalenjin 12 percent, Kamba 11 percent, Kisii 6 percent, Meru 6 percent, other African 15 percent, non-African—Asian/European/Arab—1 percent; Protestant 45 percent, Roman Catholic 33 percent, Muslim 10 percent, indigenous creeds 10 percent, other beliefs 2 percent); its rich assortment of refugees (150,000 Somalis, 77,000 Sudanese, 15,000 Ethiopians, 431,000 internally displaced); its endemic 40 percent unemployment rate; its high public debt (estimated at 48.5 percent of GDP in 2006); its highest-level graft and corruption scandals; its use as a crossroads and a platform for trafficking people and drugs; and with half of its population under the poverty line, Nairobi's voluntary partnership with the West

Ethnic/Regional Violence and Democratization: Burundi

In June 1993, Burundians chose their first popularly elected Hutu president, Melchior Ndadaye. For the Hutu majority (estimated at 85 percent of the population), there was a feeling of excitement that ethnic majority rule had become the political order of the day. The minority Tutsi (comprising approximately 14 percent), for the most part, accepted the results with trepidation, fearing a "tyranny of the majority." Many recognized the potential for retribution after 28 consecutive years of Tutsi military rule. But despite these tensions, the majority of Burundians (including many Tutsi) accepted the democratic outcome in the hope that the country would finally resolve the ethnic tensions that had led to localized bursts of violence in 1965, 1972, 1988, and again in 1991. The new democratic order rapidly disintegrated, however, following Ndadaye's assassination by Tutsi military officers, less than five months after assuming the presidency. Ndadaye had planned to restructure the army, the better to reflect the country's ethnic diversity, and this clearly had alarmed many in the Tutsi-dominated institution. The civil war that began immediately following Ndadaye's assassination resulted in the death of more than 800,000 people, while also exacting a high psychological toll from the general population.

The history of this land-locked central African country provides insight into the roots of the current crisis of democracy fueled by ethnic and regional animosities. After several centuries of localized rule, a centralized kingdom emerged in which the king—the *mwami*—was to assert regal authority over Hutu, Tutsi, and Twa (pygmy) subjects. So the royal family, while more closely related to the ethnic Tutsi, remained

---

against extremists in Kenya and in neighboring states, the use of the country as a base for NGOs in Southeast Africa, its relative stability in a war-torn region, its ability not to be drawn into any of the region's wars, and the steady growth of its economy since 2002 are strategic assets. This strategic importance remains at great risk of being adversely affected should ongoing attempts at postelectoral reconciliation fail to restore stability, despite the sense of vindication gained by the opposition upon the election of its nominee by a very small margin (105 to 101) to the third most powerful position in the country—the Speaker's chair—in the Parliament's very first session held on January, 15, 2008, following the controversial Presidential elections in December 2007.

Watching poor-looking Kenyans form patient voting queues or say they seek democracy on international TV, reminds one of Jefferson's suggestion (see Preface) that there is "no safe depository of the ultimate powers of society but the people themselves" even when the citizenry is thought "not enlightened enough" to exercise the control of the powers vested in it with "wholesome discretion." Future stances here ought not to involve acts that deprive the populace of its powers but measures tailored to edify a people-in-becoming or a citizenry-in-the-making of that very discretion.—*Ed.*

separate and distinct from the three ethnic groups until the onset of colonial rule at the end of the nineteenth century. Throughout this colonial period, ethnic differentiation was not pronounced; the *mwami* rewarded amply those who served the monarch well, regardless of their ethnic and/or clan-based lineages (Kadende-Kaiser and Kaiser 1997).[8]

From 1890 to 1919, Burundi was a German colony, until the end of the First World War, when the League of Nations placed Burundi (and the neighboring Rwanda) under Belgian trusteeship. In 1962, on the eve of Burundian independence, the son of the ruling monarch (who was also the Prime Minister-elect) Louis Rwagasore was assassinated. Less than a year after an unsuccessful Hutu-led coup attempt in 1965, the Tutsi army captain Michel Micombero assumed the presidency by overthrowing the king. In 1972, another aborted Hutu-supported coup d'état resulted in massive military reprisals, leaving at least 200,000 dead and forcing the exile of many others. Two successive military coups next resulted in continued Tutsi dominance of the government under the presidencies of Colonel Jean-Baptiste Bagaza (1976–1987) and Major Pierre Buyoya (1987–1993), lasting until the democratic election of Ndadaye. This succession of Tutsi military coups merely demonstrates that the Tutsi minority itself was not unified during this period. Regional- and clan-based differences repeatedly surfaced, especially in pursuit of the scarce resources of a fledgling economy so closely controlled by the state. After Ndadaye's assassination, brief rule by two Hutu presidents gave way to the return of Tutsi military rule. Buyoya reclaimed the presidency in 1996 with the support of the army, promising to restore calm.

International efforts to resolve the ongoing ethnic strife have been continuous, with a succession of mediators intervening with the support of multilateral organizations such as the United Nations and the Organization of African Unity. Since 1993, the Secretary-General of the United Nations has sent a series of Special Representatives to Burundi, including former Tanzanian President Julius Nyerere, who so served from 1996 until his death in 1999 (Maundi 2003; Ould-Abdallah 2000). And South Africa's Nelson Mandela brokered an accord that was signed in 2000 by the representatives of seventeen Tutsi- and

---

8. Though often portrayed as distinct "ethnic groups" or "tribes," the Hutu and Tutsi actually share a common language, culture, and traditional religion. They arguably are better described as *fluid identity groups*, with significant intermarriage and mobility occurring between the two entities (see Lemarchand, 1995).

Hutu-dominated parties. Under this agreement, Buyoya remained in power for eighteen months with a Hutu for vice president, next relinquishing the presidency to the Hutu President Domitien Ndayizeye, who governed with a Tutsi vice president. Upon the conclusion of this thirty-six-month transition, which formally began in November 2001, multiparty parliamentary elections were held with a measure of success, haltingly returning the country to the democratic trajectory that was interrupted following Ndadaye's assassination, as a consequence of the ethnic violence that ensued.

A principal obstacle to peace in the country has been the civil war waged by Hutu-armed insurgencies: the National Council for the Defense of Democracy/Forces for the Defense of Democracy (CNDD-FDD) and the National Liberation Forces/Party for the Liberation of the Hutu People (FNL-Palipehutu). Both groups subsequently splintered into subgroups, initially refused to sign the 2000 accord, opting instead for a military solution to the ongoing problems in Burundi. In December 2002, however, the government and the CNDD-FDD signed a ceasefire agreement that addressed many of the decisive military and political concerns of both parties. The CNDD-FDD ultimately decided to join the government. In July 2005, the CNDD-FDD won parliamentary elections with 58 percent of the vote. This was followed in August 2005 with the indirect election to the presidency of the former rebel leader of CNDD-FDD, Pierre Nkurunziza, who—after serving for almost two years as the Minister for Good Governance in the transitional government—received 151 of the 162 votes cast in the legislative chamber in the August 2005 election. Despite repeated ceasefires and intermittent negotiations between the FNL-Palipehutu and the government, the rebel group has continued to resort periodically to violence in pursuit of its political goals. Until the FNL-Palipehutu formally and faithfully renounces violence and joins the political process, sustainability in the recent democratic advances will continue to be very questionable.

Even if this transition returns the country to an electoral process similar to that practiced in 1993, there is little guarantee that such a move will result in a peaceful, democratic order. Ethnicity and regionalism but also proliferation of multiple understandings of the cause of, and solution for, current woes in the country, render another direct multiparty election for the presidency potentially destabilizing. Aronoff (2008) and Spinner-Halev (2008)' reinforce this assertion by elucidating how subnational divisions complicate, and often undermine, the democratic experience, and do so at the very levels of democratic citizenship and political ethics. In the case of Burundi, there is a need to develop a system of government that protects the security and the rights of the minority, while providing the ethnic majority with the political gains it has been starved of for so long.

Competing Explanations

There is little if any consensus on the specific causal factors that eased the democratizations begun in so many African countries in 1989, and even less general agreement as to their relative import. In order to identify and organize systematically the major competing explanations for success and failure in democratic transitions and consolidation, we have categorized two general sets of explanations.

Structural Explanations

These are mainly explanations informed by the impact of culture, history, and economics. They are diverse and often result in very different conclusions. Early advocates of the modernization paradigm focused on the inability of "traditional" societies to adapt to the social, economic, and political demands of modernity. In order to develop, these societies had to leave behind traditional, communal forms of social organization and in their stead embrace Western "rational" assumptions of individualism and market-based productivity (Rostow 1960). Several among the advocates of modernization also argued that economic development was a necessary precondition for the establishment of a democratic/participatory kind of political order (Huntington 1968). The early Marxist critique of this viewpoint was captured by assumptions of class-based inequality and by assertions of dependency (Leys 1974; Cardoso and Faletto 1976).

Other scholars have looked to history as the primary explanatory variable. Mamdani's (1996) comparative work on South Africa, and also on Uganda, eloquently makes this case, while the world systems theory approach pioneered by Wallerstein (1974) explicitly embraces the high import of historical legacy and, in the case of Africa, the impact of colonialism in understanding current crises of political and economic order. Much like the dependency tradition, the political economy approach also accommodates the significance of the intersection between politics and the economy based on the rationalized assumption that economic crisis foments social and political discontent, thereby leading to regime change. Some advocates of this approach have argued that economic crises reduce incumbent regimes' patronage resources, foment dissatisfaction, and hence increase demands for democratization (Joseph 1999, 64). Writing on structural adjustment in Africa, van de Walle (2001) examines how leaders, all the same, have been quite able to manipulate reform processes the longer to remain in power.

Whereas these types of explanations dominate, they do not represent the complete repertoire of possibilities that have been proffered in recent years: many scholars have placed focus also on the significance of regime type and the actions of self-interested elites. Certain regime types and some political leadership profiles are assumed to be more amenable to the democratic transition process or, alternatively, less inclined to support processes that seem to hold the potential to alter significantly the political landscape.

Voluntaristic Explanations

Instead of focusing on structural impediments to—or incentives for—democracy, voluntaristic explanations prefer to emphasize the ability of select actors to affect change. These agents of change may include rulers employing strategies designed to maintain the status quo or to transform the political system; grass-roots civil society organizations mobilized to confront (and ultimately even to dislodge) intransigent incumbent regimes (Harbeson, Rothchild, and Chazan 1994; Ndegwa 1996; Orvis 2001); members of the donor community determined to initiate or discourage regime change in an effort to respond to specific, often self-serving, interests (Brown 2001); and military personnel who often may come to believe they can do a better job of maintaining political order and promoting economic growth in divided societies than civilian leaders deriving and wielding their authority much too democratically (Malan 2000).

The four cases examined in this chapter demonstrate that none of the explanations offered above, whether structural or voluntaristic, sufficiently capture the complexities inherent in transformations and in nurturing full transitions to democratic rule. For example, in all four countries, the first generation of leaders inherited democratic polities, yet only Botswana retained a semblance of democracy. Similarly, cultural differences are insufficient to explain differing outcomes—the various cultures of one specific country have not been demonstrated to be inherently more or less democratic than in another one. Other contributing factors, such as economic crises, are also too generalized to constitute robust explanatory and/or predictive arguments across a broad set of cases. Finally, as Ndegwa (1996) and Orvis (2001) point out, the presence of civil society organizations has not served to guarantee democracy: some organizations implicitly and others, on occasion, all too explicitly, toil on behalf of the status quo and for the incumbent regime. In sum, democratizations in Africa know of no simple causal mechanism. Rather, they result from a very complex interplay of intricate conditions and compound actors.

Impediments and Prospects

Impediments to Democratization

Until the early 1990s, scholars of democratization and experts in African politics expected authoritarianism, single-party states, and military rule to continue to dominate observers' understandings and explanations of the African political landscape, as they had for decades. They were convinced that the continent lacked the structural prerequisites for democracy associated with such elsewhere: Africa was not characterized by advanced capitalism, had low literacy rates, and had no civic culture to buttress democracy. Moreover, the agents that had been found to introduce democracy in other regions—namely, the middle or working classes—were weak and/or often co-opted under authoritarian rule. The consensus was that "[d]emocratization was not supposed to happen in Africa" (Joseph 1997, 363).

It is true that impediments to democratization are stronger in Africa than in any other region of the world. The state and civilian society, two critical actors in a democracy, tend to be weak. Also, African countries generally suffer from long-standing economic crises and extreme poverty, in addition to little if any experience of democratic governance and widespread societal alienation as well. Another fundamental obstacle to democratization throughout the continent is neopatrimonial rule, described as "the *core* feature of politics in Africa" (Bratton and van de Walle 1997, 62, italics in original). Neopatrimonialism is inimical to democratization because the distribution of state resources is based on the ruling elite's petty personal ties and not on lofty principles such as the public good, national citizenship, or equal opportunities. Furthermore, the ruler's personal prerogatives all too often eclipse or override the role of formal institutions and of the rule of law. However, the economic liberalization that has developed since the 1980s has rather palpably undermined patronage-based politics.[9]

Most authoritarian leaders, experiencing growing pressure from domestic and international actors, have agreed to hold multiparty elections. They have liberalized politically but often not to extents sufficient for them to be defeated publicly. Out of forty new multiparty elections held in sub-Saharan Africa between 1989 and 1997, only fifteen were found to be significantly free and fair, and in only twelve cases did a change in leadership occur (Bratton and van de Walle 1997, 97; Bratton 1998, 54). Transitions to democracy thus remain incomplete in places such as Burkina Faso, Cameroon, Chad, Gabon, Gambia, Guinea, Togo, and Zimbabwe. In a few cases, the democratization process was at least temporarily reversed by military coups—in Burundi, the Central African Republic, Congo (Brazzaville), Côte d'Ivoire, Niger, Nigeria, and São Tomé and Príncipe, for example.

Even if a full transition to democracy does take place, the endurance of democracy will prove an even more difficult challenge. For a number of historical and practical reasons, political identity or identification in Africa tends to be organized along ethnoregional lines. Political parties often compete to be able to bring benefits to their (mostly ethnoregional) client networks. The ethnicization of politics, often reinforced by astutely divisive and self-interested politicians themselves, promotes competition for access to resources, thus crowding out the ends and means of institutionalized compromise that at least theoretically ought to characterize a democracy.

A number of authors (e.g., Ihonvbere 1996) fault African rulers' corruption and blame their feeble commitment to democratic principles once they gain power. After the defeat and replacement of former dictators, newly installed leaders often use their powers to ensure that they remain in office beyond constitutionally mandated term limits. This encourages 'backsliding' toward authoritarianism. In Malawi, Mali, and Zambia, for instance, reasonably fair elections were followed by subsequent electoral contests that were notably less transparent. Only seven of the sixteen *second* elections held between 1995 and 1997 were found to be "free and fair" (Bratton 1998, 56). To date, the alternation of parties in power (an important gauge of democracy) has occurred

---

9. For an in-depth treatment, see Brown (2005, 183–184). On enduring neopatrimonialism, see Gyimah-Boadi (2004, 22).

in four countries only: Benin, Cape Verde, Mauritius, and Madagascar, the last of which was paralyzed for several months in 2002, until the outgoing president finally conceded power.

The newer democracies face challenges that their authoritarian predecessors did not; these include the extension of citizenship to all geographic areas and social sectors (Przeworski et al. 1995, 39). This type of challenge is specially pronounced in South Africa, where racial inequalities were institutionalized by apartheid. Among the greatest problems yet to be faced are the need and means to meet the raised expectations of the electorate, let alone the Herculean task of providing good governance (which would require the limitation of executive powers, the de-emphasizing of ethnoregional ties, and the eschewal of a 'winner-take-all' mentality), of reversing the decline in the standard of living that most of the continent has suffered from, and most surely also of meeting all voters' basic human needs.

The impediments to democratization are therefore significant, but certainly not insurmountable. Numerous transitions to democracy have occurred in Africa since 1989. Many were short-lived or only presented democratic façades, but in a number of cases democracy has shown surprising endurance and resilience. Though the trajectories of many countries may be viewed as disappointing, such failures often can lead to more imaginative, more responsive systems of governance (Herbst 1999, 248–249). Moreover, the state of democracy in Africa is vastly superior to what observers expected before 1989. Among the most important gains are major advances in freedom of expression, in the entrenchment of the idea of legitimate opposition. There is some indication, furthermore, that regular electoral competition is self-reinforcing: even substandard elections stand to promote further democratization in the future (Lindberg 2006). The widespread desire for democratization cannot be easily reversed toward re-legitimizing authoritarianism. Despite the paucity of democratic success stories in Africa and the failure of democratization to improve socioeconomic conditions, today liberal democracy remains a widely shared popular aspiration across the continent (Lumumba-Kasongo 2005, 15).

Prospects: Which Way(s) Forward?

The question is often raised of the appropriateness for African countries of what is understood under the 'liberal-democratic model' (for the model's relevant aspects, see Doran, Botwinick, and Kincaid, chaps.

2, 3, and 5 in this book, for instance). Rather than trying to "engineer" African societies to fit the Western political model, might it not prove more appropriate to discover models that are better suited to Africa. Ake (1996, 132), for one, proposed a paradigm shift that would require far greater participation in decision making, greater emphasis on social policy (especially in rural areas), the promotion of collective rights, and the incorporation of marginalized groups. Mamdani (1996) and Berman (1998) both contend that the relations between rural Africans and local rulers (the so-called traditional, or customary, authorities) should be democratized. They point to need for greater local participation. What this means, in practical terms, remains yet to be developed. The national conference model launched in Benin represented an attempt to ensure that the transition to democratic rule would be an inclusive process, incorporating both marginal and dominant groups across rural/urban divides. However, as the examples of Congo (Brazzaville) and Niger demonstrate, there is no guarantee that such an approach to political transitions will result in a democratically stable order.

Culturally based arguments fare no better in presenting concrete alternatives. For instance, Ayana (2002, 50) recommends investing African democracy with "collective ceremonies and secular rituals" that would allegedly enhance grassroots participation and bolster the crucial relation between communities and the state. Osabu-Kle (2000) advocates abolishing political parties and modifying existing representational institutions in the manner to include professional entities or interest groups and to ensure that decisions are made consensually, as per "African tradition." Banning parties, however, could be a way of disguising authoritarianism. Uganda's "no-party 'movement' model," in place from 1986 to 2005, appeared to be a single-party system, all but in name. A few authors, Adediji (1995, 138) among them, suggest a return to precolonial forms of rule, despite the century-long hiatus in their practice and the uncertain applicability to the scale of the nation-state. Is it reasonable, one might ask, to conclude that in multiethnic countries, the culture and tradition of one particular group should serve as the model for democratic governance, when other groups offer competing models? In sum, the modern practicality of these suggestions remains very much in doubt.

In addition to the example of Botswana discussed earlier, a few African countries have grafted onto Western political institutions certain innovative elements. In order for its common populace to voice complaints, Mali holds a yearly forum known as the *Espace d'Interpellation*

Démocratique. South Africa and Namibia have established "councils of traditional rulers," and Ghana boasts a "council of elder statesmen." Though Malawi's constitution initially provided for a Senate composed of chiefs and other sectional representatives, this provision was repeatedly postponed and later simply abolished before ever being implemented (Brown 2008). Such alternative mechanisms are supposedly based on tradition; but, in fact, they are usually new, non-elective institutions that enjoy only consultative status. Though governments might heed some of the advice that these provide, it is likely that they will not amount to more than ineffective talk shops, at best. And, worse still, they might be manipulated into providing greater apparent legitimacy for regimes that, absent the likes of these, risk not attracting any popular support at all. Moreover, to the extent that they fortify existing power structures (chiefs were often instruments of colonial and postcolonial despotic rule), such institutions might even tend to reinforce the exclusion of women and of other participants from the political realm, in a distinctly antidemocratic endeavor. Critics of Botswana's governance model have been quick to point out the salient exclusionary characteristics of the House of Chiefs and *kgotlas* that coexist with the more powerful parliamentary institutions of national government; they stress the fact that there has been no alternation among political parties now in power since the days of independence.

Sometimes the argument is also made that many or most African countries are just 'not ready' for democracy or that they have 'other priorities'. Ottaway (1999), for one, contends that a number of African countries need to achieve greater stability and to resolve issues of 'stateness' before democratization becomes even possible. The Moi regime repeatedly made this argument before the advent of multiparty-ism in Kenya; and retrospective analyses of the violent political transition in Burundi have questioned the appropriateness of standard conceptions of democracy, given the ethnic and regional polarization that has periodically erupted into violent outbursts since early independence. Nonetheless, in many cases, democratization might actually assist in state (re)construction (see Kincaid, chap. 5 in this book).

Admittedly, democracy and democratization have an unclear causal relationship with economic growth. What may seem more certain is that democracy does and will require some economic and social development to survive. In other words, popular support for democracy will depend to a certain extent on its ability to "deliver the goods." A range of factors outside a democratic regime's control, such as debt burdens, inadequate rainfall, and low commodity prices, undermines its capacity to perform well in this respect. Alternatively, accidents of geography and change in demographics also have the potential to facilitate the democratization process, as the example of Botswana demonstrates.

The case of Kenya clearly shows that, by providing assistance for state and for civilian society, external aid donors have an important role to play in supporting African democracies. Most donors, however, no matter how committed to democratization in theory, are confronted with policy goals they consider more immediate, such as neoliberal economic reforms or strategic considerations that can involve bolstering authoritarian regimes. Broadly viewed, neither the global environment nor any of the international actors can be counted on to buttress democratizations in Africa. As Teune argues in chapter 4 of this book, the African continent does remain marginal in the far broader context of globalizations and democratizations.

Regional actors could prove more proactive. If democratic rule increasingly becomes a norm in Africa, as evidenced by the mechanisms of the African Union and the New Partnership for Africa's Development (NEPAD), greater and growing formal and informal roles will be vested in the regional hegemonies: principally Nigeria, in West Africa, and South Africa, in Southern Africa. If they are willing to assume the role, their influence and occasionally active intervention could be crucial for encouraging and sustaining democratization. Nonetheless, too much hope should not be invested in them, for their efforts could fail. South Africa, for example, was unable to negotiate an agreement in Burundi, was widely criticized for intervening militarily in Lesotho in 1998, and was faulted for failing to condemn political repression and electoral fraud in Zimbabwe. Also, both of these regional powers face important domestic challenges themselves: South Africa is struggling to overcome the legacy of apartheid, while Nigeria's own democratic survival is far from certain.

What types of African countries should prove to provide the most fertile ground for sustained democratization in the future? Making predictions is a difficult task, nowhere more so than in Africa's shifting political terrain. The performance of new democratic leaders in the areas of governance, economic growth, and poverty alleviation will all prove to be crucial in the longer term. A simple gauge for measuring the internalization of democratic rules is the respect of the presidential term limits, adopted in many countries in the early 1990s as part of the

democratization process.[10] It is evident that the paths to democratization are diverse and sinuous. Nonetheless, four factors constitute
encouraging signposts along the way: first, strong popular support for
democracy (overcoming long-standing mass suspicion of the colonial
and postcolonial state); second, an elite consensus on democracy's
desirability (encouraging election losers to accept outcomes); third, an
institutionalization of democratic governance; and lastly (and no matter
how low the starting point), a positive socioeconomic outlook.

References

Adediji, Adebayo (1995) "An Alternative for Africa," in Larry Diamond and Marc F.
Plattner, Editors, *Economic Reform and Democracy*, pp. 126–139, Baltimore, MD: Johns
Hopkins University Press.

Ake, Claude (1996) *Democracy and Development in Africa*, Washington, DC: Brookings
Institution.

Aronoff, Myron J. (2008) "Democratizations in Fissured Societies: The Makings of
Citizenship," in Jose V. Ciprut, Editor, *The Future of Citizenship*, Cambridge, MA: The
MIT Press.

Ayana, Daniel (2002) "Anchoring Democracy in Indigenous African Institutions," *African
and Asian Studies*, 1(1) (February):23–61.

Berman, Bruce J. (1998) "Ethnicity, Patronage and the African State: The Politics of Uncivil
Nationalism," *African Affairs*, 97(388) (July): 305–341.

Bratton, Michael (1998) "Second Elections in Africa," *Journal of Democracy*, 9(3) (July):
51–66.

Bratton, Michael, and Nicolas van de Walle (1997) *Democratic Experiments in Africa: Regime
Transition in Comparative Perspective*, New York: Cambridge University Press.

Brown, Stephen (2001) "Authoritarian Leaders and Multiparty Elections in Africa: How
Foreign Donors Help to Keep Kenya's Daniel arap Moi in Power," *Third World Quarterly*,
22(5) (October):725–739.

——— (2004) "Theorising Kenya's Protracted Transition to Democracy," *Journal of
Contemporary African Studies*, 22(3) (September): 325–342.

——— (2005) "Foreign Aid and Democracy Promotion: Lessons from Africa," *European
Journal of Development Research*, 17(2) (June): 179–198.

——— (2008) "Transitions from Personal Dictatorships: Democratization and the Legacy
of the Past in Malawi," in Shadrack Wanjala Nasong'o, Editor, *The African Search for Stable*

---

10. Some countries such as Namibia later amended their constitution to allow re-
election. However, several incumbents' attempts to legalize an additional mandate were
defeated, often after widespread opposition, forcing presidents Frederick Chiluba of
Zambia, Bakili Muluzi of Malawi, and Daniel arap Moi of Kenya, for example, to abandon
their campaigns to extend their rules.

Forms of Statehood: Essays in Political Criticism, pp. 187–227, Lewiston, NY: Edwin Mellen Press.

Cardoso, Fernando, and Enrique Faletto (1976) *Dependency and Development in Latin America*, Los Angeles: University of California Press.

Chazan, Naomi (1993) "Between Liberalism and Statism: African Political Cultures and Democracy," in Larry Diamond, Editor, *Political Culture and Democracy in Developing Countries*, pp. 67–105, Boulder, CO: Lynne Rienner.

Chege, Michael (2005) "Democratic Governance in Africa at the Start of the Twenty-first Century: Lessons of Experience," in Leonard A. Villalón and Peter VonDoepp, Editors, *The Fate of Africa's Democratic Experiments: Elites and Institutions*, pp. 267–289, Bloomington: Indiana University Press.

Decalo, Samuel (1997) "Benin: First of the New Democracies," in John F. Clark and David E. Gardinier, Editors, *Political Reform in Francophone Africa*, pp. 43–61, Boulder, CO: Westview.

Goode, Kenneth (2005) "Resource Dependency and Its Consequences: The Costs of Botswana's Shining Gems," in *Journal of Contemporary African Studies*, 23(1) (January):27–50.

Gyimah-Boadi, E. (2004) "Africa: The Quality of Political Reform," in E. Gyimah-Boadi, Editor, *Democratic Reform in Africa: The Quality of Progress*, pp. 5–27, Boulder, CO: Lynne Rienner.

Harbeson, John W., Donald Rothchild, and Naomi Chazan, Editors (1994) *Civil Society and the State in* Africa, Boulder CO: Lynne Rienner.

Heilbrunn, John R. (1993) "Social Origins of National Conferences in Benin and Togo," *Journal of Modern African Studies*, 31(2) (June):277–299.

Herbst, Jeffrey (1999) "Understanding Ambiguity during Democratization in Africa," in James F. Hollifield and Calvin Jilson, Editors, *Pathways to Democracy: The Political Economy of Democratic Transitions*, pp. 245–258, New York and London: Routledge.

Holm, John D., and Staffan Darnolf (2000) "Democratizing the Administrative State in Botswana," in York Bradshaw and Stephen Ndegwa, Editors, *The Uncertain Promise of Southern Africa*, pp. 115–151, Bloomington: Indiana University Press.

Huntington, Samuel (1968) *Political Order in Changing Societies*, New Haven, CT: Yale University Press.

Ihonvbere, Julius O. (1996) "Where Is the Third Wave? A Critical Evaluation of Africa's Non-Transition to Democracy," *Africa Today*, 43(4) (October–December):343–368.

Joseph, Richard (1997) "Democratization in Africa after 1989: Comparative and Theoretical Perspectives," *Comparative Politics*, 29(3): 363–382.

——— (1999) "The Reconfiguration of Power in Late Twentieth-Century Africa," in Richard Joseph, Editor, *State, Conflict, and Democracy in Africa*, pp. 57–80, Boulder, CO: Lynne Rienner.

Kadende-Kaiser, Rose M., and Paul J. Kaiser (1997) "Modern Folklore, Identity, and Political Change in Burundi," *African Studies Review*, 40(3) (December):29–54.

Lemarchand, René (1995) *Burundi: Ethnic Conflict and Genocide*, Cambridge, UK: Woodrow Wilson Center Press and Cambridge University Press.

Leys, Colin (1974) *Underdevelopment in Kenya: The Political Economy of Neo-Colonialism*, Berkeley and Los Angeles: University of California Press.

Lindberg, Staffan I. (2006) *Democracy and Elections in Africa*, Baltimore, MD: Johns Hopkins University Press.

Lumumba-Kasongo, Tukumbi (2005) "The Problematics of Liberal Democracy and Democratic Process: Lessons for Deconstructing and Building African Democracies," in Tukumbi Lumumba-Kasongo, Editor, *Liberal Democracy and its Critics in Africa: Political Dysfunction and the Struggle for Social Progress*, pp. 1–25, Dakar: CODESRIA Books.

Magnusson, Bruce A. (1999) "Testing Democracy in Benin: Experiment in Institutional Reform," in Richard Joseph, Editor, *State, Conflict and Democracy in Africa*, pp. 217–237, Boulder, CO: Lynne Rienner.

――― (2005) "Democratic Legitimacy in Benin: Institutions and Identity in a Regional Context," in Leonard A. Villalón and Peter VonDoepp, Editors, *The Fate of Africa's Democratic Experiments: Elites and Institutions*, pp. 75–95, Bloomington: Indiana University Press.

Malan, Mark (2000) "Civil-Military Relations in Africa: Soldier, State and Society in Transition," in Hussein Solomon and Ian Liebenberg, Editors, *Consolidation of Democracy in Africa: A View from the South*, pp. 139–171, Aldershot, UK: Ashgate.

Mamdani, Mahmood (1996) *Citizen and Subject: Contemporary Africa and the Legacy of Late Colonialism*, Princeton, NJ: Princeton University Press.

Maundi, Mohamed Omar (2003) "Preventing Conflict Escalation in Burundi," in Chandra Lekha Sriram and Karin Wermester, Editors, *From Promise to Practice: Strengthening UN Capacities for the Prevention of Violent Conflict*, pp. 327–350, Boulder, CO: Lynne Rienner.

Morton, Fred, Andrew Murray, and Jeff Ramsey (1989) *Historical Dictionary of Botswana: New Edition*, Metchen, NJ: Scarecrow.

Murunga, Godwin R., and Shadrack W. Nasong'o (2006) "Bent on Self-Destruction: The Kibaki Regime in Kenya," *Journal of Contemporary African Studies*, 24(1) (January):1–28.

Ndegwa, Stephen (1996) *The Two Faces of Civil Society: NGOs and Politics in Africa*, West Hartford, CT: Kumarian Press.

N'Diaye, Boubacar (2001) *The Challenge of Institutionalizing Civilian Control: Botswana, Ivory Coast and Kenya in Comparative Perspective*, Lanham, MD: Lexington.

Ngcongco, L. D. (1990) "Tswana Political Tradition: How Democratic?" in John Holm and Patrick Molutsi, Editors, *Democracy in Botswana*, pp. 42–47, Athens: Ohio University Press.

Onadipe, Abiodun (1996) "The Return of Africa's Old Guard," *Contemporary Review*, 269 (August):87–92. Organisation for Economic Co-operation and Development (n.d.) *International Development Statistics Online*, www.oecd.org/dac.

Orvis, Stephen (2001) "Civil Society in Africa or African Civil Society?" in Stephen Ndegwa, Editor, *A Decade of Democracy in Africa*, pp. 17–38, Leiden: Brill.

Osabu-Kle, Daniel T. (2000) *Compatible Cultural Democracy: The Key to Development in Africa*, Peterborough, Ont.: Broadview.

Ottaway, Marina (1999) *Africa's New Leaders: Democracy or State Reconstruction?* Washington, DC: Carnegie Endowment for International Peace.

Ould-Abdallah, Ahmedou (2000) *Burundi on the Brink 1993–95: A UN Special Envoy Reflects on Preventive Diplomacy*, Washington, DC: United States Institute of Peace.

Przeworski, Adam [with Pranab Bardhan et al.] (1995) *Sustainable Democracy*, New York: Cambridge University Press.

Robinson, Pearl T. (1994) "The National Conference Phenomenon in Francophone Africa," *Comparative Studies in Society and History*, 36(3) (July):575–610.

Rostow, Walter W. (1960) *The Stages of Economic Growth*, Cambridge, UK: Cambridge University Press.

Seely, Jennifer C. (2007) "The Presidential Election in Benin, March 2006," *Electoral Studies*, 26(1) (March):196–200.

Segal, Aaron (1996) "Can Democratic Transitions Tame Political Successions?" *Africa Today*, 43(4) (October–December):369–384.

Sklar, Richard (1999) "Africa Polities: The Next Generation," in Richard Joseph, Editor, *State, Conflict, and Democracy in Africa*, pp. 165–179, Boulder, CO: Lynne Rienner.

Somolekae, G. M., and M. H. Lekorwe (1998) "The Chieftaincy System and Politics in Botswana, 1966–95," in W. A. Edge and M. H. Lekorwe, Editors, *Democracy: Politics and Society*, pp. 186–198, Pretoria, South Africa: J. L. van Schaik.

Spinner-Halev, Jeff (2008) "Exclusion, Fear, and Identity in Emerging Democracies," in Jose V. Ciprut, Editor, *Ethics, Politics, and Democracy: From Primordial Principles to Prospective Practices*, Cambridge, MA: The MIT Press.

Throup, David W., and Charles Hornsby (1998) *Multi-Party Politics in Kenya: The Kenyatta and Moi States and the Triumph of the System in the 1992 Elections*, Oxford, UK: James Currey.

van de Walle, Nicolas (2001) *African Economies and the Politics of Permanent Crisis: 1979–1999*, New York: Cambridge University Press.

——— (2002) "Africa's Range of Regimes," *Journal of Democracy*, 13(2) (April):66–80.

Wallerstein, Immanuel (1974) *The Modern World System: Capitalist Agriculture and the Origins of the European World-Economy in the Sixteenth Century*, New York: Academic Press.

Westebbe, Richard (1994) "Structural Adjustment, Rent Seeking, and Liberalization in Benin," in Jennifer A. Widner, Editor, *Economic Change and Political Liberalization in Sub-Saharan Africa*, pp. 80–100, Baltimore, MD: Johns Hopkins University Press.

Widner, Jennifer A. (1992) *The Rise of a Party-State in Kenya: From "Harambee!" to "Nyayo!"* Berkeley: University of California Press.

Young, Crawford (1999) "The Third Wave of Democratization in Africa: Ambiguities and Contradictions," in Richard Joseph, Editor, *State, Conflict, and Democracy in Africa*, pp. 15–38, Boulder, CO: Lynne Rienner.

11

Immigration from and
Democratizations in
Latin America: Crossing
the Mexico-U.S. Border

Douglas S. Massey
and S. Mara Pérez

Backdrop

Authoritarian regimes rely on a monopolization of political resources
to perpetuate themselves in power. Within a specified territory, authoritarian officials defend their exclusive control of political resources
to foreclose a mobilization against their rule. The tactics used in this
defense typically include co-option as well as repression, with the
precise mixture of the two to be determined by historical circumstances
and the perceived severity of the potential threat. In general, any social,
political, or economic process that threatens an authoritarian elite's
monopoly on power constitutes a challenge to the regime.

Because direct political control extends only as far as a state's territorial borders, any process that transcends international frontiers carries
with it an implicit threat to the established order, as some portion of
the process occurs, by definition, outside the regime's direct internal
control. Global economic integration is thus inherently antiauthoritarian, as it exposes national populations to transnational flows of capital,
goods, information, and commodities, the social and economic consequences of which are difficult to manage (Przeworski 1991). This fact
explains why authoritarian regimes have generally sought to control
the terms of their integration into global markets and why autocratic
regimes that have opened themselves fully to trade and economic
integration have not lasted.

As the global marketplace expands and transnational linkages proliferate, international boundaries become increasingly porous not only
with respect to goods, commodities, information, and capital but also
with respect to people (Sassen 1996; Andreas 2000). Immigration is part
and parcel of the broader process of economic globalization (Hatton
and Williamson 1998; James 2001; Massey and Taylor 2004) and is

composed of two rather distinct flows (Massey 2005). A portion of what is homogeneously labeled *immigration* really represents a flow of capital, in this case human capital: the knowledge and skills inculcated in people through prior education and experience. The transfer of human capital necessarily involves the movement of people; and countries seeking to build a modern, knowledge-based economy increasingly have found themselves competing for a scarce supply of global talent. Rather than erecting barriers to keep out highly educated immigrants, most developed countries now find themselves lowering barriers and creating incentives to attract them.

"Immigration" also incorporates another flow that, in contrast to the supply of human capital, is abundant on world markets: labor. As labor markets have globalized, the relative oversupply of unskilled workers throughout the world has depressed wages in developed nations, and political officials in these countries have come under pressure to restrict the in-migration of workers (Massey 1999; Meyers 2004). As a result, most developed countries have imposed stringent numerical limitations, backing them up them with repressive sanctions, which are eased typically for humanitarian reasons only—family reunification or political asylum and the like (Freeman 1992, 1995).

A great deal of scholarly attention has been directed to the integration of immigrants, with concern for its potential influence on citizenship, politics, and culture within receiving nations (Jacobson 1997). Scholars have considered the influence of immigrants on liberal democracies, such as those in North America and Europe (see Joppke 1998; Castles and Davidson 2000), as well as on autocratic monarchies, such as those in the Persian Gulf (Shah and Arnold 1986). Relatively few scholars have considered the influence of international migration on politics in sending nations.

As a process that transcends international boundaries, migration on the international level necessarily has important implications for the politics of sending regions, particularly if they are dominated by authoritarian regimes whose monopoly of power is being challenged domestically. Large-scale labor migration toward industrially advanced countries removes citizens from the usual mechanisms of co-option and control and gives them far-reaching access to new resources—monetary, psychological, and cultural—that can be used to contest authoritarian rule at home. Here, we consider the nature of the relationship between international migration and democratization in sending nations. After considering the interrelation generally, and describing how it played out within several different Latin American nations, we use Mexico as a prime example of how international migration can, within a broader context of global economic integration, contribute significantly to a democratic transition.

Borders, Migrants, and Democratization

Borders have long played a crucial role in mobilizations against repressive regimes. By demarcating the limits of a state's legitimate authority, a border divides the world into a zone where political activities are highly constrained and subject to the direct control of ruling elites and a zone where they are not. Once citizens leave the sovereign territory of an authoritarian country, they acquire greater freedom to organize politically; to access, collect, and disseminate information; and to compile and spend resources. It is no coincidence that many of the twentieth century's revolutions were launched from abroad (e.g., in 1917, the Bolshevik Revolution began when the Germans brought Lenin back to Russia from his exile in Switzerland, and in 1959, the Cuban Revolution was launched when the *Granma* set sail from Mexico).

By providing a safe haven from coercive state powers, foreign locations offer political actors a safe space in which they can organize. Typically, however, the number of political exiles located in any one country is small. Even in the broad context of large-scale movements of refugees and displaced persons, success in a mobilization depends more on the ability of exiled leaders to mobilize the masses at home than on their aptitude in organizing them among exiles abroad, as refugees generally have few resources to contribute to 'the cause'.

International migration, however, offers dramatically different circumstances. By creating a large diaspora of autonomous, well- and long-established, secure people outside the authoritarian regime's sphere of control, mass immigration creates significant potential for an independent political mobilization. If the time, money, knowledge, and energies of a large immigrant diaspora can be mobilized against authoritarian rule, a potent dynamic for political change may ensue, particularly if it can be linked to prodemocracy movements at home.

Numbers

What sets international migration apart from other transnational movements of people are the size, duration, and stability of the flows, which eventually yield large and well-established diasporas (Massey et al.

1998). The largest and oldest migratory system in the world is that prevailing in North America, which is dominated by immigration from Latin America. In absolute terms, the largest diaspora is that of Mexico, which at nearly 8 million persons in the year 2000 dwarfs all others. However, Mexico is a very large country, home to some 100 million people, so the percentage of Mexicans living abroad is only around 8 percent. The number of Salvadorans in the United States in 2000 was only 765,000, but it constituted a much larger share of the total national population of 7 million. As a result, nearly 11 percent of all persons of Salvadoran birth lived in the United States.

In general, the Latin American immigrant populations number in the hundreds of thousands, ranging from 326,000 Guatemalans to 950,000 Cubans in the year 2000 (leaving aside the special case of Mexico). In relative terms, the diasporas range in size from 1 percent to 11 percent of the total national population, led by the relatively large populations of Salvadorans (10.8 percent), Cubans (7.9 percent), Dominicans (7.6 percent), and, of course, Mexicans (7.3 percent). Latin American immigrants offer a prime example of how sustained international migration can lead to large numbers of citizens living outside countries of origin and thus free from the control of political authorities. Such large expatriate populations represent a latent resource that opposition politicians can potentially mobilize for greater democracy at home.

Circularities

The size of an opposition movement is always important, but if the mobilized opposition is rooted outside the country of origin, an additional factor in assessing its political potential is the degree to which it remains connected to people at home. The most important connection between members of a diaspora and their origin population is regular movement back and forth. Unfortunately, data do not allow for the measurement of return migration. We therefore draw on prior research (Jasso and Rosenzweig 1982; Warren and Kraly 1985) to offer a rough classification of the degree to which international migration from various Latin American nations is circular.

The best-studied case is that of Mexico, and there is little doubt that this migratory flow has been dominated historically by massive circularity (Massey, Durand, and Malone 2002). According to estimates generated by Massey and Singer (1995), 85 percent of undocumented entries to the United States between 1965 and 1985 were offset by departures, and of all people who have ever migrated to the United States, most still live in Mexico. Although the data for Dominicans are not as precise, their migration also appears to be highly circular (Grasmuck and Pessar 1991; Levitt 2001), a pattern that is consistent with their high rate of documentation, which further enables free cross-border movement. At the other extreme are Cubans, whose political circumstances prevent their movement back and forth to Cuba. As a result, Cuban exiles in the United States are substantially cut off from their insular compatriots.

In between these two extremes are El Salvador, Guatemala, and Colombia. The former two nations lie just south of Mexico and thus have indirect access to a land border with the United States; but as relatively large shares of both groups are undocumented, they have difficulty taking advantage of this land connection. Although Colombians are mostly documented, the economic costs of moving back and forth are relatively high. Although crossing by land is theoretically possible, it is quite impractical, so the transnational movement of Colombians invariably involves air flight. As a result, the degree of circularity among Colombians is tempered.

Freedoms

Whether or not the substantial latent political potential in a demographically large diaspora can be activated also depends on the degree to which migrants can be successfully mobilized against the home regime, which depends, in turn, on political latitudes in the receiving society (see Gutiérrez 2008). In the contemporary world, immigrants flow into one of two kinds of polities. International migrants headed for North America and Western Europe enter open, democratic societies in which state authorities make little if any organized attempt to monitor the political activities of inhabitants, native or foreign. In stark contrast, migrants going to countries such as Kuwait, Saudi Arabia, or Singapore enter centralized authoritarian regimes that maintain a tight grip on the political activities of citizens and foreigners alike. The political authorities in these countries do their utmost to limit the social and political rights of migrants as a matter of state policy and may even cooperate with the authorities in the sending nations, the better to monitor the activities of migrant workers.

Even when they live and work in liberal democracies, however, the relative freedom of immigrants to organize themselves politically depends substantially on the legal status under which they entered. Little political mobilization is likely if immigrants lack the legal right to live and work in the host country. As a result, differences in the rate of documentation across immigrant groups will yield very different potentials for political mobilization. We have estimated the percentage of undocumented, among Latin American immigrants accounted for as living in the United States in the year 2000, by combining data from the U.S. Bureau of the Census (2001) with figures from the U.S. Immigration and Naturalization Service (2001).

Cubans have the most secure legal status in the United States, as virtually all are documented and free to organize as they see fit. At the other extreme are Guatemalans and Salvadorans: some 62 percent of the former and 53 percent of the latter lack appropriate documents. Under these circumstances, the odds of political mobilization are dramatically lowered because immigrants lack the freedom to organize and are loath to do anything to draw attention to themselves for fear of being arrested and deported.

With 42 percent of its members undocumented, the Mexican diaspora in the United States might still be mistaken as being also suboptimally politicized. But even if undocumented migrants constitute a large minority of all Mexicans, the base population being very large, a 58 percent documentation rate applied to a population of 8 million yields 4.6 million Mexican immigrants who are legally present and thus also free to organize and mobilize politically. Among Dominican and Colombian immigrants, the vast majority are in the United States legally: only 13 percent of the former and 18 percent of the latter were undocumented in the year 2000. Even though their populations are not large, therefore, on this dimension alone, they exhibit a high potential for political mobilization.

The ultimate freedom for immigrants to mobilize as they please is acquired through naturalization as U.S. citizens. The acquisition of U.S. citizenship puts expatriates in the best of possible positions to organize, as it does offer them not only full political rights in the United States but also all the legal protections that U.S. citizenship may provide them within their home countries. Yet the acquisition of U.S. citizenship is a double-edged sword: first, it implies a shift in allegiance away from the sending nation and toward the host society, and, second, it undermines the legitimacy of expatriates as political leaders at home. Latin American immigrants vary considerably in the degree to which they are naturalized. By far the highest percentage of U.S. citizens is among Cubans: 57 percent. The lowest rate is among Salvadorans, Mexicans, and Guatemalans, whose citizenship rates hover around a mean of 20 percent (18 percent, 20 percent, and 22 percent, respectively). Dominicans and Colombians fall in between, with corresponding rates of 33 percent and 38 percent.

Concentrations

The potential for political mobilization is affected not only by the relative number of immigrants and their legal status but also by their geographic concentration. If the vast majority of a country's expatriates are found in a single metropolitan area, for example, then the mechanics of political organization are greatly simplified. Even if the total number of migrants is small, they may constitute a potent political force if they all live in one place, compared with a larger immigrant population scattered widely throughout the country.

Latin American immigrants differ considerably in the degree of geographic concentration within the United States. The two highest concentrated groups are Cubans and Dominicans. In the former case, nearly three-quarters (73 percent) reside in the state of Florida, mostly in and around the city of Miami; in the latter case, the same percentage of Dominicans reside in New York or New Jersey—almost all in and around New York City. Although 63 percent of Guatemalans reside in the state of California, they are scattered across several metropolitan areas. Los Angeles houses the largest community, but substantial communities also exist in San Francisco and San Diego.

None of the other immigrant populations evinces a majority in any single state or region. Although 47 percent of Mexicans live in California, they find themselves scattered across an array of metropolitan and nonmetropolitan areas. Other key states of destination for Mexicans are Texas and Illinois, but during the 1990s, there was a remarkable diversification away from these historical points of attraction (Durand, Massey, and Charvet 2000). By comparison, only 44 percent of migrant Salvadorans live in California, and 33 percent of Colombians live in the New York–New Jersey area.

Resources

In addition to size, legal status, and geographic concentration, another factor determining the potential for political mobilization is the quantity of economic resources possessed by a diaspora. Most other things being equal, an immigrant population with few resources will be less effective in mobilizing politically than one potentially able to raise large sums of money from its members. Using data compiled by Meyers (1998), we derived estimates of the relative amount of money remitted from Latin American migrants in the United States to their countries of origin in 1995.

Naturally, Mexico led the pack with an estimated $3.7 billion in annual remittances, reflecting the huge number of Mexicans working in the United States as well as their high likelihood of remitting (see Massey and Parrado 1994; Lozano Ascencio 1998). Although remittances to Mexico are huge in the aggregate, the Mexican economy itself is much vaster. As a percentage of Mexican GDP, therefore, remittances are only 2 percent, and given Mexico's status as an exporter of both manufactured goods and petroleum, 'migradollars' constitute a mere 4 percent of total exports.

Nonetheless, these funds have a disproportionate effect on the Mexican economy because they flow to the bottom of the socioeconomic hierarchy and are spent relatively quickly, generating strong economic multipliers. Durand, Parrado, and Massey (1996) estimated that US$6 billion in remittances translates into US$18 billion in increased income and production once multiplier effects are taken into account. The Mexican diaspora thus possesses significant economic weight that might be tapped to bring about palpable political change at home.

The nation in which the economic leverage of immigrants is greatest, however, is probably El Salvador, where $1.1 billion in annual remittances constitutes nearly 12 percent of the country's GDP and 52 percent of its exports. El Salvador's diaspora by itself assures the liquidity of the Salvadoran economy (Funkhouser 1992). In economic terms, therefore, immigrants from El Salvador should possess considerable political leverage.

Although the US$800 million remitted annually by Cubans in the United States constitutes only 5 percent of Cuba's GDP, this sum represents 57 percent of Cuba's total exports. The entry of migradollars into Cuba is strictly regulated by the Castro regime, however. And even though Cubans in the United States might conceivably wish to withhold their remittances as an act of protest, the Castro regime correctly counts on familial interests to override political dissent and other principled imperatives. Relatives living in Cuba are critically dependent on remittances, and mainland families are thus quite reluctant to stop sending them on principle.

In the Dominican Republic, money controlled by U.S. immigrants constitutes a very critical resource: $800 million in an $11.3 billion economy, representing 7 percent of total GDP and 16 percent of exports. For the most part, this money enters the economy freely, through formal and informal channels, and the regime is relatively open to movements of people, goods, and capital back and forth between the island and the North American mainland (Levitt 2001). Remittances also figure prominently in the economy of Guatemala, where the estimated $350 million sent annually constitutes 2.4 percent of the GDP and 12 percent of exports; but they play a far more modest role in Colombia, where the $172 million in annual remittances no doubt pales in comparison with the huge annual revenues from the drug trade and, in any event, constitutes just 0.2 percent of GDP.

Economic Contexts

The foregoing considerations aside, the political consequences of immigration also depend on the broader economic context within which they occur. And in most cases large-scale emigration emerges as an adaptive response to economic development under market mechanisms. It offers poor households a means of accumulating capital and protecting themselves from forces on the home market (Massey et al. 1998). Under circumstances where a nation is creating markets and integrating them into the global economy, transnational movements of people are just one of several flows with important social, economic, and political consequences. With integration into the global economy, authoritarian regimes begin to lose control over flows of information, and with the privatization of industries, they also lose many levers of political influence. As the state recedes and yields more terrain to private enterprise, nongovernmental organizations acquire greater prominence in civic life. Across Latin America, authoritarian regimes that fully embraced markets and global economic integration (as Argentina and Brazil have done) ultimately found it quite difficult to resist the mounting pressures for democratization.

Among the countries considered here, Mexico clearly lies on one extreme of economic openness and Cuba on the other. In 1986, Mexico joined the General Agreement on Tariffs and Trade (GATT) and committed itself to deregulation, privatization, foreign trade, and investment. And in 1994, it partnered with Canada and the United States to create a continent-wide market: the North American Free Trade Agreement (NAFTA) (Massey, Durand, and Malone 2002). In contrast, Cuba was an isolated command economy until 1989, when the collapse of the Soviet Union and the ensuing elimination of subsidies forced it haltingly into global markets. Although the Castro regime has positioned certain sectors to compete globally for consumers (e.g., tourism and pharmaceuticals), Cuba remains fundamentally a centralized Stalinist state that is very substantially disconnected from the world capitalist system and even more so from both the U.S. economy and the Cuban diaspora in the United States.

Other Latin American nations lie between these two extremes. El Salvador and Guatemala historically have been governed by small land-owning elites who could preserve their economy as dependent commodity producers (bananas and coffee) linked to the global economy on unequal terms. In reaction to these historical inequalities, both nations were wracked by violence and civil war during the 1980s. And although the armed struggles ultimately did lead to peace with some structural reforms, neither Guatemala nor El Salvador experienced the neoliberal realignment that occurred elsewhere in Latin America. In these two countries, large sectors still remain substantially outside of global and even national markets.

In contrast, over the past decades the Colombian government has adopted a variety of neoliberal policies. But political and economic changes have been less far-reaching than in Mexico, Argentina, or Brazil, however, because of the weakness of the central government, which continues to experience challenges to its authority from left-wing guerillas, right-wing paramilitary groups, and narcotics cartels. As a result, the government lacks effective control over much of its territory. In the Dominican Republic, the collapse of the Trujillo dictatorship in 1965 led successive governments to dismantle the centralized political economy he had created and to open up the nation to global trade and investment, especially during the 1980s, albeit not to the same extent as Mexico succeeded in doing.

Immigrant Mobilization across Latin America

We have outlined seven influential dimensions on which immigrant diasporas seem to vary in their potential for political mobilization. Taken together, these dimensions also yield an overall assessment of the likelihood of prodemocratic mobilization among Latin American immigrants in the United States. All things considered, the conditions over the past decade have been quite favorable for political mobilization among immigrants from Mexico, Cuba, and the Dominican Republic; moderate among those from Colombia; and low among immigrants from El Salvador and Guatemala. The reasoning behind these assessments is as follows.

The high extent and effectiveness of political organization among expatriate Cubans opposed to the Castro regime is very well documented (Portes and Stepick 1993). Despite the fact that the diaspora's size, documentation, concentration, citizenship, and resources all point to a high level of mobilization, expatriate Cubans have had little if any success in promoting democratization at home. This outcome is hardly surprising given that the Cuban diaspora was created through political means and led by former elites rather than through migrant labor or via fomentation by endogenous market forces. Moreover, the low degree of circularity and the closed nature of Cuban society are such that, despite their high level of political mobilization, Cuban exiles have achieved hardly any success in putting pressure on the Castro regime.

A better example of effective democratic mobilization is provided by Cuba's Caribbean neighbor, the Dominican Republic. From 1930 to 1961, the country was ruled autocratically by Rafael Trujillo, who deliberately restricted emigration to prevent the formation of hostile exile communities overseas (Georges 1990). Trujillo's assassination in 1961 ushered in several years of political unrest, coups, and countercoups that culminated in a U.S. invasion and in the installation of a former Trujillo crony, Juan Balaguer, as president, in 1965. To defuse the tense political situation, the U.S. embassy made immigrant visas freely available, first to rid the island of left-wing activists and later to ease growing unemployment pressures on the nascent government (Grasmuck and Pessar 1991).

After 1965, the number of Dominicans in the United States rose from a few thousand to nearly 700,000 in 2000. As the community grew, it developed and organized a network that came to include branches of the principal opposition parties: the Dominican Revolutionary Party (PRD) and the Dominican Liberation Party (PLD) (Pessar and Graham 2001). After 1965, the leader of the progressive opposition, the PRD's Juan Bosch, mobilized Dominicans in New York and returned triumphantly to the island in 1978 to be elected president (Levitt 2001). In this mobilization, New York's Dominican community served as a principal resource for organization and funding; and in the 1980s, its leaders began to campaign for greater political recognition by authorities on the island, pressing for dual nationality and external voting rights.

Recognizing the growing political clout of U.S.-based Dominicans, the Dominican Senate formed a committee to investigate their concerns in the early 1990s. In 1994, the Dominican constitution was amended to allow for dual nationality. And in 1997, new laws were passed to allow expatriate Dominicans to vote in presidential elections. The influence of the diaspora on homeland politics crested in 1996, when an island-born New York–raised Dominican lawyer, Leonel Fernández, was elected president, and pledged to uphold democratic norms and to honor local constitutional rule (Levitt 2001; Graham 2001).

The case of immigrants from El Salvador and Guatemala contrasts sharply with the foregoing examples; their characteristics militate against political mobilization. The low rate of documentation, the relatively small number of citizens, economic marginality in the United States, low-to-moderate levels of geographic concentration, and very limited circulation hinder possibilities for political mobilization, despite the huge economic importance of the diaspora for the sending country, especially so for El Salvador. According to recent research (Hagan 1994; Menjívar 2000), both Guatemalan and Salvadoran immigrants have remained disconnected from home country politics and have abstained from participating materially either in resisting authoritarian rule or toward facilitating political changes.

Immigrants from El Salvador, in particular, display a very tenuous existence in the United States with rather fragmented networks that prevent effective organization (Menjívar 2000; Mahler 1995). Instead of exporting political influence back to the homeland, the Salvadoran diaspora seems to have sent back its marginality and disorganization in the form of urban gangs and rising rates of drug abuse (Thurlow 2000).

Migration and Mobilization: The Case of Mexico

Perhaps the clearest example of migrant mobilization against authoritarian rule is that of Mexico, where emigrants in the United States have played a central role in opposing, and ultimately deposing, the ruling regime (Pérez 1997, 1998). Prior to 2000, Mexico was dominated by a powerful presidency, which controlled the state bureaucracy and ran the official political party (Camp 1999) known as the PRI (Partido Revolucionario Institucional). Mexican presidents served nonrenewable six-year terms, and traditionally each president handpicked his successor, who was then duly ratified by the party. In essence, each president personally selected a successor to serve as dictator for another six years in an institutionalized system that created turnover on a regular basis and gave it great resiliency, prompting the well-known Peruvian writer Mario Vargas Llosa to label it "the perfect dictatorship" (Cothran 1994).

The foundations for this system were laid from 1920 to 1940 in the aftermath of the Mexican Revolution, by three generals, each of whom succeeded the other as president: General Alvaro Obregón created a centralized power structure based on a new constitution; General Plutarco Elías Calles founded the official party as an instrument of presidential power; and General Lázaro Cárdenas gave the party a corporatist structure while also institutionalizing the process of presidential succession (Hart 1987). From 1940 to 1970, the system functioned smoothly, keeping political peace and promoting steady economic development (Centeno 1994). The regime maintained a monopoly on power through a combination of political co-option, obfuscatory revolutionary rhetoric, and populist economic spending, backed up occasionally by the use of force (Hansen 1971).

By 1968, however, cracks were beginning to appear in the system. That year, a student revolt turned into a total political mobilization against the state. It was suppressed by a bloody massacre in downtown Mexico City (Poniatowska 1975). After 1970, in an effort to restore the regime's lost credibility, President Luis Echeverría engaged in massive foreign borrowing and increased social spending, expanding the state and distributing resources to the masses (Centeno 1994). By the time he left office in 1976, however, his massive borrowing had pushed the Mexican treasury into devaluation. The next president, José López Portillo, took office in an atmosphere of crisis and instability (Levy and Bruhn 2001).

The discovery of massive new oil reserves in Mexican waters early in 1977 seemed to promise salvation; but after a prudent start, López Portillo continued the populist spending policies of his predecessor, borrowing heavily from abroad, not only to finance oil production but also to increase social spending and continue expanding the state (Centeno 1994). A drop in oil prices during the early 1980s once again pushed the regime into default, and in 1982 Mexico was forced into a drastic devaluation that ushered in a period of economic chaos, which Mexicans labeled "the lost decade" (Sheahan 1991).

Under pressure from both U.S. banks and international lenders, a new cadre of modernizing technocrats took control of the state in late 1982 and began introducing a package of neoliberal economic reforms that called for ending public subsidies, privatizing money-losing state industries, downsizing the state bureaucracy, dismantling the protective tariffs, and generally entering the global market economy as a competitive exporter (Sheahan 1991). These reforms caused very considerable economic hardship on the poor and working classes, and that in turn led to massive political mobilization against the regime during the 1988 presidential elections—the first truly contested elections since the foundation of the PRI regime (Pérez 1997, 1998).

This mobilization proceeded from both the right and the left. While the Partido de Acción Nacional (PAN) attracted voters from the center-right under the leadership of businessman Manuel Clouthier, the newly established PRD mobilized voters from the center-left under the leadership of renegade PRI politician Cuahautémoc Cárdenas. Though both campaigns were successful in mobilizing large numbers of people, the PRD proved to have the stronger popular base, given the huge number of poor and working-class Mexicans and the instant name recognition its candidate enjoyed for being the son of the deeply revered former President Lázaro Cárdenas.

Naturally, in an effort to perpetuate its rule, the PRI resorted to its tool kit of co-optive and repressive tactics, bribing local officials, rigging polls, intimidating campaign organizers, and even threatening the candidates, trashing opposition offices, pressuring the media, and otherwise disrupting the campaign operations of the PRD and the PAN (Centeno 1994). But in 1988, a new mobilization arose, out of the reach of Mexico's local machinations. Until then, the Mexican diaspora had little or no role in Mexican presidential politics, but that year the political mobilization sweeping Mexico spread northward into the United States (Pérez 1997). It is the fractures in the Mexican regime that led to the establishment of the PRD. And it is this that eased the transnational connection, by activating a preexisting but latent diaspora and incorporating that U.S.-based entity in a now-concerted binational effort vying to democratize Mexico: soon enough, the PAN would launch a transnational political campaign (Pérez 1998).

In Mexican communities throughout the United States, migrants established offices for both the PAN and the PRD, mounted local fundraisers, and organized campaign rallies often attended in person by the candidates. Substantial funds were raised north of the border and channeled into party coffers for use against the PRI. Political ads were purchased in Spanish-language newspapers and television stations in the United States, and these reached out not only to immigrants who responded with additional donations but also to the millions of Mexicans living in cities along the border, notably in Tijuana and Juarez (Pérez 1998). Party officers in the United States organized caravans to allow voters to be driven to and from Mexico in order to exercise their voting rights.

In the end, the PRI preserved its power through massive fraud (Centeno 1994). Most likely, Cárdenas did win a plurality of the vote, and possibly even a decisive majority; but once it became clear that the PRD had swept electoral districts in Mexico City, the government announced a "computer failure," suspending the tabulation of votes. Ballots were secretly "counted" by election officials. And several days later, the PRI candidate, Carlos Salinas de Gortari, was declared the "winner" with 50.4 percent of the popular vote.

Angry street demonstrations and massive protests in Mexico did not prevent Salinas from taking office and quickly consolidating his political control. He was to become one of the most powerful leaders modern Mexico had ever known (Centeno 1994). Salinas accelerated the pace of neoliberal reform and brokered Mexico's entry into NAFTA, thereby making it impossible for a successor to undo the political and economic changes he had put in motion. At the same time, Salinas developed what Dresser (1991) has called a "neopopulist solution to neoliberal problems," through the National Solidarity Program, which came to be known by its Spanish acronym, PRONASOL (Programa Nacional de Solidaridad).

This program targeted government funding to local communities, provided they also contributed materially to the project in question and formed a local "solidarity committee." Thus it became a mechanism for political patronage that tied grassroots organizations and local communities directly to the regime. Moreover, PRONASOL's funds were disproportionately allocated to regions that had mobilized against the PRI in the 1988 elections. This 'neopopulist' measure proved to be remarkably effective in restoring political support for the regime by the midterm elections of 1991 (Dresser 1991).

Although PRONASOL may have been 'neopopulist' it was no more than a variation on a very old political theme in Mexico, creating a new co-optive mechanism that was consistent with neoliberal principles. What was truly revolutionary and unprecedented was the creation, in 1990, of an international wing of PRONASOL as part of an explicit attempt to extend the regime's co-optive mechanisms across the border to the Mexican diaspora in the United States (Smith 1995). The international initiative had two basic prongs: the Program for Mexican Communities Abroad (PCME), administered by the Foreign Ministry and implemented through its U.S. consulates to maintain relations with Mexicans living north of the border, and the Programa Paisano, which was designed to improve the circumstances of returning immigrants by protecting them from abuses by Mexican police and customs officials (Smith 1998, 2001; Goldring 1998; Zabin 1995). Both programs represented a deliberate effort to neutralize the success enjoyed by the PRD and the PAN in mobilizing Mexicans in the United States during the 1988 campaign (Pérez 1997, 1998).

By 1993, it appeared to most observers that President Salinas's neoliberal restructuring had succeeded in reestablishing the hegemony of the PRI, but his carefully crafted solutions began to unravel during the last year of his presidency (Oppenheimer 1996). On January 1, 1994, Indian peasants in the state of Chiapas rose in armed revolt against the neoliberal political economy. A few months later, his would-be successor, Luis Donaldo Colosio, was assassinated during a campaign stop in Tijuana, forcing Salinas to substitute a politically inexperienced economist as his heir. Finally, in September 1994, the Secretary General of the PRI (the President's former brother-in-law) was unceremoniously shot and killed in downtown Mexico City.

Amidst this political chaos, nervous Mexican voters elected the PRI candidate, Ernesto Zedillo, despite vigorous mobilization by the PAN and a weaker showing by the PRD. Just three weeks after Zedillo's inauguration, his Minister of Finance botched a devaluation of the peso, thereby unleashing another round of hyperinflation and economic turmoil, followed by the arrest of President Salinas's brother and the exile of the former president himself. As the PRI's grip on power declined, the political mobilization of the Mexican diaspora in the United States continued, and its power and influence in Mexican affairs never ceased to rise (Levy and Bruhn 2001).

As early as 1988, the PRD had proposed that Mexicans attaining U.S. citizenship be allowed to remain Mexican citizens and to continue to have the right to vote in Mexican elections. This position proved to be extremely popular with the Mexican diaspora. Thus, to preempt the opposition, President Zedillo and the PRI threw their support to the concept of dual nationality, even as they continued to drag their feet on voting rights. In March 1998, a constitutional amendment was enacted, allowing Mexicans who acquired U.S. citizenship to retain their Mexican passports. In principle, this granted them the right to vote in Mexican elections.

Although specific mechanisms to permit voting had not been worked out by the time of the 2000 presidential elections, Mexicans in the United States once again played an active role in contesting the PRI's hegemony (Levy and Bruhn 2001). This time, however, popular support swung over to the center-right PAN party under the new leadership of Vicente Fox Quesada. Whereas the PAN party historically had been dominated by conservative Catholic interests, these traditional power brokers were outflanked by Fox, a multinational executive who tried his luck at an unauthorized run for the party's nomination and, to the surprise of many, succeeded in capturing it in an open primary.

Candidates of the PAN historically had come from Monterrey, and those of the PRI and the PRD from Mexico City, neither of which are major historical sources for emigration to the United States (Durand, Massey, and Zenteno 2001). Despite their endorsement of dual nationality and improved conditions for returning migrants, candidates from the PRI and the PRD were therefore disconnected from migrants and their woes and had otherwise no real understanding of the centrality of U.S. migration in the life of Mexican communities at home and abroad.

In contrast, Vicente Fox is from Guanajuato, a key sending state with a hundred-year history of heavy involvement in large-scale out-migration (Durand, Massey, and Parrado 1999). Fox understood migrants and their communities; he reached out to them as no candidate ever had, campaigning vigorously in Mexican communities north of the border, referring to Mexican immigrants as "heroes" and throwing his support behind voting rights for dual-nationals. Support for Fox surged across the diaspora in the 2000 elections, and immigrants in the United States contributed heavily to his campaign, assuring his victory and thus ending the PRI's seventy-year monopoly on presidential power. With Fox's inauguration in December 2001, democracy finally came to Mexico, thanks to the major role played by the Mexican diaspora in the United States, who became decisive elements in the broader process of Mexican democratization.

Conclusion

Because international migration necessarily involves the crossing of borders, it cannot but hold considerable potential for challenging authoritarian rule within migrant-sending countries. It achieves this by removing large numbers of people from exposure to the co-optive and repressive tactics employed by authoritarian regimes vying to maintain political control. Drawing on examples from Latin America, we showed how extended international migration can produce conditions favorable to political mobilization against repressive regimes, and we enumerated and exemplified the specific characteristics likely to propagate a movement for democratization among the members of a diaspora. Cuba, the Dominican Republic, El Salvador, Guatemala, and Colombia served as examples to illustrate the role played by international migrants in the prodemocracy movement compared to Mexico, whose diaspora is the largest and whose long history of migration and settlement north of the border has created conditions particularly favorable to popular mobilization.

The contribution of international migration to democratization is not limited to Latin American nations, of course, and the potential for immigrant diasporas to contribute to democratic transitions elsewhere remains a very real possibility. By far the biggest and most important case is China, whose participation in the global economy is growing, and which has emerged as a major contributor to international migratory systems throughout the world, including those based in North America, Europe, and the Pacific (Massey et al. 1998). Immigrants still represent a small proportion of China's 1.4 billion people, but their numbers are growing rapidly, and their influence is inordinately high by comparison to immigrants of other origin because a significant proportion of those emigrating are entrepreneurial and professional and thus in possession of significant financial resources. Whether Chinese authorities will be able to maintain authoritarian control over an increasingly free and open market remains to be seen, and whether and how the Chinese diaspora mobilizes to promote democracy at home will be a question of the highest importance in the years to come. With Fox's inauguration in December 2001, of course, democracy finally did come to Mexico. As this chapter has shown, not all immigrant entities in the United States can be key players in the broader process of democratization in the sending countries, but because their own political rights have grown through their change in circumstances, as in the case of the Mexican government's recognition of the right of Mexicans living in the United States to vote in national elections, diasporas can become increasingly influential in introducing greater adoption of democratic principles in their countries of origin. To wit, Mexican democracy is becoming more inclusive and open than it has ever been in the history of that nation and, in a very palpable way, it is Mexico's migrants that have catalyzed these internal changes.

References

Andreas, Peter (2000) *Border Games: Policing the U.S.-Mexico Divide*, Ithaca, NY: Cornell University Press.

Camp, Roderic (1999) *Politics in Mexico: The Decline of Authoritarianism*, New York: Oxford University Press.

Castles, Stephen, and Alastair Davidson (2000) *Citizenship and Migration: Globalization and the Politics of Belonging*, New York: Routledge.

Centeno, Miguel Angel (1994) *Democracy within Reason: Technocratic Revolution in Mexico*, University Park: Pennsylvania State University Press.

Cothran, Dan A. (1994) *Political Stability and Democracy in Mexico: The "Perfect Dictatorship"?* New York: Praeger.

Dib, George (1988) "Laws Governing Migration in Some Arab Countries," in Reginald T. Appleyard, Editor, *International Migration Today*, Vol. I: *Trends and Prospects*, pp. 168–179, Perth: University of Western Australia for the United Nations Educational, Scientific, and Cultural Organization.

Dresser, Denise (1991) *Neopopulist Solutions to Neoliberal Problems*, La Jolla, CA: Center for U.S.-Mexican Studies, University of California, San Diego.

Durand, Jorge, Douglas S. Massey, and Fernando Charvet (2000) "The Changing Geography of Mexican Immigration to the United States: 1910–1996," *Social Science Quarterly*, 81:1–15.

Durand, Jorge, Douglas S. Massey, and Emilio A. Parrado (1999) "The New Era of Mexican Migration to the United States," *The Journal of American History*, 86:518–536.

Durand, Jorge, Douglas S. Massey, and René Zenteno (2001) "Mexican Immigration to the United States: Continuities and Changes," *Latin American Research Review*, 36:107–127.

Durand, Jorge, Emilio A. Parrado, and Douglas S. Massey (1996) "Migradollars and Development: A Reconsideration of the Mexican Case," *International Migration Review*, 30:423–444.

Freeman, Gary P. (1992) "Migration Policy and Politics in the Receiving States," *International Migration Review*, 26:1144–1167.

——— (1995) "Modes of Immigration Politics in Liberal Democratic States," *International Migration Review*, 29:881–902.

Funkhouser, Edward (1992) "Mass Emigration, Remittances, and Economic Adjustment: The Case of El Salvador in the 1980s," in George J. Borjas and Richard B. Freeman, Editors, *Immigration and the Workforce: Economic Consequences for the United States and Source Areas*, pp. 135–175, Chicago: University of Chicago Press.

Georges, Eugenia (1990) *The Making of a Transnational Community: Migration, Development, and Cultural Change in the Dominican Republic*, New York: Oxford University Press.

Goldring, Luin (1998) "The Power of Status in Transnational Social Fields," in Michael Peter Smith and Luis Eduardo Guarnizo, Editors, *Transnationalism from Below*, pp. 165–195, New Brunswick, NJ: Transaction.

Graham, Pamela M. (2001) "Political Incorporation and Re-Incorporation: Simultaneity in the Dominican Migrant Experience," in Héctor R. Cordero-Guzmán, Robert C. Smith, and Ramón Grosfoguel, Editors, *Migration, Transnationalization and Race in a Changing New York*, pp. 87–108, Philadelphia: Temple University Press.

Grasmuck, Sherri, and Patricia R. Pessar (1991) *Between Two Islands: Dominican International Migration*, Berkeley: University of California Press.

Gutiérrez, David G. (2008) "Citizenship Dispersed: A Third Space Looking for Its Proper Place," in Jose V. Ciprut, Editor, *The Future of Citizenship*, Cambridge, MA: The MIT Press.

Hagan, Jacqueline Maria (1994) *Deciding to Be Legal: A Maya Community in Houston*, Philadelphia: Temple University Press.

Hansen, Roger (1971) *The Politics of Mexican Development*, Baltimore, MD: Johns Hopkins University Press.

Hart, John M. (1987) *Revolutionary Mexico: The Coming and Process of the Mexican Revolution*, Berkeley: University of California Press.

Hatton, Timothy J., and Jeffrey G. Williamson (1998) *The Age of Mass Migration: Causes and Economic Impact*, New York: Oxford University Press.

Jacobson, David (1997) *Rights across Borders: Immigration and the Decline of Citizenship*, Baltimore: Johns Hopkins University Press.

James, Harold (2001) *The End of Globalization: Lessons from the Great Depression*, Cambridge, MA: Harvard University Press.

Jasso, Guillermina, and Mark R. Rosenzweig (1982) "Estimating the Emigration Rates of Legal Immigrants Using Administrative and Survey Data: The 1971 Cohort of Immigrants to the United States." *Demography*, 19:279–290.

Joppke, Christian (1998) *Challenge to the Nation-State: Immigration in Western Europe and the United States*. Oxford, UK: Oxford University Press.

Levitt, Peggy (2001) *The Transnational Villagers*, Berkeley: University of California Press.

Levy, Daniel C., and Kathleen Bruhn (2001) *Mexico: The Struggle for Democratic Development*, Berkeley: University of California Press.

Lozano Ascencio, Fernando (1998) "Las Remesas de los Migrantes en Estados Unidos: Estimaciones para 1995," in *Binational Study: Migration between Mexico and the United States*, pp. 1189–1214, Washington, DC: U.S. Commission on Immigration Reform.

Mahler, Sarah J. (1995) *American Dreaming: Immigrant Life on the Margins*, Princeton, NJ: Princeton University Press.

Massey, Douglas S. (1999) "International Migration at the Dawn of the Twenty-First Century: The Role of the State," *Population and Development Review*, 25:303–323.

——— (2005) "Social and Economic Aspects of Immigration," in Stephen G. Kaler and Owen M. Rennert, Editors, *Understanding and Optimizing Human Development: From Cells to Patients to Populations*, Annals of the New York Academy of Sciences, vol. 1038, pp. 206–212, New York: New York Academy of Sciences.

Massey, Douglas S., Joaquín Arango, Graeme Hugo, Ali Kouaouci, Adela Pellegrino, and J. Edward Taylor (1998) *Worlds in Motion: International Migration at the End of the Millennium*, Oxford, UK: Oxford University Press.

Massey, Douglas S., Jorge Durand, and Nolan J. Malone (2002) *Beyond Smoke and Mirrors: Mexican Immigration in an Era of Economic Integration*, New York: Russell Sage Foundation.

Massey, Douglas S., and Emilio A. Parrado (1994) "Migradollars: The Remittances and Savings of Mexican Migrants to the United States," *Population Research and Policy Review*, 13:3–30.

Massey, Douglas S., and Audrey Singer (1995) "New Estimates of Undocumented Mexican Migration and the Probability of Apprehension," *Demography*, 32:203–213.

Massey, Douglas S., and J. Edward Taylor (2004) *International Migration: Prospects and Policies in a Global Market*, Oxford: Oxford University Press.

——— (2005) "Social and Economic Aspects of Immigration," *Proceedings of the NICHD 40th Anniversary Scientific Symposium*, New York: New York Academy of Sciences.

Menjívar, Cecilia (2000) *Fragmented Ties: Salvadoran Immigrant Networks in America*, Berkeley: University of California Press.

Meyers, Deborah W. (1998) "Migrant remittances to Latin America: Reviewing the Literature," Working Paper, Tomás Rivera Institute, San Antonio, Texas.

Meyers, Eytan (2004) *International Immigration Policy: A Theoretical and Comparative Analysis*, New York: Palgrave Macmillan.

Oppenheimer, Andrés (1996) *Bordering on Chaos: Guerillas, Stockbrokers, Politicians, and Mexico's Road to Prosperity*, Boston: Little, Brown.

Pérez, S. Mara (1997) "Transnational Migration and the Institutionalization of Mobilization: The Role of a Political Party in a Social Movement," *Revista/Review Interamericana*, 27:1–4.

——— (1998) "Social Movements and International Migration: The Mexican Diaspora Seeks Inclusion in Mexico's Political Affairs, 1968–1998," Ph.D. dissertation, Department of Sociology, University of Chicago.

Pessar, Patricia R., and Pamela M. Graham (2001) "Dominicans: Transnational Identities and Local Politics," in Nancy Foner, Editor, *New Immigrants in New York*, pp. 251–274, New York: Columbia University Press.

Poniatowska, Elena (1975) *Massacre in Mexico*, New York: Viking Press.

Portes, Alehandro, and Alex Stepick (1993) *City on the Edge: The Transformation of Miami*, Berkeley: University of California Press.

Przeworski, Adam (1991) *Democracy and the Market: Political and Economic Reforms in Eastern Europe and Latin America*, New York: Cambridge University Press.

Sassen, Saskia (1996) *Losing Control? Sovereignty in an Age of Globalization*, New York: Columbia University Press.

——— (1999) *Guests and Aliens*, New York: The New Press.

Shah, Nasra M., and Fred Arnold (1986) "Government Policies and Programs Regulating Labor Migration," in Fred Arnold and Nasra M. Shah, Editors, *Asian Labor Migration: Pipeline to the Middle East*, pp. 65–80, Boulder, CO: Westview Press.

Sheahan, John (1991) *Conflict and Change in Mexican Economic Strategy*, La Jolla, CA: Center for U.S.-Mexican Studies, University of California at San Diego.

Smith, Robert C. (1995) "Los Ausentes Siempre Presentes: The Imagining, Making and Politics of a Transnational Migration Community between New York City and Ticuani, Puebla, Mexico," Ph.D. dissertation, Department of Anthropology, Columbia University.

——— (1998) "Reflections on the State, Migration, and the Durability and Newness of Transnational Life: Comparative Insights from the Mexican and Italian Cases," *Soziale Welt*, 12:197–220.

——— (2001) "Current Dilemmas and Future Prospects of the Inter-American Migration System, in Aristide Zolberg and Peter Benda, Editors, *Global Migrants, Global Refugees*, pp. 121–170, New York: Berghahn Books.

Thurlow, George (2000) "Remilitarizing El Salvador," *Alternet*, http://www.alternet.org/story.html?StoryID=9760, September 11.

U.S. Immigration and Naturalization Service (2001) *1998 Statistical Yearbook of the Immigration and Naturalization Service*, Washington, DC: U.S. Government Printing Office.

U.S. Bureau of the Census (2001) "The Foreign Born Population," *U.S. Bureau of the Census Website*. http://www.census.gov/population/www/socdemo/foreign.html.

Warren, Robert, and Ellen P. Kraly (1985) "The Elusive Exodus: Emigration from the United States," *Population Trends and Public Policy*, no. 8, Washington, DC: Population Reference Bureau.

Zabin, Carol (1995) "Mixtecs and Mestizos in California Agriculture: Ethnic Displacement and Hierarchy among Mexican Farm Workers," in Michael Peter Smith, Editor, *Marginal Spaces: Comparative Urban and Community Research*, pp. 114–143, New Brunswick, NJ: Transaction Press.

12

Voice, Participation, and the Globalization of Communication Systems

James Patrick McDaniel,
Timothy Kuhn,
and Stanley Deetz

The Globalization of Communication

The so-called "globalization of communication" intensifies dreams of connection with others, dreams that have long and tangled legacies in the social and intellectual history of our talkative species. From the notion that through technologically extended communication we can "reach out and touch someone" in McLuhan's "global village" to visions of world peace and harmony achieved by obviating traditional boundaries, fantasies of techno-mechanically facilitated communion with others decorate such dreams. At the same time, this globalization of communication intensifies nightmares of a systematically colonized world in which the economic interests of the few dominate the representational practices that should, ideally, reflect the needs of the many. Such hopes and fears have initiated, and perhaps confounded, debates on policy issues concerning the highly contested relationships between new communication technologies (NCTs) and democracy, not as merely national but also as global political projects.

Key to understanding more fully the practical and theoretical stakes involved in these broad issues is reclamation of the term *communication* from the distended notion of "globalization of communication." Conflating specific technical apparatuses and processes with such a notoriously flexible term as *communication* misplaces hopes for democracy in an age of increasingly comprehensive and world-shaping network technology. New communication systems must be analyzed in light of a theory of communication that can contribute to a normative foundation for analysis and policy development. In the perspective we elaborate in this chapter, communication and communications are not the same. Indeed, depending on how richly the root concept is developed and deployed, the two can be deeply at odds. We believe that typical uses of the notion of "globalization of communication" refer less to increases in our ability to coordinate collaborative action and to cope with otherness—two strong norms of a rich communication theory—than they do to the thrusting of particular modes of culture-specific and technologically extended subjectivities onto the world. This is not to say that new media lack democratic potential or that technologically extended communication is somehow bad. Rather, the point is that current NCTs are developed, deployed, and understood within a more or less coherent 'ideology of use'. Today, as Fredric Jameson (1991) has argued, it is within the cultural logic of late capitalism that new media are invented, marketed, operationalized, and selectively comprehended. A communication theory capable of contributing to a normative foundation for policy development must reckon with the promises and perils of NCTs as they are drawn out from—to reduplicate and possibly to resist—this cultural logic.

The current development and implementation of communication technologies are both rapid and uneven. The rapidity of development is clear in a number of cases. Computer-assisted communication systems such as the Internet have greatly increased the speed and quantity of data transmission, the storage of large quantities of potential information, and the efficient retrieval of stored data by relevant users. In addition, the development of optical fiber and satellite transmission capacities has greatly expanded the size, integration, and possible interactivity of these evolving systems. Further still, technological developments have greatly reduced the cost of such systems so that both corporations and individuals now can own or have access to equipment necessary for participation in these much larger networks. Put together, these technological advances have had a great impact on the data available through the mass media, the nature of home entertainment, and the increases in size and the growth in controls by corporations. These developments are clearly transforming aspects of modern life, even though debate continues on the nature and extent of the changes. Few if any aspects of everyday life and culture are left untouched, an influence so extensive that Poster (1990) calls for an analysis of "modes of information," and particular configurations of communication analogous to Marx's "modes of production," to serve as explanatory devices when scrutinizing the development of societies in relation to processes of globalization and democratization. A potent challenge to critical analysis and to policy-oriented thinking is that new technologies replace older ones even before most consequences of the preceding implementation can begin to be understood.

Consequently, we argue for more intense focus on communication technologies in the processes of globalization and democratization. Doing so must involve critically defining communication and drawing out the implications of alternative conceptions of human interaction. Such a focus should direct attention to NCT development and discourse and show the social shaping of communication media, while, importantly, also pointing to the opportunities that they tend to present. One of the important intentions of this chapter, therefore, is to avoid an 'a-contextualization' of NCTs. Hence, we submit, it is not the case that communication technologies (a) deterministically lead to democratic utopia or dystopia nor that (b) these technologies are neutral, their impacts depending simply on how they are employed. Rather, ours is an account that sees NCTs as being developed and introduced in an already-structured web of social relations, such that they possess certain features (and their users possess certain preferences), which shape subjects and communities in specifiable, yet nondeterministic, ways. This chapter's final section builds on the communicative and technological foundations to propose a set of normative considerations for policy applied to existing and future NCTs.[1]

Two Views of Communication: Transmission and Dialogue

A first step in developing an understanding of the development and use of NCTs is to clarify the potential senses of the term *communication* and what each implies for our understanding of democracy. If our concern is to develop policy orientations regarding the design and use of technological systems in ways that foster the creation of democratic communities, we need a theory explaining the connections between interaction, interactants, and media. Although there are many alternatives in defining *communication* (see Craig 1999), all emanate from a fundamental distinction between dialogue and transmission (Clark 2008). In addition, each carries ideologically loaded important assumptions about subjectivity and community, both of which are basic to democratization.

A transmission view, first, conceives of communication as an act of message sending, or conveyance. Exemplified in Shannon and

---

1. For a complementary perspective, grounded on an ethics-based worldwide approach, see Cooper and Christians (2008).

Weaver's (1949) information theory, it holds that meanings come to be exchanged between actors as they manipulate symbols, that senders simply insert their thoughts into those symbols, and the process ultimately results in a correspondence consisting of exchanges in meaning-laden symbols. These actors may be individual or collective, hence we may conceive of corporations or governments as participants in communication acts. In effect, therefore, communication is a conduit (Reddy 1979) for making mental content manifest to others—a view that draws attention to and interest in the capacity of the channel to carry more messages or to move messages more efficiently. With the advent of mass media, the ability to transmit messages across space means that the controllers of the channels can manipulate the mental contents of the receivers and thus shape public opinion by choosing "appropriate" symbols, as participants are assumed to be operating by using common codes, premises, and inference rules (see Sperber and Wilson 1995). The key problematic addressed by this model is a breakdown in efficiency or effectiveness (both defined in terms of transmission and information receipt); when problems are detected, participants can alter the encoding or decoding choices for ideas, alter the channels they use, or reduce noise interferences. For our purposes, the transmission view's most important assumptions are that the sources of messages are conscious agents bringing pre-given sets of ideas to interaction and, as if operating a hypodermic needle, insert their consciousnesses into others to create shared meanings. Meaning, then, is inside minds and is expressed in the symbols used, but the formation of ideas and human subjectivity as well as construction of community is not and largely cannot be problematized.

The second model contrasts sharply with the first, for framing communication as dialogue between actors who do not necessarily carry fully formed meanings into interaction. Thus, in the transmission model, it is appropriate to say that one can communicate to another, as the issue is merely one of transmission. In the dialogic model, however, transmission is a secondary concern at best; what assumes center stage is the negotiation of meanings and subjectivities. Here one can communicate with another, and communicating to another clearly violates its essential conception of communication. This is because communication here is a dynamic process of emergent intersubjective meanings and is defined by the coordination and control of knowledge and activity. Here symbols themselves do not contain meaning; symbols are but elements in a larger ongoing negotiated system in which sociohistorically constructed contexts, intentions, artifacts, events, and actors are mutually and recursively determinative. These symbols often are quite ambiguous and indeterminate (see Gross 2008), and often strategically so (Eisenberg 1984): actors' subjective meanings shift with the changes in systemic relationships. Communication is then seen as the symbolic/linguistic process by which actors make sense of their "thrownness" in the world (Heidegger 1962; also Williams and Barber 2008) while they simultaneously participate in its communities (Dewey 1927).

A key distinction of the dialogic model is its vision of the construction of a communicating subject. Attention shifts to the ways individuals interpret the world and meaningfully participate in it, suggesting that we must theorize the shaping of the consciousnesses of the subjects to understand communication. Specifically, "The question of communication is how certain processes serve to constitute our experience in terms of a relationship between individual and social meaning . . . through communication, we interpret our existence in terms of a continuous process of relating our individual meanings to those of others within the context of an already meaningful social world" (Grossberg 1982, 227).

In other words, the dialogic model necessarily considers the orientations and interpretive predilections of actors, asserting that the consciousness that allows us to engage in communication is "always and already" socially formed. More to the point, our orientations are shaped by institutionalized practices that enable some interpretations of experience while constraining others (see Urban 2008). Most people are "subject to" a variety of competing institutionalized practices (such as are experienced in the family, workplace, and school), such that significant fragmentation and fluidity in subjectivity is to be expected (Gergen 1991). These institutionalized practices are also thoroughly political in that they involve groups and interests competing over subjects' understandings of their worlds. Communication is a social institution that not only is a carrier of ideas but also embeds "historically developed dimensions of interests, the lines along which things will be distinguished" (Deetz 1992, 130). Symbol using (and misusing) is the fundamental means by which we engage with the world and thus is the material from which our subjectivity is molded (Althusser 1971). Language—in use—activates a structure that embodies a system of distinctions that provide rules and resources for the construction of subjectivity, but these rules and resources shape actors in patterned and nonneutral ways. Although actors retain agency in their use of language, they enter into, and must orient themselves to, institutionalized linguistic practices (Bhaskar 1979). If communication is ideological in this way, and if it is intricately involved in subjectivity formation, then all communication with others is political in the sense that interactants may reproduce and/or transform both subjective and institutional structures in dialogue.

The important point for effective social analysis is, then, not to attempt to strip away all discourse so as to locate the "essential nature" of the subject, or to reintegrate the individual into an idealized community (Putnam 2000). On the contrary, the task here is to recognize that seemingly independent thoughts, feelings, and orientations are in fact (re)produced in quite ideologically specified ways. The effective analyst's task thus becomes one of identifying and characterizing those very conditions that lead particular discursive, psychosocial, and socioeconomic formations to gain dominance over how "others" (i.e., subjects) are "positioned." The preferred outcome (consequence) of effective critique should then be to suggest possible avenues to disrupt sedimented structures, in the hope that conflict will lead to a more integrated or rational dialogue. The point is to pry open the process of social construction to enable the conflictual interaction that can lead to more informed and integrated identity choices and, ultimately, to more rational and thoughtful dialogues that build stronger democratic communities. Lacking a strong normative framework for policy analysis, deliberation, and development, such critical processes tend to stall at the level of description or characterization.

Recognizing their disparate notions of subjectivity, the two models of communication confronted and compared here are accompanied by dramatically different conceptions of democratic participation. The transmission model, with its focal concern for message conveyance, is equipped to guide participation under conditions of liberal democracy. In liberal democracy, three principal assumptions of the communicative construction of the public sphere are paramount. First, an autonomous individual is seen to be the origin of perceptions and meanings that have already been worked out in his or her private life. Second, freedom of speech and access to speaking forums provide for equitable participation in decision making (Tambini 1999). It is assumed that good decision making requires that all relevant perspectives are aired, and voting comes to be seen as the vehicle to express one's interests while evincing the collective's true desires. Third, the mode of communication in these forums is rhetorical: persuasion, identification, and interest advocacy are the ways democracy is best achieved.

This model of democracy is significantly flawed in that it equates the subject's voice to the mere airing of interests, making expression and transmission the pivotal concerns. If one has a preformed and stable identity (the discursive "I") and the opportunity to speak and have access to media that exhibit self-authentically to others, then it is assumed that the fundamental element of democratic participation has been achieved. However, the focus on representing group interests through codified messages fails to recognize the high likelihood of unequal influence over actual decision—making while also somehow ignoring the political nature of interest (subjectivity) formation. Similarly, potential proliferation of opinions neither allows nor, indeed, creates conceptual space for meaningful discussion and deliberation. An expressionist (liberal) ideal and its concomitant valuing of adversarial interactions are unlikely to lead to more fully democratic communities because they rest on a deeply flawed conception of communication. Expression may be an important element in any communication theory, as surely also in democracy, but it can neither support nor contribute to the social reconstruction of collective experience. In favoring expression over other norms of communicative activity, liberal democracy disavows inequities of voice and participation characteristic of anything but dreamy utopian public life.

The dialogic model cultivates an alternate sense of democratic participation premised on civic republican (rather than liberal) values. Here democracy is concerned with the process by which the collective decides what it shall become, and voting is only one (limited) element of that process. Communication analysis then turns to the process of negotiating moral questions in decision making in a way that decreases not only dominance of particular interests but also communicative distortions that interfere with the pursuit of community goods (or lesser community evils, depending on which side of the ambiguity one happens to favor). Subject positions and voices are not seen as necessarily fixed, such that the configuration of self, other, and world are opened up for scrutiny, self-legislation, and the development of new configurations. The nature of the public and the private are always open for negotiation, as are the emergent structures that shape community life. Consequently, unhinged from the liberal/expressionist ideal of communicative interaction, mediation, and participation, these social domains can be rethought in far more flexible and politically inventive ways.

The dialogic model, moreover, forces a conception of the 'other' as a central constituent of human communication. In dialogue, we find and recognize the other's subjectivity while also knowing that our own identities are rooted in the narratives of a wealth of others that are temporally, culturally, and geographically both near and far (Langsdorf 1997). Whereby, from this perspective, the process of democratization is much less about interest representation to create sustained agreement and that much more about reclaiming conflict to establish a community, marked not only by overlapping identities but interrogating alternatives and continuously deliberating. Democratic participation is therefore not about merely making interests manifest but (more) about recognizing (and rethinking) the humanness of others in constructing the interactions and institutions that comprise our shared worlds.

In sum, the transmission and dialogic models of communication present very divergent views of communication. Each carries its very own implications for subjectivity and democratic participation. And although we do favor the dialogic over the transmission model, we must explicitly stress that each has its place in shedding light on complex communication processes. Expression and participation are not always or necessarily at odds, even though the latter appears more inclusive, more democratically charged than the former. Yet, as we discuss in the next section, one model (that of "transmission") has unfortunately dominated the design, development, and use of NCTs, with detrimental consequences for democratization.

Transmission, Dialogue, and Communication Technologies

Current NCTs and their socially privileged uses clearly embody a conceptualization of communication predicated upon communication—as transmission. True, computer-assisted communication systems such as the Internet have greatly increased both the speed and the quantity of data transmission, storage capacity for large quantities of potential information, and stored-data retrieval efficiency for relevant users. Although both the computer and the Internet were originally designed for manipulating and exchanging data, the "interpretive flexibility" (Pinch and Bijker 1989) of either has led to uses in human communication that are now seen as integral to their existence. The dramatic expansion, capabilities, and adoption of computer technology and the exponential growth of Internet access for both corporations and consumers now impact almost every aspect of our everyday life, world, and culture. New technologies keep replacing older ones before most implications and/or consequences of prior implementations can be understood.

Equally clear is the uneven nature of this swift development. As certain types of technologies move ahead rapidly, others lag behind. Developments have been more rapid where there is a ready market, where the technology supports basic values, and where technical change is most cost effective. Choices are not random but follow identifiable patterns. Some of these are so obvious and appear so insignificant as to escape notice. For example, despite great strides in mediating and technologically extending our hearing and vision, smell and motion sensation have relatively few accompanying technologies. High-fidelity transmission of visual images and acoustic data enter our homes daily, but we lack even the most elementary extension of other senses. Few scholars studying communication would suggest that these other senses are trivial, even in the U.S. culture. Whereas it can be argued that there are technological reasons why such development remains limited, suffice it to remember that 200 years ago no one could imagine that the sight and sound technologies we consider commonplace today would have been developed. There are cultural reasons why development has focused on certain senses, and that very focus has had collective consequences (Ong 1967). It would not be difficult to conceive a human society in which other developments could have occurred. But the very notion that it could have happened differently helps us refocus our attention on the central issue: the choices made and the possibilities foreclosed.

Given our interest here in analyzing communicatively constructed realities that shape both the design of NCTs and their engagement with democratization, and our desire to avoid a-contextualizing technology (thinking of NCTs either as the strongest determinants or as the mere instruments of social processes, for instance), an investigation of the features of their contextual shaping and, by implication, of their challenges to policy-making, should be in order. In particular, our concern now shifts to the discourse surrounding NCTs as their meanings and capabilities are shaped by the social context in which they are designed, used, and transformed (DeSanctis and Poole 1994; Jackson 1996). This discourse is the basis of the choices we have made and the possibilities we have foreclosed but also of alternatives available in the future. As McLuhan and Fiore (1967, 74–75) have noted, "When faced with a totally new situation, we tend always to attach ourselves to the objects, to the flavor of the most recent past. We look at the present through a rear-view mirror. We march backwards into the future." Specifically, there are three themes in NCT development and discourse that shape its present and future influences on democratic participation.

A first theme is the inevitability of NCTs (thus implying inevitability's excluded opposite, rational choice). NCTs often come to be portrayed as necessary accoutrements for daily life, part of an evolutionary march of "progress" and increased control over nature (see Feenberg 1999; Habermas 1971). Because capitalistic progress is ineluctable—there is no alternative (Giddens 1998)—subjects should not only learn to adapt to new realities but also hone "technological skills" to become "new barbarians" of sorts, a ruling class that controls the keys to the technological kingdom in Angell's (2000) expressly undemocratic vision of a brutish brave new world. Although framing new technological developments in this way may be expected from marketers, when inevitability becomes a dominant motif of social thought, choice making (so central to democracy) is foreclosed. Moreover, this sort of discourse pushes off problem solving (yes, also problems of domination and unequal access when they are recognized) to an amorphous future in which even better technologies will be able to solve present problems. As Finlay (1987, 49) argues, "Futurology is carte blanche for actions in the present which need never be accounted for: if everything is just about to happen rather than having already happened or being in the process of happening, then the need for policy and decisions can constantly be put off until tomorrow."

A second theme evident in NCT development and discourse speaks to individualist traits opposed to potential roles for collectivism. Electronic monitoring and surveillance, for instance, are frequently framed as intrusions on personal privacy and individual liberties (Botan 1996; Spears and Lea 1994). Cyberspace and virtual reality are heralded as locales for individuals to explore alternative identities through free movement from site to site to site (Biocca and Levy 1995; Rheingold 1993), although the degree to which such sojourners actually challenge existing identities is questionable. Some scholars (Fernback and Thompson 1995; Hassan 1999, for example) have argued that nascent cyber-communities actually create more fragmentation than ever before. Similarly, when authority is called for on some important technological issue, journalists tend to turn to individual experts, corporate heads, or technical specialists (Finlay 1987). Even though in Western cultures such individualism is not surprising at all, it does preclude subjects' awareness of the impacts of NCTs on social structure as also subjects' understanding of the broader social responsibilities for the incorporation of technologies into individual and collective settings (Trethewey and Corman 2001). In addition, identity persistence rather than identity fluidity is taken to be key to cooperative relations and dependable interactions in public spheres (Kollock 1998). Such perdurance of identity is the sort of responsibility and participation that proves central to conceptions of strong democracy (Barber 1984).

The third theme in NCT discourse is the emphasis on transmission and flow of data. It reduces knowledge to information while limiting both knowledge and information to mere "know-what" or "know-how" (Webster 2000). Other categories of knowledge—intuition, contextual insight, self-understanding, and emotional knowledge, for instance—are generally overlooked because the information society's focus is on speed and objectivity in information transmission, in decision making, and in learning (Castells 1996; Hassan 1999). If more computerization, along with the physical infrastructure that feeds it, is deemed so necessary, this is because of the ever-growing need and desire for the faster transactions that have been increasingly replacing face-to-face interactions. At the same time, this distinct preference for information over knowledge calls for the production of subjects capable of becoming "nodes" in that new, ever faster-paced and electronically enhanced world (Davis and Meyer 1998). Connecting with the previous two themes, Poster (1990, 7) has argued that "the 'informed' individual is a new social ideal, particularly for the middle class, a group to which in the United States everyone but the homeless claims to belong." Also, organizations develop knowledge management systems around technologies that allow them to collect, store, and transfer information, but these do little to enhance processes of knowing (Jackson, Poole, and Kuhn 2002; Zuboff 1988) or to advance the interests of strong democracy (Deetz 1995). Organizational knowledge that is easily codified and classified is duly entered into such systems, whereas tacit knowledge, intuition, emotions, and cultural insights somehow are not.

Thus, technical/scientific/instrumental rationality has become privileged while other categories of discernment have been marginalized, and the ascendancy of this form of reasoning dovetails with those of NCTs: its values are their values. Such domination narrows concepts of communication and subjectivity to their vanishing points. Measured with the yardstick of effectiveness and efficiency, "communication" is identified with the values embedded in the ascendant media of dissemination (namely, computers). Deprived of alternative ways, means, and forms for the development of self-interest and self-identity, "subjectivity" now suffers a similar fate: it becomes either an inwardness that cannot be expressed within the dominant discursive regime or an impersonal outwardness characteristic of all signs. In this way, communication is reified; it is received as an entity that may be employed and enhanced, especially when subjects are granted access to the touted "information superhighway." In addition to forming individuals and collectives along the lines of a transmission model, the need to produce and to consume information takes precedence over calculations of social costs and considerations of alternatives. Of course, this sort of reification enables NCTs to exercise their computational and channeling abilities more adroitly; the danger comes, however, when we fail to recognize this influence on other spheres of life. Because NCTs are gradually being exchanged for other modes and forms of human interaction, the likelihood that these characteristics will ever more profoundly shape both subjectivity and community rises.

Currently, technologies are being developed where there are preexisting markets for them, where the new technology is in line with existing concepts and values, and where technological developments are cost effective (Hassan 1999). Rarely are human needs considered when financial resources are limited. Rarely are social, noneconomic factors assessed in choosing where foremost to place resources for development. For example, the innovative pace of large, sophisticated databases for investment firms offer a stark contrast with the slower development of computer-assisted data retrieval systems for nonpromotional consumer information. Profit-making companies are making most of the decisive development choices, while differences are settled in the marketplace. Understanding this relation can clarify why technological development takes a certain direction and what motives drive it in that direction. An important step in advancing this sort of understanding would be the examination of the three themes in NCT development and discourse discussed: inevitability, individualism, and knowledge reduction—each of which is likely to enhance the dominance of the transmission view of communication and to conduce to limited versions of democracy. More simply put, the colonization of public realms (Habermas 1984) commands the resources necessary for freely forming self and self-interest. Note that such colonization also (and massively) constrains all social opportunity for expressing identity and interest in any manner that can have a bearing on public affairs. Resources and opportunities for self-invention and for public articulation are not distributed equally. Based on these insights and the foundations of communication and democracy introduced above, we offer a set of principles that can guide subsequent design, development, and use of NCTs to promote democratization.

Toward a Normative Foundation for Communication Technology Policy

We submit that NCTs need to be evaluated on the grounds of their contribution to the equitable representation of human interests, to reaching communicative understanding, to overcoming decision-making dominance, and to opening up subjectivity formation for reflexive and critical analysis. Unfortunately, to date most researchers have studied communication as strategic influence within the transmission model only, which provides few resources for reflexive awareness of self and other. Comparatively little is known about communication as participation, or partaking, even though provocative assertions by progressive theorists of communication and of democracy such as John Dewey (1927) and, more recently, John Durham Peters (1999) contribute much to this gaping need. For the most part, however, even studies of participation in decision making have tended to be structured around concepts of effectiveness and influence. Examining the structure of interaction aimed at reaching understanding reveals much about the depth and durability of our moral commitment. One social theorist who has written extensively on communication and democratic participation in a variety of public spheres is Jürgen Habermas (1984, 1987, 1992). Habermas's "universal pragmatics" asserts that communication includes an implicit normative dimension that affords several characteristics of a situation liberated from barriers that obstruct communication processes. Here communication is defined along the lines of the dialogic model, richly reconstructed as collaborative activity aimed at producing the understanding necessary to constitute a just society. In this section, we draw on Habermas's work to advance four elements of a normative foundation to policy in the realms of NCT analysis, NCT development, and NCT administration—elements that promote the cause of democratization.

First, Habermas holds that the attempt to reach interpersonal understanding in the public sphere is one that presupposes symmetric distribution of the chances to choose and to apply speech acts. In technologically mediated interpersonal communication, this would mean specification of the minimal conditions of skills and opportunities for expression. When extended to a consideration of new technologies, such specifications place initial focus on equal access, distribution of training opportunities, or development of technologies with ease of access and low skill requirements. They hence also suggest that democracy is more than the systematic measurement of preferences through voting or polling. This draws up issues of information availability and suggests consideration of information as a public utility that includes public management. In addition, ownership and management structures, both as controls 'for', and as products 'of', technologies, need to be investigated in the spirit of the concept of symmetrical distribution of chances.

Second, Habermas argues that our understanding and representing of the external world needs to be freed—liberated—from privileged preconceptions in the social development of truth. Ideally, all of the participants have the opportunity to express interpretations and explanations, with conflicts being resolved in reciprocal claims and counterclaims, but without privileging particular epistemologies of forms of data. Here freedom from preconception implies examining ideologies that privilege one form of discourse, disqualify certain possible participants, and universalize any particular sectional interests. Communication technologies need to be examined as to how they function ideologically to privilege certain perceptions and forms of data, while obscuring historical processes. Identifying ideological frames of inevitability, individualism, and knowledge reduction, and examining their impacts on democratic action is a first step in this direction.

Third, participants in a democratic public sphere need to have the opportunity to establish legitimate social relations and norms for conduct and interaction. The rights and responsibilities of people are not given in advance by nature, or by some privileged universal value structure; rather, they are negotiated through interaction. Acceptance of certain views, because of an individual's privilege or authority or because of the nature of the medium, hints to a possibly illegitimate relation. Authority itself is legitimate only if redeemable by appeal to an open interactional formation of relations freed from any appeal to authority. Values and norms legitimately exist in human society by the achievement of rational consensus, subject to appeals to warrants supporting the social relations assumed. To the extent that particular technologies embody values, hide authority relations, or reify social relations, they participate in domination.

Finally, interactants need to be able to express to the fullest their own authentic interests, their needs and their feelings, while simultaneously acquiring an experience of others' subjectivities. In other words, the ways in which communication technologies promote or subvert subjects' self-knowledge becomes a key plank in theoretical and policy considerations (Woodward 1993); concomitantly, however, attention needs to be given to the capacity to apprehend the other with whom oneself is in interaction. Enhancing self-knowledge would require freedom from various coercive and hegemonic processes by which the individual is rendered unable to form experience openly, let alone to understand its self, and to form expressions presenting such. Technology can aid the formation of self or other, as images, as it can also magnify a distance that denies the formation of otherness and the interrogation of selfness. Presently, NCTs seem to discourage this sort of self-knowledge, be it by reducing agency to consumption and/or by disrupting the coherence of self-identity: "If I can witness political and cultural events without leaving my home, if a database at a remote location contains my profile and informs government agencies which make decisions affecting my life without any knowledge on my part of these events, if I can shop in my home by using the TV or computer, then where am I and who am I? In these circumstances I cannot consider myself centered in my rational, autonomous subjectivity or bordered by a defined ego, but I am disrupted, subverted, and dispersed across social space" (Poster 1990, 16).

An examination of NCTs' capacity and extent of structuring 'the interior' of subjects would be an important step toward understanding their effects on the accomplishment of a communicative ideal. True, the ideal communication situation is a fiction; but Habermas may be correct when he says that "on this unavoidable fiction rests the humanity of relations among" people.

Computer technologies that provide for identity exploration and for interpersonal discussion do not necessarily increase knowledge of self or of other. Vast technological strides in the ease and speed of interactivity do not a priori contribute to deeper understandings of communicative others; also, the elegance and acceleration of sign-exchange systems such as Internet chat rooms may do more to maximize aesthetic (rather than epistemic or sociological) experiences. Note that the "virtual communities" in cyberspace are most often based on demographic or psychographic similarities and therefore are unlikely to promote the sort of interaction that challenges existing practices. One crucial element of discovering otherness is the ability to trace or to make sense of the source of messages as a historically material point in social time-space. This must involve not only access to the other's "actual" identity but also availabilities for insight into the conditions of information production. These involvements are not just a call for greater transparency in the development and in the use of communication technologies. They also suggest the need to incorporate a far deeper multisensual experience of otherness in technologically mediated communication. Although, for long, there has been much talk about developing tools that combine visual, aural, tactile, and even olfactory stimuli, the prevailing ideology of linear transmission suggests that technologies catering to these multiple senses will do precious little—through extant processes of exploration and conflict—to contribute to the creation of the array of intersubjective meanings, and of the trust, that a conception of communication, as dialogue, requires. It is only through dialogue that participants can understand differences and similarities, moving away from sectional concerns with "I" or "us" to a more universal interest in the "we" (Gunson and Collins 1997).

Such a policy orientation for communication theory and for NCTs may have more than the limitations ascribed to Habermas. Elevating understanding to the status of an end-all of communication threatens to obscure other motives (including strategic action) available to analysis, whereby understanding can also threaten to become the be-all of communication. To the extent that Habermas aims precisely at this pattern of elevation and exclusion, he and his intellectual heirs can plead guilty as charged, or remain silent. Habermas's "distrust of representation" (Peters 1999) presents us with both a subtler and a tougher problem, particularly as we attempt to derive a policy orientation for social theory and for NCTs amid the ongoing processes of globalization, where the vastness and complexities of the world can only, if ever, be "represented" via media of sensual extension in the form of a reduction. When deeply embedded in one or another notion of the ideal speech situation, universal pragmatics and systematically distorted communication may provide a structure of preference that clings too tightly to proximate 'embodied' exchange to be capable of assessing the discarnate 'action-qua-understanding-at-a-distance' that the electronic connection privileges.

In the end, what we are advocating is much greater reflexivity into the conditions for rational action and interaction through the media of new communication technologies. A problematization of the processes of subjectivity formation, voice, and participation would place these terms in play, thereby potentially disrupting the more traditional concerns with transmission, access, voting, speed, and ease discussed in this chapter. The social impacts of communication technologies are determined neither by their objective features nor indeed simply by the contexts of their use. Our use of these can foster greater control by powerful ideologies or advance the cause of strong democracy (and a multitude of possibilities in between): the route to pursue depends acutely on our collective conception of "communication." We have argued that broadening our understanding of communication in ways to include dialogue as well as transmission provides alternative ways of thinking about subjectivity formation, voice, and democratic participation. Built on such a normative framework, optimized possibilities for fuller progressive critiques of social discourses with regard to the newer roles of communication technologies in individual and collective decision-making processes become clearer. Not least, this perspective conduces to a normative foundation that can guide NCT analysis, development, use, as well as administration, in a fashion that holds hope for the development of greater democracy.

References

Althusser, L. (1971) "Ideology and Ideological State Apparatuses," in *Lenin and Philosophy and Other Essays*, B. Brewster, Translator, London: New Left Books.

Angell, I. (2000) *The New Barbarian Manifesto: How to Survive the Information Age*, London: Kogan Page.

Barber, Benjamin (1984) *Strong Democracy: Participating Politics for a New Age*, 2nd ed., Berkeley: University of California Press.

Bhaskar, R. (1979) *The Possibility of Naturalism: A Philosophical Critique of the Contemporary Human Sciences*, Atlantic Highlands, UK: Humanities Press.

Biocca, F., and M. R. Levy, Editors (1995) *Communication in the Age of Virtual Reality*, Hillsdale, NJ: Erlbaum.

Botan, C. (1996) "Communication Work and Electronic Surveillance: A Model for Predicting Panoptic Effects," *Communication Monographs*, 63:293–313.

Castells, M. (1996) *The Rise of the Network Society*, vol. 1, Oxford, UK: Blackwell.

Clark, Robin (2008) "Reliable Cribs: Decipherment, Learnability, and Indeterminacy," in Jose V. Ciprut, Editor, *Indeterminacy: The Mapped, the Navigable, and the Uncharted*, Cambridge, MA: The MIT Press.

Cooper, Thomas W., and Clifford G. Christians (2008) "On the Need and the Requirements for a Global Ethic of Communication," in Jose V. Ciprut, Editor, *Ethics, Politics, and Democracy: From Primordial Principles to Prospective Practices*, Cambridge, MA: The MIT Press.

Craig, R. T. (1999) "Communication Theory as a Field," *Communication Theory*, 9: 119–161.

Davis, S., and Meyer, C. (1998) *Blur: The Speed of Change in the Connected Economy*, New York: Warner Books.

Deetz, S. A. (1992) *Democracy in an Age of Corporate Colonization: Developments in Communication and the Politics of Everyday Life*, Albany: State University of New York Press.

—— (1995) *Transforming Communication, Transforming Business: Building Responsive and Responsible Workplaces*, Cresskill, NJ: Hampton Press.

DeSanctis, G., and M. S. Poole (1994) "Capturing the Complexity in Advanced Technology Use: Adaptive Structuration Theory," *Organization Science*, 5:121–147.

Dewey, J. (1927) *The Public and Its Problems*, Athens, OH: Swallow Press.

Eisenberg, E. M. (1984) "Ambiguity as Strategy in Organizational Communication," *Communication Monographs*, 51:227–242.

Feenberg, A. (1999) *Questioning Technology*, London: Routledge.

Fernback, J., and B. Thompson (1995) "Computer-Mediated Communication and the American Collectivity: The Dimensions of Community within Cyberspace," paper presented in May 1995 at the Annual Meeting of the International Communication Association in Albuquerque, NM.

Finlay, M. (1987) *Powermatics: A Discursive Critique of New Communications Technology*, New York: Routledge and Kegan Paul.

Gergen, K. (1991) *The Saturated Self: Dilemmas of Identity in Contemporary Life*, New York: Basic Books.

Giddens, A. (1998) *The Third Way*, Cambridge, UK: Polity.

Gross, Steven (2008) "Vagueness, Indeterminacy, and Uncertainty," in Jose V. Ciprut, Editor, *Indeterminacy: The Mapped, the Navigable, and the Uncharted*, Cambridge, MA: The MIT Press.

Grossberg, L. (1982) "Intersubjectivity and the Conceptualization of Communication," *Human Studies*, 5:213–235.

Gunson, D., and C. Collins (1997) "From the 'I' to the 'We': Discourse Ethics, Identity, and the Pragmatics of Partnership in the West of Scotland," *Communication Theory*, 7:277–300.

Habermas, J. (1971) *Knowledge and Human Interests*, J. J. Shapiro, Translator, Boston: Beacon.

————— (1984) *The Theory of Communicative Action*, vol. 1: *Reason and the Rationalization of Society*, T. McCarthy, Translator, Boston: Beacon.

————— (1987) *The Theory of Communicative Action*, vol. 2: *Lifeworld and System*, T. McCarthy, Translator, Boston: Beacon.

————— (1992) "Further Reflections on the Public Sphere," in C. Calhoun, Editor, *Habermas and the Public Sphere*, pp. 421–461, Cambridge, MA: The MIT Press.

Hassan, R. (1999) "Globalization: Information Technology and Culture within the Space Economy of Late Capitalism," *Information, Communication, and Society*, 2(3):300–317.

Heidegger, M. (1962) *Being and Time*, John MacQuarrie and Edward Robinson, Translators, London: SCM Press.

Jackson, M. H. (1996) "The Meaning of 'Communication Technology': The Technology-Context Scheme," in B. Burleson, Editor, *Communication Yearbook 19*, pp. 229–267, Thousand Oaks, CA: Sage.

Jackson, M. H., M. S. Poole, and T. Kuhn (2002) "The Social Construction of Technology in Studies of the Workplace," in L. A. Lievrouw and S. Livingstone, Editors, *Handbook of New Media*, pp. 236–253, London: Sage.

Jameson, F. (1991) *Postmodernism, or, the Cultural Logic of Late Capitalism*, Durham, NC: Duke University Press.

Kollock, P. (1998) "Design Principles for Online Communities," *PC Update*, 15(5): 58–60.

Langsdorf, L. (1997) "Refusing Individuality: How Human Beings Are Made into Subjects," *Communication Theory*, 7:321–342.

McLuhan, M., and Q. Fiore (1967) *The Medium Is the Message*, New York: Random House.

Ong, W. J. (1967) *The Presence of the Word: Some Prolegomena for Cultural and Religious History*, New Haven, CT: Yale University Press.

Peters, J. D. (1999) *Speaking into the Air: A History of the Idea of Communication*, Chicago: University of Chicago Press.

Pinch, T., and W. Bijker (1989) "The Social Construction of Facts and Artefacts: Or How the Sociology of Science and the Sociology of Technology Might Benefit Each Other," in T. Pinch, T, T. Hughes, and W. Bijker, Editors, *The Social Construction of Technological Systems*, Cambridge, MA: The MIT Press.

Poster, M. (1990) *The Mode of Information: Poststructuralism and Contexts*, Chicago: University of Chicago Press.

Putnam, R. D. (2000) *Bowling Alone: The Collapse and Revival of American Community*, New York: Simon and Schuster.

Reddy, M. J. (1979) "The Conduit Metaphor—A Case of Frame Conflict in Our Language about Language," in A. Ortony, Editor, *Metaphor and Thought*, pp. 284–324, Cambridge, UK: Cambridge University Press.

Rheingold, H. (1993) *The Virtual Community: Homesteading on the Electronic Frontier*, New York: Addison-Wesley.

Shannon, C. E., and W. Weaver (1949) *The Mathematical Theory of Communication*, Urbana: University of Illinois Press.

Spears, R., and M. Lea (1994) "Panacea or Panopticon? The Hidden Power in Computer-Mediated Communication," *Communication Research*, 21:427–459.

Sperber, D., and D. Wilson (1995) *Relevance: Communication and Cognition*, Cambridge, MA: Blackwell.

Tambini, D. (1999) "New Media and Democracy: The Civic Networking Movement," *New Media and Society*, 1:305–329.

Trethewey, A., and S. R. Corman (2001) "Anticipating K-Commerce: E-Commerce, Knowledge Management and Organizational Communication," *Management Communication Quarterly*, 14:619–628.

Urban, Greg (2008) "Freedom and Culture," in J. V. Ciprut, Editor, *Freedom: Reassessments and Rephrasings*, Cambridge, MA: The MIT Press.

Webster, Frank (2000) "Information, Capitalism, and Uncertainty," *Information, Communication, and Society* 3:69–90.

Williams, David R., and Jacques P. Barber (2008) "Freedoms Lost, Freedoms Regained," in Jose V. Ciprut, Editor, *Freedom: Reassessments and Rephrasings*, Cambridge, MA: The MIT Press.

Woodward, W. (1993) "Toward a Normative-Contextualist Theory of Technology," *Critical Studies in Mass Communication*, 10:158–178.

Zuboff, S. (1988) *In the Age of the Smart Machine: The Future of Work and Power*, New York: Basic Books.

13   Democratic Prospects in Undemocratic Times

Patrick J. Deneen

The chapters of this book rightly alert us to the many ways in which the process of 'democratization' has been pursued, is currently accomplished, and might yet take place in subnational, national, and international contexts around the world. The book itself challenges the blinkered view that 'democratization' necessarily unfolds in the same uniquely predetermined process for all and, once again, rightly reminds us that considerations of structure, scale, economic scope or organization, the state of institutions, constitutional forms, and specific cultural histories—among many other considerations—can be expected to vary widely as the variegated process continues to carve its meanders in the years and decades ahead.

Yet, by dint of their interrelatedness, the chapters in this book also reveal an implicitly shared fundamental understanding of democratization that can go unnoticed amid the emphasis on the term's plural form. Despite the wide range of approaches and interpretations covered, there is, by and large, a singular underlying conception of democracy that informs practically all of the chapters in this book. Such a conclusion should not be too surprising, as the chapters do reflect widespread, quasi-universal agreement over what constitutes the basic modern political philosophical features of democracy.

Democracy seems to be one of those words affording infinite plasticity and applications; yet, at a deep, largely invisible level underlying the many apparent distinctions that are claimed to define modern democracy, there are a set of widely shared assumptions that point toward a more uniform conception of democracy than otherwise might be suspected.

As the ancient Greek etymology of the term reminds us, democracy is a political concept meaning "rule of the people." Thus, almost by universal agreement, modern democracy is understood to mean rule of the people by means of ongoing and periodic elections. This reflects the modern Enlightenment assumption that all government fundamentally rests on consent: that governments are to be chosen freely by persons who are citizens—autonomous individuals—who, while recognizing the need for government in the preservation of order, suspiciously guard against any illegitimate encroachments on their own personal freedoms by that otherwise legitimate authority. In this view, government is held to be fundamentally conventional, that is, constituted by a set of institutions resulting from contractual agreements reached among freely consenting individuals. Regardless of its many manifestations and combinations in the world today, modern democracy is conceived essentially in the shadow of this liberal political philosophy (see, for instance, Ciprut, Doran, Botwinick, and Kincaid, chaps. 1, 2, 3, and 5, respectively, in this book).

Modern democracy's emphasis on popular rule through an electoral process can be seen to share a fundamental similarity with the most ancient forms of democracy, in which deliberations used to result in a show of hands among citizens, when assembling over one or another judicial or legislative decision. Yet does modern democracy not represent a fundamental shift from this ancient practice, were it for introducing representation as a key component of modernity? Elections, whether held within a parliamentary or congressional system, on a fixed or more flexible schedule, and at a federal or central level, are almost always held for the purpose of choosing 'representatives' who, once chosen, become responsible for crafting and passing legislation on behalf of the citizenry. The brute fact of this immutable equation of "democracy" with representation results from the enlarging scale of contemporary democracies. Today, no ruling assembly conceivably can be composed of the active citizenry of even the smallest unit within contemporary federal or confederal systems, let alone in national or international regimes. Guided by individually held conceptions and priorities of self-interest, the citizens are called upon to (s)elect their representatives and thereafter, periodically, to approve or to disapprove of them, based on the effectiveness of the representatives in upholding and promoting the citizenry's (i.e., the electorate's) preferences.

Given this strong, quasi-exclusive political idea of democracy as a practice grounded on an electoral process meant to assure the free selection of citizens' representatives, 'democracy' finds itself marked no less by a particular emphasis on the civic equality implied by electoral rights. Universal suffrage is one of the central defining features of modern democracy: where suffrage is arbitrarily or ascriptively restricted, a polity is held to be insufficiently or incompletely democratic (Smith 1997; Keyssar 2000). Manifold other rights, too, are deemed just as essential in the liberal democratic framework, comprising an array of individual civil liberties that include protecting the individual from government (in matters of speech, assembly, conscience, property, and the like) and in a number of basic civil rights that permit making good on claims that citizens can place on government (basic welfare, safety, and due protection from encroachments of private forms of power among them, particularly though not exclusively in the form of private industry). These rights must be respected and protected by governments: for only in order to secure such rights do people agree to the institution of government in the first instance. Therefore, those governments that do not adequately respect or secure the rights of their people risk being replaced, whether by electoral change or via revolutionary action when necessary (Zuckert 1999).

Among the preeminent reasons advanced to justify modern liberal democracy is the extent to which such a regime allows the flourishing of individual autonomy in myriad spheres. The sphere given pride of place by early liberal thinkers especially was in the economic arena. Liberal democracy makes few demands on citizens; instead, it frees them to pursue private interests and to cultivate personal talents that contribute to great and growing prosperity across the society at large (Constant [1819] 1988). As Locke writes, given the prosperity that eventually could be expected in the modern order, which placed a priority on economic liberation, one should be materially better off as a day laborer in England than the mightiest king among the Native Americans (Locke [1698] 1960, 296–297 and II.5 generally; Macpherson 1964). In contrast to ancient democracy—in which every citizen was expected regularly to sit in the Assembly, to attend and contribute sufficiently to public deliberations, and assiduously to vote in an informed manner—modern democratic citizenship consists of the formal extension of the vote to every eligible citizen but without an actual expectation that one must (or will) exercise one's right to vote, or demonstrate some evidence of attentiveness to, or any proficiency in, public affairs. Representation tended to be recommended for one major reason: it exonerated modern democratic citizens from the burdens of public deliberation and allowed them to place their full attention on private economic and personal pursuits (Constant [1819] 1988). One must not forget that politicians come to be judged almost exclusively based on the performance of the economy or overlook the fact that the expansion of prosperity and the growth of mankind's dominion over nature support greater leisure for the pursuit of personal forms of autonomy and pleasure and that this is vital enough to justify and sustain modern liberal democracy.

Modern liberal democracy sets up a dynamic in which individuals are freed from political, feudal, religious, or other constraints and pointed toward pursuits of individual private satisfaction. The very success of this liberation has led, especially in the West, to the monumental rise of modern expansive and globalized capitalism.[1] The free market system derives its fundamental motivation from private interests and gives rise to increasing bounty and material comfort, in ways echoing Bernard Mandeville's eighteenth-century dictum, "private vices, publick benefits" ([1732] 1988). Modern forms of capital accrue such substantial power, however, that they pose a threat to the liberty of individuals, because they permit the manipulation of political outcomes through subtle lucre or outright bribery, but also because they encroach in innumerable ways on the private spheres of individual life—for example, in the domain of personal information. Governments now empowered to protect citizens from the predations of large-scale private economic organizations take on arrays of duties and activities that were unimaginable by early liberal theorists (Jouvenel 1949). The success of modern liberal democracy's liberation of individual self-interest and its ability to redirect it toward the Enlightenment project of conquering nature, toward increasing human power, have resulted in the rise of public and private organizations that are both baffling in their power and expanse and dizzying in their complexity and interdependence (Polanyi 1944). People are asked to vote for representatives who by themselves can barely grasp the complexity of modern institutions and economies and who then respond by surrounding themselves with layers of advisers, experts, and large bureaucracies as the sole resources affording adequate capacity for crafting policy. This in turn makes government ever more encompassing and ever more complex, seemingly divorced from the daily concerns of ordinary citizens

---

1. Sheldon Wolin has written perhaps more profoundly than any other commentator on this transformation and on the attendant decline of 'the political'. See Wolin's *Politics and Vision* (1960), especially chapter 7 and his more recent work *Tocqueville between Two Worlds* (2001), especially chapters 1 and 2. He calls the current environment "post-democracy" (2001, chap. 26).

(McConnell 1966). And, consequently, many citizens choose simply not to exercise that singular formal sign of political citizenship, as they are either too bewildered or too disenchanted to cast a ballot they perceive to have become an insignificant opinion (Patterson 2002).

It is within this paradigm of modern liberal democracy in which most discussions over 'democratization' occur. Should democracy be more centralized or federal? Should governments have greater or less oversight over free markets? Should democracy become fully identified with globalization and internationalization, or should it remain wed at some level to the nation-state? To what extent should subnational cultural differences be respected and protected, even if the costs to be borne are inconsistent with the benefits expected from provisions of the sort, and even with the potential of injustice to be suffered by cultural entities otherwise? These and innumerable other questions are by no means trivial, and without exception, they are asked and at least provisionally answered in the framework of the ruling paradigm of modern liberal democracy. From inside the prevailing paradigm of modern liberal democracy, the range of differing answers to these manifold questions results in the perception of 'democratization' as 'democratizations'—the possibility of many different manifestations of contemporary democracy across the expanse of the globe. Stepping outside of the paradigm, however, one sees these questions rather as negotiations within a firmly entrenched project of democratization— a societal process that takes its cues from the philosophical project of modernity. True, from this perspective, there may be many possible paths to democratization but little if any significant evidence of competing conceptions of democracy that might make a true plurality of democracy possible. Indeed, stepping outside the dominant paradigm of modern democratization, it becomes possible to raise the question whether, by another standard, modern 'democracy' can be considered to be fundamentally democratic at all.

Another Kind of Democracy

For ancient political theory, questions fretted over by modern democrats—say, concerns over economics and international relations— concerned matters deemed to be political in nature and therefore not essential to the definition of democracy as such. To begin with, they were queries secondary to the more fundamental contemplation over the nature of regimes. A regime was not considered to be "democratic" by dint of its particular system of exchange, or on the grounds of some prevailing theory of jurisprudence, or yet because of its willingness to cede sovereignty to an international order; but in the first and overarching instance, a regime was deemed to be so always by reason of a certain conception of citizenship. At first blush, similar to modern liberal democratic conceptions, the vision of the ancients insisted on the fundamental political equality of citizens. Democracy, Aristotle wrote, consisted of "ruling and being ruled in turn"; hence, for the ancients, democracies were defined, above all else, upon the basis of a conception of equal citizenship and shared rule (Aristotle 1984, 1277b). Aristotle pointed out that representation, at some level, contained a deeply undemocratic premise inasmuch as it implied that one citizen saw in one other someone better qualified to "re-present" fully one's own views in public (1282b–1283b). Modern representation contains an aristocratic element. Even when on grounds of expediency the need was recognized for smaller assemblies that by definition did exclude most citizens, democracies nevertheless elected members of their assembly on the basis of the lot and not on the basis of campaigning over qualifications and abilities.[2]

Modern democracy emphasizes the major role of rights, especially of rights intended to protect minorities against the depredations of majorities. Based fundamentally on self-interest, modern democracy's insistence on the central need for rights reflects the intuition that, without such rights, democracy would simply result in arbitrary rule of one larger group of people pursuing self-interest against a smaller group motivated by divergent interests (Ely 1980). Ancient political theory did not dwell on the role of rights in a democratic order. Why? Because it was predicated not on politics poised on self-interest but on an insistence that the good of the whole supersede the good of the parts.[3] In democracy so conceived, majorities do not intend tyranny.

---

2. The *Federalist* consistently argues that representation at the national level will result in the election of gentlemen with more discernment and wisdom than the populace that elected them. See *Federalist 10* (Hamilton, Madison, and Jay 1999 [1787–1788]): "[Representation will] refine and enlarge the public views by passing them through the medium of a chosen body of citizens, whose wisdom may best discern the true interest of their country and love of justice will be least likely to sacrifice it to temporary or partial considerations. Under such a regulation, it may well happen that the public voice, pronounced by the representatives of the people, will be more consonant to the public good than if pronounced by the people themselves, convened for the purpose" (50).
3. Nevertheless, Josiah Ober (2000) has argued that Athenian democratic practices resulted in the practical existence of rights, notwithstanding that they were not self-understood as such.

Because of this preliminary dedication to the public good, citizens in the minority would not assume that majorities acted out of a desire to advance solely their exclusive interests (Winthrop 1978, 156). A prior commitment to the good of the whole in effect acts as a potent restraint upon the ambitions born wholly of unharnessed self-interest. For as Wilson Carey McWilliams has written of ancient understandings of democracy, "Citizenship rules partisanship, and public principles govern private interest" (1980, 81).

Modern democratic theorists have difficulty understanding this core justification of democracy, beginning, as they do, with priority on the individual over the polity, of the part(s) over the whole. In a much-discussed essay titled "A Paradox in the Theory of Democracy," published in 1962, the political theorist Richard Wollheim pointed out the difficulty that democracy posed to modern assumptions: on the one hand, as a citizen of a democracy, one may come to believe that Policy A ought to be enacted; whereupon one might try to articulate that preference by means of one's vote. However, it may come about that a majority of one's fellow citizens vote for Policy B, thereby defeating the enactment of one's own preference. As an individual, I might continue to prefer Policy A—(perhaps its electoral defeat has not persuaded me otherwise), but as a democratic citizen, I am also empowered to think "Policy B" ought to be enacted, because, being a democrat, I defer to the will of the majority. Wollheim paraphrases the apparent paradox in a question: "How can the citizen accept the [democratic] machine's choice, which involves his thinking that B ought to be enacted when, as we already know, he is of the opinion, of the declared opinion, that A ought to be enacted?" (1962, 78).

Of course, this is only a paradox to the extent that a priority is placed on individual self-interest as in modern liberal theory. Wollheim justifiably notes that, in a democratic age, one might merely appear to prefer Policy B, while in fact harboring the secret wish to parlay that appearance into a position of power within the democracy. A person motivated at every point by self-interest would merely use the machinery of democracy to achieve power, at which point "he would probably try to end the democratic process." Wollheim concedes that here the problem "arises [of] how we are to distinguish such a man from the genuine believer in Democracy" (1962, 84). Given Wollheim's basic premise that one is fundamentally motivated by self-interest, it naturally remains unclear whether in reality there could exist a "genuine believer in Democracy," to begin with. He concludes by suggesting that both conditions can apply—that is, one can genuinely prefer Policy A without thereby necessarily repudiating Policy B. He thereby implicitly acknowledges that a democrat cannot begin with any fixated policy preference that stands to eclipse the more fundamental dedication to equal citizenship and shared rule. A citizen's primary allegiance in the first instance is to democracy because that citizen sees in democracy a form best suited to how humans ought to live and to promoting an apprehension of the whole even while recognizing that political differences will be manifested within even such a regime. Nevertheless, democracy is incomprehensible unless there is a shared conception that the democratic (systemic) civic whole supersedes the (elemental) single parts without suppressing them (Aristotle 1984, 1253a).

Wollheim recognizes that ancient democracy was able to maintain this 'awareness of the whole' by limiting democracy to small regimes. Classical theory, even early modern theorists such as Montesquieu, recognized that a distinctive feature of democracy was its physically small scale. More than voting—the sine qua non of modern democratic citizenship, even though defended in the main as a formal right—for ancient democracy, 'citizenship' was much more closely equated with deliberation. Voting was the mere conclusion of a more comprehensive activity: that of speaking and of listening in turn. In contemporary democracy, "freedom of expression" is protected because any form of expression is seen to be central to one's authenticity and autonomy, regardless of whether anyone is attending to one's articulations or even whether such 'expression' is political in nature.[4] Conversely, for ancient-mode democracy, political speech presupposed "listeners" who would accord a speaker the respect they expected to be shown them when they in turn would rise to the rostrum and speak. Rather than viewing speech principally as a means for airing one's differences—nowadays in the form of 'opinions begging to differ'—political and democratic speech in this ancient understanding first and foremost was premised on its basic commonness, a virtuous core asset of human nature that was able to bind together even political antagonists. Superficially, speech appears to divide, but Aristotle suggested that speech is a manifestation of a deeper and more fundamental common nature of human-

---

4. Perhaps the most exemplary form of protected modern expression is found in the U.S. Supreme Court's decision, *Buckley v. Valeo* (424 U.S. 1 [1976]), in which it deemed personal campaign expenditures to be a protected form of expression, and thus equates "speech" and "money." Given the logic of this decision, bribery also and rightly might be considered a form of protected "expression."

ity, one that naturally signals a commonality that precedes artificial distinctions (Aristotle 1984, 1253a).

Finally, ancient political theory held a conception of freedom that was largely rejected and reversed by modern liberal theory. For modern theorists, freedom is manifested by an absence of restraint and the ability to pursue one's interests to the fullest extent possible (Mill [1859] 1972, especially chaps. 1–3). For Hobbes and Locke, man is free in the State of Nature precisely because there are no formal external restraints preventing him from fulfilling his every desire. Yet one's freedom is also radically constrained by the exact same freedom enjoyed by every other human in the State of Nature. Hence, a social contract is agreed upon, to prevent the anarchy and even the slaughter that can result from such a condition of universal freedom. The creation of government is only a second-best solution: implicit in liberal theory is the first-best solution—one according to which every other human remains constrained by the agreements of the social contract, while I act freely if secretly (to preempt or prevent other backsliders and free riders), the better to fulfill my every desire.[5] Theoretically, this possibility is forestalled by the existence of the State, which will 'catch and punish' me, but unless it is Hobbes's Leviathan—in which case it hardly can be a liberal state, let alone a democratic one (see Botwinick, chap. 3 in this book)—citizens who do not break the law too flamboyantly, or much too visibly, and are not reputed to do so habitually, reasonably can hope to "get away with it." In sum, liberal theory suggests that every person's fondest dream is to be a tyrant, effectively capable of satisfying one's innermost appetites, without fear of punishment or restraint from State or fellow citizen.

For the ancients, this conception of freedom was tantamount to a form of slavery. Marked by a disordered soul, a tyrant is unable to restrain his desires: he craves without limit and pursues without end (Plato 1968, chaps. 8–9). He is enslaved by the desires of the body, unable to prevent the disfigurement of the soul. In contrast, the ancients understand freedom to be the mark of one's ability to deny one's most primitive desires and to forego the many aimless cravings that mark man's physical and psychic nature—to choose between alternatives, to the extent of invoking nobility and self-sacrifice as a standard of

---

5. The "myth of Gyges" related in Plato's *Republic* is an early version of this tyrannical dream, describing the ability of Gyges to fulfill his every desire (by means of a ring of invisibility) while others continue to abide by the law, all the while believing Gyges to be a just man (Plato 1968, 359b–361d)

conduct, elevating some pursuits while debasing others. To be sure, politics makes possible the cultivation of a division of labor, thus allowing for the possibility not only of 'mere life' but of the 'good life'; yet Aristotle recognized that the pursuit of physical goods without restraint was an abnegation of good living (Aristotle 1984, 1252b). For him, unrestrained souls "are serious about living but not living well, and so since their desire for that is infinite, they desire also an infinite amount of things that produce it" (1257b). Modern democratic citizens, as Tocqueville described them centuries later, are noteworthy rather for their persistent 'restlessness': "[Democratic man] grasps those [goods] that pass within his reach that one would say that he fears at each instant that he will cease to live before he has enjoyed them. He grasps them all but without clutching them, and soon allows them to escape from his hands so as to run after new enjoyments" ([1840] 2000, vol. 2, part. 2, 13:512). By contrast, ancient political theory pointed to self-knowledge as the source of limits to the restless pursuit of any and all desires; it suggested that self-rule was the result of such examination, and it held that, as such, self-rule is the single overarching requirement of true democratic governance.

Whereas moderns viewed democracy in almost purely formal terms, ancients held fast to a conception of active and shared ruling; where moderns sought to unleash self-interest as a means to increase their prosperity and power, ancients viewed restraint and self-governance as the highest form of liberty; and wherever moderns conceptualized democracy to be manifest primarily inside organizations capable of protecting, preserving, and enhancing the fulfillment of individual autonomy, ancients insisted on the primacy of democracy first for the personal cultivation of internal self-rule and, extended outward, for the collective cultivation of shared rule by active political equals.

Its seeming implicit promise of progressing plurality aside, the widespread embrace of 'democratization' is in fact informed almost wholly by modern conceptions of democracy aimed at the liberation of the citizenry from the basic demands of self-rule recommended by the ancient political theorists. 'Democratizations,' on the other hand, in implying or recognizing differing conceptions of democracy, would invite contrasts, comparisons, and confrontations that, if seriously conducted, might very well raise doubts on the democratic claims of modern forms of governance. Curiously, in the very effort to embrace the possibility of 'democratizations' it is quite possible, if not plausible, that modern conceptions of democracy could be rejected or at least significantly modified on the grounds that they are, in the final estimation, insufficiently democratic. That is, if we accept ancient teachings that equate democracy with a robust understanding of political self-governance and with a more cultivated acquiescence of democracy's prior recognition of common civic purposes, then all of the contemporary theories of 'democratization' that place emphasis on privatism, free choice, and growth in the economic sphere, and only occasional and superficial attention to political activity regarding distant political entities, might begin to look like sadly inadequate versions of democracy.

The Paradox of "Democratizations"

The ancient conception of democracy is rejected out of hand for its historical association with inequality, particularly for its use of slavery and its complete omission of a public role for women. Ancient democracy held a robust and committed conception of citizenship, but that vision relied extensively on the effective disenfranchisement of large segments of the population. Modern democracy, on the other hand, strips citizenship of its substantive expectations and, by making it foremost a matter of formal recognition, extends universal suffrage. Wollheim formulates the difference: "In classical theory the people is identified with a section or part of the population, whereas in modern theory the people is identified with population as a whole" (1962, 72). However, if ancient democracy—in practice—required this radical division as a means for making possible political liberty for relatively few citizens, there is nothing endemic to ancient theory that makes this the case. Aristotle suggested that the distinctions between citizen and slave would evaporate if the work of 'mere life', of 'basic survival', could be performed by mechanized 'tools': "For suppose that each tool could complete its work either by being told to do so or because it perceived what was to be done in advance . . ."—in such case, "managers need not assistants . . . masters need not slaves" (Aristotle 1984, 1253a–1254a).[6] Aristotle readily admitted that a scenario of the sort was

---

6. Critics rightly point out that Aristotle took some distinctions to be natural and not merely the product of social circumstance. Although any defense of slavery is lamentable, many readers sensitive to Aristotle's "defense" of natural slavery have noted its peculiarity, beginning with the fact that his justification would have made all existing forms of ancient slavery illegitimate. For many readers, it is difficult to conceive of what being would qualify as a "natural slave" (see, for example, Swanson 1992).

more the fancy of poets than remotely within the power of realization extant in Hellenic civilization. Yet the larger point here is that the inequalities marking ancient democracy were the result of material circumstance, not a fundamental failure of ancient political theory.

Modern theory resolves the problem by releasing humankind from restraints that formerly pointed humans away from the domination of nature. Francis Bacon inaugurated the tradition aimed at providing 'relief to the human estate' by promoting the useful arts and sciences as the handmaiden of modern politics, thus unleashing at once creative energies hitherto unseen and a transformation of nature breathtaking in its thoroughness (Bacon [1605] 2001; White 1968). Yet herein lies the paradox of 'democratizations': if the modern project aimed at the 'conquest of nature' now makes possible those material conditions that Aristotle could only fantasize about as being capable of making the realization of universal civic equality feasible, those very same conditions appear to require a fundamental transformation of philosophy that actually points people away from that ancient conception of civic equality and shared rule. The same argument that emphasizes the priority of individual self-interest, the pursuit of material goods without limit, and the elevation of private goods over public goods at once promotes also the very material conditions imagined by Aristotle and by the Greek poets as potentially capable of emancipating people from brute drudgery. Yet, concomitantly, this philosophy also undermines those democratic beliefs that at base inspired the ancients' fantasy of 'tools' that could relieve human drudgery in the first place. In order to realize the conditions that might make ancient democratic forms universally possible in our time, history suggests that moderns must develop an alternative philosophy aimed at human mastery of nature that in effect makes the realization of robust democracy implausible if not impossible.

In light of this recognition, it becomes likely that there is no plausible chance of 'democratizations.' The great complexity and interdependence of modern peoples, the massive expansion of the world population, and the inability of most contemporary democratic citizens to rely extensively on their own economic products make even the most well-intentioned efforts to instantiate such ancient conceptions of democracy as too frightful to contemplate: their outcomes may likely resemble the era of French terror than a realm of beatific vision. Yet the fact remains that, at least in the domain of theory, one can envision a form of democracy distinctive from the modern form, upon beginning to see more clearly the radical insufficiencies of modern democracy, both at the fringes of social policy and on democratic grounds as such. Ancient political theory does offer a corrective principle that points to the need for attentiveness to political democracy itself, rather than to the lip service being paid its pale shadow comprising economic choice and personal satisfaction. Ancient conceptions remind us of the nobility of rule and of the even greater majesty of assent to rule (given that such assent may work against one's perceived 'self-interest' in the immediate), of those first grounds for democracy involving ruling and being ruled, and of the civic whole that deserves precedence over its parts. The ancient teachings do afford an encounter with a justification of democracy on the basis of human equality rather than as a utilitarian arrangement that best suits the modern project of nature's domination and that reinforces the belief that democracy is the fulfillment of the misguided claim "to live as one likes" (Aristotle 1984, 1317b).

Prospects for Democracy in Undemocratic Times

In these overly self-congratulatory of all democratic times, the prospects for democracy according to its more ancient understanding are meager if not irrevocably moribund. The most ardent proponents of democracy in contemporary times largely eschew alternative democratic commitments of the ancient kind. On the right, many equate democracy with the opening of markets and with the continued growth of human mastery over nature.[7] On the left, many embrace noneconomic liberation as the sine qua non of democracy, equating democracy wholly with personal autonomy in all of its forms and reserving distrust for economic libertarianism, because the manifold forms of personal autonomy that it does recommend rest extensively on the material advances and greater leisure afforded by modern economics.[8] While

---

7. American policy toward China best reflects how extensively this belief is now held: by encouraging Chinese economic development, democracy is sure to follow. Democracy is the result of, and hence subordinate to, economic development, not vice versa (see deLisle, chap. 9 in this book).

8. To this extent, many on the left continue to evoke, if only implicitly, the fond portrait of human life at the end of history described by Karl Marx in which one could combine multiple forms of work and nearly unlimited leisure. See *The German Ideology* ([1888] 1972): "In communist society, where nobody has one exclusive sphere of activity but each can become accomplished in any branch he wishes, society regulates the general production and thus makes it possible for me to do one thing today and another tomorrow, to hunt in the morning, fish in the afternoon, rear cattle in the evening, criticize after dinner, just as I have a mind, without ever becoming hunter, fisherman, shepherd or critic" (160). Marx would be the first to admit that this condition becomes possible only after superseding the stage of capitalism and the material wealth provided initially by a market economy.

the left voices more explicit commitments to political forms of democracy than does the more economics-oriented right, more often than not civil devotions of the sort are manifested by calls for participation in movements and (or) for dramatic democratic 'action', all in all evincing impatience for the hard discipline and even for the inglorious quotidian grind of democratic attentiveness (Mansbridge 1986; Kelly 2001). Perhaps more significantly, whatever their differences over that phenomenon's specific defining character, both the right and the left seem wedded to the project of globalization.

A conception of democracy that focuses instead on citizenship—not merely formal extension of electoral rights, but also substantive commitments to shared civic life and to public deliberation as daily undertakings—somehow finds less obvious support in these purportedly democratic times.[9] Modern peoples schooled and groomed in a conception of democracy that recommends, above all, individual satisfaction, and that is likely to equate the word *politics* with the distant cynical exploitation and manipulation of interests, are not easily amenable to embrace a conception of democracy that stresses discipline, values sacrifice, and lauds the willingness to reconsider one's self-serving interests in the light of the good of the polity.[10] The very absurdity of the notion that there can ever be a single 'good' to be expected of an impersonal polity of such vastness and overwhelming anonymity should suffice to reveal the utterly foreign, even incomprehensible, tenor of such a conception of civic democracy.

At the same time, one must marvel at the near-universal embrace of democracy and the manifestly widespread ambition to effect various 'democratizations' throughout the globe. Such belief in the promise of democracy, even in these times of pallid democratic forms, flows deep nevertheless. Beneath modern democracy's latter-day commitments to rights-based citizenship, to jurisprudential political activity, and to representative democratic forms, and behind its recommendation of individual self-concern, there may lurk nevertheless a devotion to democracy in its more robust civic conception.

---

9. This is surely not to say that such a conception is lacking proponents, if merely that they tend to fall outside the prevailing mainstream political categories. See, for example, Barber (1984, 1996), Putnam (2001), and Lasch (1995), among others.

10. Hannah Arendt begins her essay entitled "What Is Authority?" with the statement that its subject might better be rendered as "What Was—and Not What Is—Authority?" (1961, 91). On the central importance of "expanded mentality" for democratic life, see Arendt's "Truth and Politics" and "The Crisis in Culture" (1961).

This possibility was disclosed particularly in the United States on September 11, 2001, and in the days that followed. That morning, fanatics opposed to democracy flew above the skies of New York City and Washington, DC, searching for suitable targets, the destruction of which would symbolize their hatred of and ephemeral triumph over the products of modern democratic processes. In New York City, they chose two towering skyscrapers, the Twin Towers of the World Trade Center. In Washington, DC, they targeted the Pentagon. In short, they set their sights on an 'America' they perceived primarily and maybe solely as a "military-industrial complex"—that very 'thing' President Dwight Eisenhower had warned America to beware of, as he addressed the nation in his Farewell Address of 1961. Forty years later, the attackers concluded that America manifested the complete triumph of modern forms of democracy expressed through economic expansion and military domination, altogether overlooking the nobler democratic commitments that even more meaningfully characterize the civilization they so deeply despised and wished to harm.

Were one to have asked any American what structures or symbols best represented his or her own self-conception of America in either of those two cities, on the evening of September 10, 2001, it is doubtful that many would have named the buildings that were attacked on the following morning. Instead, one modestly may speculate that most would have named, in New York City, the Statue of Liberty, and in Washington, DC, the Capitol, the White House, or possibly the Lincoln Memorial. That most U.S. citizens likely would have chosen as the paramount symbols of their nation the more value-laden edifices and politically significant monuments over any financial or military structures is all the more noteworthy, because many Americans have been tutored to think of democracy as a system that allows for the fullest expression of personal preference and many U.S. citizens quite often lack strong admiration for politics in its day-to-day practice. The overwhelming and spontaneous willingness to donate blood, time, and treasure especially for those civilian victims in New York City—a place that many throughout the country had been rumored to love to hate before September 11—momentarily revealed the residue of civic commitments that continues to persist in spite of modern democracy's prevailing commitments to self-gratification. Like a palimpsest, the ancient devotions of democracy—shared political equality and a deep belief in the citizenry's interlinked common fates—linger below the surface of its contemporary redefinitions, leaving those more robust civic forms legible for those with the willingness and patience to discern their presence and to make their subdued teachings a tad more visible amid the more obvious commonplace manifestations of modern democracy.

Tocqueville, more explicitly than others, discerned this dual nature of democracy in modern times. He noted that Americans tended to justify their actions in terms of self-interest, even when their true motivations were considerably more selfless than they would care to admit. He noted that modern democrats—captured by the influence of liberal and individualist philosophy and capable solely of expressing even their noblest actions in the cramped language of self-interest—all too often "would rather do more honor to their philosophy than to themselves" ([1840] 2000, vol. 2, part. 2, 8:502). Yet he worried that actual motivations eventually would conform to the more explicit language in which those motivations were framed and justified, perhaps ultimately undermining the nobler motivations of the people in favor of their philosophical claims.

Nevertheless, Tocqueville also hoped that even such explicit emphasis on self-interest could be moderated through participation in democratic politics itself. He noted that citizens might understand their initial engagement in political activity as a practical means of advancing their perceived self-interest, but that interaction with other citizens, sustained exposure to countervailing concerns and to varied backgrounds or alternative proposals, democratic politics in and of itself should foster the likelihood that each citizen's "heart is enlarged" ([1840] 2000, vol. 2, part. 2, 5:490). Above all, he said, democracy might come to flourish where there persists a commitment to cultivating "the arts of association"—the formal/informal political activities through which individuals are transformed into citizens and in virtue of which a conception of the common good could result through dynamic interaction among democratic citizens. Tocqueville predicted the rise of 'individualism' and the decline of active civil life. But the more hopeful aspects of his analysis—a hopefulness that was momentarily justified in the civic response to the terrorist attacks on the United States, in 2001—suggests that perhaps multiple forms of 'democratization' are possible, after all. Tocqueville kept up this hope in spite of the formidable paradox that exists at the core of modern democracy: the fact that the very embrace of modern forms of material progress via emphasis on economic freedoms that ease human liberation from the drudgery of 'mere life' simultaneously also undermines the human capacity to acknowledge a common civic purpose and a shared fate. The truth is that even contemporary democratic faith rests most fundamentally on a belief in democracy's potential and in the wishful expectation of the sheer possibility of a political whole that transcends the many parts that comprise it. Like any faith, it offers grounds and it inspires justifications for greater humility—in this instance, for a form of civic humbleness that points to the fact that democracy is neither easy nor automatic, and that in fact, all too often it requires extensive, even heroic civic commitments.[11]

Although commentators from William James (1897) to Jean Bethke Elshtain (1995) have insisted that democracy remains "on trial," it perhaps would be more effective instead to conceive of democracy itself as trial. For, according to its ancient conception, democracy's trial takes the form of hard discipline. It involves the cultivation of civic capacities of ruling and being ruled as well as the restraint of immediate self-interest. It requires the hard task of discerning a common purpose underlying manifold disparate interests. In its modern form, democracy's trial inheres in a double temptation: its in-built inclination to lose sight of its basic commitment to political self-rule and its innate tendency to surrender wholly to its unmistakably explicit foundation on self-interest. Owing to citizens' increasing inability to resist these temptations, and because of the absence of statesmen and leaders to remind citizens of the ancient teachings, contemporary democracy is increasingly imperiled. By attending to the fragility of democracy despite its seemingly power-laden reigning modern forms, we modern men and women can relearn to recognize it as a shared civic project—an activity, not a set of institutions—thereby also rediscovering good reason to carve out a possibility for democratizations in these otherwise undemocratic times.

References

Arendt, Hannah (1961) *Between Past and Future: Eight Exercises in Political Thought*, New York: Penguin Books.

---

11. George Santayana understood the heroic nature of democratic citizenship, even as he despaired that it was implausible for a polity to achieve as a whole: "If a noble and civilized democracy is to subsist, the common citizen must be something of a saint and something of a hero. We see, therefore, how justly flattering and profound, and at the same time how ominous, was Montesquieu's saying that the principle of democracy is virtue" (1954, 148).

Aristotle (1984) *The Politics*, Carnes Lord, Translator, Chicago: University of Chicago Press.

Bacon, Francis (2001) *The Advancement of Learning*, New York: Modern Library.

Barber, Benjamin (1984) *Strong Democracy: Participatory Politics for a New Age*, Berkeley: University of California Press.

——— (1996) *Jihad vs. McWorld: How Globalism and Tribalism Are Reshaping the World*, New York: Ballantine Books.

Constant, Benjamin (1988) "The Liberty of the Ancients Compared to That of the Moderns," in *Political Writings*, Biancamaria Fontana, Editor/Translator, Cambridge, UK: Cambridge University Press.

Elshtain, Jean Bethke (1995) *Democracy on Trial*, New York: Basic Books.

Ely, John Hart (1980) *Democracy and Distrust: A Theory of Judicial Review*, Cambridge, MA: Harvard University Press.

Hamilton, Alexander, James Madison, and John Jay (1999) *The Federalist Papers*, Clinton Rossiter, Editor, New York: Mentor.

James, William (1897) "Robert Gould Shaw," *The Works of William James: Essays in Religion and Morality*, Cambridge, MA: Harvard University Press.

Jouvenel, Bertrand de (1949) *On Power: Its Nature and the History of Its Growth*, J. F. Huntington, Translator, New York: Viking Press.

Kelly, Christine A. (2001) *Tangled Up in Red, White and Blue: New Social Movements in America*, Lanham, MD: Rowman and Littlefield.

Keyssar, Alexander (2000) *The Right to Vote: The Contested History of Democracy in the United States*, New York: Basic Books.

Lasch, Christopher (1995) *The Revolt of the Elites and the Betrayal of Democracy*, New York: W. W. Norton.

Locke, John (1960) *Two Treatises of Government*, Peter Laslett, Editor, Cambridge, UK: Cambridge University Press.

Macpherson, C. B. (1964) *Political Theory of Possessive Individualism: Hobbes to Locke*, Oxford, UK: Oxford University Press.

Mandeville, Bernard (1988) *The Fable of the Bees: or, Private Vices, Publick Benefits*, 2 vols., Indianapolis: Liberty Press.

Mansbridge, Jane J. (1986) *Why We Lost the E.R.A.*, Chicago: University of Chicago Press.

Marx, Karl (1972) "The German Ideology," in *The Marx-Engels Reader*, 2nd ed., Robert C. Tucker, Editor, New York: W. W. Norton.

McConnell, Grant (1966) *Private Power and American Democracy*, New York: Knopf.

McWilliams, Wilson C. (1980) "Democracy and the Citizen: Community, Dignity, and the Crisis of Contemporary Politics in America," in Robert A. Goldwin and William A. Schambra, Editors, *How Democratic Is the Constitution?* Washington, DC: AEI Press.

Mill, John Stuart [1859] (1972) *On Liberty*, in *Utilitarianism, On Liberty and Considerations on Representative Government*, H. B. Acton, Editor, London: J.M. Dent and Sons.

Ober, Josiah (2000) "Quasi-rights: Participatory Citizenship and Negative Liberties in Democratic Athens," *Social Philosophy and Policy*, 17:27–61.

Patterson, Thomas E. (2002) *The Vanishing Voter: Public Involvement in an Age of Uncertainty*, New York: Knopf.

Plato (1968) *The Republic of Plato*, Allan Bloom, Translator, New York: Basic Books.

Polanyi, Karl (1944) *The Great Transformation: The Political and Economic Origins of Our Time*, Boston: Beacon Press.

Putnam, Robert D. (2001) *Bowling Alone*, New York: Touchstone Books.

Santayana, George (1954) *The Life of Reason, or The Phases of Human Progress*, one-volume edition, London: Constable.

Smith, Rogers M. (1997) *Civic Ideals: Conflicting Visions of Citizenship in U.S. History*, New Haven, CT: Yale University Press.

Swanson, Judith A. (1992) *The Public and the Private in Aristotle's Political Philosophy*, Ithaca, NY: Cornell University Press.

Tocqueville, Alexis de (2000) *Democracy in America*, Harvey C. Mansfield and Delba Winthrop, Translators and Editors, Chicago: University of Chicago Press.

White, Howard B. (1968) *Peace among the Willows: The Political Philosophy of Francis Bacon*, The Hague: Martinus Nijhoff.

Winthrop, Delba (1978) "Aristotle on Participatory Democracy," *Polity*, 11:151–171.

Wolin, Sheldon S. (1960) *Politics and Vision: Continuity and Innovation in Western Political Thought*, Boston: Little, Brown.

——— (2001) *Tocqueville between Two Worlds: The Making of a Political and Theoretical Life*, Princeton, NJ: Princeton University Press.

Wollheim, Richard (1962) "A Paradox in the Theory of Democracy," in Peter Laslett and W. G. Runciman, Editors, *Philosophy, Politics and Society: Second Series*, New York: Barnes & Noble.

Zuckert, Michael P. (1999) *The Natural Rights Republic: Studies in the Foundation of the American Political Tradition*, Notre Dame, IN: University of Notre Dame Press.

14

Pictures at an Exhibition in the Guise of an Epilogue

Jose V. Ciprut

"We want Absolute Democracy!"
(Poster borne during the "Protests of '88" in Burma)

In Afterthought, as It Were

Having examined the theoretical underpinnings and commonplace practices of different modes of democratization around the world, we think it useful to add an album of narrative snapshots in the guise of an epilogue: these telling close-ups might prove helpful in revealing how the smallest of daily details can serve as powerful deterrent, potent reinforcement, or subtle multiplier, for both democracy and democratizations, in hues and sounds that often elude qualifications in theoretical explanations and easily evade rigid quantifications in empirical understandings. These 'verbal drawings' were crayoned in the United States in various epochs of the country's history, by discerning French intellectuals—three of them assiduously jotting down 'from the inside', and one perspicaciously conjecturing, comparing, and commenting 'from the outside'—in ways that sound still fresh, even disquietingly appropriate, if surprisingly timely as well.

Despite their steadily augmenting magnitude around the world to date, rare are the advanced actors among the established democratic systems who are engaged in ceaseless self-questionings that somehow spur continual self-transformations via processes that thereby are in turn deepened, broadened, and accelerated, with strengthening effects. For being all-azimuth in their aggregate thrust, such practices shape the mentality of democracy and reinforce the indigenous character of democratization—nay, democratizations—pursued in those spaces from within. The United States, as the oldest of young democracies, provides a good example of a nation engaged in just such a dynamic. It therefore may prove enlightening, we thought, as we conclude, to compare notes with three noteworthy visitors who, having visited "America" at different periods of its history and having made trenchant comments about its democracy in eloquently simple if insight-arousing contrasts, might help us further distance ourselves from stylized understandings based on too clear-cut explanations, and thereby spare us hasty conclusions along one or another of the traditional dimensions.

Of Democracy and Democratization—Also in America

In 1831–1832, an independently wealthy French country gentleman and intellectually curious frequent traveler by the aristocratic Christian surname of Alexis Henri Charles Maurice Clérel, vicomte de Tocqueville was sent by Louis-Philippe's administration on a mission to scrutinize and report on the penitentiary system in "America." Following an intense nine-month visit that allowed this emissary to penetrate levels of U.S. society and to visit places that otherwise he could not have gotten to know,[1] his purposive undertaking gave us two products: one (with de Beaumont as first coauthor, in 1833) titled *Du système pénitentiaire aux États-Unis et de son application en France,* and the other, *De la démocratie en Amérique* (volume 1, in 1835, and volume 2, in 1840, currently known to U.S. undergraduates as *Democracy in America* [1945, among others]).

From January 25 to May 20, 1947, a self-styled French feminist, born and raised as a bourgeois Catholic, but by now a fervent atheist and 'liberated' Frenchwoman by the name of Simone de Beauvoir, toured the United States for four intensively introductory months organized for her by an entourage all too avid to expose her to what they

---

1. "[T]he characters who influenced Tocqueville during his journey and in his later writing . . . held a particular weight or influence in American society. In truth, his letters of introduction took him to powerful sources. He and Beaumont met two of the seven men who had been President of the United States up to that time, three of the men who had been President of Harvard University, a signer of the Declaration of Independence, men who fought in the Revolutionary War and the War of 1812, men who led major religious movements of the day (especially Unitarianism), men who developed American systems of imprisonment and slavery, prisoners who enjoyed and feared the fruits of those imprisonment theories, pioneers, Native Americans, slaveholders, slaves, and former slaves. They also met historians, professors, authors, merchants, innkeepers, military leaders, politicians at every level of government, other European visitors, French [émigrés], and many, many lawyers. This type-cast is far from a comprehensive list, but it truly contextualizes what their journey was like. They met the common and the uncommon man. In short, they were in heavy company." (For details, see the Web sites of the University of Virginia, at http://xroads.virginia.edu/~HYPER/DETOC/home.html in general and, in particular, at http://xroads.virginia.edu/~HYPER/DETOC/tvox/comm.html.)

concluded she must see if ever she was to begin to understand 'democratic' America in its blossoming complexity through and beyond its McCarthyite Black Listing days. Result? A detailed diary[2] turned into a book: *L'Amérique au Jour le Jour* (1948, 1954), also known as *America Day by Day* (1952, 1999).

In 2004–2005, more than seventeen decades after de Tocqueville's year-long exploration, and fifty years after de Beauvoir's four-month-long on-the-job indoctrination, an exuberant French secular Jew—a neoprogressive conservative critic of the Old Left, with explicit philosophical reservations on global-capitalist ideology—set out 'to retrace de Tocqueville's steps.' The outcome: a series of impassioned articles in *The Atlantic*, titled "In the Footsteps of Tocqueville," now a book by French philosopher-journalist Bernard-Henri Lévy.[3]

So what did the 'elephant' look like to the wide-eyed very early on, much later, and—at long last—now? Were all three looking at one and the same behemoth and catching a glimpse of the beast's babyhood, adolescence, and maturity, respectively, or were they in fact eyeing a different creature each time they took yet another look? The question still stands: Is there 'one America', embodied in what now exceeds a population of 300 million individuals, each of whom is dynamically distributed about a perpetually moving median? Or are there as many Americas as there are observers, each trusting to have witnessed 'the truth' directly, firsthand, through one's very own mind's eye?

As to 'democratization in America', the open-ended process to which that labile term refers was, is, and remains a project under perpetual construction. And although the very pursuit might be emulated elsewhere, never could it be reproduced identically. Why? Well—and this is the very question examined worldwide in this book—because perspectives and prospects, both, are context related; moreover, they cannot wholly shed the effects of their initial conditions. In retrospect, it is also evident that neither responsive systems nor fickle environments ever have been coextensive or coterminal with one another's

---

2. The diary, published in France in 1948, appeared in English in 1952, following the publication of *Le Deuxième Sexe* (1949), for which she became far better known, and which might have eclipsed both *L'Amérique au jour le jour* and *America Day by Day*.
3. The bicentennial of de Tocqueville's birth was on July 29, 2005. Part 1 of Lévy's seven articles, offering his personal experiences, observations, and insights while traveling in the United States, appeared in *The Atlantic*'s May 2005 issue; followed by Parts 2 (June 2005), 3 (July/August 2005), and 4 (October 2005), complemented by three articles, before appearing as a book published by Random House, under the title *American Vertigo: Traveling America in the Footsteps of Tocqueville*, in January 2006.

in-built proclivities to change and transformation, not that they ever could be.

All three French observers, brought up in an educational milieu unavoidably alimented by Cartesian clarity, not only undertook the tough effort of methodically questioning 'the natives' in sincere antic-ipation of firsthand understandings but also kept detailed diaries lest they forget or misrepresent those tiny je-ne-sais-quois liable to lose what at first blush might have seemed to them to hold great salience. Remarkable for de Tocqueville's time, perhaps a tad less so for post–World War II teacher-philosopher de Beauvoir's, and certainly far more commonplace in Lévy's own lifetime, all three observers made use of a sociologically tilted politico-economic-cultural lens for their inquiry into the confounding marriage of blind injustice and bland equality under law, in a dynamic societal environment, which—as all three admit—nonetheless unmistakably radiates a credible likeness of freedom: one of democratic liberty.

If Alexis de Tocqueville's 'impartially' intrusive, 'neutrally' inquisi-tive opus, seeking tips for the advancement of the French mode of governance, swiftly received worldwide attention—even praise "by radicals and conservatives alike"—this was not least also because "[i]ntense interest at this time was constantly refueled by English fears of the possible Americanization of British life, French fears of American radicalism, and [not least?] American satisfaction over the unantici-pated respectability [that the opus] conferred upon them. Significantly, it was Volume 1 with its greater specific detail, its flattering and opti-mistic coloration, its political and institutional focus—all suitable as an introduction to the American system—which enjoyed the greatest pop-ularity" (Riessman 1971, 175–176, 174; reproduced also in Kerschner 1983, xviii). Simone de Beauvoir was not as lucky. Her journalistic reportage appeared as a book in the years when the world was preoc-cupied with the first atomic test explosions by the United States and the USSR, the first hydrogen bomb drop by the United States, China's emergence as both nuclear power and tacit Russian ally in the after-math of the Korean conflict, and the creation of the Warsaw Pact, which added fuel to the Cold War at a time when the mood in Europe in general, and in France in particular, was rather center-left and not exactly pro-American. It went almost unnoticed. Lévy's essays, too, conducive to a book in 2006, happened to be penned in a period when the war in Iraq did not especially endear America to French public opinion. History has its uncanny ways of revisiting the world.

Among the leitmotivs spread across these three observations over a span of 174 years, there are continuities and changes in opinions that nevertheless come closest to voicing the very questions raised by a majority of non-Americans today: Founded on life, liberty, and the 'pursuit of happiness', is *Démocratie à l'Americaine* truly foremost tied to high mobility, facilitated by intense commerce and industry; by economic success based on cheap oil, low postage, ease of transport and communications; on a work ethic that is competitive in its search for efficiency and productivity; on a social ethic that seeks to lift the underdog but is tough on the chronic 'loser' who lacks the skills and the education; on motivated and self-reinventing self-interest, yet a sense of self-centeredness that is not sinful nor incompatible with religiosity; on pride in work, fear of laziness and idleness, and the kind of self-respect that obtains from the self-liberating spirit of enterprise conducive to material comfort, and requiring a delicate balance to be struck between unequal inner insecurity and equal rights under law, the better to prequalify for opportunity, given a visibly deep-rooted, widespread lust for dignity and fame, only too readily evident for discerning outside observers?

American democracy manages explicit recognition of the people's sovereignty in every aspect of, and application to, everyday societal life, although there always lurks the natural danger of mediocrity in any democracy's leadership, as also lurks the menace of tyranny by the majority, exacerbated by partisan winner-takes-all elections, or by electorates inclined to isolationist individualism, introverted self-reliance, and a proneness to mistake for freedom the virtual reality of absolute equality under law. True, where it overrides inequality or outflanks rank, compassion may conduce to some fraternity that can lead to patriotism and to 'good citizenship'. And there is virtue in, as well as tangibles to be reaped from, decentralized government. Not least, there also always exist intangibles to be gleaned from letting the collective yearnings of the citizenry to remain in touch with its soul in "Amazing Grace," and to reaffirm its pride and to refresh its hope in "America the Beautiful." No matter that the highest notes of "O-oh say . . ." are hard to negotiate, they do propel young Americans to faraway places not only to fight, but also to help and in selfless ultimate sacrifice, even to die for their flag and their anthem. The lesson here is that democratic pluralism seems capable of begetting patriotic nationalism of a caliber that none of the self-purifying nationalisms lacking pluralism have seemed able to afford for long.

It is the unfathomable mystery discernable in this and in many other similar paradoxes (all too easily mistakable by foreign eyes to be voluntarily coexisting as the deliberate outcome of a nationwide social compact), which prompts first the curiosity, then promptly, the anticipatory scrutiny, and finally the begrudging admiration accruing from a misguided sense of firsthand understandings that fascinate the stranger's usually predisposed gaze from outside in. Thus, for all such self-indoctrinated outsiders, the spontaneous aid extended by democratic America to tsunami victims in faraway places comes to be seen as natural: the 'perfectly American thing' to do . . . until, that is, they switch their television on and behold armed looters taking advantage of flood victims in their own city, somewhere much closer to base, say in New Orleans, and then quite sheepishly ask themselves what in American democracy's name has gone 'wrong'. Was not democracy supposed to be of, for, and by 'the people', especially so in America? Might they have missed something somewhere?

Of Spaces and Places with Familiar Faces

"Our contemporaries are constantly excited by two conflicting passions: they want to be led, and they wish to remain free. A[nd a]s they cannot destroy either the one or the other of these contrary propensities, they strive to satisfy them both at once. They devise a sole, tutelary, and all powerful form of government, but elected by the people. They combine the principle of centralization and that of popular sovereignty; this gives them respite: they console themselves for being in tutelage by the reflection that they have chosen their own guardians. Every man allows himself to be put in leading-strings because he sees that it is not a person or a class of persons, but the people at large who hold the end of his chain" (*Democracy in America*, vol. 2, p. 337). How anachronistic or depleted is this piercing contemplation made some 174 years ago by an 'alien' stopping over for a look-see? And if that perception is still valid, then what has the 'average' democrat anywhere in the world or in the United States (assuming any 'average' can subsist for long in that Land of Number Ones) learned or heeded to greater advantage since, were it toward improving his or her 'pursuit of happiness' in the shorter and/or longer run?

Writing *Of Democracy in France* in 1849, a contemporary of Alexis de Tocqueville's, and a Minister to French King Louis-Philippe for eleven years, Monsieur F. Guizot,[4] pondered aloud: "A people who has staged a revolution overcomes its perils and picks its fruits only if itself bears upon the principles, the interests, the passions, the words that have presided the revolution, the sentence of the last judgment that 'separates the grain from the chaff and the wheat from the hay good only for fire.' . . . As long as that judgment is not rendered, there is chaos. And if chaos prolongs itself in the bosom of a people, this would be death. Chaos hides itself today under one word: *Democracy*. It is the sovereign, universal, word. All of the parties invoke it and would like to appropriate it as a talisman. The monarchists have said: 'Our monarchy is a democratic monarchy. It is thus that it essentially differs from the old monarchy and that it suits the new society.' The republicans say, 'The republic is democracy governing itself. This government alone is in harmony with a democratic society, with its principles, with its sentiments, with its interests.' The socialists, the communists, and the *Montagnards*[5] want the Republic to be a pure, absolute democracy. It is for them the condition of its legitimacy. Such is the empire of the word *democracy* that no government, no party dares live, and disbelieves to be able to, without inscribing this word on its flag, and the

---

4. *De la Démocratie en France* (1849:8–15), my translation, his italics. In 1829–1830, de Tocqueville attended Guizot's courses, to acquire political and intellectual acumen (Lamberti 1983, 15–16); Volpilhac-Auger (2005) suggests that just like Montesquieu's concern for 'the spirit of laws', de Tocqueville's preoccupation was with the spirit of democracy, namely, the scrutiny of a nation by examining the relations between a political state and an intellectual movement of mores and sentiments—in effect the very substance that adds up to content, in the second part of *Democracy in America*.

5. "In French history, the label applied to deputies sitting on the raised left benches in the National Convention during the French Revolution. Members of the faction, known as *Montagnards* [Mountain Men] saw themselves as the embodiment of national unity. Its followers included Jacobins elected from Paris as well as the Cordeliers and the followers of Jacques Roux. Approximately 300 of the 750 deputies associated themselves with the Mountain. Although party lines were not sharply drawn, the Mountain's opponents were the more moderate Girondists. Prominent *Montagnards*—like Robespierre, Georges Danton, and Jean Paul Marat—were elected from Paris. The fall of the Girondists (June 1793) was a victory for the Mountain, whose members ruled France under the Reign of Terror (1793–1794). The Mountain sponsored the Revolutionary Tribunal, the surveillance committees, the Committee of Public Safety, and the *levée en masse*. Its deputies went on missions, wielding unlimited powers, to defend the Revolution in the provinces and at the fronts. It was supported by Jacobin propaganda. The fall of Robespierre, 9 Thermidor (July 27, 1794), supported by some of the Mountain, split the Mountain . . . led to its downfall. The romance of the Mountain led the revolutionary left of 1848 to call themselves the Mountain as well." (See also http://www.answers.com/topic/the-Plain).

ones who carry that flag the highest and the farthest believe themselves to be the strongest. A fatal idea, which unceasingly raises or foments war among us: a social war. It is this idea that one must extirpate. For this is the price of social peace. And with social peace, liberty, security, prosperity, dignity, all the goods, moral and material, that only it can guarantee. These are the sources from which democracy draws its might. It is the flag of all hopes, of all of humanity's social ambitions, pure or impure, noble or base, sensible or senseless, possible or chimerical. . . . For all these parallel and contrary instincts, for all confusedly, bad and good, the word *democracy* holds infinite perspectives and promises. It pushes at every slope, it speaks to all the passions of the human heart, to the most moral and the most immoral, to the most generous and the most shameful, to the sweetest and the toughest, to the most uplifting and the most destructive. To the ones it offers the highest, while to the others, sotto voce, it allows a glimpse of their satisfaction. Therein rests the secret of its force. I am wrong to call it a secret. The word *democracy* is not new, and all the time it has said what it says today. This is what is new and proper in our time. The word *democracy* now is pronounced every day, at every hour, everywhere; and it's heard all over and endlessly by everyone. This awesome call to the mightiest there is of good and of evil, in man and in society, used to resonate in passing, locally, within certain classes, united with other classes in the bosom of one and the same fatherland, albeit deeply diverse, distinct, and limited. They lived separated by distance, obscure to one another. Now there is only one society, and in this society no more are there such high barriers, long distances, mutual obscurities. False or true, fatal or salutary, when a social idea arises, it penetrates, it acts everywhere all the time. It is a never-extinguishing torch. It is a voice that neither stops nor shuts up anywhere. Universality and never ending publicity, such is henceforth the character of all of the grand provocations, and of all great movements addressed to mankind. It is there that these sovereign 'faits accomplis,' no doubt, enter God's own designs on humanity. At the heart of this fact, the empire of the word *democracy* is not a local accident, nor is it transient. It is the development—others would say the unleashing—of human nature as a whole, across the board and at every depth of society. And as a result the flagrant, general, continual, inevitable struggle of these evil proclivities, these virtues and vices, all of these passions and all of these forces, towards perfecting and corrupting, elevating and debasing, and creating and destructing. This is henceforth the social state and permanent condition of our [French] nation" (Guizot 1849, 8–15; my translation, his italics).

In his retrospective "inquiry into the working of democratic ideals and institutions in France under the Third Republic," meant to "explore the special meaning, character, and working of democracy in France" now that greater "experience of the Fourth and Fifth Republics can also be drawn upon to assist in this purpose," David Thomson[6] (1969, 133) saw democratization[7] in France to have evolved even more ambivalently than that: ". . . the Third Republic may be said to have both a negative and a positive aspect. . . . [one, of:] suspicion, distrust, watchfulness, resistance, hostility to all governments however democratic in origin . . . closely connected with the intense individualism of the French people. It produced the hierarchy of checks which was favored by the Republic—the Deputy checking the Minister, the constituent checking the Deputy, elected councils checking the Prefect and the Mayor, and so on. It meant the disparagements of all politics . . . in the cynicism shown towards all politicians by the average French elector . . . [while the other:] democracy [as] independence and self-help, the readiness of the citizen armed to defend the nation, the Republic and himself by recourse to violence when necessary—[something that] springs from very similar national characteristics. Intellectually, it takes the form of restless, incessant demand that the 'revolutionary tradition' be carried out to its logically complete conclusion with the effective establishment of liberty, equality, fraternity, sovereignty of the people, and the addition of social and economic democracy to political democracy. Practically, it merges into the demand for real national security and abolition of class privileges or oligarchic power."

Now "[t]he most important substantial differences [of the French Fourth Republic] from the Constitution of the Third Republic were only two: the great weakening of the second chamber (the *Conseil de la République*) in legislative power and in relation to the other chamber (the *Assemblée nationale*) and the abolition, by Article 13, of the former

---

6. See also his *Democracy in France: The Third Republic*, 2nd edition (1949).
7. Setting an example of Republican government for the whole of Europe promptly after the Revolution of 1789–1792, France nevertheless had to traverse three additional revolutions (1830, 1848, 1870–1871) and five republics (1792–1804, 1848–1852, 1870–1940, 1946–1958, 1958– to date) before settling down in a stabilized and enduring (semi-)presidential mode of rule, a self-suiting pursuit of democratization, and an idiosyncratically evolving—but hardly devolving—form of democratic governance. On the social/cultural groundings of republican values in France, see Nord (1995).

system of *décret-lois* [decree-laws]. Even so, the Council of the Republic was given a voice in the election of the President, and in constitutional revision . . . its 'opinion' was required on legislation and for declarations of war. . . . Executive powers grew, but in isolation of parliamentary life. Thus developed the gap between government and democracy that . . . haunts the record of democracy in France. To bridge this gap, to encourage cohesion and coherence without destroying freedom and diversity, to produce balance . . . not deadlock . . . compromise without stalemate, is the perennial function of democratic regimes in France. Under the Fifth Republic the great experiment went on, with emphasis now on the side of authority and discipline more than on the side of freedom and diversity. But it is the same experiment, the inescapable mission to which the French people is dedicated" (Thomson 1969, 239–258).

Guizot had attributed differences in the evolution of democracy and in the pursuit of democratization in the United States and France at least in part also to 'initial conditions': "Democratic France owes much to Emperor Napoleon. He gave [France] two things of immense price: on the inside, a solidly constituted civil order; on the outside, a national independence established strongly through glory. . . . Napoleon concerned himself merely with raising power, with imparting to it the conditions and its force and its grandeur. For one democratic society as for any other, he saw therein a national interest of the first order, indeed, according to him, the first of interests. But Napoleon was a despot . . . how, being so hostile to liberty himself, could he have been favorable to the political instincts of democracy? . . . [George] Washington does not resemble Napoleon. He was not a despot. [Washington] founded political liberty at the same time as the national independence of his fatherland. He made war to serve peace. Brought to supreme power without ambition, he left it without regret, as soon as the safety of his country permitted it; he is the model for democratic republican leaders. . . . Democratic societies do not have the privilege of seeing the spirit of government to be less necessary, or its vital conditions to be other or less elevated than in any other [kind of society]. As an infallible consequence of the struggle that infallibly [*sic*] establishes itself in their bosom, the powers-that-be incessantly are called upon to decide between contrary impulses which solicit them to become the artisan of good, or the accomplice of evil, the champion of order . . . the slave of disorder. . . . Any government, whatever its form or name, that—owing to the vice of its organization or situation, or due to the corruption or weakness of its will—cannot prove itself equal to that inevitable task, soon will pass as a malfeasant ghost, losing democracy instead of founding it" (Guizot 1849, 26–30).[8]

Of Times Ahead, in Hindsight

"I spent four months in America—very little time. As a private individual, I crossed this great industrial country without visiting its factories . . . seeing its technical accomplishments . . . making contact with the working class. Nor did I enter the elite circle where U.S. politics and economics are hammered out. Yet alongside the fuller pictures the more competent people have drawn, it does not seem useless to me to recount, day by day, how America revealed itself to one consciousness—mine." So begins the diary of Simone de Beauvoir (1954, 1999, xvii): "New York is here; everything is real. . . . Fifteen years ago I was leaving the train station, and from the top of the monumental staircase I saw all the rooftops of Marseille at my feet. I had a year or two to spend alone in an unknown city. I didn't move; I just looked thinking: 'This strange city is my future; it will be my past'. . . . Beyond Washington Square, the grid begins to bend. The right angles break down; the streets are no longer numbered but have names. The lines curve and tangle together. I'm wandering through a European city. . . . Everything amazes me, both the unexpected sights and those I've anticipated. . . . Yesterday I had dinner . . . with some French people. This evening . . . dinner at the home of more French people . . . When I am with French people, I sense the same disappointment I felt when I was with my parents during my childhood, that nothing was completely real. There was a glass wall between things and me . . . I don't like the taste of whiskey . . . Yet until three o'clock in the morning, I drink scotch docilely because scotch is one of the keys to America. I want to break through the glass wall. . . . All these French people I meet are pleased to explain America to me—according to their experience, of course. Nearly all of them have a strong bias: either they hate it and can think only of leaving or they shower it with excessive praise, as the collaborationists did with Germany. R., a university professor, is one of these. As soon as he shakes my hand, he asks me to 'promise' to write nothing about America. . . . America is so vast that nothing people say about it is true. In any case, I must 'promise' to write nothing about the blacks. . . . V., who is anti-American, explains . . . scornfully that

8. My translation from the original (first edition, January 1849).

this attitude is the only feasible one for a Frenchman living in this country; otherwise, he would live in a state of intolerable anger and revolt. No European values are acknowledged here [says V., who] acknowledges no American values . . . [and] despises New York" (de Beauvoir 1999, 8–17).

"I read a sign in a drugstore, 'Not to grin is a sin.' Everyone obeys the order, the system. 'Cheer up! Take it easy.' Optimism is necessary for the country's social peace and economic prosperity. If a banker has generously lent fifty dollars without any guarantee to some young Frenchman in financial straits, if the manager of my hotel takes a slight risk by cashing his customers' checks, it's because this trust is required and implied by an economy based on credit and expenditure" (de Beauvoir 1999, 23). "I don't want to rush to judge America. But one thing I'm already sure of—aside from the beauty of New York—is that there is a human warmth in the American people. . . . I don't pass up the chance to meet Americans" (25–29). "Those among the French who get down on their knees to worship all-powerful America adopt all its prejudices even more obsequiously than Americans do. One of them says to me, 'If you like, we'll go through Harlem by car; you *can* go through Harlem by car, but you must never go on foot.' A bolder Frenchman declares, 'If you're determined to see Harlem, in any case stick to the large avenues. If something happens, you can always take shelter in the subway. But above all avoid the small side streets.' . . . I deliberately walked . . . toward Harlem, but my footsteps are not quite as carefree as usual; this isn't just a walk but a kind of adventure. A force pulls me back, a force that emanates from the borders of the black city and drives me back— fear. . . . It's because of this moral discomfort, not timidity, that I'm happy to be escorted this evening to the Savoy by Richard Wright; I'll feel less suspect. He comes to fetch me at the hotel, and I observe that in the lobby he attracts untoward notice. If he asked for a room here, he would surely be refused. We go eat in a Chinese restaurant because it's very likely that they wouldn't serve us in the uptown restaurants. Wright lives in Greenwich Village with his wife, a white woman from Brooklyn, and she tells me that every day when she walks in the neighborhood with her little girl, she hears the most unpleasant comments" (34–37).

I wonder what de Beauvoir would say if she saw Harlem today or attended Martin Luther, Jr., Day mass in Washington, DC, or took time to stroll in the new Old South. Democratizations are incremental processes: those lynched by the hundreds, the three young men[9] who died for that ideal, among the thousands of others who gave valiant speeches,[10] all are integral to the price a society, any society, must have the courage and determination to acquit if, as, when, and wherever the need arises, in the name of its own greater good. In the hands of the self-replenishing, the dogged pursuit of democracy in the private mind proves to be continually self-emancipating for the public soul.

Democratizations in a Globalizing International Political Economy

For Guizot, the personality and leadership styles of Washington and Bonaparte had much to do with the nature at birth and the early traits of character featured by their two nations' idiosyncratic quest for liberty and distinct pursuits of democratization. But de Beauvoir's notes would seem to contradict his hypothesis that initial conditions might predetermine contextualized evolutionary outlooks: "[T]here is a tradition of self-criticism in America, as there was not long ago in France. And the people who speak most harshly of the country here are not those who are least attached to it. The French who, in prosperous times, objected to jingoism were those most loyal to their conquered country. The Americans who attack a certain moral, political, and economic position are showing that they insist on a destiny worthy of this great land where they are citizens; their demands and their lucidity are the highest forms of love. [Those of my friends who] have thrust their roots into this soil . . . expect harvests worthy of it. To label as anti-American books, films, statements that imbue Jefferson's ideal with a living reality . . . is to mutilate America. The day America is forbidden to question itself, America will be no different from the totalitarian regimes it claims to oppose" (de Beauvoir 1999, 271).

[Despite frequent events to the contrary, the calumny] "that the democratic ideal in the U.S.A. is no more than a cynically exploited hypocritical lie . . . would not be entirely fair . . . [for] as expressed in

---

9. Human rights activists, Michael Schwerner, Andrew Goodman (both white), and James Chaney (an African American) were murdered at the hands of the Ku Klux Klan in Mississippi during the summer of 1964. At a trial held in 1967, an all-white jury deadlocked 11 to 1 in favor of convicting Edgar Ray Killen and 17 other men. On June 21, 2005, however, Killen, now an old Baptist preacher and sawmill operator, was sentenced (sixty years in jail on manslaughter charges) for ordering the deaths.

10. "What haven't we all done for this Land," remarks the Turkish poet Orhan Veli Kanık (1914–1950): "Some of us gave our lives; some of us gave our speeches."

the Declaration of Independence . . . and each day through speeches and official documents, [this ideal] is more than empty chatter. A class hierarchy is not superimposed on inequalities of wealth. . . . Each person can disguise the mediocrity of his fate by thinking that he participates in the life of a great nation. . . . Americans have never demanded an *actual* economic equality; they accept there are different living standards, as long as every citizen has the possibility of rising from one level to another through his own efforts. But this is where the deception begins. . . . At a time when the economy is no longer indi-vidualistic, it's a lie to continue regarding every individual as a singular case: he has only the singularity of a number. Without knowing it, he is subject to the law of averages. . . . This is what makes 'participation' in the life of the country assume the guise of a lure. This means that freedom has no more concrete reality than equality" (de Beauvoir 1999, 292–296). May 19 [1947]: "Two days of shopping and good-byes . . . I go to declare the money I've earned these past four months and to pay the required taxes. In France this operation would have taken days of coming and going. Here, the business is transacted one-on-one, as always, and it's settled in half an hour. The official sitting across from me examines the sheet of paper I've submitted and asks me for my word of honor as verification—nothing more. Then he helps me deduct . . . [:] transportation, secretarial help, receptions, hotels, laundry? He's the one who makes all these suggestions with touching enthusiasm. . . . Two imprints from the rubber stamp and I'm free to leave America. . . . Hardly a day has passed that I haven't been dazzled by America; hardly a day that I haven't been disappointed. I don't know if I could be happy living here; I am sure I'll miss it passionately . . . . You have the exhilarating feeling that anything can begin here. But what, in fact, is beginning? . . . I don't know the ruling class . . . but it constitutes only a tiny minority. The majority of Americans are like those I've rubbed shoulders with—. . . content to leave their lives go round in the same circle . . . this world that's full of generous promise is crushing them . . . they think they can isolate the part from the whole, as evidenced by the preference for specialization one finds in technol-ogy, the sciences, and culture. . . . This is the paradox of all positivisms, of all pseudorealisms that turn away from men to affirm the thing—they miss the thing itself and attain only concepts. . . . They want to know only a present that's cut off from the flow of time, and the future they project is one that can be mechanically deduced from it, not one whose slow ripening or abrupt explosion implies unpredictable risk. . . . One of the things that's most striking to me is how much they hate questioning themselves and the world as it is. They need to believe that Good and Evil are clearly divided categories and that Good is or will be brought about readily. . . . America is one of the pivotal points of the world, where the future of man is being played out. To 'like' America, to 'dislike' it—these words have no meaning. It is a battle-field, and you can only become passionate about the battle it is waging with itself, in which the stakes are beyond measure" (de Beauvoir 1999, 381–389).

Fifty years later, writing probably only just before Hurricane Katrina transformed New Orleans, Louisiana, into a flooded plain, in Bangladesh, Bernard-Henri Lévy entered the following thought in his diary: "For a European, one of the most enigmatic characteristics of the American ethos is its relationship with nature. . . . People in the United States don't need to imagine: they know . . . this knowledge feeds their extreme sensitivity to . . . cataclysm when it takes the form of a tsunami and devastates a destitute country . . . [yet,] the most striking aspect for a European when faced with this implacable recur-rence of natural catastrophes some of which (Hurricane Andrew; the Mississippi flood of 1927) . . . have shaped the construction of the American landscape—the most incomprehensible thing—is the rela-tively passive roles of politicians and citizens . . . *in New Orleans, I saw the ingenuity deployed to avoid a repetition of the 1927 scenario.* But let me tell you about Homestead . . . [a] town on the road to the Everglades, in a landscape of fake trees painted yellow, orange, blue, and red as if to liven things up, this town devastated a dozen years ago by Hurricane Andrew, and also hit by many of the ensuing hurricanes. What takes you by surprise in Homestead is the vulnerability of the houses. What bewilders and stuns you is that everything has been rebuilt just as it was before, with the same prefab kits and the same kinds of trailers, which look as if they've been set down ready-made, patched together, a little rickety. You wonder what will keep them from flying apart in the same way when the next Andrew, Mitch, or Allison comes along. America has the means to protect Homestead. . . . Just as I've never seen a European airport as profoundly paralyzed as the major American airports can be by a snowstorm . . . I can't imagine the principle of precaution so poorly applied in my country as it is here in Homestead. Why is it so neglected? . . . No pity for our enemies, the American of the twenty-first century seems to be saying. No mercy for terrorists, certainly, or even for opponents of the country's economic supremacy. But we'll let nature take her best shot" (Lévy 2005, 96; my italics).

What to make of these observations? What is the dilemma facing the enigma of 'democracy' in the world at large and the interrogation faced by 'democracy' in America, at this critical juncture in human history, that is, in the dusk of a long millennium and in the immediate aftermath of an exhausting century putatively preceding the dawn of a less-murderous tomorrow inside yet another new world order rumored to be in the making?

While agreeing that "the fact of American power is a reality, perhaps the central reality" [since the U.S.] "today is the first global power," Zbigniew Brezinski (2000, 150–151) has warned us that "preponderance [of power] should not be confused with omnipotence. . . . The first question that comes to mind is whether a democracy can, in the long run, assume a quasi-imperial role on the world scene: a role into which the United States has now been cast. . . . The key challenge is whether . . . American global preponderance can be translated into effective global cooperation based on the realities of power."

One could not end with a better forewarning in afterthought: for the future of all democratizations around the world may depend on it.

References

Brezinski, Zbigniew (2000) "Epilogue: Democracy's Uncertain Triumph," in Marc E. Plattner and Aleksander Smolar, Editors, *Globalization, Power, and Democracy*, pp. 149–154, Baltimore, MD: Johns Hopkins University Press.

de Beaumont, G., and A. de Tocqueville (1833) *Du système pénitentiaire aux Etats-Unis, et de son application en France; suivi d'un appendice sur les colonies pénales et de notes statistiques*, Paris: H. Fournier Jeune.

de Beauvoir, Simone (1954) *L'Amérique au Jour le Jour*, Paris: Editions Gallimard.

——— (1999) *America Day by Day*, Berkeley: University of California Press.

de Tocqeuville, Alexis (1836) *De la démocratie en Amérique*, 5. éd. revue et corrigée, Paris, Librairie de Charles Gosselin (vol. 1, first published in 1835; vol. 2, first published in 1840).

——— (1945) *Democracy in America*, the Henry Reeve text, revised by Francis Bowen, further corrected and edited with a historical essay, editorial notes, and bibliographies by Phillips Bradley, New York: Vintage Books (Random House).

Guizot, M. (1849) *De la Démocratie en France*, Paris: Victor Masson.

Kauders, Anthony D. (2004) *Democratization and the Jews: Munich, 1945–1965*, Lincoln: University of Nebraska Press for the Vidal Sassoon International Center for the Study of Antisemitism (SICSA), Hebrew University of Jerusalem.

Kerschner Frederick, Jr., Editor (1983) *Tocqueville's America—The Great Quotations*, Athens: Ohio University Press.

Lamberti, Jean-Claude (1983) *Tocqueville et les deux démocraties*, Paris: Presses Universitaires de France.

Lévy, Bernard-Henri (2005) "In the Footsteps of Tocqueville (Part 4): From The Storm Systems of Florida to Those of Washington, D.C.," Charlotte Mandell, Translator, *The Atlantic*, October:94–109.

——— (2006) *American Vertigo: Traveling America in the Footsteps of Tocqueville*, Charlotte Mandell, Translator, New York: Random House.

Nord, Philip (1995) *The Republican Moment: Struggles for Democracy in Nineteenth-Century France*, Cambridge, MA: Harvard University Press.

Riessman, David (1971) "Tocqueville as Ethnographer," *American Scholar*, 30 (Spring): 174–187.

Rimanelli, Marco, Editor (1999) *Comparative Democratization and Peaceful Change in Single-Party Dominant Countries*, New York: St. Martin's Press.

Schraeder, Peter J., Editor (2002) *Exporting Democracy: Rhetoric vs. Reality*, Boulder, CO: Lynne Rienner.

Thomson, David (1946) *Democracy in France Since 1870*, 1st ed., London: Oxford University Press (1949), Royal Institute of International Affairs (1958, 1964, 1969).

——— (1949) *Democracy in France: The Third Republic*, London: Oxford University Press (1946, 1949).

Volpilhac-Auger, Catherine (2005) "Tocqueville et Montesquieu: récrire l'histoire?" in François Mélonio and José-Luis Diaz, Editors, *Tocqueville et la littérature*, pp. 221–232, Colloque de la Sorbonne, Paris: Presses de l'Université Paris-Sorbonne.

About the Authors

Aryeh Botwinick (PhD Princeton) is Professor of Political Science at Temple University. A graduate of the London School of Economics and Yeshiva University, he is the (co)author of many books, chapters, articles, and reviews in his fields of specialty, which span political philosophy, Jewish and rabbinical thought, as well as negative theology, skepticism, political participation, justice, ethics, postmodernism, power, democratic theory, liberalism, and the gamut of justifications for democracy. He serves on editorial boards of numerous academic journals.

Stephen Brown (PhD New York University) is Associate Professor at the School of Political Studies, University of Ottawa; has conducted extensive field work in Kenya and Malawi on foreign aid and democratization; and has published widely on those topics, as well as on conflict and conflict prevention in Africa. His current work is on "transitional" violence in Africa, with particular focus on the cases of Angola, Kenya, Mozambique, and Zimbabwe. He is also conducting research on new trends in Canadian development assistance.

Jose V. Ciprut (PhD Penn), an industrial technologist and international businessman, educated in the humanities, with postgraduate degrees in the social sciences, has authored articles and chapters and edited a number of books. He works on international relations, geopolitical economics, regional development, comparative international political economy, and national/regional/international/global security. His current research dwells on the theoretical, empirical, and historical ties among democratic citizenship, relational ethics, and governance.

Stanley Deetz (PhD Ohio University) is Professor of Communication and Director of Peace and Conflict Studies at the University of Colorado at Boulder. He studies organizational communication from a critical/cultural/philosophic perspective. He specializes in communication theory, organizational communications, and qualitative research methods; and has held positions of international import. He continues to offer community consulting services and serves on the editorial boards of a number of scholarly journals. He is a Fellow and past President of the International Communication Association.

Jacques deLisle (JD Harvard) is Professor at the Law School of the University of Pennsylvania, where he teaches, researches, and writes on contemporary Chinese law, the politics of the People's Republic of China, China's take on international issues, Taiwan's international status, the politics and law of Hong Kong, and issues of transnational legal import and public international law, with a particular focus on China's international relations. He directs the FPRI's Asia Programs and is a member of the National Committee on U.S.–China Relations.

Patrick J. Deneen (PhD Rutgers) is the M.&N. Tsakopoulos-Kounalakis Associate Professor of Government at Georgetown University and the author of two books, numerous articles, and several reviews on ancient and American political thought, religion, and politics and literature. He has co-edited a volume on democracy in literature and is writing a book on the division of labor in Western political thought. As holder of a Leo Strauss Award, he taught politics at Princeton before moving on to join the tenured faculty of Georgetown University.

Charles F. Doran (PhD Johns Hopkins) is Andrew W. Mellon Professor of International Relations, Director of the SAIS International Relations Program and its Theory and History subfield, as well as Director of the Center of Canadian Studies within the new Western Hemisphere Program at the Paul H. Nitze School of Advanced International Studies (SAIS). His research dwells on security policy, conflict analysis, and environmental/energy issues, with an emphasis on benefits and costs. He pioneered work in political risk analysis.

Andreas Heinemann-Grüder (PhD Free University Berlin) is a political scientist, historian, and senior researcher at the Bonn International Center for Conversion. He teaches political science at the University of Bonn and has been affiliated with Humboldt University, Duke University, the University of Pennsylvania, and the University of Cologne. He works on post-Soviet politics, comparative federalism, and post-conflict dilemmas. One of his six books looks at European federalism between integration and separation.

Paul Kaiser (PhD Indiana) was Associate Director of African Studies and Adjunct Associate Professor of Political Science at Penn before relocating to Malawi. He has penned a number of journal articles and book chapters on African politics relating to economic and political reform, to the politics of identity, conflict prevention, and environmental policy making. He has written a book on the Asian community in Kenya and also co-edited two volumes on the democratic transition process in East Africa and on the phases of conflict on the continent.

John Kincaid (PhD Temple) is the Robert B. and Helen S. Meyner Professor of Government and Public Service and the Director of the Meyner Center for the Study of State and Local Government at Lafayette College, where he has served as Acting Head of the Department of Government. He was the editor of *Publius: The Journal of Federalism;* is editor of a 50-book series on the Governments and Politics of the U.S. American States; and lectures and consults on issues of local and regional governance, constitutionalism, and–especially–federalism.

Timothy Kuhn (PhD Arizona State University) is Associate Professor and Director of Graduate Studies in the Department of Communication at the University of Colorado at Boulder. His work, teaching, research, and writing focus on organizational communication, organizational knowledge, learning and change processes, communication networks, small group decision making, communication, and information technology. His ongoing projects dwell on cross-functional teams in workplace settings, as well as on textual analysis procedures for use in organizations large and small.

Douglas S. Massey (PhD Princeton) is the H. G. Bryant Professor of Sociology and Public Affairs at Princeton University's Woodrow Wilson School. He was trained as a demographer and specializes in migration and human ecology. Before joining Princeton, he was Dorothy Swaine Thomas Professor and Chair of the sociology department at Penn. He is a member of the National Academy of Sciences, the American Academy of Arts and Sciences, past President of the Population Association of America and of the American Sociological Association. He is prolific.

James Patrick McDaniel (PhD Iowa), Assistant Professor in the Communication Department of the University of Colorado at Boulder, passed away recently. He taught rhetorical theory and criticism, wrote in specialized journals, and co-edited *Judgment Calls: Rhetoric, Politics,* *and Indeterminacy*. His "democratic aesthetic" depicted an attitude to authority and to otherness characterized by civic discourses of awe and rebellion, of concomitant respect and ridicule radiated by 19th-century philosophies, and also by historic texts and actual practices of participation.

S. Mara Pérez   (PhD Chicago) is a sociologist. She currently serves as President and Chief Executive Officer of Development and Planning Services, a body that cooperates with local nonprofit organizations with the objective of strengthening both their stability and their overall longer-term effectiveness when dealing with the issues in the sphere of Latino affairs, which includes diversity, health, the arts, education, the environment, and—notably—international affairs. Her specialty area is Central and South America.

Vladimir Shlapentokh   (Dr. Econ. Moscow) is Professor of Sociology at Michigan State University. As Senior Fellow at the Sociological Institute in Moscow, he conducted the first nationwide public opinion survey to be held in the U.S.S.R. He has published close to 30 books and dozens of essays on social, sociological, and methodological topics and has examined Soviet/post-Soviet issues since 1982. He has served as a consultant to the U.S. government on social processes, on ideology, and on public opinion in Russia and the C.I.S.

Henry Teune   (PhD Indiana) is Professor of Political Science and was the Undergraduate Chair of the Political Science Department at Penn. His work is on national and regional growth and development, democratic values and governance, political development, and local democracies in a globalizing international setting. He has (co)authored a number of volumes and numerous essays and chapters on these specific topics. He was President of the International Studies Association, a cross-disciplinary interprofessional entity he served in its infancy.

Jerzy Wiatr   (PhD Warsaw) is a political-military sociologist. He has served at Jagiellonian University, the Military Political College, and the University of Warsaw as Professor/Chair of Sociology, Dean of Social Sciences, and also as Director of the Socio-Political Studies Center at the Baltic College of Humanities. As founding member of the new Social Democracy Party of the Polish Republic and its National Council/Presidium, he was elected Parliamentary Deputy and later named Minister of National Education. He is the Editor in Chief of a leading Polish political quarterly.

Name Index

Abraham, the patriarch, 53–60
Abromeit, Heidrun, 125, 130
Abuladze, Tengis, 176
Ackerman, Bruce A., 67
Adams, John, 37
Adams, John Quincy, 43
Adedjiji, Adebayo, 252
Adorno, Theodore, 184
Agranoff, Robert, 97
Ake, Claude, 252
Akheiser, Alexsander, 173
Al-Jilani, Shaikh Abd Al-Qadir, 55
Allison, Graham, Jr., 33
Almond, Gabriel, 49
Althusser, Louis, 285
Amin, İdi, 235
Andreas, Peter, 259
Angell, Ian, 290
Arango, Joaquín, 267, 276
Archimedes, 31
Arendt, Hannah, 184, 314
Aristotle, 32–33, 306, 308–313
Arnold, Fred, 260
Aronoff, Myron J., 108, 246
Aslund, Anders, 12
Ayana, Daniel, 252

Babosov, Evgenii, 176
Bachrach, Peter, 4
Bacon, Francis, 312
Bagaza, Jean-Baptiste, 245
Bahcheli, Tozun (Bahçeli, Tosun), 105
Balaguer, Juan, 269
Balcerowicz, Leszek, 159

Bao Tong, 208
Barber, Benjamin R., 314
Barber, Jacques P., 285, 291
Barnes, Samuel H., 156, 157
Bartkowski, Jerzy, 155
Baum, Richard, 206, 219, 224, 225
Beauvoir, Simone de, 322–323, 324, 331–335
Beck, Ulrich, 141
Bellamy, Richard, 136
Belokovskii, Stanislav, 187
Benda, Julien, 188
Bennett, Robert J., 98
Berger, Peter L., 199
Berisha, Sali, 155
Berman, Bruce J., 235, 252
Bernier, Lynne Louise, 109
Bernstein, Thomas P., 224
Beschel, Robert, Jr., 33
Bhaskar, Roy, 286
Bijker, Wiebe, 288
Biocca, Frank, 291
Blair, Tony, 10, 122
Blecher, Marc, 201
Bokassa, Jean-Bédel, 235
Bonaparte, Napoleon, 330, 333
Bonner, Elena, 177
Borisov, Vadim, 175
Borodin, Pavel, 182
Borodin, Vladimir, 169
Bosch, Juan, 269–270
Botan, Carl, 290
Botwinick, Aryeh, 3–5, 53–72, 109, 208, 251, 302, 309

Boulding, Kenneth E., 79
Boylan, Delia M., 39
Bratton, Michael, 236, 249–250
Brazauskas, Algirdas, 150, 155
Breton, Albert, 102
Brezinski, Zbigniew, 336
Brooks, David, 180
Brown, Stephen, 25–26, 89, 108, 207,
    233–258
Brugmans, Henri, 109
Bruhn, Kathleen, 271, 274, 275
Bruszt, Laszlo, 157
Brym, Robert J., 168
Brzezinski, Zbigniew, 166
Buchanan, James M., 114
Bukovsky, Vladimir, 184
Bunce, Valerie J., 11
Bush, George W., 96, 137
Butrin, Dmitri, 182
Butterfield, Jim, 176
Buyoya, Pierre, 245

Calder, Kent E., 199
Calhoun, Craig, 224
Calles, Plutarco Elías, 271
Cameron, Fraser, 137
Camp, Roderic, 270–271
Cárdenas, Cuahantémoc, 272
Cárdenas, Lázaro, 271, 272
Cardoso, Fernando, 247
Castells, Manuel, 291
Castles, Stephen, 260
Castro, Fidel, 266–269
Centeno, Miguel Angel, 271–273
Chai, Joseph C. H., 201
Chan, Ming K., 200
Chang, Maria Hsia, 225
Charvet, Fernando, 265
Chazan, Naomi, 235, 248
Chege, Michael, 236
Chelysheva, Oksana, 169
Cheney, James, 333
Cheng, Joseph S. Y., 219
Cheng, Lucie, 223
Chen Liangyu, 223
Chen Xitong, 223
Chen Yun, 206

Chiluba, Frederick, 255
Chirac, Jacques, 135
Chiu, Hungdah, 211
Chrétien, Jean, 97
Christians, Clifford G., 28, 283
Chua, Amy, 166
Chubais, Anatolii, 167, 181, 182
Ciprut, Jose V., 1–30, 35, 38, 78, 91,
    99, 109, 110, 188, 204, 302, 321–337
Clark, Robin, 58, 283
Clarke, Donald C., 213, 215, 223
Cleisthenes, 33, 45
Clifford, Mark L., 200
Clinton, William Jefferson, 97
Clouthier, Manuel, 272
Collier, David, 119
Collins, Chik Revista, 296
Colosio, Luis Donaldo, 274
Conn, Christine, 93
Constant, Benjamin, 303
Cooke, Jacob E., 110
Cooper, Thomas W., 28, 283
Corman, Steven R., 291
Corne, Peter H., 215
Cornford, Francis MacDonald, 32
Cothran, Dan A., 271
Craig, Robert T., 283
Crossick, Stanley, 130

Dahl, Robert A., 4, 49, 119, 120
Dakhin, V. N., 173
Dalin, Alexander, 168
Dallmayr, Fred, 65, 70
D'Anieri, Paul, 11
Danilov, A., 176
Danilov, Victor, 173
Danton, Georges, 327
Darnolf, Staffan, 236, 237–238
Davidson, Alastair, 260
Davies, James Chowning, 78
Davis, Michael C., 104
Davis, Stan, 291
Decalo, Samuel, 239
Deetz, Stanley A., 28, 281–300
deLisle, Jacques, 13, 15, 20, 22–23, 31,
    104, 197–232, 313
Demeš, Pavol, 12

Deneen, Patrick J., 28, 301–319
Deng Xiaoping, 22, 206, 208, 226
Derbyshire, Denis J., 93
Derbyshire, Ian, 93
Dermer, Ron, 166
Dernberger, Robert F., 201
DeSanctis, Gerardine, 290
Dewey, John, 285, 293
Diamond, Larry, 33, 94, 98, 218
Dickens, Charles, 47
Dickson, Bruce J., 208
Ding, Xueliang, 213, 224
Djindjic, Zoran, 148
Dominguez, Jorge, 220
Doran, Charles F., 2–3, 31–52, 208,
    251, 302
Doyle, Michael, 35
Dresser, Denise, 273
Dubin, Boris, 168, 178
Duchacek, Ivo D., 105
Duck, Raymond, 168
Durand, Jorge, 262, 265, 266, 268,
    275
Du Xichuan, 211

Echeverria, Luis, 271
Eckstein, Harry, 168
Eder, Klaus, 140
Eisenberg, Eric M., 285
Eisenhower, Dwight, 315
Elazar, Daniel J., 94–96, 102
Elshtain, Jean Bethke, 317
Ely, John Hart, 306
Evans, Peter C., 39

Faletto, Enrique, 247
Fedotova, Valentina, 173
Feenberg, Andrew, 290
Ferguson, Niall, 166
Fernández, Leonel, 270
Fernback, Jan, 291
Fewsmith, Joseph, 206
Finifter, Ada, 168
Finlay, Mark, 290, 291
Fiore, Quentin, 290
Fischer, Joschka, 122
Forbig, Joerg, 12

Fox Quesada, Vicente, 275
Franklin, Benjamin, 37
Freeman, Gary P., 260
Friedman, Edward, 23–25, 226
Fromm, Erich, 184
Fukuyama, Francis, 32, 166, 197
Funkhouser, Edward, 266

Gaddis, John Lewis, 166
Gaidar, Egor, 189
Gaidar, Yegor, 180, 181, 182
Galileo, 33
Gallarin, Juan Antonio Ramos, 97
Garten, Jeffrey E., 219
Gaubatz, Kurt Taylor, 40
Geddes, Barbara, 81
George I, 37
Georges, Eugenia, 269
Gergen, Kenneth, 285
Gibson, James, 168
Giddens, Anthony, 290
Gill, Graeme, 168
Gilley, Bruce, 206, 220
Gilpin, Robert, 218
Gold, Thomas B., 200
Goldman, Merle, 224, 225
Goldring, Luin, 274
Goode, Kenneth, 236
Goodman, Andrew, 333
Gorbachev, Mikhail, 13, 150, 174–177,
    189
Gordon, Leonid, 175
Gorshkov, Mikhail, 172
Graham, Pamela M., 269, 270
Grande, Edgar, 141
Grasmuck, Sherri, 263, 269
Grimm, Dieter, 126
Gromov, Andrei, 170
Gross, Steven, 285
Grossberg, Lawrence, 285
Gudkov, Lev, 168
Guillen, Mario F., 73
Guizot, François, 110, 326–331, 333
Gunson, Darryl, 296
Gurov, Alexander, 179
Gutiérrez, David G., 27, 263
Gyimah-Boadi, E., 250

Haas, Richard N., 197
Habermas, Jürgen, 9, 28, 119, 127, 290, 293–296
Hackney, Sheldon, 35
Hagan, Jacqueline Maria, 270
Haggard, Stephan, 199, 200, 226
Haight, Roger, 64
Haley, John O., 210
Halperin, Morton H., 197
Hamilton, Alexander, 306
Hansen, Roger, 271
Harbeson, John W., 248
Hart, John M., 271
Haskelevitch, Levi Y., 56
Hassan, Robert, 291, 292
Hatton, Timothy J., 259
Hedlund, Stephen, 172
Hegel, G. W. F., 148
Heidegger, Martin, 285
Heilbrunn, John R., 239
Heinemann-Grüder, Andreas, 4, 7–11, 95–96, 119–144, 161, 207
Held, David, 94
Hempstone, Smith, 241
Herbst, Jeffrey, 251
Hesli, Vicki L., 168
Heyd, David, 3
Hirschmann, Nancy J., 216
Hobbes, Thomas, 54, 57–62, 67, 309
Hobsbawm, Eric, 166
Hofheinz, Roy, Jr., 199
Holm, John, 236, 237–238
Holmes, Kim R., 100
Holt, Robert T., 19
Hormats, Robert, 219
Horn, Guyla, 155
Hornsby, Charles, 241
Howse, Robert, 96
Hsiao, Michael, 199
Hugo, Graeme, 267, 276
Hugo, Victor, 47
Hu Jintao, 22, 206, 208, 211
Hume, David, 37, 61–62
Huntington, Samuel P., 32, 94, 219–220, 226, 247
Husak, Gustav, 149

Huther, Jeff, 98
Hu Yaobang, 208

Ignatieff, Michael, 166
Ihonvbere, Julius O., 250
Iliescu, Ion, 150, 152, 155–156
Illarionov, Andrei, 186
Inglehart, Ronald, 33, 180, 181
Inozemtsev, Vladislav, 186
Isaac, 54
Ishmael, 54
Ivanov, Nikolai, 167
Ivanov, Sergei, 17
Ivan the Terrible, 178

Jackson, Michele H., 290, 291
Jacobson, David, 260
James, Cyril, 166
James, Harold, 259
James, William, 317
James II, 62
Jameson, Frederic, 282
Janos, Simon, 156, 157
Jaruzelski, Wojciech, 155
Jasso, Guillermina, 262
Jay, John, 306
Jefferson, Thomas, 35, 37, 188, 244
Jiang Zemin, 201, 206, 208
Johnson, Chalmers A., 42, 199, 200
Johnson, Ian, 224
Jopp, Mathias, 136
Joppke, Christian, 260
Joseph, Richard, 248, 249
Jospin, Alain, 122
Jouvenel, Bertrand de, 304

Kadende-Kaiser, Rose M., 245
Kagan, Robert, 166
Kaiser, Paul J., 25–26, 89, 108, 207, 233–258
Kalinina, Yulia, 182
Kanet, Roger E., 166
Kanık, Orhan Veli, 333
Kantner, Cathleen, 140
Karasimeonov, Georgi, 156
Karatnycky, Adrian, 97, 100, 101, 103
Kashin, Vasilii, 170

Kasianov, Mikhail, 173
Kasparov, Garry, 173
Kaufman, Robert R., 226
Kazhdaia, Valerii, 185
Kekes, John, 54, 65–67
Kelly, Christine A., 314
Kennedy, John James, 207
Kenyatta, Jomo, 241, 242
Kenyatta, Uhuru, 242
Kenyon, Daphne A., 102
Kérékou, Mathieu, 239–240
Kerschner, Frederick, Jr., 324
Keyssar, Alexander, 303
Khama, Seretse, 237
Khodorkovsky, 170
Khrushchev, Nikita, 185
Kibaki, Mwai, 242, 243
Killen, Edgar Ray, 333
Kim, Byung-kook, 218, 219
Kincaid, John, 6–7, 37, 93–117, 131,
    200, 208, 251, 253, 302
King, Martin Luther, Jr., 332
Kinsky, Ferdinand, 109
Kirchoff, Paul, 126
Kisilev, Evgenii, 181
Kitchelt, Herbert, 156
Kohler-Koch, Beate, 127
Kollock, Peter, 291
Kolodziej, Edward A., 166
Konchalovsky, Andrei, 173
Korzhakov, Aleksandr, 185
Kotkin, Stephen, 14–16
Kouaouci, Ali, 267, 276
Kraly, Ellen P., 262
Kramer, Andrew, 169
Kramer, Heinz, 139
Krauthammer, Charles, 166
Krippendorff, Klaus, 58
Kristoff, Nicholas D., 201
Krugman, Paul R., 218
Kucan, Milan, 149, 155–156
Kudelin, Aleksandr, 175
Kuhle, Gesa-S., 136
Kuhn, Timothy, 28, 281–300
Kurpas, Sebastian, 136
Kuzio, Taras, 11
Kwasniewski, Aleksander, 156

Lam, Willy Wo-Lap, 206
Lamarck, Jean Baptiste, 37
Lamberti, Jean-Claude, 327
Lampton, David M., 207
Landes, David S., 41–42
Lane, Kevin P., 219
Langsdorf, Lenore, 288
Lardy, Nicholas R., 205, 221
Lasch, Christopher, 314
Latukhina Kira, 170
Lawal, Amina, 110
Lawson, Kay, 156
Lea, Martin, 290
Lebedeva, Oksana, 169
Lee, Junhan, 226
Leff, Carol Skalnik, 40
Lefort, Claude, 70
Lehoucq, Fabrice Edouard, 41
Lekorwe, M. H., 237
Lemarchand, René, 245
Lenin, V. I., 261
Leung, Shao-chuan, 211
Levada, Yurii, 172, 176, 177, 179,
    184
Levinas, Emmanuel, 54
Levitsky, Steven, 11, 119
Levitt, Peggy, 263, 267, 269, 270
Lévy, Bernard-Henri, 323, 324,
    335–336
Levy, Daniel C., 271, 274, 275
Levy, Mark R., 291
Leys, Colin, 247
Li, Lianjiang, 207
Liao Gailong, 208
Lieberthal, Kenneth G., 207
Lieven, Anatol, 166
Limongi, Fernando, 42
Lindberg, Staffan, 251
Linz, Juan J., 151, 226
Li Peng, 206, 224
Lipset, Seymour Martin, 32, 220
Liu Guoguang, 201
Locke, John, 37, 102, 303, 309
Loewenhardt, John, 168
Long, Norton, 87
Lopatin, Leonid, 175
López Portillo, Jose, 271

Louis-Philippe, French King, 322,
  323, 326–327
Louis XIV, French King, 33
Lozano Ascencio, Fernando, 266
Lu, Xiabo, 224
Lubinski, Marek, 158
Lubman, Stanley B., 211, 223
Lumumba-Kasongo, Tukumbi, 251

MacFarquhar, Roderick, 225
Machiavelli, Niccolò, 102
MacLennan, Hugh, 38
Macpherson, C. B., 303
Madison, James, 4, 110, 306
Madsen, Deborah, 166
Magnusson, Bruce A., 238, 239
Mahler, Sarah J., 270
Maimonides, Moses, 53–57, 61, 62
Mair, Victor, 19–21
Majone, Giandomenico, 127
Malan, Mark, 248
Malone, Nolan J., 262, 268
Malthus, Thomas, 43–44
Mamdani, Mahmood, 247, 252
Mandela, Nelson, 245
Mandelbaum, Michael, 166
Mandeville, Bernard, 304
Manion, Melanie, 21–22, 224
Mansbridge, Jane J., 314
Mao Zedong, 21, 206
Marat, Jean Paul, 327
Markov, Sergei, 170
Markwick, Roger D., 168
Marx, Karl, 32–33, 282, 313
Mary II, 62
Massey, Douglas S., 26–27, 99,
  259–280
Maull, Hanns W., 126
Maundi, Mohamed Omar, 245
Maurer, Andreas Peter, 130, 135
Mazowiecki, Tadeusz, 148
McConnell, Grant, 304–305
McCormick, Barrett L., 207
McDaniel, James Patrick, 28, 281–300
McFaul, Michael, 11–12, 166, 168, 176
McInerney, Jeremy J., 33
McLuhan, Marshall, 281, 290

McWilliams, Wilson Carey, 307
Meciar, Vladimir, 152
Medvedev, Dmitry, 17, 170
Meisner, Maurice, 201
Mendelson, Sarah E., 172
Menjívar, Cecilia, 270
Merkel, Angela, 8
Meyer, Christopher, 291
Meyers, Deborah W., 260, 266
Mickiewicz, Ellen, 168
Micombero, Michel, 245
Midlarsky, Manus F., 44
Migranian, Andranik, 170
Mikhailov, Stoian, 154–155
Milekhin, A., 182
Mill, John Stuart, 309
Miller, Arthur H., 168
Miller, Leszek, 156
Milosević, Slobodan, 148
Miners, Norman, 200
Mlinar, Zdravko, 75, 78, 79, 85
Mobutu Sese Seko, 235, 237
Mogae, Festus Gontebanye, 237
Moi, Daniel arap, 241–243, 253, 255
Monnet, Jean, 121
Montesquieu, Baron de (Charles-
  Louis de Secondat), 317
Montinola, Gabriella, 104
Moore, Barrington, Jr., 219–220
Moreno, Luis, 97
Morton, Fred, 236
Moskvy, Ekho, 173
Mo Zi (Master Mo), 20–21
Muluzi, Bakili, 255
Munro, Neil, 180
Murray, Andrew, 236
Murunga, Godwin R., 243

Nagel, Thomas, 63
Nano, Fatos, 155
Napoleon Bonaparte, 330, 333
Nasong'o, Shadrack W., 243
Nathan, Andrew J., 206, 207
Naughton, Barry, 203
Ndadaye, Melchior, 244–246
Ndayizeye, Domitien, 246
Ndegwa, Stephen, 248, 249

N'Diaye, Boubacar, 238
Nemtsov, Boris, 170
Ngcongco, L. D., 237
Nicolaidis, Kalypso, 96
Niebuhr, Reinhold, 38
Nkurunziza, Pierre, 246
Nord, Philip, 329
Novy, Leonard, 140
Nye, Joseph S., Jr., 166
Nyerere, Julius, 245

Oakeshott, Michael, 54, 57, 62,
   67–69
Ober, Josiah, 306
Obregón, Alvaro, 271
O'Brien, Kevin J., 207
Odinga, Raila, 243
O'Donnell, Guillermo, 32, 161, 226
O'Driscoll, Gerald P., 100
O'Grady, Mary Anastasia, 100
Oksenberg, Michel, 207
Onadipe, Abiodun, 239
Ong, Walter J., 289
Oppenheimer, Andrés, 274
Orvis, Stephen, 248, 249
Osabu-Kle, Daniel, 234, 252
Ottaway, Marina, 253
Ould-Abdallah, Ahmedou, 245

Packenham, Robert A., 197
Paine, Thomas, 31
Park Chung Hee, 203
Parrado, Emilio A., 266, 275
Parvanov, Grigorij, 156
Patterson, Thomas E., 305
Pavlovsky, Gleb, 170
Pechenev, Vadim, 176
Peerenboom, Randall, 211
Pei, Minxin, 215, 219, 225
Pelinka, Anton, 155
Pellegrino, Adela, 267, 276
Penn, William, 35
Pérez, S. Mara, 26–27, 99, 259–280
Perlez, Jane, 197
Perry, Elizabeth J., 224, 225
Pessar, Patricia R., 263, 269
Peters, John Durham, 293, 296

Petrov, I., 176
Petrov, Nikolai, 172, 181
Petrova, A., 180
Pfaff, William, 135
Piano, Aili, 145
Piasheva, Larisa, 176
Pinch, Trevor, 288
Pisistratus, 39
Plato, 46, 70, 309
Plattner, Marc F., 124
Polanyi, Karl, 304
Poliakov, L. V., 172
Politov, Yurii, 169
Polterovich, Victor, 187
Poniatowska, Elena, 271
Ponomarev, Aleksander, 187
Pontusson, Jonas, 42
Poole, Marshall S., 290, 291
Popov, Gavriil, 175, 177
Popov, N., 182
Popov, Vladimir, 187
Portes, Alehandro, 269
Poster, Mark, 282, 291, 295
Potter, Pitman B., 211
Pound, Ezra, 37
Privalov, Kirii, 170
Prodi, Romano, 122, 129
Prokhanov, Aleksandr, 173
Przeworski, Adam, 42, 146, 151, 160,
   161, 251, 259
Puddington, Arch, 145
Putin, Vladimir, 14–17, 158, 168–172,
   183, 185–186
Putnam, Robert A., 49, 286, 314

Qian, Yingyi, 104

Raciborski, Jacek, 157
Radishchev, Alexander, 187
Radzikhovsky, Leonid, 173
Ramo, Joshua, 198, 220
Ramsey, Jeff, 236
Rashi (Rabbi Shlomo Yitzchaki), 53,
   56–57
Rau, Johannes, 123
Rauer, Valentin, 140
Rawls, John, 46, 67

Ray, Amal, 110
Reddy, Michael J., 284
Régnier, Philippe, 200
Reisinger, William H,, 168
Reissner, William, 166
Rheingold, Howard, 291
Richter, Frank-Jurgen, 219
Riessman, David, 324
Rigger, Shelley, 218
Risse, Thomas, 140
Robert, Lionel, 166
Robespierre, Maximilien Marie
    Isidore, 327
Robinson, Pearl T., 240
Rodriquez, Victoria E., 99
Roemmele, Andrea, 156
Rose, Richard, 153–154
Rosenbaum, M., 56
Rosenberg, Tina, 155
Rosenzweig, Mark R., 262
Rosett, Arthur, 223
Ross, David, 39
Ross, Lester, 213
Rostow, Walter W., 247
Rothchild, Donald, 248
Rousseau, Jean-Jacques, 109
Roux, Jacques, 327
Rudneva, Elena, 169, 170
Rwagasore, Louis, 245
Rybakov, Anatolii, 176

Sakharov, Andrei, 176, 177
Salinas de Gortari, Carlos, 273, 274
Samarina, Aleksandra, 170
Sandel, Michael, 62, 63
Sanger, David E., 197
Santayana, George, 317
Sarkozy, Nicolas, 8, 10
Sassen, Saskia, 259
Scalapino, Robert A., 39
Scharpf, Fritz, 127
Schell, Orville, 224
Schmitter, Philippe C., 32, 94, 126,
    141–142, 216, 226
Schram, Stuart R., 224
Schuman, Robert, 121
Schwerner, Michael, 333

Sedaitis, Judith B., 176
Seely, Jennifer C., 240
Segal, Aaron, 240
Semigin, Gennadii, 187
Sen, Amartya, 166
Seymour, James D., 224
Shah, Anwar, 98
Shah, Nasra M., 260
Shaka (Zulu chief), 234
Shanker, Thom, 197
Shannon, Claude E., 283–284
Sharansky, Natan, 166
Sheahan, John, 271–272
Shelokhaev, V., 173
Sherbinin, H. G., 173
Shevstova, Liliiaa, 172
Shin, Doh Chull, 31
Shirk, Susan L., 203, 207
Shklar, Judith N., 62, 217
Shlapentokh, Vladimir, 4, 13, 17–19,
    96, 158, 165–196, 207
Shleifer, Andrei, 189
Shoup, Paul, 146
Shubkin, Vladimir, 178
Siegle, Joseph T., 197
Silitski, Vitali, 11
Silvermann, A. M., 56
Singer, Audrey, 262–263
Skinner, Quentin, 61
Sklar, Richard Peter, 238
Slider, Darrell, 172
Smith, Adam, 102
Smith, Hedrick, 176
Smith, Robert C., 274
Smith, Rogers M., 303
Sobchak, Anatolii, 175
Soglo, Nicéphore, 239–240
Solinger, Dorothy J., 207
Somolekae, G. M., 237
Spears, Russell, 290
Sperber, Dan, 284
Spinner-Halev, Jeff, 48, 108, 246
Stalin, Joseph, 44, 147, 177, 183, 185
Starovoitova, Galina, 177
Štepan, Alfred, 151, 226
Stepick, Alex, 269
Steyn, Mark, 166

Stiglitz, Joseph, 180
Strauss, Leo, 57
Sun Zi, 20
Surkov, Vladislav, 170
Su Shaozhi, 208
Swanson, Judith A., 311

Taine, Hippolyte, 188
Tambini, Damian, 286
Tanner, Murray Scot, 207
Taylor, J. Edward, 259, 267, 276
Tedin, Kent, 168
Teune, Henry, 5–6, 73–92, 94, 208,
    233, 254
Theophanus, Andreas, 105
Thompson, Brad, 291
Thomson, David, 329, 330
Throup, David W., 241
Thurlow, George, 270
Tito, Marshall, 158
Tocqueville, Alexis de, 107, 310, 316,
    322–324, 326–327
Tolz, Vera, 176
Travin, Dmitrii, 183, 188–189
Trethewey, Angela, 291
Triska, Jan, 146
Tsipko, Aleksandr, 170, 177
Tudjman, Franjo, 152
Tumanov, Boris, 170
Turner, John E., 19

Unger, Roberto M., 217
Upham, Frank K., 210
Urban, Greg, 77, 285

van de Steeg, Marianne, 140
van de Walle, Nicolas, 47, 236, 248,
    249–250
van Doren, Carl, 37
Vargas Llosa, Mario, 271
Varshavchik, Sergei, 170
Verba, Sidney, 49
Veretennikova, Kseniia, 169
Voegelin, Eric, 63–65
Vogel, Ezra F., 199
Volpilhac-Auger, Catherine, 327
Voltaire, 34

Wachman, Alan M., 218
Wade, Robert, 199, 220
Wallerstein, Immanuel, 247
Walsh, David, 54, 63–65
Wang Mengkui, 201
Warren, Robert, 262
Washington, George, 37, 330, 333
Watkins, J. W. N., 59
Watts, Ronald L., 94
Way, Lucan A., 11
Weale, Albert, 129
Weaver, Warren, 283–284
Webster, Frank, 291
Wehler, Hans-Ulrich, 139
Weingast, Barry, 104
Weinsten, Michael M., 197
Wen Jiabao, 22, 206
Westebbe, Richard, 239
White Howard B., 312
Wiarda, Howard J., 216
Wiatr, Jerzy J., 12–13, 128, 145–163,
    207
Wibbels, Erik, 100
Widner, Jennifer A., 241
Wilcox, Philip, 53
William III, 62
Williams, R. David, 38, 285
Williamson, Jeffrey G., 259
Wilson, Dierdre, 284
Windsor, Jennifer L., 197
Winthrop, Delba, 307
Wolchik, Sharon L., 11
Wolf, Sebastian, 130
Wolin, Sheldon S., 4, 54, 68–69,
    304
Wollheim, Richard, 307–308, 311
Woodward, Wayne, 295
Woronov, Victor, 156
WuDunn, Sherryl, 201

Yan Jiaqi, 208
Yayi, Boni, 240
Yeltsin, Boris, 13, 167, 175–176,
    180–186
Young, Crawford, 235
Young, Michael K., 210
Yu Guanghua, 213

Zabin, Carol, 274
Zabrodina, 170
Zasorin, S., 176
Zedillo, Ernesto, 97, 274–275
Zenteno, René, 275
Zhang Lingyuan, 211
Zhao Ziyang, 201, 208
Zhong Jianhua, 213
Zhou Enlai, 226
Zhuravlev, V. V., 173
Zhu Rongji, 206, 223
Zipko, Alexander, 176
Zorkaia, Natalia, 180
Zuboff, Shoshanna, 291
Zuckert, Michael P., 303
Zudin, Aleksei, 169
Zweig, David, 213

Subject Index

absolute intolerance, 38
accountability
  corruption versus, 98
  economic, 101
Afghanistan, war in, 96–97, 138
Africa, 233–255
  authoritarian rule in, 108, 235–238,
    239, 249–251
  colonialism in, 234–235, 236, 245,
    246, 252
  corruption in, 240–243, 254
  democratizations in, 25–26, 82,
    233, 234–255
  economic development in,
    236–240, 241–243, 254
  human rights in, 243
  law in, 241
  resurgence of democracy in, 25
  See also names of specific states
African Union, 254
agnosticism
  generalized, 60–63, 66–70
  liberalism and, 60–63
Agricultural Revolution, freedom
  and, 33
Akeidah (sacrifice of Abraham's
  son), 53–60
  Hobbes' analysis of, 57–59
  Maimonides' analysis of, 54–57
  Rashi's analysis of, 56
Albania, democratization process
  and, 147, 149–152, 155, 158–159
All Union Center for Public Studies
  (VTSIOM), 176, 177

America Day by Day (de Beauvoir),
  322–323, 324, 331–335
anarchy, inclusion and, 76
Angola, social cohesion and, 41
Argentina
  economic integration of, 267, 268
  federalism in, 93, 95, 103–104
assimilation process, 37
Australia, federalism in, 93, 94,
  103–104, 107
Austria
  EU and, 138, 140
  federalism in, 93, 94, 96, 110
authoritarianism
  in Africa, 108, 235–238, 239,
    249–251
  in China, 22–25, 201–209
  in East Asia, 206
  federalism following, 95, 108, 110
  migrant populations and, 259, 261,
    263, 267, 276
  in Russia, 14, 17–19, 166–167,
    172–175, 177–189
  in suppression of diversity, 105
  See also totalitarian systems
autonomy
  in democratizations, 3, 74
  as goal of democracy, 28
  of groups in global system, 74
  in liberalism, 65–66

Balkan states, 12
  democratization process and,
    159

Balkan states (cont.)
  EU and, 129, 133–134, 136, 138,
      139, 141
Baltic states, democratization process
      and, 145–147, 150, 158
Bangladesh
  corruption in, 98
  social cohesion in, 40–41
Belgium
  federalism in, 93, 98–99, 104
  social cohesion and, 40, 48–49
Belorussia, democratization process
      in, 186
Benin, 25–26, 233, 234, 238–240, 252
Berlin Wall, fall of, 7, 94
bigotry, 35
birth rates, diversity and, 2, 3
Bloodless Revolution, 62
body politic, in democracy, 68–69
Bosnia-Herzegovina
  democratization process and,
      150–151, 152, 159
  federalism in, 93, 106
Botswana, 25–26, 233–234, 236–238,
      252–253
Brazil
  economic integration of, 267, 268
  federalism in, 93, 95, 103–104
Buckley v. Valeo, 308
Bulgaria, 13
  democratization process and, 149,
      150, 151, 152, 154–155, 158–159
  EU and, 138, 141
Burma, old elites in, 90
Burundi, 25–26, 233, 234, 244–247,
      254

Canada
  federalism in, 93–97, 98–99,
      103–104, 107, 109, 113–114
  political freedom in, 44
  social cohesion and, 40, 48
  trade agreements, 268, 273
capitalism
  communism versus, 166–167
  crony, 42
  federalism and, 101–103

new communication technologies
      (NCTs) and, 290
  ownership rights in, 102–103
  requirements of, 102–103
  U.S., 102, 166–167
Central Europe, 11–13, 145–162
  corruption in, 153–154
  democratization challenges in,
      148–157
  EU and, 13–14, 153, 161–162
  experiments with democracy, 11,
      31
  human rights and, 153–156
  international diffusion and, 11–12
  law and, 151–153
  nature of, 145–148
  party systems in, 156–157
  political participation in, 41
  as post-communist, 12, 13
  social malaise in, 157–162
  transition from communism,
      145–151
chaebols, 203
change, dialectic of, 84–85
charity, 37
Chechnya
  intolerance and, 38
  social cohesion and, 41
child labor, industrial revolution
      and, 36
China, 19–25, 197–226
  authoritarian system of, 22–25,
      201–209
  communism in, 21–22, 201–209
  Confucianism and, 20–21, 23–24
  corruption in, 214–216, 223–224
  decentralization of economic
      power, 22, 201–209
  "democracy movements" in,
      208–209, 224
  democratization avoidance in,
      22–25, 201–226
  East Asian model and, 22–23,
      198–201, 203–205, 209–211,
      217–220
  economic growth and, 201–209,
      211, 220–226

elections in, 207, 225
federalism and, 100–101, 104,
     114–115
historical perspective on, 201–209
human rights in, 36, 208–209,
     211–217
international migration and,
     276–277
law in, 198, 211–217, 224, 225–226
Mohism and, 20–21
nationalism in, 24–25
opening the world to, 81
Qin Dynasty, 21
socialist market economy of, 198,
     201–209, 211, 220–226
Taoist philosophy and, 20–21
U.S. policy toward, 313
Christians and Christianity
Akeidah (sacrifice of Abraham's
     son), 53–60
liberal democracy and, 64–65
citizenship, democracy and, 314
civil wars, social cohesion versus,
     40–41
Cold War, end of, viii, 11, 16, 17, 31,
     40, 95, 107, 138, 166–167
collectives, tolerance and, 38
Colombia, 26
circularities of migration from, 263
economic context of migrant
     populations, 268
geographic concentration of
     migrants from, 265
legal status of immigrants in U.S.,
     264–265
political participation of migrants
     from, 267
colonialism
in Africa, 234–235, 236, 245, 246,
     252
American Revolution, 68–69
federalism and, 107
COMECON, 158
Committee of Permanent
     Representatives (COREPER), 125
communication, 281–297
consciousness in, 285

as dialogue, 28, 284–286, 287–288,
     293–296
globalization of, 281–282
philosophy of communication
     (Oakeshott), 67–68
as term, 281, 283
as transmission, 28, 283–284,
     286–287, 288–297
voting as, 286–287
See also new communication
     technologies (NCTs)
communism
capitalism versus, 166–167
in China, 21–22, 201–209
collapse of, viii, 11, 16, 17, 31, 40,
     81
as old elite, 90
post-communist states, 12, 13
in Russia, 174–183
see also China; Cuba; Soviet Union,
     former
Comoros, federalism in, 93, 106
conflicts
among economic and social strata,
     84–85, 89–90
between old and new elites, 84,
     90–91
among regions, 84, 88–89
Confucianism, 20–21, 23–24
consciousness
in communication process, 285
workplace as locus for raising,
     4
constitutionalizing of democracy
EU and, 8, 9–11, 119, 122–123, 126,
     127–136
Wolin and, 69
conversation, philosophy of
     (Oakeshott), 67–68
corruption
in Africa, 240–243, 254
in Central Europe, 153–154
in China, 214–216, 223–224
federalism and, 98
in modern democracy, 304
in Russia, 17, 98, 179, 181–183,
     186–187

counter-Reformation, freedom and, 33

creativity, liberation of individuals and, 77–79

Croatia
democratization process and, 149, 151, 152, 158–159
EU and, 136, 141

crony capitalism, 42

Cuba, 26
circularities of migration from, 263
economic integration and, 267–268
geographic concentration of migrants from, 265
immigrant mobilization in, 269
legal status of immigrants in U.S., 264–265
number of migrants from, 262
old elites in, viii, 90
political participation of migrants from, 266–267
Soviet Union and, 268

culturologists, authoritarianism in Russia and, 14, 17–19, 166–167, 172–175, 177–189

Cyprus, cultural diversity and, 105, 139

Czechoslovakia
collapse of, 95, 146, 147, 149
democratization process and, 149
social cohesion and, 40

Czech Republic, democratization process and, 151, 154, 158

Dahomey. see Benin

Dao De Jing, 20–21

Darfur (Sudan), social cohesion and, 41

Dayton Peace Agreement (1995), 150–151

decentralized unitary systems
demographic bases of, 103–106
economic performance of, 99–103
federalism versus, 93, 97–103
human rights and, 97–99, 111
list of, 93

quality-of-life performance of, 99–103

deconstruction, 67

de facto theory of revolution, 61–62

democracy
ancient versus modern views of, 301–313
central goals of, 28
citizenship and, 314
core values of, 32–46
de Beauvoir and, 322–324, 331–335
deepening of, 41–42
de Tocqueville and, 322–324, 325–326
diversity/assymetry and, 1–2
European Union (EU) democratic deficit, 7–9, 119–120, 122, 124–127, 140
failure in Russia, 17–18, 168–175, 177–189
federalism and, 93–99, 101–103, 106, 108–109
flaw in majoritarian, 108–109
in France, 326–332
globalization as threat to, 94
Guizot and, 326–332, 333
as history, 80–84
as ideology, 1–2
just society and, 46–47
as learning, 79–80
Lévy and, 323–324, 335–336
liberal. See liberal democracy
minority rights and, 4, 306–307
nature of regimes and, 305–306, 308
near-universal embrace of, 314–315
participatory, 3–4, 69
as philosophy of modern liberalism, 28
plasticity of, 301–305
as popular rule, 3–4, 302–303
prospects in undemocratic times, 28–29, 313–317
pursuit of physical goods and, 310
requirements for, 119–120
self-interest and, 305–306, 310, 316
struggle within Mexico, 27

women and, 311, 322–324, 331–335
  see also democratizations
Democracy in America (de
    Tocqueville), 322, 325–326
"democratic deficit," 7–8, 119–120,
    122, 124–127, 140
democratic pluralism
  importance of, 2–3, 49–51
  political tolerance and, 3, 49–50
Democratic Republic of Congo,
    economic growth of, 237
democratizations
  in Africa, 25–26, 82, 233, 234–255
  anti-democratic movement in
    Russia, 168–175, 177–189
  avoidance in China, 22–25,
    201–226
  avoidance in East Asia, 198–201
  in Central Europe. *See* Central
    Europe
  challenges of, 148–157
  defined, 2–3, 31
  determinants of, 1
  as development, 75–79
  dialogic model of communication
    in, 287–288
  emplacement of value as
    multiplicative process, 43–44
  of European Union. *See* European
    Union (EU)
  federalism and, 93–99, 101–103,
    106, 108–109
  fundamental processes of, 39–42
  globalizations and. *See*
    globalizations
  immigration to U.S. and, 26–27,
    259–277
  impediments to, 249–251
  liberal democracy and. *See* liberal
    democracy
  as localization of globalizations,
    78
  "mature" democracy and, 42–43,
    48, 49
  in Mexico. *See* Mexico
  in modern conception of
    democracy, 310–311

multiple forms of, 316–317
nature of, 2
near-universal embrace of
    democracy and, 314–315
new communication technologies
    (NCTs) in. *See* new
    communication technologies
    (NCTs)
as open-ended processes, 1
openness and, 80–84
in paradigm of modern liberal
    democracy, 28, 305
paradox of, 311–313
processes of, 3
rate of increase of, 42
in Russia. *See* Russia
societal core values in, 38–42
transforming, 1–2
unfinished nature of, 47–49
waves of, 94–97, 103–104, 107
as Western conspiracy, 22–25,
    40–41
Denmark, EU and, 134, 138
dependence, globalizations and, 74
détente, 138
development. *See* democratizations;
    economic growth and
    development; globalizations
dialectics
  of change across levels of human
    organization, 84, 85–87
  of different rates of change, 84,
    87–88
dialogic model of communication,
    28, 284–286, 287–288, 293–296
diasporas, 26–27, 262. *See also*
    immigration
direct democracy, 53
diversity
  closed systems versus, 77
  contributing factors, 2, 3
  federalism and, 6, 104–106, 111
  globalizations and, 5, 77–80
  importance of, 2–3
  law of attractiveness of variety, 84,
    85–87
  varying rates of change, 84, 87–88

Dominican Republic, 26
  circularities of migration from, 263
  economic context of migrant
    populations, 268
  geographic concentration of
    migrants from, 265
  immigrant mobilization in,
    269–270
  legal status of immigrants in U.S.,
    264–265
  number of migrants from, 262
  political participation of migrants
    from, 267

East Asia
  Asian Financial Crisis of 1990s,
    198, 217–220
  China compared with, 22–23, 198–
    201, 203–205, 209–211, 217–220
  democratization avoidance in,
    198–201
  difficulty of economic model, 22,
    23, 198, 205–206, 217–220
  economic growth of, 22–23, 76, 81,
    198–201, 203
  emergence as key economic player,
    81
  law and, 209–211, 219
  "tiger" economies of, 22–23, 76,
    198–201
Eastern Europe, EU and, 10, 12, 128,
    136–139
East Germany. See also Germany
  democratization process and, 149
economic growth and development,
    75–79
  in Africa, 236–240, 241–243, 254
  in Central Europe, 157–162
  change across levels of human
    organization, 84, 85–87
  in China, 201–209, 211, 220–226
  conflicts among economic and
    social strata, 84–85, 89–90
  conflicts among regions, 84, 88–89
  conflicts between old and new
    elites, 84, 90–91
  democratic pluralism and, 49–50

  in democratization process, 39,
    41–42
  dimensions of integration in,
    75–77
  in East Asia, 22–23, 76, 81,
    198–201, 203
  economic context of migrant
    populations, 267–268
  equality of opportunity and, 36, 44
  failure in Russia, 178–180
  federalism and, 99–103
  foreign direct investment and,
    83–84
  freedom and, 44
  in globalization, 75–79
  as goal of democracy, 28
  industrialization process in, 36, 44,
    47
  inequalities in, 78
  just society and, 46–47
  in Mexico, 272–275
  stresses of, 88
  varying rates of change, 84, 87–88
efficiency, as goal of democracy, 28
El Salvador, 26
  circularities of migration from, 263
  economic context of migrant
    populations, 268
  geographic concentration of
    migrants from, 265
  immigrant mobilization in, 270
  legal status of immigrants in U.S.,
    264–265
  number of migrants from, 262
  political participation of migrants
    from, 266
empiricism, of Hobbes, 58–59
emplacement
  nature of, 39
  of societal core values in
    democratization, 38–46
  of value as multiplicative process,
    43–44
Enlightenment, democracy and, 302
equality
  as core value of democracy, 32–33
  evolution of, 35–36

before the law, 32–33
liberal democracy and, 64
of opportunity. *See* equality of
opportunity
equality of opportunity
economic growth and, 36, 44
freedom and, 44
nature of, 32–33, 35–36
social cohesion and, 45–46
tolerance and, 45–46
equilibrium, in democracy, 32
Estonia, democratization process
and, 145–147, 150, 151, 158–159
Ethiopia, federalism in, 93, 106, 114
EU. *See* European Union (EU)
Euro, 121
European Coal and Steel Community
(ECSC), 7–8
European Commission (EC), 7–8, 10,
120, 124–125, 130
European Council, 10, 12, 124–125,
128, 130, 132, 153
European Court of Justice, 125
European Economic and Monetary
Union, 121
European Economic Area (EEA),
7–8
European Economic Community
(EEC), 7, 122
European Free Trade Association
(EFTA), 7–8
European Union (EU), 7–11, 119–142
as alternative to U.S. hegemony, 9,
123, 137–139
candidate states, 7, 133–134, 135,
136, 139, 140, 141
Central Europe and, 13–14, 153,
161–162
Common Foreign and Security
Policy (CFSP), 137–140
constitutionalization of democracy
in, 8, 9–11, 119, 122–123, 126,
127–136
as delegative democracy, 120
democratic deficit in, 7–9, 119–120,
122, 124–127, 140
digestive integration and, 11

Eastern Europe and, 10, 12, 128,
136–139
economic migration and, 11
in Euro-optimist point of view, 9
in Euroskepticalist point of view, 9
federalism in, 95–96, 107, 109, 110,
114–115, 122, 131–132
formation of, 7–8
globalization and, 123
in Intergovernmentalist point of
view, 9, 125–127, 131–132, 142
Iraq war and, 137, 138
legitimization of, 121–124
member states, 7, 122, 124, 132,
134–136. *See also names of specific
countries*
pillars of, 132
Qualified Majority Vote and, 132,
133
as supranational state, 9, 131–132,
142
types of laws, 133
extension, as dimension of
integration, 75–77

fascism, collapse of, 109
fear, in negative theology of
Maimonides, 55–56
federalism, 6–7, 93–115
asymmetrical, 95–96
capitalism and, 101–103
centrifugal versus centripetal, 95
challenges to, 110–111
China and, 100–101, 104, 114–115
communitarian identity and,
109–111
corruption and, 98
creeping international treaty, 96
decentralized unitary systems
versus, 93, 97–103
defined, 93
democracy and, 93–99, 101–103,
106, 108–109
demographic bases in, 103–106
economic performance and,
99–103
empirical perspective on, 94–95

federalism (cont.)
  as highest stage of democracy, 106,
    107, 114–115
  historical perspective on, 94–97,
    103–104, 107, 110, 111
  human rights performance and,
    97–99, 109–114
  individualism and, 109–111
  justice and, 112–114
  key interests in, 94
  list of federalist polities, 93
  normative perspective on, 106–107
  quality-of-life performance and,
    99–103
  security and, 107
  territorial scope and, 107
  theoretical perspective on, 106–107
  U.S. and, 93, 94, 96–97, 98–99,
    103–104, 107, 109, 110–111, 113
Federalist No. 10, 3–4, 306
Federalist No. 51, 110
First Democratic Revolution, 74
Forum of Federations, 97
France
  Africa and, 239
  democracy in, 326–332
  EU and, 122, 128, 131, 134,
    135–136, 137–138, 141
  French Revolution, 188, 226, 227
  human rights in, 34
  Jacobins in, 108–109, 110, 327
  social cohesion and, 40
  Vichy Regime of, 34
freedom
  capitalism and, 102
  as core value of democracy, 33,
    309
  in democratizations, 3, 33
  economic growth and, 44
  equality of opportunity and, 44
  evolution of, 35
  of expression, 308
  federalism and, 99
  immigration and, 263–268
  liberal democracy and, 64, 65–66
  political participation and, 45
  tolerance and, 45

Freedom House, 97, 101–102, 105,
    169–170

Gazprom, 15, 17
General Agreement on Tariffs and
    Trade, 267
generalized agnosticism, 60–63,
    66–70
Georgia
  democratization process in, 169,
    186
  EU and, 136
Germany
  in Africa, 245
  democratization process and, 149,
    154, 165
  EU and, 122, 123, 127, 128, 131,
    137–138, 141
  fall of Berlin Wall, 7, 94
  federalism in, 93–97, 114
  intolerance in, 36
globalizations
  change across levels of human
    organization and, 84, 85–87
  communication in. *see*
    communication
  in democratizations, 5, 47, 73–91
  as development, 75–79
  empires of conquest and, 73
  as history, 80–84
  immigration and. *see* immigration;
    international migration
  as learning, 79–80
  openness and, 80–84
  resistances to, 5–6
  Second Democratic Revolution
    and, 73–74
  theoretical approaches to, 5
  as threat to democracy, 94
  varying rates of change and, 84,
    87–88
Glorious Revolution, 62
God
  monotheism and, 59–60
  as Other, 54, 56, 58
  See also religion
Gosplan, 15

Great Britain
  colonies of, 107, 234–235, 236
  EU and, 134
  Iraq war and, 137
  social cohesion and, 40, 48–49
  as union versus federation, 107
Greece, ancient
  constitutionalization of democracy
    and, 69
  democracy in, 301–313
  economic productivity and growth
    in, 39
  freedom in, 33
  tolerance in, 45
  virtue in, 32
Greece, modern, EU and, 136
Guatemala, 26
  circularities of migration from, 263
  economic context of migrant
    populations, 268
  geographic concentration of
    migrants from, 265
  immigrant mobilization in, 270
  legal status of immigrants in U.S.,
    264–265
  political participation of migrants
    from, 267
Guide of the Perplexed, The
  (Maimonides), 53–57

Habsburg Empire, 146
Hanseatic League, 107
hedge funds, international financial
  crisis and, 24
Hong Kong
  in East Asian model, 198, 204, 205,
    210, 217, 218–219, 221
  as "tiger" economy, 22–23
human rights
  in Africa, 243
  in Central Europe, 153–156
  in China, 36, 208–209, 211–217
  democratization as, 43
  federalism and, 97–99, 109–114
  liberal democracy and, 64
  minority rights in democracy, 4,
    306–307

  in Russia, 16, 169–170
  slavery and, 36–37, 110–111,
    309–310, 311
  tolerance and, 33–34, 37
  in the U.S., 33–34, 36–37, 110–112,
    333
Hungary
  democratization process and, 146,
    147, 149, 151, 158
  social cohesion and, 40
Hutu-Tutsi conflict, 234, 244–247

immigration
  borders and, 261–263
  China and, 276–277
  circularities in, 262–263
  diversity and, 2, 3
  economic contexts of, 267–268
  equality of opportunity and, 36
  flow of human capital in, 260
  flow of unskilled labor in, 260
  freedoms and, 263–268
  geographic concentrations of,
    265
  immigrant mobilization across
    Latin America, 26–27, 259–277
  integration of immigrants in,
    259–260
  numbers involved in, 261–262
  resources of migrants and,
    265–267
  Russia and, 14
inclusion, as dimension of
  integration, 75–77
India
  castes in, 36
  democratic challenge in, 45–46
  federalism in, 93, 94, 100–101,
    103–104, 107, 108, 110
  social cohesion in, 40–41
individuality
  democracy and, 316
  development and, 78–79
  federalism and, 109–111
Indonesia
  authoritarianism in, 82
  social cohesion in, 40–41

industrialization process
  equality of opportunity and, 36, 44
  just society and, 47
International Criminal Court, 137
international financial crisis, 24, 198
international migration, 259–277
  borders and, 261–263
  China and, 276–277
  circularities in, 262–263
  economic contexts of, 267–268
  flow of human capital in, 260
  flow of unskilled labor in, 260
  freedoms in, 263–268
  geographic concentrations of, 265
  immigrant mobilization across
    Latin America, 268–275
  integration of immigrants in,
    259–260
  numbers in, 261–262
  resources of migrants and, 265–267
International Monetary Fund (IMF),
  96, 239, 241
intolerance. *See* tolerance
Iraq
  democratic challenge in, 45–46
  war in, 96–97, 137, 138
Ireland, EU and, 134
Islam. *See* Muslims and Islam
Israel, social cohesion and, 40
Italy
  EU and, 122
  social cohesion and, 40

Japan
  in East Asian model, 198, 203, 204,
    211, 218, 220, 221
  federalism in, 96
  intolerance in, 36
  political freedom in, 44
Jews and Judaism, Akeidah (sacrifice
    of Abraham's son), 53–60
justice
  federal democracy and, 112–114
  Hume's theory of, 62–63
just society
  nature of, 46–47, 67
  theory of justice, 62–63

Kashmir, social cohesion and, 41
keidanren, 203
Kenya, 25–26, 233, 234, 241–243,
    253–254
Kremlin Inc., 14, 16, 183–187
Ku Klux Klan, 333
Kuwait, migrants to, 263
Kyoto Protocol, 137

Latin America
  democratizations in, 82
  immigration process and, 26–27,
    259–277
  See also names of specific countries
Latvia, democratization process and,
    145–147, 150, 158–159
law
  in Africa, 241
  capitalism and, 102–103
  in Central Europe, 151–153
  in China, 198, 211–217, 224,
    225–226
  within democracy, 31–32, 46–47
  in East Asian model, 209–211, 219
  equality before, 32–33
  evolution of legal foundation for
    democracy, 32–33
  federal democracy and, 112–114
  just society and, 46–47, 67
  Russia and, 19
  status of migrant populations,
    263–268
learning/ecological approach
  to democracy, 79–80
  to globalizations, 79–80
  theory of rational learning, 80
Lebanon, social cohesion and, 40,
    41
Leviathan (Hobbes), 54, 57–62, 309
liberal democracy, 3–5, 53–70
  advancement of, justifications for,
    303–305
  in Africa, 251–252
  Akeidah (sacrifice of Abraham's
    son), 53–60
  ancient democracy compared with,
    301–313

constitutionalism and. *see*
    constitutionalizing of democracy
dialogic model of communication
    and, 293–296
Kekes critique of, 65–67
metaphysical backdrop to, 4–5
nature of, 3–4
Oakeshott critique of, 67–68
representation in, 53, 302–303,
    306–307
skepticism and, 69–70
transmission model of
    communication and, 286–287
Walsh critique of, 63–65
Wolin critique of, 68–70
See also democracy;
    democratizations
liberalism
agnosticism and, 60–63
democracy as philosophy of
    modern, 28, 305. *see also* liberal
    democracy
of Hobbes, 59–60
of Hume, 62
Lithuania, democratization process
    and, 145–147, 150, 151, 158–159
love, in negative theology of
    Maimonides, 55–56

Macau, in East Asian model, 204
Macedonia, democratization process
    and, 149–150, 152, 159
Malaysia, federalism in, 93, 106, 108
Mali, 252–253
Marxism, 166–167, 247, 282
"mature" democracies, 42–43, 48, 49
media, in Russia, 176, 185
Mexico
economic growth in, 272–275
economic integration and, 267–268
elections in, 27
federalism in, 93, 95, 99
geographic concentration of
    migrants from, 265
historical perspective on, 270–275
immigration across U.S.-Mexico
    border, 26–27, 259–277

legal status of immigrants in U.S.,
    264–265
political participation of migrants
    from, 41, 266
trade agreements, 268, 273
Micronesia, federalism in, 93
military-industrial complex, 315
minority rights, 4, 306–307
modern liberal democracy. *see* liberal
    democracy
Mohists, 20–21
Moldova, democratization process
    and, 152
Monnet method, 121
monotheism, negative theology and,
    59–60
Montenegro, democratization
    process and, 148, 149–150
morality, 37–38
Moral Man and Immoral Society
    (Niebuhr), 38
Mozambique, 34
Muslims and Islam
Akeidah (sacrifice of Abraham's
    son), 53–60
terrorist attacks of 2001, 29, 53,
    197, 315

nationalism
in China, 24–25
as old elite, 90
NATO, 12, 96, 138
Nazi Germany, intolerance in, 36
negative theology
of Hobbes, 57–59, 61, 62
of Maimonides, 54–57, 61, 62
neopatrimonialism, 249–251
Netherlands, EU and, 134, 135–136,
    141
new communication technologies
    (NCTs), 27–28
a-contextualization of, 283
development and implementation
    of, 282–283
individualist traits and, 290–291
inevitability of, 290
preexisting markets for, 292–293

new communication technologies
 (NCTs) (cont.)
 representation of human interests
  and, 293–297
 in transmission model of
  communication, 28, 283–284,
  286–287, 291–297
 universal pragmatics (Habermas)
  and, 293–294, 296–297
 virtual communities and, 296
New Partnership for Africa's
 Development (NEPAD), 254
New World
 evolution of equality and, 35–36
 evolution of freedom and, 35
 migration to, 35, 36
 revolution and, 74
Nigeria
 corruption in, 98
 economic growth of, 237, 254
 federalism in, 93, 94, 98, 104, 107,
  108, 110
nominalism, of Hobbes, 58–59
North American Free Trade
 Agreement (NAFTA), 268, 273
North Atlantic Treaty Organization
 (NATO), 12, 96, 138
North Korea, old elites in, 90

Of Democracy in France (Guizot),
 326–332, 333
Olympic games, 33
orange revolution, in Russia, 18, 186
Organization of African Unity, 245
organized crime, in Central Europe,
 153
Other
 in Akeidah (sacrifice of Abraham's
  son), 53–60
 in dialogic model of
  communication, 288
 God as, 54, 56, 58
 as One Absolute Being, 58

Pakistan
 corruption in, 98
 federalism in, 93, 106
 social cohesion and, 41

participatory democracy, 3–4, 69
Pentagon terrorist attack (2001), 29,
 53, 197, 315
People's Republic of China (PRC).
 See China
perestroika, 13, 179
Philippines, social cohesion and, 41
pluralism
 in democracy, 32
 in liberalism, 65–67
Poland, 12, 33
 democratization process and,
  146–149, 151, 155, 156–157, 158,
  160–161
 EU and, 134, 138
 Solidarity Union, 156–157
political development, social
 cohesion in, 39–40
political economy, in democracy,
 68–69
political participation
 in democratization process, 39, 41,
  47–48
 freedom and, 45
 just society and, 46–47
 of migrant populations, 265–267
 tolerance and, 45, 49–50
 voting as communication,
  286–287
politicization, 4
popular rule, democracy as, 3–4,
 302–303
Portugal
 African colonies of, 235
 EU and, 134, 136
 fall of dictatorship, 94
poverty
 in Central Europe, 159–160
 tolerance and, 38
 See also social class
power
 Dao De Jing and, 20–21
 democratizations and, 1, 68–69
 dispersed, 6–7
 federalism and, 6–7
power cycle theory, 32
privacy, communication and,
 290–291

procedural republic, 62–63
professionalization of politics, as
    goal of democracy, 28
Puritan Revolution, 61

Qin Dynasty, 21
quality of life
    federalism and, 99–103
    in Russia, 178–180

Reformation, freedom and, 33
relative intolerance, 38
religion
    Akeidah (sacrifice of Abraham's
        son), 53–60
    conservative theories of revolution
        and, 61–62
    freedom and, 33
    freedom of, 35
    generalized agnosticism and,
        60–63, 66–70
    liberal democracy and, 64–65
    negative theology of Hobbes,
        57–59, 61, 62
    negative theology of Maimonides,
        54–57, 61, 62
    in Russia, 184, 185
    See also God; specific religious
        groups and religions
renminbi, 222
representation
    in liberal democracy, 53, 302–303,
        306–307
    in popular rule, 3–4, 302–303
retroactive justice, democratization
    process and, 154, 155–156
revolution
    American, 68–69
    conservative theories of, 61–62
    First Democratic Revolution, 74
    French, 188, 226, 227
    international migration and, 261
    religion and, 61–62
    Second Democratic Revolution,
        73–74, 81–82
Romania
    democratization process and, 147,
        148, 150, 152, 158–159

EU and, 138, 141
    social cohesion and, 40
Russia, 13–19, 165–189
    anti-communist revolution and,
        17, 165, 167–168
    anti-democratic movement in,
        168–175, 177–189
    authoritarian system of, 14, 17–19,
        166–167, 172–175, 177–189
    corruption in, 17, 98, 179, 181–183,
        186–187
    culturologist views of, 172–175,
        188–189
    democratization process and, 31–
        32, 146–147, 158, 159–160, 165,
        167–168, 174–177
    failure of democracy in, 17–18,
        168–175, 177–189
    federalism in, 93, 95, 96, 103–104
    historical perspective on, 174–183
    human rights and, 16, 169–170
    immigration and, 14
    Kremlin Inc. and, 14, 16, 183–187
    new assertiveness of, 15
    orange revolution and, 18, 186
    social class in, 16, 183–185
    social cohesion and, 41, 178–180
    spontaneous elites in, 18–19,
        183–187
    stability of, 14–16
    structuralist views of, 167–168,
        171–172, 187–188
    See also Soviet Union, former
Rwanda, 24, 34, 38

St. Kitts and Nevis, federalism in,
    93
Saudi Arabia, migrants to, 263
Second Democratic Revolution,
    73–74, 81–82
self-defense, justice and, 114
self-interest, in democracy, 305–306,
    310, 316
self-knowledge, 295, 310
September 11, 2001, terrorist attacks,
    29, 53, 197, 315
Serbia, democratization process and,
    148, 149–150, 152

Singapore
  in East Asian model, 198, 204, 205,
    209, 210, 219, 221
  migrants to, 263
  as "tiger" economy, 22–23, 76
Single European Act of 1986, 121
skepticism, 53–54
  connection between political
    liberalism and, 64–66
  EU and, 9
  in negative theology of Hobbes,
    57–59, 61, 62
  in negative theology of
    Maimonides, 54–57, 61, 62
  participatory democracy and,
    69–70
  in skeptical idealism, 58
slavery
  democracy and, 309–310, 311
  federalism and, 110–111
  intolerance and, 36–37
Slovakia, democratization process
    and, 151, 152, 158
Slovenia, democratization process
    and, 12, 149, 151, 155–156, 158
social class
  conflicts among economic and
    social strata, 84–85, 89–90
  poverty and, 38, 159–160
  in Russia, 16, 183–187
  slavery and, 36–37, 110–112,
    309–310
social cohesion
  in Central Europe, 157–162
  collective memories and, 48–49
  in democratization process, 39–42,
    48–49, 157–162
  economic problems and, 178–180
  equality of opportunity and, 45–46
  just society and, 46–47
  problems with, 40
  tolerance and, 45–46
societal core values, 32–46
  emplacement in democratization
    process, 38–46
  evolution of, 34–38
  nature of, 32–34

South Africa, 93, 254
Southeast Asia, economic collapse of,
    82–83
Southern Europe
  democratizations in, 82
  EU and, 128
South Korea
  in East Asian model, 198, 203, 204,
    205, 210, 217, 219, 220, 221
  as "tiger" economy, 22–23, 76
sovereign democracy, 170
Soviet Union, former
  collapse of, viii, 11, 16, 17, 31, 40, 95,
    108, 109, 145–148, 165, 241, 268
  Cuba and, 268
  federalism in, 106–107
  intolerance in, 36
  U.S. versus, 166–167
  See also Chechnya; communism;
    Georgia; Russia
Spain
  EU and, 136
  federalism in, 93, 95–97
  social cohesion and, 40, 48
Sri Lanka, social cohesion and, 41
Stockholm Convention, 8
strength, as dimension of integration,
    75–77
structuralism
  Africa and, 247–248
  Russia and, 167–168, 171–172,
    187–188
Sweden, EU and, 134
Switzerland, federalism in, 93, 94,
    96–97, 98–99, 109

Taiwan
  in East Asian model, 198, 204, 209,
    210, 217, 218, 219, 220, 221
  as "tiger" economy, 22–23
Taoism, 20–21
terrorist attacks of September 11,
    2001, 29, 53, 197, 315
Thailand, authoritarianism in, 82
tolerance
  as core value of democracy, 33–34
  democratic pluralism and, 3, 49–50

equality of opportunity and, 45–46
evolution of, 36–38
freedom and, 45
political participation and, 45,
49–50
social cohesion and, 45–46
totalitarian systems
in Central Europe, 145–148
extension and, 76
See also authoritarianism
trade
regional trade agreements,
267–268
social cohesion and, 39–40
transmission model of
communication, 28, 283–284,
286–287, 291–297
Transparency International, 98
Treaty of Amsterdam (1997), 121, 124
Treaty of Lisbon (rejected), 8
Treaty of Maastricht (1993), 7, 114,
121, 127
Treaty of Nice (2000), 121
Treaty of Paris (1952), 7
Treaty of Rome (1957), 7
Turkey, EU and, 133–134, 135, 136,
139, 140, 141
Two Solitudes (MacLennan), 38

Ukraine, 12
democratization process in, 168,
169, 186
EU and, 136
United Arab Emirates, federalism in,
93, 106
United Kingdom, EU and, 10, 122,
131, 137
United Nations, 96, 245
Human Development score,
99–100
Security Council, 138
United States
American Revolution, 68–69
anti-Americanism and, 22–25, 29,
53, 197, 315
capitalism in, 102, 166–167
Cold War and, 166–167

EU as alternative to hegemony of,
9, 123, 137–139
federalism in, 93, 94, 96–97, 98–99,
103–104, 107, 109, 110–111, 113
global power of, 90
Great Depression, 178–179
humanistic record of, 33–34
human rights in, 33–34, 36–37,
110–112, 333
immigration from Latin America,
26–27, 259–277
international financial crisis and,
24, 197
Iraq war and, 96–97, 137, 138
legal status of immigrants in,
263–268
as liberal democracy, 3
military-industrial complex and,
315
output of, 90
policy toward China, 313
political freedom in, 44
slavery in, 36–37, 110–112
Supreme Court rulings, 111, 113,
308
terrorist attacks of September 11,
2001, 29, 53, 197, 315
tolerance in, 33–34
trade agreements, 268, 273

Vaduz Convention, 8
values
consensus on, 295
societal core values, 32–46
Venezuela
corruption in, 98
federalism in, 93, 95
Vichy Regime, 34
violence, intolerance and, 38
virtual communities, 296
virtue
Dao De Jing and, 20–21
law-making and, 32
voluntarism, Africa and, 248–249
voting
as communication, 286–287
in democracy, 303, 308, 311

voting (cont.)
   in European Union, 132, 133
   universal suffrage, 303, 311
   See also political participation
women
   democracy and, 311, 322–324,
      331–335
   equality of opportunity and, 36
   feminist view of democracy,
      322–323, 324, 331–335
workplace
   glass ceilings for women, 36
   international flows of human
      capital and, 260
   international flows of unskilled
      labor and, 260
   as locus for raising consciousness,
      4
World Bank, 96, 239, 241
World Trade Center terrorist attacks
   (2001), 29, 53, 197, 315
World Trade Organization (WTO),
   205, 211, 221, 222–223
World War II, democratizations
   following, 94, 96

Yom Kippur War (1973), 81
Yugoslavia
   collapse of, 40, 95, 147, 149
   democratization process and,
      149–151, 159
   federalism in, 93